WINNING THE RACE

WINNING THE RACE

Beyond the Crisis in Black America

JOHN McWHORTER

GOTHAM BOOKS

GOTHAM BOOKS
Published by Penguin Group (USA) Inc.
375 Hudson Street, New York, New York 10014, U.S.A.
Penguin Group (Canada), 90 Eglinton Avenue East, Suite 700, Toronto, Ontario,
Canada M4P 2Y3 (a division of Pearson Penguin Canada Inc.); Penguin Books Ltd,
80 Strand, London WC2R 0RL, England; Penguin Ireland, 25 St Stephen's Green,
Dublin 2, Ireland (a division of Penguin Books Ltd); Penguin Group (Australia), 250
Camberwell Road, Camberwell, Victoria 3124, Australia (a division of Pearson Aus-
tralia Group Pty Ltd); Penguin Books India Pvt Ltd, 11 Community Centre,
Panchsheel Park, New Delhi - 110 017, India; Penguin Group (NZ), cnr Airborne and
Rosedale Roads, Albany, Auckland 1310, New Zealand (a division of Pearson New
Zealand Ltd); Penguin Books (South Africa) (Pty) Ltd, 24 Sturdee Avenue, Rosebank,
Johannesburg 2196, South Africa

Penguin Books Ltd, Registered Offices: 80 Strand, London WC2R 0RL, England

Published by Gotham Books, a division of Penguin Group (USA) Inc.

First printing, January 2006
10 9 8 7 6 5 4 3 2 1

Gotham Books and the skyscraper logo are trademarks of Penguin Group (USA) Inc.

Library of Congress Cataloging-in-Publication Data

McWhorter, John H.
    Winning the race / John McWhorter.
        p.   cm.
    Includes bibliographical references (p.).
    ISBN 1-59240-188-0 (hardcover : alk. paper)
    1. African Americans—Social conditions—1975–   2. African Americans—
Psychology.   3. Alienation (Social psychology)—United States.   4. Inner cities—
United States.   5. African Americans—Economic conditions.   6. United States—
Race relations.   I. Title.
    E185.86.M427   2006
    305.896'073—dc22   2005023472

Printed in the United States of America
Set in Giovanni Book

Contents

ERASING IT

WINNING THE RACE

Introduction

Condoleezza Rice and Colin Powell? Well, good for them.

There are more middle-class black families than poor ones? Well, okay—but still.

There are eight times more black-white married couples than there were in 1960? Yes, but.

The editor in chief of *Newsweek*, the president of Brown University, and the CEO of AOL-Time Warner are black people? Nigger, please.

There is so much good news in black America today that if we could transport a black American into our era from even as recently as the 1960s, they would wonder whether some trick had been played. But in certain quarters of black America, people are almost embarrassed to see such things brought up and can only celebrate them in a backhanded fashion. These people, as well as white fellow travellers, give the impression that if race conditions improved to the point that it would no longer make sense to say "We've come a long way, but we have a long way to go," they wouldn't quite know what to do with themselves and would even be a little irritated.

Stanley Crouch tells us, "One should always keep a hot poker ready for the backside of injustice, but it is important to polish the crown when you've damned well earned it." Yet so many find it distasteful to even go near that crown, much less polish it—at least in public.

What they want us to think about is Robert Parsons.

On a June night in 2005, Parsons, a black father of four, was at a barbecue on a public playground in Brooklyn. Two men drove up and suggested a private conversation in a grassy area not far from the playground. The first gunshot got Parsons in the stomach. The force spun him around and the murderer finished Parsons off with a shot in the back. He died at the hospital.

Parsons was hoping to make a mark as a rapper, and to the best of people's knowledge, the people who killed him, who were rappers as well, decided they could use a little less competition. Or maybe they had mistaken him for someone else. In any case, he would have had his thirtieth birthday two days later. "It's like I'm walking around without a heart anymore," his mother said.

Parsons's murder took place in a struggling ghetto setting sadly familiar to us all. In his case, it was Brooklyn's Crown Heights, infamous as the neighborhood where in 1991 blacks rioted for days and killed a young Jewish scholar after a young black boy was killed by a Hasid in a traffic accident. Looming over the playground was the Ebbets Field Apartment housing project, hideous twenty-five-story towers plain and tall that, bafflingly today, passed as visionary public architecture in the early 1960s when they were thrown up (so to speak). The project was built for low-income people, and there is no shortage of them in the district they are in: Every fourth person in the zip code lives below the poverty level. Crown Heights has been one of the neighborhoods identified by the New York City Health Department as most in need of aid for substance abusers. Segregation? Indeed—the area where Parsons died is 85 percent black.

That the middle school near the housing project is named after icon of integration Jackie Robinson qualifies as an irony today. Middle School 320 has been one of those tragic inner-city schools we hear so much about, with the graffiti, the broken windows, and the threatened takeover by Edison. At one point it had a single guidance counselor for 1,400 kids, and it has had an extended school-day program aimed at distracting students from violence.

And then, Parsons's murder was, as it happened, one in a string of three that took place in blue-collar black New York that week. Two days before, fifteen-year-old Phoenix Garrett was selling homemade CDs in West Harlem when a thirteen-year-old from Queens shot him dead after an argument; the killer sat unfazed at his arraignment. Then, the day after Parsons was killed, just twenty blocks from where Garrett died, a twenty-one-year-old black man was shot dead while waiting for his food at a McDonald's.

So—Condoleezza Rice, Brown University, jungle fever marriages? Mere abstractions in Crown Heights, which is, we are often told, the real state of black America.

And that means that there is still, as Randall Robinson so deftly had it in the title of his best seller of 2000, a *debt* that America owes to black people despite the Civil Rights Act of 1964. The American government did not do enough, the argument goes. Black America needs a Second Civil Rights Revolution.

Ask people who think this way whether they think black America's problems will sit unchanged until there is a Second Civil Rights Revolution, and they will usually deny it. But then ask them what they think needs to happen, and note when they start reciting the usual historical grievances and decrying the "persistence of racism" that their views logically imply, whether they consciously parse it this way or not, that "revolution" is indeed the only way out. For our informed race warriors, black America's problem is white people.

The white people who moved their factories to the suburbs starting in the sixties and left urban blacks without dependable low-skill jobs. The white people who enforced under-the-table housing covenants even after the Fair Housing Act of 1968 and kept blacks from moving to follow the jobs. The white people who built sterile towers like the Ebbets Field Apartments, which discouraged residents from developing a sense of community and, with their dark staircases and remove from sidewalks, provided cover for criminal activity. The white people who pumped crack into poor black communities. Okay, it's not about individual whites standing right in front of you anymore. But there is still that Old Devil Systemic Racism that creates and preserves the world that Robert Parsons lived and died in.

For such people, black America's problem, then and now, is The Man. This is the fundamental message of countless prominent thinkers in scholarship and punditry on black issues, such as Michael Eric Dyson, Douglas Massey, Sheryll Cashin, Elijah Anderson, William Julius Wilson, Ishmael Reed, Cornel West, Deborah Mathis, Manning Marable, Tavis Smiley, Ellis Cose, Tricia Rose, Robin D. G. Kelley, and Troy Duster. These people differ in tone, but not in basic revolutionary ideology. This viewpoint is taught in colleges and universities. It is given an ample place at the table by the liberal wing of the media. It is treated as enlightenment by what we might call Blue America.

The argument that the world of Robert Parsons is the result of a fatal combination of economics, racism, architecture, and the cheapness of crack is a deeply considered one, promoted by people with a sincere concern for black Americans left behind.

It is also wrong.

This book is dedicated to explaining why this argument is wrong, and what this means for how we will chart black America's future.

What created Robert Parsons's world was exactly what these writers so indignantly insist did not: culture. Note: It's not that there is "something wrong with black people," but rather, that there is something wrong with what black people learned from a new breed of white people in the 1960s. It's something that manifests itself in many ways, generating a range of tendencies and events and customs that can seem unconnected but are rooted in the same source. We'll get to its role in black history since the sixties. But understanding that is easier with a quick look at one of its manifestations in the here and now, an episode of a type familiar to us all.

In the fall of 2003, a white supervisor at the University of Virginia's medical center was heard to say: "I can't believe in this day and age that there's a sports team in our nation's capital named the Redskins. That is as derogatory to Indians as having a team called Niggers would be to blacks."

Here was a white person who had gotten the message about respect for minority groups, right? Apparently not. Some of her black subordinates decided that this was a "hurtful" statement because the woman had deigned to mouth the word *nigger*—hurtful enough to be worth a meeting with their union president, who in turn contacted the university administration. According to modern university ritual, the administration dutifully reprimanded the supervisor for her "offensive" moral lapse.

That alone was far enough from any connection to basic logic. But what's more, the union president suggested that she be fired outright, and spearheaded a protest by black hospital staff against the supervisor and "racism" at the University of Virginia in general. Soon, none other than Julian Bond, history professor at the school but also chairman of the national NAACP, joined in, prescribing that the woman apologize publicly and undergo sensitivity training.

Quite simply, what happened at the University of Virginia that fall was divorced from any conception of human reason; it did not follow from A to B. This administrator was showing her awareness of the hurtfulness of the word *nigger*, and sticking up for exactly the heightened sensitivity that her opponents consider an urgent missive to white America. Little did she know that her mere utterance of the word, even in condemnation, would set off the same trip wire that actually hurling it at a black staff member would have. She fell that afternoon into a kind of Wonderland, where common sense no longer applied.

The union president, clearly aware on some level of a certain disjunction between how healthy human brains process the world and the rhetoric of the protest, announced, "It doesn't really matter in what context this word was used." And that, too, made about as much logical sense as saying that two times two equals pi. When the person was condemning the word's usage, context indeed mattered a great deal—that is, it determined, with perfect clarity, the very meaning and intent of what the woman said.

People like these objectors at UVA leave many of us perplexed. A common response to them, most associated with conservatives, is to assume that they are being cynically manipulative, or that they are curiously "stuck in the past." Another common response is most associated with the left. This supposes that the person is responding to genuine, present-day abuse. Under this approach, it is considered a kind of higher wisdom to understand that racial progress is mere window dressing, and that modern versions of discrimination stain all black lives in ways that are subtle but decisive, best explained in college courses or ticklish conversations about "the race thing." To question this is blaming the victim or black-bashing.

Both of these responses to these people are mistaken. People like this are not opportunists. They are not mysteriously unaware that America in 2006 is not America in 1956. Nor, however, are they responding to real life.

What do they want?

What they want is central to what, in other guises, created the world of Robert Parsons. The nut of the issue is that these people want neither justice nor healing. What people like this are seeking is, sadly, not what they claim to be seeking. They seek one thing: indignation for its own sake.

And that means that the alienation that they are expressing is disconnected from current reality. We can only truly understand black America's past forty years, its present, and its prospects for the future if we grasp that this kind of disconnection is very common, can have seismic effects upon the fate of a group, and can inhabit even the most brilliant of minds.

However, people do not behave this way to seek money or power. The reason this way of thinking has such a foothold in black American ideology is pain.

To black leaders a hundred years ago, that UVA episode would have looked as anthropologically baffling as sacrificing virgins. There was, however, one area of shared understanding between black leaders of yore and the UVA protesters. Centuries of slavery and segregation left a stain on the black American psyche, as well-known to blacks in 1903 as 2003. There are so very many books and articles exploring the damage that the White Man did to black Americans' self-esteem that I will assume that even people far to the left of me will not even begin to dispute this simple proposition.

That insecurity about being black is why this kind of alienation for its own sake—curiously exaggerated, melodramatic, and heedless of reason—is so attractive to so many black Americans today. It assuages a person who is quietly unsure that they are worthy or okay, by giving them something or someone to always feel better than. They seek this because slavery and segregation left black America with a hole in its soul—and why would it have not? But the fact remains that there is little connection between today's America and their alienation. It survives on its own steam.

This is *therapeutic alienation*: alienation unconnected to, or vastly disproportionate to, real-life stimulus, but maintained because it reinforces one's sense of psychological legitimacy, via defining oneself against an oppressor characterized as eternally depraved.

Therapeutic alienation is, itself, blind to race, and it was hardly unknown before the late 1960s. Alienation has always sometimes been as much theatrical as proactive. Therapeutic alienation can be as white as Anton Chekhov's Masha in *The Seagull*, "in mourning for her life" mostly because it is an endlessly interesting way of being. Therapeutic alienation is the pigs in George Orwell's *Animal Farm*. Even those most sympathetic to the countercultural movement of the sixties know that there was a goodly amount of performance for its own sake involved. It's part of how human beings are.

Therefore, the question at hand is why therapeutic alienation acquired such a hold on black America only in the sixties. Insecurity alone could not have been the reason. Therapeutic alienation was not as widespread or influential in black America in 1903, or 1943, or even 1963, the year of the March on Washington—at which times black people had plenty of clear and present reasons to feel insecure. Back in the day, the idea that it was progressive to obsessively tabulate black failure and propose that the only solution was for whites to become blind to race was rare to unknown in leading black ideology. Those who purported that blacks were incapable of surmounting the obstacles were generally tarred as defeatist—witness the reaction of much of the black punditocracy to Richard Wright's work.

Most blacks were more interested in fighting the concrete barrier of legalized *discrimination* than the abstract psychological happenstance of *racism*.

Two new conditions were necessary for alienation among blacks to so often drift from its moorings in the concrete and become the abstract, hazy "race thing" that whites just "don't get."

One condition was that blacks had to be prepared to embrace therapeutic alienation, and ironically, this could only have been when conditions improved for blacks. When racism was omnipresent and overt, it would have been psychological suicide for blacks to go around exaggerating what was an all-too-real problem.

Second, whites had to be prepared to listen to the complaints and assume (or pretend) that they were valid. This only began during the countercultural revolution, within which a new openness to blacks and an awareness of racism were key elements. Certainly this frame of mind was not true of all or even most whites. But it became a common wisdom especially among educated and influential ones, such that it quickly infused university curricula and grounded governmental policies intended as progressive.

Even though there were still plenty of white bigots, the nature of black life in America changed. Many whites were now, for the first time, ready to nod sagely at almost anything a black person said. And in that new America, for many blacks, fetishizing the evils of the White Man beyond what reality justified was a seductive crutch for a spiritual deficit that we would be surprised that they did not have. It was the only way to feel whole. Even blacks less injured were still injured enough to let the loudest shouters pass, as bards of their less damaging, but still aggravating, pains.

So, there is nothing to deplore about "black culture" in itself—our issue is what happened when black America met the New Left. And in the 1960s, black America's social consensus underwent a shift as transformative as the Reformation or the Enlightenment. Alienation drifted from being a spur to action to being a form of self-medication. Here is where legendary Civil Rights activist Bayard Rustin became dismayed as a new generation of black activists began embracing the "heroics" of idle protest and theatrical rage, uninterested in rolling their sleeves up and working out concrete plans for change. Episodes like the one at UVA are today's expressions of that mood.

Importantly, though, our problem is emphatically not the foibles of a few highly visible black leaders, though therapeutic alienation surely motivates them. Therapeutic alienation has hijacked millions of ordinary managers, homeowners, educators, union leaders, diversity consultants, performers, local journalists, students, local activists, and other people, all quite unconnected to leadership posts in the NAACP or the Rainbow Coalition, and who usually seek no celebrity. This has included whites, including, as it happens, the union president at UVA. I refer not to escapades on high, but to a national mood channeling thought on the ground all over black America and among many whites seeing themselves as on our side.

Therapeutic alienation demands our attention because it has had effects far beyond lurid sideshows like the one at UVA. Once established among the thoughtful and influential in America in the sixties, therapeutic alienation began setting off chain reactions that made the difference between the seedy but stable black ghettos of 1950 (*A Raisin in the Sun, Lackawanna Blues*) and the hopeless deathscape black ghettos of 1990 (*Boyz n the Hood, The Corner*).

The keystone example here is when therapeutic alienation transformed welfare into a multigenerational dependence program. Until the late sixties, welfare allowed one to eat but was very hard to stay on for very long and was harder for black people to get than whites. The welfare world we now recall so easily was born only when white activists such as Columbia social work professors Frances Fox Piven and Richard Cloward devoted themselves to bringing down the American financial system by dragging as many people, especially poor black ones, onto the welfare rolls as possible. Their goal was to bankrupt the Treasury so that the Feds would give a guaranteed income to poor people. But in the end, all that happened was that generations of poor blacks idled on the dole, getting just enough money that they were doing better than they could in entry-level jobs.

But the activists were unperturbed by this. Writings and interviews by Piven and Cloward since show a crucial hole: They do not regret that their actions created generations of black people for whom working for a living is an abstraction. They claimed to be seeking something positive. So why was thirty years of self-destructive idleness in black inner cities an acceptable alternate outcome?

Because whether their efforts improved the lives of the *people* was less important than whether it lent *them* satisfaction, feeling that they were Good People fighting an Evil System. Their actions were really about them, not justice or compassion: Their alienation was therapeutic.

The problem was the wreck that their therapeutic alienation left behind: a transformation of what responsibility meant to poor black Americans. In poor black Chicago in the 1920s, it was considered alarming that just 15 percent of babies were born out of wedlock. But by the late seventies, a whole generation of black people had grown up in neighborhoods where it was peculiar if a baby *was* born to a married couple, women living on the government was the norm, and as such, young men had no reason to take care of children they created. In other words, this was the type of environment that Robert Parsons grew up in.

On which: Let's leave the statistics and look at an actual life. While the media reports regularly billed Parsons as a "father of four," we must not imagine that he was the head of a household raising said four children. Parsons had the kids with three different mothers and lived with none of them. One might expect that someone with four offspring would work nine to five (at least?), but Parsons worked only part-time. He was a "free spirit," apparently, and then he also had injured one of his hands. But really, there are so very many ways one can work full-time without having full power in one hand, and there remains the simple question as to why a man with four kids worked only part-time.

Upon which we cannot help but think about the view common among underclass black men that punching a clock is working for "chump change," regularly documented even by sympathetic sociologists. It sounds so "normal" now—but until the late sixties, this orientation was typical only of a bottom fringe of black "corner men," not a *norm*. Alienation caught fire. Parsons, for instance, seems to have at least flirted with stealing money instead of earning it: He had been arrested twice for robbery (as well as two other times for arms possession and drunk driving).

Yet, Parsons was not exactly an absent father; he visited his kids regularly and lit up whenever he was around them. And viewing him in context, *it is impossible to condemn him* because where he grew up, life trajectories like his have long been norms. Family and friends mourning his death spoke of his four kids by three mothers and his fitful employment as casually as women in Scarsdale talk of where their children are going to college. Born in 1975, Parsons grew up long after a new welfare culture had become established starting in 1966, and long before welfare was discontinued as an open-ended dependency program in 1996.

Big surprise that he made his first baby at seventeen—his mother had him at eighteen.

Again, *it is impossible to condemn him*. It's all he knew. But all he knew only began when whites, comforting themselves by fighting The Man and showing that they were not racists, decided that it was a form of higher wisdom to teach poor black people not to work. "Conservative rhetoric"? In this book we will take a good look at this lost chapter in black history and find out whether it is or not.

Middle School 320 sheds light on another example of alienation taking on a life of its own beyond contact with reality. By the late 1990s, 60 percent of its students were reading below grade level, and by 2001, just 6 of 357 students met the state math standard. A typical claim has been that low scores like this are because of insufficient funds. But before the sixties, black schools often gave solid educations on shoestring budgets; it is tragic how almost unseemly some find it to bring up schools like Dunbar High in Washington, DC, where black students performed excellently for decades. There were plenty of other schools like this, that blacks of a certain age regularly recall. These were the schools that educated the heroes of the Civil Rights movement. What happened to schools like Middle School 320 was not a matter of economics, but of culture.

Namely, a major difference between then and now is the sense among many black teens that doing well in school is culturally inauthentic, "acting white." This only became common coin among young blacks in the late 1960s, as the national mood embraced an especially open disidentification with the Establishment in the wake of the Vietnam War and the Civil Rights victories. Once again, whites lit the torch on college campuses and beyond, but it took on a special life among blacks, as a new badge of racial authenticity. One prong in this was the "acting white" sentiment in school.

This distrust of school as "white" was thoroughly understandable among black people living just past legalized segregation, in an America where the social color line was still heavily policed. But forty years later, this "acting white" notion lives on even under *circumstances that would no longer create it*, such as in school districts where successful blacks are a norm and white administrators are deeply committed to minorities' achievements. Today, the alienation is no longer connected to reality. Rather, it hangs around instead because of its alternate usefulness, as a handy in-group sentiment. All teens, riddled with the uncertainties of an awkward age, cultivate alienation to express identity in various ways. Being "not white" is a way that is available to black kids.

But it is no longer a response to racism, and it comes at the price of scholarly failure and narrowed opportunities. Some leftist scholars have come up with studies supposedly proving that the "acting white" idea is a myth, but this oeuvre is advocacy masquerading as science, which a smart seventh grader could see the fatal flaws in. In this book, we will look at how neglecting the reality of self-generating alienation scuttles engagement with this and other issues in race and education.

Finally, there is Parsons's career goal as a rapper. Here is music cherished for being confrontational in the goal of fostering some kind of "revolution"—but full of aimless black-on-black violence and heartless abuse of women that makes no sense as politics of any kind. What the anger, the violence, and the sexism have in common is not political intent, but alienation—and of an aimless, self-medicating variety. Acting up is the goal in itself; the "revolution" idea is a fig leaf. One is in opposition, and that is enough. *To* what and *for* what is unimportant, an almost annoying question.

For example, Parsons belonged to a group called "The Brooklyn Hooligans"—but why, exactly, must the name hold the "thug" front and center? It's easy to forget how local to our times such music-group names are. The Mills Brothers, The Temptations, The Spinners . . . The Hooligans? Why would a group portray itself as criminals? Because it's a norm now: In Robert Parsons's black America the antiauthoritarian holds a special and proud place—but for its "feel," not out of intention to change anything. If rap were progressive, then by definition, very few groups would have criminal names because crime is not very progressive.

Yes, most of rap's buyers are white. But how many blacks would be comfortable to hear that the music is *not* a black American creation and *not* a reflection of black American concerns? Whites swoon to the antiauthoritarian too? Yes, but how dominant on the market is white pop that is all about singers giving America the upturned middle finger and backing it up with threats of violence—other than some white hip-hoppers who are imitating a model provided by, again, people we are taught are "authentic" blacks?

And then, what is "revolutionary" about how common murder is in the rap world, so much so that it is a news cliché? Parsons's murderers felt no shame in killing him over what was likely a trifle. This was normal to them. For the record, the person driving the getaway car was a woman. Black musicians were not known for shooting at and killing one another so frequently and casually until the hip-hop "revolution."

Yet, a common wisdom lately has it that because hip-hop is "in your face," it must be an urgent political statement. It is, in fact, therapeutic alienation set to a beat: infectious as hell and just as trivial. I will make my case in this book, which will also get to a common idea that the more considered lyrics of "conscious rap" contradict this kind of assessment (preview: they don't).

My goal in this book is a revision of how we see black America's past and present. They sound clever enough, claims that Robert Parsons's world is the product of factories moving away from Brooklyn, the Ebbets Fields Apartments being too high, too many black people living in one place, and so on. But they are based on a logical lapse. Life for most blacks before the late 1960s was endurable at best, in ways very concrete. Why did we not have the inner-city plagues so familiar to us when the best that all but a few blacks could expect was menial labor, whites were hanging black men from trees on a regular basis, and the police—or even just a gang of real "hooligans"—could beat a black person senseless without it even making the papers?

We need not pretend that poor black districts before the sixties were sociological paradises. Parsons's grandmother, for example, gave birth to his mother at about fifteen in the late fifties. Nor, however, will we pretend that there hasn't been something uniquely hideous going on in poor black America since—ironically—the War on Poverty. *If the four hundred–plus years of black American history from the early 1600s to 2006 were compressed into twenty-four hours, something went seriously wrong only at about ten o'clock P.M.* Why?

My purpose will be to show that it must stop being considered "controversial" to acknowledge that cultural change played a central role here. Specifically, I believe that we cannot understand our past without fully facing that alienation and disidentification can thrive independently of modern causes because they can serve other psychological purposes. There can be no useful perspective on black America's trajectory that neglects the impact of therapeutic alienation. To move forward, we must trace it, face it, and erase it. This book, section by section, is about how we can do all three.

Tracing It. Young blacks started checking out of the workforce in the 1960s when the economy was roaring; the unemployment problem among them barely moved for decades regardless of how the economy was doing. At the exact same time, two things happened. One, rejecting mainstream norms became vibrantly fashionable in young America, and in black America this often translated into a bone-deep wariness of "white" norms. Two, welfare became an open-ended opportunity, led by people actively seeking people to bring onto the rolls. From now on, millions of poor blacks grew up in places where few people worked regularly and even fewer considered this especially unusual.

Yet, informed wisdom is that these developments had nothing significant to do with the social breakdown of the inner cities and that the main culprit was whitey and his "systemic racism." This makes no sense: It helps no one, and it will not do. The first half of this book makes this case.

Facing It. What turned black America upside down in the sixties was a new value placed on resistance as a fashion statement rather than resistance as a foundation for building. We will explore the roots and impact of therapeutic alienation, showing that it can shape history even when racism is no longer a significant obstacle. Of course, there are people who would disagree that racism has decreased enough to matter for most blacks. There are middle-class blacks who assert that their daily lives are still grinding battles against racism, asserting the "Black Middle-Class Rage" that Ellis Cose and others have chronicled. Also, there is a massive orthodoxy among social scientists that modern black America is much less different from black America a century ago than we might suppose. Engaging these views as closely as I am able, I find them invalid. They are further demonstrations that alienation can persist beyond its stimulus. The second section of this book addresses both positions.

Erasing It. In the final section, I will show that understanding therapeutic alienation is crucial for understanding not only our past but also our present and future. This is especially clear regarding three issues central to race discussions today: the performance gap between black and white students, the place of hip-hop in black identity and activism, and what constitutes black leadership in our times.

Leftist scholars and writers are frustrated that Joe Barstool has yet to understand that black America's problems are all responses to external evils beyond the control of any but a few superstars. But their paradigm has reached poor black America to the extent that as I write, young ghetto blacks who have revived the art of break dancing, or developed a new competitive dance craze called krumping, are telling the media that if they weren't doing this, they would probably be gangbanging. They have internalized the message that evil inequities all but force blacks below the middle class to go wrong. But this was not considered an informed or acceptable message in black America until, as it were, ten o'clock at night.

We must turn back the clock. The faster we do, the faster we will truly get past the race dilemma in this country.

TRACING IT

On the Saturday afternoon of October 9, 2004, fourteen-year-old black ninth grader Byron Lee in South Central Los Angeles was riding his bike down a small street when two men in a car shot him. He fell to the ground. The men got out of the car with their guns at the ready. Byron got on his knees and begged for his life, but the men still shot him nineteen times in the face and body, killing him.

The men were apparently gang members, but Byron had nothing to do with gangs. People in the neighborhood avoid wearing red or blue, because these are colors the Bloods and Crips wear to identify themselves. Byron was wearing black—but was shot down like an animal anyway. The hoods were doing what they call "work"—hunting someone down randomly just to show their rivals that they control the area and mean business.

Quite a few people want you to think that what did this to black communities was The Man. They think that black communities must stay like this until The Man changes his ways.

But was it The Man?

It would be better if it wasn't, since The Man will always be with us. So, if it wasn't The Man, then that means more hope for a better future.

Well, guess what? It wasn't The Man.

CHAPTER ONE

The Birth of the Inner City:
The Conventional Wisdom

Until I was eleven, my family lived in Philadelphia, and my mother worked at Temple University downtown. From our neighborhood, one way to Temple was a scenic route down lovely, winding Lincoln Drive. But when Mom drove me and my sister to Temple to sit in her office as faculty brats while she worked (such as in the summer) or to take us swimming at the campus pool, she would often take a longer route, through the tough North Philly ghetto.

One day I asked her why we went this long way through stop-and-start traffic so often. She said she wanted me to have a sense of how other black people lived and how lucky we were to be middle class.

It was a "scenic" route of a different kind, including boarded-up houses, crumbling sidewalks, and too many chintzy little liquor stores. But what stood out for me was the people. Countless people were sitting on front stoops. Young black men congregated on street corners and in front of bars at two in the afternoon. Young black women were pushing baby carriages, with it rare that a man was anywhere near a child: The women were raising the children themselves.

Maybe some of them had night shifts. But the contrast at two in the afternoon between these neighborhoods and integrated, middle-class West Mount Airy where I lived was plain. There, few people were on the streets at all because they were either in school or at work, and if a teenage girl was pushing a baby carriage, that the baby was her sibling rather than her child was plain. Basically, one sensed that proportionally, many more people in North Philly did not have full-time jobs than in West Mount Airy.

In the 1970s, drugs were not yet the basis of the economy of these neighborhoods or others like them across the nation. But within ten years, in districts like these crack addiction would become epidemic, and young black men would be killing one another without a thought over turf wars related to the drug trade. By then, social scientists, followed by the media, would refer to the people in areas like this as the underclass. Quickly, the underclass would attract intense academic analysis and become the subject of a string of violent gangster films in the early 1990s, as well as of the "gangsta" strain of rap music that thrives today.

In her position as a professor in a department training social workers, Mom taught courses that ushered students into an awareness of societal racism. Growing up around her and her colleagues, I naturally breathed in a basic assumption: The reason that black people in North Philly were idling midday, having children too early, and rarely getting much of anywhere with their lives was because racism condemned them to this fate.

Yet, even at ten and eleven, I was always nagged by a sense that this explanation didn't quite work.

THE HIGHER AWARENESS

Of course, that sense was merely visceral at the time. But I couldn't help asking myself: Is there really *no* work for them? One thing really stood out for me, even as a kid. What struck me was that the people in this neighborhood did not exactly have the air about them that we associate with the downtrodden, with thwarted ambition. One thinks of old photos of men on breadlines in the Depression; they look haggard and, especially, ashamed and despondent. But it was hard not to notice a certain insouciance—even an exuberance—among the people we would pass in the car on those weekday afternoons.

Never could I have fallen into simply condemning the people as lazy and unworthy—it would have been impossible for me to grow up under my mother's care and come out thinking that way, especially since like most black Americans, I have some relatives not unfamiliar with this side of life. But I still could not help thinking now and then: Were these men and women really doing their utmost to find work, only to find doors closed? Or had welfare and having children early without getting married become a lifestyle few were inclined to change because it was all they had known? I couldn't help noticing that in my own life as a black person by the seventies and eighties, "racism" was at best an occasional inconvenience—an attitude here, a way someone put something there—but not barring me from anything I wanted. Also, I knew legions of young blacks just like me, and I hardly grew up in rarified luxury.

By the time I was in my twenties, I began learning that the questions that had always nagged at me were a result of an ignorance of larger sociohistorical currents. In college and graduate school at this time, and as someone coming into a larger awareness of national and world events, I received the idea that black communities disintegrated when low-skill factory jobs, once mainstays of black communities, moved into the suburbs or overseas. This left poor blacks with little access to employment. Meanwhile, it is also supposed that the departure of middle-class blacks from poor black districts after overt redlining was outlawed left poorer blacks without role models. Presumably, the double punch of factories and middle-class people moving away left poor blacks penned into crumbling districts, with no choice but to descend into idle misery.

The factory relocation part of the thesis traces back to academic work of the late 1960s, with an article by John Kain in 1968 having been read especially widely. But its most prominent exponent has been Harvard sociologist William Julius Wilson, whose work on the subject, encapsulated in his *When Work Disappears* in 1996, has played a key role in establishing the idea as common consensus among thinking people. It was also Wilson who stressed the second prong, the departure of middle-class "role models," arguing it first in his *The Truly Disadvantaged* in 1987 and returning to the idea in *When Work Disappears*, broadcasting to a wider public an idea that was once largely heard only among ordinary blacks.

Hence today, thinkers regularly write assuming that where black people live with gunshots echoing day and night, it's because the Ford plant moved away and George and Weezy moved up to the East Side (with, in their case, a pit stop next door to the Bunkers in Queens). Manning Marable, history professor and head of the black studies department at Columbia, writes in passing: "As middle-class outmigration increased, many businesses relocated outside of the city or simply shut down." Elijah Anderson, a black sociologist at the University of Pennsylvania, again concerned with larger points and just briefly flagging the factory explanation as a given, mentions: "Younger and poorer blacks who are left behind have little chance to participate in the regular economy. The jobs that do exist for them are usually low paying or many miles away."

Columnist and commentator Deborah Mathis quotes Boston College theologian David Hollenback: "There are so few decent jobs in most urban ghettos that many people simply give up looking for work. This amounts to the institutionalization of despair." Marable is a radical, Anderson is a leftist, and Mathis is angry, but even more moderately inclined writers make the same assumption. For example, Henry Louis Gates Jr. gives a quick sketch of Buffalo's decline: "The glory days for the black working class were from 1940 to 1970, when manufacturing boomed and factory jobs were plentiful. But when the manufacturing sector became eclipsed by the service economy, black workers ended up—well, stuck in a demographic Buffalo," that is, "a boarded-up central city and a few lakefront mansions."

Scholars on the subject have their disagreements, but within a consensus upon the basic assumption. Sociologists Douglas Massey and Nancy Denton specify that segregation of poor blacks is the key factor—but that the segregation was still, of course, created by factories and middle-class blacks moving out. Wilson's thesis actually has a third major prong: that marriage is so rare in underclass communities because pregnant teenage women see little value in marrying unemployed young men. But other writers addressing the subject do not appear to have picked up on this thread to any serious extent. (Nor will I, simply because it would be a result of the first two causes rather than a primary factor; besides, urban American teens have never married in large numbers—even in 1960, before black ghettos took their bad turn, only 3.5 percent of black teens were married.)

That none of these scholars or writers would see factory relocation and the middle-class exodus as the *only* causes is beside the point. They are comfortable referring to just these two factors, and especially the factories, as a kind of shorthand. They choose them when seeking rhetorical power, or when confined by editorial-page word limits. This shows that they consider them not just two factors out of many equally important ones, but as the decisive ones. We can reasonably suppose that they would assume the following: If the factories were still down the street and Dr. Jenkins still lived across the street, the ghettos would not have become deathscapes, and any other factors would have had little significant effects.

Today, Wilson's thesis is the explanation of the underclass to which the informed person is expected to subscribe. God, how I tried to. I recall my first exposure to the gospel when I eagerly read an issue of *The Nation* after the Rodney King riots in Los Angeles, showcasing various writers tracing inner-city pathology to factory relocation and the absence of middle-class black role models. I wanted to accept this account as truth, but year after year it just didn't quite sit in my mind.

In the physical sense, Philadelphia even illustrates the factory closings especially vividly. The ghostly hulks they left behind are still very common in the city's poor black neighborhoods, and I had grown up seeing them from car windows assuming that they were a normal part of an urban landscape rather than a sign of historical transformations. So okay, the Fred Flintstone jobs moved away. But were the goings on in the shadows of those buildings today really an inevitable result?

THE CRUCIAL QUESTION

After all, black Americans have always known poverty, underemployment, injustice, and social dismissal. Yet, the North Philly scene I was so familiar with was not business as usual. Certainly, ghettos hardly came into existence in 1970. Mom had made sure I read my Claude Brown and Richard Wright, whose work makes it quite clear that there was a vast underbelly in black communities long before our times; another useful example is Ann Petry's novel *The Street*, which often sounds like 1985 but depicts a Harlem forty years before. But there was a sea of change in poor black communities starting in about 1970. Illegitimacy rates skyrocketed, as did drug use and violence.

Starting in the nineties, I was nagged by a simple question. If blacks during the Great Migration of the teens and twenties picked up stakes and moved from the South in dogged search for employment, then why did their children and grandchildren not just move when factories moved to the suburbs? Sure, there were discriminatory housing policies, but were these so conclusive that blacks could move nowhere near any of these suburbs, when, after all, plenty of middle-class blacks did? As Shelby Steele put it in 1998, "When, as Wilson puts it, 'work disappears,' the common human response is migration."

Obviously blacks of yore knew a racism much more overt and oppressive than today, and yet even poor blacks coped with a bad hand to an extent that today is rare and treated as heroic. From the late nineteenth century to the 1940s, black communities in large cities tended to get by and then some, despite the same remorseless segregation and racism and significant numbers of poor people.

The question of what distinguished 1910 from 1980 is, ultimately, rather obvious. Yet, it is almost strange how rarely it is addressed in discussions of race on any level. This is because our times teach us to look always to explanations under which blacks are victimized.

The factory-and-flight thesis is uniquely well suited to settle in as common wisdom. For a radical fringe, it allows one to characterize globalization as "racist" in depriving inner-city blacks of jobs. This frame of reference is even more attractive in allowing one to frame one's racial concerns within a perspective that is broader, even more sophisticated and humanitarian, perhaps: One champions not only black Americans, but also the "little man" worldwide.

But the thesis meanwhile comforts even those disinclined to extremity or conspiracy theories. Without veering into fanciful notions of evil operators pulling strings from on high, it traces black ills to a broad, societal factor beyond the individual's control. Whites, especially, are protected from any charge of racism. After all, one can even think globalization is good, or just inevitable, and still "acknowledge" that it leaves inner-city blacks with nowhere to turn. Lani Guinier's metaphor, brilliant in itself, of the miner's canary becomes useful. Exposed to polluted air, the canary drops dead quickly, serving as a warning to miners, to whom the air would be harmful but not lethal. Guinier compares the canary with blacks, uniquely vulnerable to demise when conditions are tough, while others, although hardly having a good time of it, will stumble a bit but right themselves in good time.

In embracing the idea that poor black communities had no way of avoiding falling to pieces without factories or middle-class role models, the indignant radical, the disappointed leftist, and the concerned moderate have all arrived at ways of making sense of a very challenging post–Civil Rights racial landscape in America. They are not hysterical, they intend no condescension, and they are sincere. However, I find myself convinced that they have also been misled. The modern inner city emerged for reasons that simply do not fit the patterns of thought that we have been taught as the only way to be compassionate. I hope to show in this book that there is a more realistic account of the birth of the inner city, which, although of a sort that makes a certain cadre uncomfortable, allows every bit as much compassion and hope for the future.

WHATCHOO TALKIN' 'BOUT, UNDERCLASS?

However, my argument requires that we spend some time on a common argument from the left that one is either racist or stereotyping to even speak or write of an "underclass." A number of writers on race object that there have always been plenty of poor black people, but that only over the last few decades have they been "essentialized," as it is often put, as a pathological phenomenon.

But other scholars, including black ones, have presented careful justifications for seeing something especially alarming about today's poor black communities. William Julius Wilson, a black man whose career is devoted to helping, not slandering, blacks, has noted, "There is a heterogenous grouping of inner-city families and individuals whose behavior contrasts sharply with that of mainstream America," and as a definition, specifies that the underclass occupy neighborhoods where at least 40 percent of the residents live below the poverty line and adults are more likely not to work than to work. Elijah Anderson also stresses another factor in such neighborhoods that crucially distinguishes them: a breakdown of civic order such that the "old heads" lose prestige while role models are criminals who are successful in selling drugs. A poor neighborhood is one thing, but a war zone where drug vending, drug addiction, early childbirth, absent fathers, unemployment, violence, and murder are all norms is another.

A potential objection here is that the modern analyst is unaware of what conditions were often like in black slums back in the day, unjustly abusing modern "thugs" out of a nostalgic idealization of the old days. Falling into that nostalgia could indeed tempt the unwary. For one thing, in more formal times, photographs tended to be posed and commemorative: groups standing in front of buildings in their Sunday best, people posed in studios waiting for the bulb to flash. Casual photos catching people smoking in a bar, "hanging out" on a corner, or in the middle of a live, spontaneous human gesture were less ordinary. Photography was more expensive, and so only the rich and famous could leave behind endless stacks of photos; the poor were lucky to have only a few by the end of their lives. Plus, in times more openly classist, there was less interest in documenting the lives of the people on the bottom in pictures: Indeed, there was Walker Evans or Richard Wright's *12 Million Black Voices*, but they were received as unique and eye-opening, not as ordinary. Thus in our moment, what we *see* of the black past skews away from its poorer aspects.

This applied as well to literature, journalism, and mass culture. In none of these realms was our sustained interest in "the real" established yet. Books about the poor were written, like John Steinbeck's *The Grapes of Wrath*, but their focus was considered against the grain, departing from the usual middle-class or wealthy mise-en-scène that novelists usually wrote of, and even books like Upton Sinclair's *The Jungle* were stylized rather than documentary. Few clamored for books written by the poor about themselves. Only in flashes did movies give us a look at life beyond those realms, and even then, usually in a sanitized fashion (Sam Goldwyn refused to even let trash be shown on the streets in the slum drama *Dead End* in 1937). Poverty was for all extents and purposes nonexistent on what we now know as old radio, and on television before the mid-sixties, and flashed by only in the occasional documentary or special series episode.

Especially given that all of this also tended to hide black people of *all* classes from national awareness, it is not surprising that the urban black poor do not exactly leap out at one in a casual survey of the black American past. Whites weren't interested in them, and quite a few middle-class and wealthy blacks were embarrassed by them.

Various black writers have been eager to remind us that this does not mean that old-time black communities were populated exclusively by women in high collars having "teas" and men with three names and hair parted down the middle smoking cigars in three-piece suits at civic organization meetings. They remind us that these people were lucky ducks, while the basic inequities of American society have meant that "thugs" have always been with us.

One even gleans a sense that some of these writers have a quiet sense of pride in the "thug" as a healthy rebel against the racist Establishment, and thus want to make sure the thug has his place in the black history diorama as a figure with a noble and ancient lineage. This perspective is not limited to black writers: Massey and Denton note that in 1960s ghettos, if a woman got pregnant, the man usually married or at least lived with her; "by the late 1980s, however, this bow to conventional culture had been eliminated in black street culture." Get that: a "bow" to "conventional culture"—part of them sees the rise in out-of-wedlock births among poor blacks as a laudable escape from puritanism, even though it was triple the rate of that among whites.

SOMETHING DIFFERENT:
EARLY BLACK GHETTOS VERSUS MODERN
BLACK INNER CITIES

In this light, I must make clear that whatever one's verdict on this book, its argument is constructed in full awareness that the black lower class is not new in American life. We must always recall Louis Armstrong's childhood in the violent, crowded, filthy Storyville section of New Orleans, descriptions of which will leave no one nostalgic in the least, or Ethel Waters's early life in the "bloody Eighth" ward in Philadelphia.

Middle-class blacks in the old days had no hesitation in mentioning this side of the black community. In Cleveland of 1915, we hear of the black man who "only works for the wherewithal to buy a gaudy creation of the tailor's art, some six-for-a-quarter so-called Havanas, and a rakish bowler, which he dons with the inevitable tilt. With this necessary equipment . . . he is then at peace with the world." In gaslight-era Chicago, a black newspaper huffed that "a number of our girls and boys are on the road to ruin," complaining of "the boys rioting in the Clark and 4th Avenue dives, laying the foundation for lives of thieves, thugs, and murderers, and the girls walking the streets in gaudy attire." In the mid-1960s in Detroit, black middle-class people in one neighborhood complained of "rowdy people," "hoodlums," "transients," and "ADC [welfare] people and their boyfriends" moving in and "lowering the tone," so to speak.

The claim in this book, then, is not that black neighborhoods in 1965 were uniformly sweet old places where everybody held their head up high and gave one another cakes and pies on Sunday, and then on New Year's Day in 1966 the neighborhoods became nightmares where the thug ruled the roost and people gave one another crack and gunshot wounds every day. My point is that poor black life was old news by the late sixties, but took an especially desperate, violent, hopeless, and narcoticized turn after that time. Given a choice between living in the old black slum districts and today's inner cities, just about anyone would choose the former.

The kind of description of early black neighborhoods that seems to make certain black thinkers nervous is positive ones of Bronzeville, Chicago. It's an easy score to list the usual examples of self-sufficiency that made Bronzeville a victory in the face of naked racism and segregation: several newspapers including the famous *Defender* of national influence; $100,000,000 in black-owned real estate by 1929 including several magnificent buildings; "the Finest Colored Hotel in the World," the Brookmont;

192 churches by 1929 that doubled as thriving social agencies helping to get poor black migrants on their feet; 731 black-owned businesses as early as 1917; the hot jazz scene and a crackling literary world-within-a-world; Provident Hospital; and so on.

It is important to know of these things because it shows what black people in America could achieve despite entrenched bigotry and segregation, questioning the current idea that "racism" condemns all but a few black supermen to misery. But those celebratory portraits are indeed incomplete. All blacks in Bronzeville were not gliding around in a glimmering sepia reproduction of middle-class white life—in fact, most weren't.

Legions of blacks in Bronzeville, recent migrants from the South with little education and no job skills, lived in outright squalor. Tiny "kitchenette" apartments, carved out of normal-size ones as migrants arrived by the thousands every year and were barred from living in other neighborhoods, were as nasty as the ones in which white immigrants lived in New York. Martinette Apartments was a seven-story building with a thousand people living in it, including two hundred children. A few blocks down was a building where people had to cook in the hallway and trash was picked up only every three weeks.

Unsurprisingly, there was an underworld side to this layer of Bronzeville. Black boys drifted into gangs that could break bread with their "gangsta" crew equivalents today, with early deaths common. Then there were boys who skirted the line, never getting arrested but qualifying as "cats" wearing zoot suits and impregnating the occasional woman. When St. Clair Drake and Horace Cayton in the mid-1940s write from Chicago, "The men, insecure in their economic power, tend to exalt their sexual prowess. They cultivate an attitude of 'love 'em and leave 'em'," we see a clear ancestor to the underclass men William Julius Wilson writes of today. Drake and Cayton chronicle the life of "Slick": "Nearly 30, Slick was a floater with two deserted wives behind him, an insatiable appetite for liquor, and spirochetes in his veins." Substitute crack for liquor and AIDS for VD and Slick is any number of unfortunate inner-city black men of today, and as they often do, Slick goes to prison for assault with a weapon and does not stay straight for long once he gets out. //

Richard Wright noted that "more of our girls have bastard babies than the girls in any other sections of the city," and that "many of our black women drift to ruin and death on the pavements of the city; they are sold, by white men as well as black, for sex purposes." There were also "good-time girl" black women who, while not formally selling their bodies, supported themselves partially on "favors" from men.

So when journalist Alan Ehrenhalt surveys the neighborhood and concludes, "What Bronzeville had, and so many of its graduates continue to mourn, was a sense of posterity—a feeling that, however difficult the present might be, the future was worth thinking about and planning for in some detail," he goes a bit far. He gets much of his sense of the time from poring through microfilms of the *Defender*. But the tone of editorialists and advertisements was a staged one, a public presentation of the black community, certainly quite different from how the typical person felt in the kitchenette apartments. Ehrenhalt is also taken by reminiscences from old people who grew up there, but the people most likely to be available for interview and harboring broad-horizon perspectives on how the neighborhoods changed are the successful ones, who had the means or special spirit to work their way out as soon as they could. Certainly they had this optimism, but how can we know that the woman who spent forty years doing laundry and raising kids in a tumbledown walk-up and died living with one of her daughters in a cramped housing project apartment ever thought much about "posterity"?

And yet, we cannot utterly discount one of the former residents saying "Fifty-first and Dearborn was a bunch of shacks. We didn't have hot water—and the houses were torn down for slum clearance to build Robert Taylor Homes. But in those shacks, there was something different from what there is now." This person lived in those shacks heating bathwater on the range, and yet joins in with a chorus of countless black people of her vintage and experience who make similar observations. We believe them when they tell us about the special task force of white police officers assigned to Bronzeville in the fifties, "the flying squad" that harrassed blacks of all classes, stopping them for moving violations and roughing them up, almost always when they were alone so there would be no witnesses. If so, we must temper a possible impulse to dismiss them as stuck in nostalgia when they also give us positive reminiscences.

After all, even statistics show this "something different." In 1950, almost everybody in Bronzeville who could work did. But by 1990, employment rates in the three districts of the neighborhood were four in ten, one in three, and one in four. This was, indeed, something different. In Drake and Cayton's survey, three out of five poor blacks were married—or at least in common-law marriages—and most people of age had at least tried marriage. Also saliently missing from even the most detailed and honest accounts of black slum districts in the old days is widespread drug addiction and its sale led by bands of young men killing one another and bystanders over turf. Not even the glummest accounts of Bronzeville give any indication that young black men were killing one another so frequently that their funerals were a monthly occurrence, as is so commonly reported from black inner cities today.

The story was similar in cities across the nation. Blacks made the best of segregation by developing their own world-within-a-world. If you scratched the pretty surface of the news accounts and lodge bulletins, you found a black lower class who would not have looked so good in photos—but then, even this part of the community had yet to tip into utter chaos and despair. One of black Cleveland's main historians, as interested in class and injustice as any responsible modern historian, depicts Cleveland's poor black district before the sixties as the "quiet ghetto," contrasting it with what would happen later.

BLACK GHETTOS BEFORE THE CHANGE: CLOSER UP

So we can be aware that there have always been black slums and also that today's black slums are very different places. But next we must assess whether I am correct in placing the time of the change in the late sixties. Here, what is most useful is surveys of poor black communities written just as they straddled the line between then and now. Sources like these reveal crucial differences between the modern underclass and yesterday's black "ruffians" and unfortunates.

Washington, DC

For example, in *Tally's Corner* Elliot Liebow studied black life at the very bottom in Washington, DC, in 1962 and 1963, chronicling the lives of "street corner men." Yet, from our modern perspective, they seem more like harmless chuckleheads than "thugs."

They are marginally employed if at all and have an ambivalent relationship to mainstream expectations. But they are a world apart from the black men so common in modern underclass communities. For example, the "don't-work-and-don't-want-to-work" contingent among them, who basically refuse to work at all, are a minority. Most of the men work at piecemeal "gig" jobs, on and off, even if "getting a job, keeping a job, and doing well at it is clearly of low priority." Moving to seek work is common: "Here a man loses a job and moves out; another one finds one and moves in . . . there goes a man who wants to try his luck in New York." This contrasts with the underclass men that, for example, William Julius Wilson chronicles, among whom moving to seek work is extremely rare, and who are less likely to see finding a job as "luck" than as knuckling under to "working for chump change." /

Sea Cat typifies how these men are hardly Cliff Huxtables or even Rocs, but still do what they have to do. Sea Cat has six weeks to pay his ex-wife $200 of alimony. He leaves his grocery-store job for higher-paying work as a laborer, but quits after four days because the work is too hard. But he doesn't stop here and spend the next few years dodging court officers: He goes back to the grocery-store job and washes dishes at night, working at both jobs until he pays off the debt.

And then notice also that Sea Cat was married at one point. To be sure, wife and kids are not what these men are about. "Most of the men have tried marriage and found it wanting," Liebow observes—but then most of them did at least try it. Middle-class norms still have some part in these men's self-conceptions, even if distantly. For the street corner man, "his behavior appears not so much as a way of realizing the distinctive goals and values of his own subculture, or of conforming to its models, but rather as his way of trying to achieve many of the goals and values of the larger society, of failing to do this, and of concealing his failure from others and from himself as best he can." That is, on some level these guys felt a certain sense of having failed at being "respectable," rather than proudly nurturing a thug persona. And yet many of these men can still refer to the South as "back home"—that is, they grew up under Jim Crow.

Then in *Soulside*, Ulf Hannerz gives a broader view of a black neighborhood in DC from 1966 to 1968, during the twilight of the era when middle-class blacks still lived among poorer ones. The "street corner" men are the bottom rung in a stratified portrait in which "mainstreamers" own their homes and read books, "swingers" are young adults who party a lot but have jobs, and "street families" are the kinds of people today often called "ghetto," scraping by in menial jobs and no strangers to welfare. The street corner men are the ones who have more or less checked out of respectability of any kind.

Crucially, though, they are not a simple equivalent to today's gangbangers. They fall afoul of the law here and there, yes, but their lives are not based on violence. Their addiction is not to heroin, stealing and killing to get the next fix, but to "getting a taste" of cheap liquor. They neither terrorized the neighborhood nor set its tone: They were riffraff, delinquents.

Chicago

Also useful is Elijah Anderson's portrait of lower-class black men who congregate in a seedy bar in Chicago, *A Place on the Corner*. Although Anderson studied them in the early seventies, these men, long past their teens and twenties, were products of the poor black America before the late sixties. Anderson eloquently sets the scene:

> Passengers sometimes gawk at the people of Jelly's. From the safety of their cars, often with rolled-up windows and locked doors, passersby can see wineheads staggering along, a man in tattered clothing "nodding out," leaning on Jelly's front window, and a motley, tough-looking group of men gathered on the corner . . . those on foot hurry past, not wanting to be accosted by the people of Jelly's.

The bar is home to "lowlives" who make only token gestures toward marriage, responsibility to their children, or steady work, and then below even them are the "hoodlums" who take the criminal path, and "wineheads" who don't do much of anything but drink.

But the bar also has a group of "regulars." These men are not middle-class burghers by any means, but they have steady jobs and value "decency," "strong character," and being of "some 'count." They also value having "a clean slate downtown," as opposed to the virtual pride in having done time that today's "thug" often brandishes. By the early seventies, unemployment and welfare could get one by as well as working a low-level job, but the regulars see people who resort to this as "something less than full men," as one explains:

> For a man to be al'right in my book, he got to work, or at least be tryin' to get some work. That's the first thing. . . . See, 'cause when we was comin' up, my daddy always told us, 'Don't be afraid of work. Don't be too proud to shovel shit all day, if you have to.' . . . When a man is workin' hard all day, 'stead of layin' 'round these here streets, well, he showin' me a good side of hisself.

Notice from this man's dialect that he is no bow-tied member of the black bourgeoisie whom some might accuse of wishing he were white or not liking black people. He is clearly as "authentic" as he can be: He is, roughly, television's Fred Sanford, who had a bar that he regularly went to with his friends.

Most important, at Jelly's the regulars like him set the tone, not the others: They are not considered squares or chumps but possess a solid status in the bar's pecking order. The notion that for black men checking out and living on the criminal side is noble, cool, or even just no big deal did not exist yet among these men.

For example, the "hoodlums" tend not to overtly see themselves that way; Anderson notes, "until they are reminded, they often attempt to pass themselves off as regulars. The term 'hoodlum' is considered derogatory and consequently is used more often to describe someone else rather than oneself." Compare this with the note of proprietary pride that the word *thug* has become infused with over the past twenty years, even for many middle-class black people. Among the men at Jelly's, the description "down" refers to someone who is good at avoiding a violent situation—and is a compliment!

The contrast is obvious with the Philadelphia ghetto that Anderson himself covered fifteen years later in *Streetwise*, where a man can get shot for just looking at another one for too long, marriage is a rarity, most people are either drug sellers or users, and a woman who gets a new refrigerator puts small pieces of the cut-up box in the trash each week to keep from advertising that she got something new. In the *Streetwise* world, the very designation "no 'count" has currency only among moralistic iconoclasts, since making one's way in the white man's world where "It's like a jungle out there, it makes you wonder how we keep from going under" is considered a sign of capitulation to racism and injustice. In *Streetwise*, Anderson, apparently as deeply affected by changes in the black word on the street as the people he studies, repeatedly frames men with the ideology of the Jelly's regulars as naïve and self-inflated.

Even the world of Jelly's was not one that most of us would enjoy hanging out in. But in that little bar, old-fashioned mores of "respectability" swayed some more than others but they had juice, in a way that indicated our "something different," soon to become a memory in black communities across the country.

St. Louis

An especially revealing study of the black urban transformation is Lee Rainwater's *Behind Ghetto Walls*, a portrait of the Pruitt-Igoe housing projects in

St. Louis on the early side of the mid-sixties, before the Watts riots. Life in these buildings showed "respectability" playing a less dominant role long before 1970 than it did even at Jelly's in Chicago ten years later. But still . . .

There is no doubt that conditions in Pruitt-Igoe gave ample fodder for someone seeking an argument that today's black underclass is nothing new. One resident said, "If you go downstairs now and step on someone's foot then the first thing you would hear is the popping of the case [knife being opened]." Just a list of residents' complaints about the buildings shows that they knew a world that no one who grew up in the "PJs" twenty years later would find unfamiliar.

> There's too much broken glass and trash around outside
> The elevators are dangerous
> People use the elevators and halls to go to the bathroom
> People who don't live in the project come in and make a lot of trouble by fights, stealing, drinking, and the like
> Little children hear bad language all the time so they don't realize how bad it is
> Holding somebody up and robbing them
> Teenagers yelling curse words at adults
> Boys or girls having sexual relations with a lot of different boys or girls

On that last issue, while rates of out-of-wedlock births among blacks exploded nationwide after the late sixties, rates were already rising somewhat before then, and this trend was evident in interviews with girls in Pruitt-Igoe. Asked whether they would be ashamed to get pregnant without being married, each of five teenage women said no, one saying, "It's really no reason to feel shame because there are a lot of people walking around here unmarried and you'll just be one more in the crowd," observing further, "Now girls don't be ashamed and you just expect a girl to get pregnant now because so many girls do, but before 1960 it was something for everybody around the corner to talk about and everything."

Now, it must be noted that even before 1960 (I've always wondered just what led this girl to specify that year as if she were a historian), out-of-wedlock birth was hardly something that got a poor black woman shunned from her community. In the 1940s, Drake and Cayton noted that poor black Bronzeville "not only tolerates illegitimacy, but [also] actually seems almost indifferent to it," tracing this to similar attitudes on plantations, where under any conditions, a child was considered a useful extra hand for fieldwork. But the fact remains that in both mid-century Bronzeville and this St. Louis girl's hypothetical pre-Kennedy poor black America, to have a child out of wedlock was "talked about," and crucially, was nothing approaching a norm.

And even in Pruitt-Igoe after 1960, views on the subject were hardly monolithic. Asked, "In a home what do you think is most important?" a fourteen-year-old says, "Having a mother and a father and a good family." That was just one girl, true, but then in a sample of fifty, responses about virginity included, "It's very important. Her husband would think more of her," "It means she took care of herself," and "It gives the husband something he hasn't had." I think most will agree that these statements would be much rarer today among young inner-city black people.

Now, indeed, they would be much rarer among all Americans of all colors. I, for one, born in 1965 and reaching puberty in the late seventies, certainly did not grow up with such old-fashioned ideas about premarital sex. The point is, however, that sexual mores in Pruitt-Igoe around 1964 were not already the ones we are so familiar with in the black underclass. That is, it is not true that the black underclass in 1964 was the same as it was in 1994. Nor is it that the difference between 1964 and 1994 in the black underclass was just a matter of the same sexual revolution that occurred nationwide. By 1994, national rates of out-of-wedlock births were three-quarters for blacks and only one-quarter for whites. In Pruitt-Igoe of this time, despite the changes that were clear from the interviews, women raising several children from several fathers was not yet a *norm*.

Rainwater traces the life of Thomas Coolidge, twenty-one years old and married to his nineteen-year-old wife (note that marriage among people this young is virtually nonexistent among poor blacks today). Coolidge's trajectory nicely illustrates a transitional stage between then and now. He starts out with old-fashioned "bootstraps" assertions: "People don't act the way they used to and I'm not saying that the way they used to act was the best, but at least they showed respect for others," or "People move in here with a chip on their shoulder against the white man and against anybody who has any kind of authority."

But Coolidge's story is no parable of making lemons out of lemonade. His life falls apart with a series of employment setbacks and his wife leaving him, and he starts drifting into Black Muslim activity including plans for a violent attack on whites. Yet he remains, in the end, someone with one foot in the old days and one foot in the new.

For one, nothing comes of the plans, and the ideology they are based on never becomes more than a kind of Lee Press-On Politics for Coolidge: "He observes that Negroes are not ready for equality, but at a later time argues even more persuasively that Negroes are ready and that it is only the whites who stand in their way. He argues that Pruitt-Igoe is a jungle in which each man's hand is turned against the other, later says that it is a solidary community which can bring itself together against the whites." Coolidge has little interest in jazz or the blues or "black is beautiful" statements, and ultimately values conventional "respectability." His basic nature survives: Before his bad times, he seemed to sense himself as American first and black second.

There are two even more glaring absences in the study, given the norm today. Drugs did not rule Pruitt-Igoe at this time, and gunfire is not its sound track—note the absence of shootings from the list of residents' complaints on page 32.

Overall, Rainwater's portrait of Pruitt-Igoe is one of the effects of poverty on communities and even the way high-rise buildings can worsen its manifestations—Pruitt-Igoe was in fact the inspiration for Oscar Newman's work on the subject. No one can deny that poverty often leads to levels of violence, illegitimacy, and unemployment higher than those in quiet middle-class communities, and hence the underbelly of Bronzeville, black Cleveland, black DC, and black St. Louis long before the Los Angeles riots after the Rodney King verdict. But black poverty had different results before the 1970s than it did later. None of the surveys of poor black realms in the sixties even begins to depict what we today would recognize as an underclass milieu equivalent to today's. Instead, the main impression that they give is that of "the quiet ghetto."

I feel it necessary to point out that none of the authors of these surveys was driven by a desire to stress the positive. These were not studies in the vein of bourgeois boosterism or old-fashioned white paternalism, hoping that whites would reconsider their racism if they saw blacks' basic industriousness and moral uprightness.

Rainwater, for example, gives us one of the Pruitt-Igoe buildings' "good boys" named Joe who writes in an essay: "Occupants in the Pruitt-homes district have very few jobs because most of the women just sit up on their butts getting welfare checks better known as 'Mother's Day checks,' on the tenth of every month. Jobs for youths are not too easy to find but if you really want a job you can get one. There are a lot of jobs for youths and adults also. Employment is pretty darn close to us too, because you can go down on Sixth to the Missouri Employment Agency." But for Rainwater, Joe is a problem, "unable to stand aside from the action of the project without moralistically condemning all those who participated in it."

Rainwater's perspective, then, is modern PC through and through, as is especially clear in his sharp words for little Joe: "His route to respectability makes him sound like a Junior Uncle Tom. Perhaps only a sense of revulsion bolstered by moralistic self-congratulation is adequate for resisting his temptations." The other chroniclers would also fit right in ideologically with most of today's social scientists.

Which is what makes it so important that their chronicles still show a different world from the same kinds of places just a decade-and-change later and in ways far beyond fashions and slang. There is a tragic difference between the "wino" and the crackhead, both in terms of what he does to himself and what he does to his community. There is a tragic difference between the snap of a switchblade and the crack of the cocking of a gun.

CONCLUSION

Vigilance against stereotyping is a hallmark of being a civilized American today—to a point. Writers old enough to have known black ghettos before the sixties, or who are familiar with the relevant literature, who fashion themselves as "disapproving" of the term *underclass* are, ultimately, more concerned with shielding black people from bad PR than facing a tragic reality. Others uncomfortable with the term either were not alive to see the old black ghettos or have not had occasion to consult the sources. Regardless of their intent, they mislead us in implying that their dismissal of the term is an informed one.

So Michael Eric Dyson is correct in noting that "black communities weren't the idyllic places that nostalgic black folk make them out to be," noting W.E.B. Du Bois's documentation of pre–World War I black leaders' decrying of young blacks who "hang around the corners in great numbers, especially the boys. Many of them are becoming gamblers and idlers." But he is wrong in supposing that this means that noting the "weakness, fragmentation, and collapse of black communities today" is a mere matter of a snobbish black bourgeoisie dumping on poor black people.

"Nostalgia" for old-time black ghettos can be heard from black people whom Dyson would be hard-put to dismiss as dismissive of black folk of humble origins. For example, I assume that *Invisible Man* silences anyone who would accuse Ralph Ellison of lack of sympathy with poor blacks. As such, we must hear him out on his own upbringing as he described it in 1958, in which he and fellow blacks were stuck on the other side of the tracks but took heart not in reading Edna St. Vincent Millay, but in listening to the blues-shouting of little Jimmy Rushing.

> We were pushed off to what seemed to be the least desirable side of the city (but which some years later was found to contain one of the state's richest pools of oil), and our system of justice was based upon Texas law; yet there was an optimism within the Negro community and a sense of possibility which, despite our awareness of limitation (dramatized so brutally in the Tulsa riot of 1921), transcended all of this, and it was this rock-bottom sense of reality, coupled with our sense of the possibility of rising above it, which sounded in Rushing's voice.

Rushing's voice was one "from below," equivalent in its era to the hip-hop that Dyson so cherishes. And it was that "authentic" voice from which Ellison drew support and hope—not as fodder for dreams of a revolutionary overturning of the American polity, but as a beacon for blacks he knew were making the best of themselves despite the obstacles they knew all too well.

The fact that there was a seamy black underworld in Ellison's Oklahoma City does not render him an old man forgetting the reality of what he grew up in. That optimism that he mentions, while surely apportioned to differing degrees among individuals according to circumstances, experiences, and sheer luck, was a guiding element in black communities' fabric, rendering even their seamier sides much less stained by "weakness, fragmentation, and collapse" than they would be later.

The point here is neither moralizing nor contempt, but constructive historical analysis. If we agree that there is a definite difference between poor black America then and now, then we come back to our central question. What made the difference?

CHAPTER TWO

The Birth of the Inner City, Part One: Indianapolis

In presenting a revision of our conception of why underclass culture became so widespread in America, I have chosen to take us on a historical trip to Indianapolis. And if the reader wonders why Indianapolis, that's exactly why. Indianapolis will be useful to us because of how neutral it is to almost anyone who did not grow up there. I want to avoid the subjective resonance of black communities with so many stories endlessly told, such as Harlem, the South Side of Chicago, and South Central Los Angeles. Let's put aside the rappers "shouting out" from Bushwick and Bed-Stuy, the ghetto LA that John Singleton branded in our minds with Ice Cube in *Boyz n the Hood* and Tupac Shakur in *Poetic Justice*, Marion Barry with his "Bitch set me up!" in DC, Sonny Carson fighting the school board establishment in New York, and Harold Washington turning heads in Chicago. No legends, no lore, no famous photos, no local schools of hip-hop and the blues. Just the facts.

For that, we need a city that rarely appears on the national scene in a racial context—where just as elsewhere, a black underclass took root and made a detour as tragic as it is familiar.

But for that, there are any number of cities I could have chosen, including my hometown, Philadelphia. Indianapolis is crucial to us for another reason. We are told that a key factor in inner cities going haywire was that factory jobs moved away. Okay—but before being accepted as theory, a hypothesis must submit to verification. The factory thesis makes the following simple prediction:

> If factory jobs did not move beyond blacks' reach in a city, then employment levels among blacks would not drop, and poor black

neighborhoods would not undergo an epidemic of crime, drug use, illegitimacy, and multigenerational welfare dependence.

That does not mean that black neighborhoods would be paradise. Some people would still be better off than others. There would be a criminal element, as well as a layer of "shiftless" sorts hovering somewhere between respectability and the street. Unemployment would be higher than in a middle-class suburb.

But black neighborhoods would be fundamentally stable, as they are so often recalled by older blacks who saw what happened after the sixties. Figures like the neighborhood "Mayor" that Ossie Davis played in Spike Lee's *Do the Right Thing* would unofficially reign supreme. The neighborhoods would be a little down-at-the-heels, but hardly the tragic hellholes that rappers "teach" us about and have concerned so many blacks and whites for the past few decades.

In that light, Indianapolis contradicts the prediction. Low-level manufacturing jobs never deserted this city as they did Chicago, Philadelphia, and other better-known ones. In Indianapolis, at best, a good number of such jobs moved a few miles away from the city center. Yet, before long, an underclass culture, of a sort well-known nationwide, took root, rued by mature black residents as deeply as in New York, Chicago, and Los Angeles.

INDIANAPOLIS FROM THEN TO NOW

Indianapolis Now

Summer 1993 in Indianapolis lent a vivid example. Let's start at SoulFest that year, which was supposed to be a celebration of black culture and commercial enterprise. SoulFest is one of many events at the annual Indianapolis Black Expo, which began in 1971. The Expo was billed at its debut as "a positive expression of what blacks can do in the community," in "a spirit of accomplishment, achievement and aspiration." That year, as in future ones, there were dozens of booths representing black businesses and organizations and a fine arts show. The SoulFest event had begun in 1989, and featured music, food, and carnival games, all in a grand celebration of black people in their glory. Here in 1993 was its fifth annual edition.

But a certain taint was in the air. For years, at SoulFest and other Black Expo events, for too many young black men, celebrating black culture apparently meant regaling the crowd with the "vitality" of black people at their worst. Over a hundred people had been arrested over the past four years as onlookers enjoyed their cotton candy.

The petty thefts and nasty scuffles had been bad enough. But in 1993 a young black man was shot dead at Soulfest, in a gang set-to among about twenty. The victim, twenty-year-old Marcus Clasby, was shot in the head. His murderer, Curtis Baker, was all of sixteen.

SoulFest was cancelled the following year and reopened in 1995 under a heavy police presence hard to square with a sense of community achievement. Three years later, in the days before the 1998 Expo, black columnist Lynn Ford tried to distract whites from associating the black gathering with carnage: "If you visit the Indiana Convention Center and RCA Dome, you'll see us as the loving, creative, spiritual, beautiful, nonviolent, goal-oriented, knowledge-seeking souls we are." That year's Expo's theme was "Strengthening Our Youth."

But a few days later, SoulFest witnessed another black-on-black homicide, and there was no SoulFest the following summer.

These episodes were the spawn of a violent inner-city culture that had grown in Indianapolis over the past few decades, much as in other American cities. Concerned people, black and white, wondered why this segment of Indianapolis's black community had gone so wrong. Crime and juvenile delinquency are age-old problems, but there was something new in the savagery and nihilism of events like those at SoulFest, and in the rampant unemployment, fatherlessness, and desolation in the city's inner-city neighborhoods.

Now, according to the factory analysis we saw in the previous chapter, we are to assume that the SoulFest events and the subculture they came from were due, ultimately, to an employment problem. Smart people often term it "deindustrialization." The idea is that once the factories pick up stakes, Marcus Clasby's death, bitterly mourned by his mother, was only to be expected. The implication of this analysis, explicitly spelled out by William Julius Wilson, is that inner-city Indianapolis's woes are the white man's fault and the only humane solution is a vast restructuring of American society.

That way of thinking is so very much in the air that a great many of us may genuinely imagine that bullet entering Marcus Clasby's skull as the end of a chain reaction that traces back to racist white men smoking cigars in office buildings. But if we really look at the history of black Indianapolis, we start to wonder.

Indianapolis Then: Auld Lang Syne

Blacks began moving to Indiana from the South in large numbers just after the Civil War, but during the Great Migration of the teens, so many blacks poured into Indiana that there were 80,810 black residents in 1920 compared with 11,428 in 1860. Immigrants flocked in particular to the cities: From 1900 to 1920 Indianapolis's black population jumped from 15,931 to 34,678, and ten years later, a full 90 percent of the state's blacks lived in Indianapolis or Gary.

But these migrants did not sit on their hands and devolve into an underclass problem case. Overt racism was a harsh reality, but their response to this was, as in most American cities, to create their own world-within-a-world.

An energetic business district grew up on "The Grand Ol' Street" of Indiana Avenue. Madame C. J. Walker, whose hair-care empire made her one of America's first self-made female millionaires, moved her operation to Indianapolis in 1910, employing 3,000 people. Her yellow-brick Walker Building anchored "the Avenoo," housing a theatre, restaurant, and ample office space. There were six elegant square blocks that housed the city's black bourgeoisie, Ransom Place. By 1920, Ransom Place was 96 percent black, and homeowners included doctors such as Henry W. Furniss, who doubled as a diplomat and was appointed ambassador to Haiti.

By the turn of the twentieth century, Indianapolis had no fewer than four major black newspapers, the *Leader*, the *World*, the *Freeman*, and the *Recorder*. This was despite the fact that slavery, when blacks were routinely denied learning how to read, was as recent to black Indianapolis residents as the Nixon Administration is to us. The *World* and the *Freeman*—probably America's first illustrated black newspaper—both had national audiences. The *Recorder*, in its 110th year at this printing, is now the third-oldest black newspaper in America.

In its early days, the *Recorder* had a strutting tone that today's PC black orthodoxy would condemn as insufficiently contemptuous of "white supremacy," even though blacks at that time knew white supremacy of a kind that would wear out most of today's black Americans in about a week. The *Recorder* editors had their feet on the ground, to be sure, diligently reporting incidences of racism and discrimination, and calling on blacks to boycott businesses that refused to advertise in the black community. But the general tone was one of a glass half full, not half empty. In 1902, one issue proudly listed all of the city's black-owned businesses, hoping that "if after reading the facts and figures as succinctly presented an inspiration comes to any who may be considering embarking on some business enterprise or renews hope in those who are now struggling to attain success we shall feel gratified." An issue the year before had listed the four dozen blacks who were worth $5,000 or more, duly noting that some few were worth as much as $40,000.

In some ways, the black movers and shakers' quests to show themselves worthy of white esteem went into directions that make us squirm today: The *Recorder* ran an uncomfortable number of ads for hair straighteners and skin lighteners week after week. But the editors clearly had a deep-seated sense of recoil from the idea that a leading black weekly would put doom and gloom front and center, as if degradation and abuse were the soul of blackness. As human beings focused on survival in a nasty America, they felt a primal urge to shout their victories to the heavens and put their best and brightest front and center. Ancient issues of the *Recorder* are mesmerizing accounts of a kind of alternate black universe.

Branches of the National Association of Colored Women, the National Negro Business League, and various lodges thrived, as well as innumerable churches. In 1946, the McArthur Conservatory opened, offering black students lessons in voice, orchestra, piano, music theory, and composition, and it was Indiana's first conservatory to train students in jazz. "The Avenoo" was also home to a crackling hot music scene.

There was no wariness of "the miseducation of the Negro" in early black Indianapolis. These people were hungry for mainstream education, and black leaders' struggles against school segregation were stage-center on the city's black scene for decades. An ironic benefit of this segregation, however, was the all-black Crispus Attucks High School. High school teaching positions were among the only ones available to intellectually talented blacks, which meant that Attucks students learned from demanding, college-educated black teachers. The school was established to great fanfare in 1927, and demand was so high that 1,300 students showed up for instruction in a school built for 1,000. Beyond Attucks, night schools were popular among blacks unable to attend school in the daytime, while the local NAACP fought against school segregation, seeking for blacks to have as much access to top-quality education as possible.

The Bad Old Days

Yet, black people in Indianapolis were no strangers to racism. We tend naturally to think first of the South in terms of the worst of racism back in the day, but bigotry had always been notoriously virulent in Indiana. Despite the Fifteenth Amendment of 1869, black suffrage was not officially condoned until twelve years later, and blacks were barred from joining state militias until 1936. In the 1920s, the Indiana Chamber of Commerce recommended that schools be segregated.

Then there were the usual housing covenants. As in most American cities, while blacks were at first distributed fairly evenly in the city, in the 1920s after the black population had vastly increased during the Great Migration, whites began penning blacks into a single, overcrowded district. Neighborhood "associations" sprouted up devoted to keeping blacks out of white neighborhoods, such as the Capitol Avenue Protective Association that supported the building of "spite fences" around black homes on white blocks, surrounding the house with high walls on three sides. In 1924, a black family moved into a white neighborhood only to have a grenade thrown through their window; white residents then received a leaflet asking "Do you want a nigger for a neighbor?" Such episodes were sadly typical, and there was soon a "white supremacy dead line" at Twenty-seventh Street, above which no blacks were allowed to live. By 1940, almost all of Indianapolis's 44,000 blacks were corralled into one area, in which crumbling quarters without modern electricity or indoor plumbing were common.

If the grenade episode sounds like something the Ku Klux Klan would do, then it is germane to note that in the 1920s the Klan was the largest and most powerful social organization in Indiana; 40 percent of the native-born white adult male population were members. Indianapolis's mayor John Duvall was a known Klansman, and the Klan controlled the legislature and the governor's office—the Democratic Party in Indiana was essentially the Klan at the polls. In 1924, 6,500 Klansmen paraded downtown after their election victories. There was a reason that there was an Anti-Lynching League in black Indianapolis—one of the last recorded lynchings north of the Mason-Dixon line happened in nearby Marion in 1930.

All but a few blacks had work, not careers, and little hope for better. Most blacks were stuck in the lowest-paying jobs with the least prospects for advancement. Employment discrimination was a fact of life for all blacks, who before World War II were largely barred from most unions and rarely allowed to advance beyond low-skill blue-collar jobs. The typical black worker in Indianapolis was a laborer, shelf-stocker, custodian, food-service worker, or domestic (in the 1920s, 90 percent of black women who worked outside of the home were maids). In factories, blacks were vastly overrepresented in low-level positions and indefensibly underrepresented as craftsmen. The occasional promotion of a talented black into a higher position sometimes even sparked revolts among white workers.

Yet, despite the injustice of this discrimination, the basic fact was that black people took the jobs that were available, and as such, black Indianapolis *worked*. Proportionately, more blacks were unemployed than whites—but that will surprise no one. What might be more surprising is that even amid such stark racism, there was no unemployment "crisis" in black Indianapolis per se. The crisis was about the quality of the jobs blacks could get, not about whether they took them. In fact, black unemployment was lower in Indianapolis in this era than in some other cities: 90 percent of blacks were employed in 1940.

Ominous Developments?

For the "deindustrialization" theorist, the slide downhill to the Indianapolis of the SoulFest shootings begins twenty years later in the sixties, when two developments coincided.

First was the "Second Great Migration" of Southern blacks in the 1960s. In Indianapolis, two-thirds of the migrants were under twenty-five, most had not graduated from high school, and three-quarters were women, most from broken marriages and now saddled with children. These people naturally settled in the black neighborhoods in the center of the city.

Second was that, indeed, at this time many low-skill manufacturing jobs were moving away from the city center into the more spacious suburban ring. Only 15 percent of the new migrants had cars to get to the new plants, while the local bus system, developed for the more centralized city of yore, often did not run early or late enough to adequately serve factory workers. Manufacturing jobs were even, on the average, located a few miles farther from the center of town than service jobs that often did not pay as well.

Black Power Gets to Indy

And indeed, the late sixties saw stirrings of a new black Indianapolis, where twenty-five years later the typical black citizen would see the SoulFest murders more as "same-old same-old" than as an aberration. I have referred to those particular murders for the purpose of starting from the particular and proceeding to the general; in themselves, they were by no means headline events by 1993.

The city saw its first race riot in 1969, on, as it happened, Indiana Avenue. Police officers arrived to break up a fight in an apartment complex one Thursday night, and a young black man stole one of the officers' guns and fled. Blacks on the scene later reported—although the officers denied—that the officer fired three shots in his direction, upon which the young man dropped the gun. But what is certain is that when more officers came to the scene, black onlookers pelted them with bricks and bottles.

In the wake of this, the Big 10 market was firebombed, and Newbauer's department store was looted (and after this, closed up shop for good). Unrest continued for the next few days. The next day a sniper fired shots from a rooftop at police officers, and two patrolmen were attacked by a crowd, with one officer stomped on as others threw rocks and bottles at passing cars. On Sunday a church was set on fire.

Although eventually about a thousand policemen worked twelve-hour shifts to avoid an outright conflagration, the Indianapolis riot was a low-key one as riots went at the time. The police made no arrests on the first night, calling on black community leaders to step in—which they did, including the local Black Panthers. Property damage amounted to just $90,000, there were only about ninety-five arrests, and there were no civilian injuries.

But a new tone was set. There was something new in the air. In a town meeting with Mayor Richard Lugar after the riots, blacks presented bitter complaints justifying what had happened, such as there being too many fatherless men, too few male teachers in the schools, excessive discipline in the schools, inadequate recreational facilities for blacks, and a general problem of unemployment. Maybe none of those things were ideal. But then, the tendency for teachers to be women had not been considered a problem before. And as for the other problems, they had existed since the nineteenth century.

One might say that blacks were exploding after decades of frustration—but one would then be obliged to recall an earlier response to frustration, the old black Indianapolis with its "Grand Old Street." Racism was as bad then as it was in 1969; worse, really. Just what determined that blacks got "fed up" in the sixties instead of, say, in the twenties when the Klan was running things? Also, supposing that blacks "finally" got fed up sounds as if the blacks who took to the streets in 1969 were people ninety and older who recalled the grand sweep of racist oppression in Indianapolis since the late nineteenth century. In fact, however, they were young people, most of whom barely remembered the forties (no account or photograph of the riot I have consulted indicates participants in wheelchairs).

So what, then, do we make of the angry young black men telling Mayor Lugar, "We have no place but the corners"? These men's fathers and grandfathers hadn't felt that way—or, they knew a number of black men who made that choice, but the black community as a whole was not representing itself that way to the powers that be. Was the tone of that town meeting really a natural, step-by-step result of discrimination? Or was it a tone only possible in a new era, different from 1925 in that now mayors like Lugar were open to listening to black people vent rage? Was it about a pot coming to boil, or was it just about a new fashion?

Fashion seemed a better answer at least in terms of some of the new black "leaders" coming out of the woodwork. They made good press and good TV, but little else, and the old black Indianapolis would have run them out of town in a week. Especially well remembered today is Charles "Snooky" Hendricks, a reformed petty criminal who got the ear of a local white establishment jittery from seeing the race riots erupting elsewhere. Hendricks claimed that he was in a unique position to "maintain stability" among blacks, such that, for example, he acted as an intermediate between blacks and the police on the scene of the riot. He fashioned himself as the head of a Black Radical Action Project and was granted a municipal position including office space—only to turn out to be dealing in drugs on the side, get shot on the street, and end up in prison. He died there decades later, having been a regular caller on a local black talk radio show that dwells liberally in anti-whitey rhetoric.

The Turning Point

A culture rarely turns upside down overnight. The late sixties in Indianapolis saw a brief overlap between the old and the new ways, with Civil Rights in its final gasps as Black Power was in the ascendant.

Black schoolteacher Mattie Coney embodied the "old school" approach to a bad hand. Three years before the riot she had established the Citizen's Forum, dedicated to helping blacks clean up their neighborhoods and point their children toward success. Coney was from a solid working-class family that taught her that blacks' path to salvation was to "quit feeling sorry for ourselves and take advantage of opportunities." She established the Citizen's Forum with a start-up grant from E J Lilly and used her organization to found more than 3,000 block clubs over the years dedicated to clearing trash and a "de-RAT-ification" effort against vermin. The Forum distributed a pamphlet urging black parents to teach their children to stress cleanliness and polite conduct and to have pride in themselves.

Coney was granted a special award by president Lyndon B. Johnson and elicited accolades from presidents Dwight D. Eisenhower and Gerald Ford.

Just a year before Coney founded the Citizen's Forum, it had seemed like a few white housewives with some good old-fashioned "civic spirit" could take care of what crime there was in Indianapolis. It is almost sad looking back at the national attention Margaret Moore, a white woman, got by lowering the crime rate with her Indianapolis Anti-Crime Crusade in 1965, enlisting local citizens to interface with the police, attend court hearings, have streets better lit, and watch for truant kids. Reporters and pundits purred over this effort, convinced that a problem had been solved, along the lines of the period's radio and television shows where officers, clergymen, and old heads could make short work of "juvenile delinquency" in half an hour. But the die was cast. By 1973, central Indianapolis's black streets were often so threatening that the Citizen's Forum had added a program escorting black children to school in safety.

One vignette in the 1969 riot had neatly shown where black Indy was going. A black twenty-something-year-old and fifteen of his comrades from a local neighborhood center had circulated advising the rioters to "Cool it," saying that "Violence won't do anybody any good," and "Let's think about what we are going to do." They were lauded as playing a significant part in spreading some sense.

But they also offered another piece of counsel, this one historically revealing, in that 1969 was about the very last time that any black person could walk the ghetto streets and say it with any illusion that it would be received as constructive: "Remember that we are residents of Indianapolis and Americans first." Ah, but "authentic" black identity has long since relegated sentiments of that kind to the margins. Today, black people who fashion themselves as blacks second and Americans first better be prepared to defend themselves; these days, "real" black people feel the other way around. And these guys very much straddled then and now, in that they refused to release their names to the media.

They had one foot in 1949, but were savvy enough to know that 1969 was a very different time. The word on the street was changing. Fred Crawford, a Black Panther member from Oakland, was setting up shop in Indianapolis with rhetoric along the lines of, "I don't feel we can gain our freedom without a revolution. This could only happen if the white man raised his fist off the black man's neck, but I don't think he'll ever do that."

Editorialists black and white of a certain age tsk-tsked over this sort of thing. Andrew W. Ramsey, a black editorialist at the *Recorder* wrote,

"Unfortunately to many of those who have cried the loudest about black power and black beauty, these slogans have been only the shibboleths of negatives. They have with reason denounced the actual racial situation in the United States and have decided that it must go but they have done very little thinking about what is to succeed it and how the change is to be brought about . . . many of the youthful parturient of black power have acted as if blackness alone were the end rather than merely a rallying point for a meaningful program for America." Pointedly, however, his column was titled "A Voice from the Gallery." Ramsey was an activist as well as editorialist, serving as president of the Indiana state chapter of the NAACP. "A continued program of negativism will not help to solve the plight of the black minority in America," he wrote, but his voice was lost in the maelstrom of an era that had no use for him and his "parturient."

And one can just imagine how young blacks in Indianapolis received columns like white Grover C. Hall's over in the mainstream *Indianapolis Star*, touting Booker T. Washington's *The Future of the American Negro* and admonishing blacks that "Washington understood the mischief of rigorists: 'There is danger that a certain class of impatient extremists among the Negroes . . . may do the entire race injury by attempting to advise their brethren . . . to resort to armed resistance or the use of the torch, in order to secure justice.' " Decidedly unhip. ⁄

From Slum to Inner City

The rest of the story is sadly familiar. In the wake of the construction of highway route 65, thousands of blacks were placed in housing projects, which were 96 percent black by 1993 when the SoulFest murders happened and, to put it lightly, were in no sense demonstrations of black dignity of a kind that the *Indianapolis Recorder* would have celebrated back in the day. And in these buildings and beyond, black Indianapolis became a very different place from what residents around "The Grand Old Street" in the old days would have recognized.

By 1992, the Indianapolis Commission on African American Males was established to address a dismaying subculture of depravity. The statistics were as tragic as they were familiar. By 1993, the black unemployment rate was three times the white one, as was the rate of black children in one-parent homes. In 1990, blacks committed 56 percent of Indianapolis's violent crimes despite constituting only 21 percent of the population. One in ten black men aged sixteen to twenty-four were in jail, black boys made up 43 percent of those in juvenile detention, and 48 percent of adult men in prison were black. Indianapolis saw 68 homicides in 1989, 109 in 1991, and 160 in 1998, and in that year, a study showed that three-quarters of the victims were acquainted with their killers. Sadly, no, it was not "stereotyping" to treat this as a black issue: Gun-driven savagery was sharply higher in predominantly black poor neighborhoods. A young black man stood up at one town meeting on the crisis and said, "Why bother? I probably won't be around anyway."

These statistics make it obvious that lax parenting had become typical in a community that had once held its children on a short tether. By 1987, the Children's Defense Fund announced that Indianapolis had the highest rate of infant mortality of any city in America with 500,000 residents or more.

Meanwhile it became common for black educators to embrace the idea that traditional teaching "miseducates" black children. Back in 1922, a letter from "16 progressive colored citizens" of the Better Indianapolis League had insisted that "no one section of the population can be isolated and segregated without taking from it the advantage of the common culture." But by the 1990s, some predominantly black Indianapolis schools were proposing that black students would benefit from "Afrocentric" materials. And this was partly in response to another crisis: In the nineties, black community sixth graders were failing basic skills tests at rates as high as 82 percent, and dropping out of high school was common. Whatever one attributes this to, one must compare it with the stampede on Crispus Attucks High School in 1927—when Indiana was run by the Klan and all but a sliver of black workers were menials. Something in black Indianapolis had changed, deeply and decisively.

A 1993 report concluded, "There is lack of black male adult participation in the lives of young black males that contributes to a violent street culture, gang activities, and drug trafficking." Sadly ordinary today. But blacks in Indianapolis in 1950, seeing the slow but sure successes of the Civil Rights movement, would have been stunned to find out that a statement like that would apply to their community at *any* point in the future—and certainly not just forty years later.

WHAT HAPPENED?
THE FACTORY ANALYSIS

To return to our main question: Was all of this brutality and alienation really the result of factories changing their addresses?

It is hard to think so when low-skill jobs never deserted central Indianapolis to remotely the degree that they did in many other cities. The phantom hulk buildings I grew up seeing all over Philadelphia were due to the fact that between 1963 and 1987, manufacturing facilities there had gone from 4,618 to just 1,887, and this was not just from within the city but from the surrounding suburbs as well. Factory jobs truly flew the coop. Detroit's factory count went from 4,546 to 2,843 during the same period, again including surrounding Wayne County.

But in Indianapolis, the only significant factory relocation was from the central city to nearby suburbs within the county containing the city, Marion County, which only radiates about ten miles outward in all directions from central Indianapolis. One study documented that in 1972 the average distance of manufacturing jobs from central Indianapolis was a mere 3.2 miles. In fact, from 1963 to 1987, within Marion County itself— that is, the nearby environs of central Indy—manufacturing facilities *increased* from 1,130 to 1,254. We can say, then, that the number of factories basically stayed the same.

Without a doubt, Indianapolis in the 1950s had been a city where solid low-skill jobs were ripe for the picking right within the city, generally a bus ride away from the west side black district. The largest companies included Coca-Cola, Pepsi, and Canada Dry bottling facilities; Nabisco; Stokley-Van Camp; International Harvester; Indianapolis's traditional mainstay E J Lilly; and car manufacturers Chevrolet and General Motors. All offered blue-collar jobs upon which one could found a decent existence.

And equally without a doubt, manufacturing jobs no longer anchor central Indianapolis today as they did back then. In the wake of the nationwide suburban development after World War II, corporations began relocating their factory headquarters in more spacious quarters beyond downtown. A map of Indianapolis in 1955 shows countless factories large and small clustered around the city center, but a map of Indianapolis today shows the same kinds of factories mostly hovering in a ring beyond.

But only in that ring beyond, a few miles away. Not in India. Not over in Ohio. Not even in the counties next door. Just a few miles away from downtown Indianapolis. And our question is whether this difference caused the change from the old days to the new. In the 1920s, on "the Grand Old Street" Indiana Avenue, miscreants were around, but they acted on the margins of society. The black community *norm* was one of decorum and making the best of the least. But in 1993, at SoulFest, young black teens committed cold-blooded murder as punctuation to a mere scuffle—and this was so ordinary that it barely made news. Equally ordinary was drug addiction, the life devoted to drug sales, the father who barely knew his children by multiple partners, and the multigenerational black family on the dole.

Was this because factories moved a few miles down the road?

That's all it was. Today, the Coke bottling plant is five miles northwest of where it was in 1955. Other factories have moved eastward—but not to, say, Pittsburgh, but in the case of Nabisco, seven miles east from where it was in 1955, International Harvester about five miles, and General Motors about two-and-a-half. And then some plants have stayed put since 1955, such as Stokley-Van Camp and Chevrolet, while E J Lilly's plant has moved, but to a location no farther from central Indianapolis than its site in 1955. To be sure, some plants have moved farther—Pepsi is now a good ten miles out in the 'burbs, and Canada Dry a tad farther out (although still within Greater Indianapolis). But then naturally, new facilities have come in since the days of *I Love Lucy*, such as a Ford plant five miles east of central Indy, and Daimler-Chrysler three miles to the southwest, hard by the Olin brass foundry.

All of these companies are within the same telephone area code as central Indianapolis. Almost all are accessible via principal streets stretching from the city center, rather than being outposts planted alongside highways endless miles away, barely processible as part of the municipality of Indianapolis. The bus route grid of Indianapolis covers an area that thoroughly encompasses all but the few especially distant factories. Yes, routes outside of central Indianapolis are not as thickly concentrated as they are downtown, but buses there still run at least on the hour throughout the day and into the evening.

So yes, factories in Indianapolis moved "to the suburbs." But what kind of distance did this entail? What is, after all, a mile? From the top of the Empire State Building in New York, on a clear day you can see *eighty* miles. At the edge of their ability, humans can *run* a mile in a few minutes. Hardly would we expect black people in Indianapolis to sprint to work, but the point is simply that a mile is only so far. And then, we are not medievals—we have not only horses and oxen but also motorized transport. Certainly, a city bus can manage even several miles—and definitely three, or four, or even seven, or even ten. And then there are cars—no, not BMWs, but even the jalopy, the beater, the lemon, the 1988 Nissan. Imagine someone saying, "Well, I'm not working because now the GM plant is almost *three miles* from downtown." How can we sagely agree that for inner-city blacks whose dignity is at stake, travelling more than one bus ride from home is such a chore that the crack pipe, the gun, and fatherless children are inevitable?

Academia Chimes In

Two studies in the early seventies, early examples of the deindustrialization hypothesis, examined the factory relocations in Indianapolis and their possible impact on black employment patterns. Both began with description, but then essentially came up short in giving any concrete reason why factories moving a few miles away would bar blacks from getting jobs in them. One study, with assiduous statistical analysis, showed that blacks' presence in a factory's workforce was lower in factories farther from the city center than in those closer in. But correlation does not demonstrate cause. Was it that blacks could not possibly get to these factories or that other factors made them less likely to try?

Granted, the transportation situation was far from optimal. But then we must ask, if millions of blacks had picked up stakes from the South and moved thousands of miles from their homes in search of work for decades, why did a core of their children suddenly lapse into criminality and generations of living on the dole when work moved a twenty-minute drive away? The studies dance around that question in a sense, stating—just stating, mind you—that whites in Indianapolis were more likely to own cars than blacks. But what about carpooling? One conceivable scenario is that blacks might have often pooled their resources and bought cars at least viable enough to make the modest trip out to the suburbs to work. If we were to read today that struggling black Indianapolis residents had done precisely this starting in the late sixties, we would hardly consider it as awesomely perplexing and counterintuitive as the construction of the pyramids in Egypt—"My *God*, they *scraped together* their money and bought *used cars* to *get to work*????" We would just see it as an ordinary demonstration that people who want to put food on the table chase sources of employment. But the 1972 analysts offer only that, well, blacks were less likely to carpool to work than whites. But anthropologists record no folk wariness of carpooling endemic to black American culture.

Today, in Indiana's third poorest county, rural Crawford, where the black population is basically nil, 70 percent of its workers commute outside of the county by hook or crook. In 1946, black Lawrence Brookins in

Indianapolis got a job at the Union Carbide plant and commuted an hour by bus from his home in Martindale-Brightwood northeast of center city. What made the difference among inner-city blacks in Indianapolis from the seventies onward?

Aware that the figures alone did not provide a real argument, the researchers groped at speculations: that the distance subjected poor Indianapolis blacks to "lack of job information," or even that there was a "hard-core unemployed's conception of distance" different from other people's. But the Great Migration itself leaves these guesses dead in the water. The person who gleans "job information" from across state lines will presumably have little trouble honing in on it from a few miles off. The person who readily negotiates the "distance" from Mississippi to Indiana will not be stymied by a few miles of asphalt.

No Place but the Corners?

And in any case, it's not as if the factory jobs, however far they happened to be from the dead center of the city, were the only jobs available. For example, just when black Indianapolis's streets were taking a nasty turn as the sixties became the seventies, it is hard to glean from classified ads in that era's *Indianapolis Recorder* a city that barred uneducated blacks from employment.

Yes, I know—some companies were certainly still opposed to black applicants; legalized segregation was just a few years in the past. But that's exactly why we look to the *Recorder*—a black newspaper. We assume that companies advertising there were more progressive. After all, capitalism alone would militate against their spending money to post ads in a paper read by people they did not want to hire.

So—take the *Recorder* want ads in 1969 when Indiana Avenue erupted. "Help! We need men to work today! GENERAL LABORERS WAREHOUSE YARD WORKERS," said one ad. Indiana Bell wanted repairmen, installers, cable splicers' helpers and specified "will train." Another company wanted shipping clerks, and again, "will train"—it wasn't that lack of skills completely barred Indianapolis's blacks from jobs that required more than lifting and screwing on bottle caps. Elsewhere, the call was for "nonexperienced assemblers, heli arc welders, process inspectors, stock handlers, experienced wirers, fork lift drivers, punch and brake press operators, brazers, spray painters, electricians." Note that "nonexperienced"—no one could read this ad and reasonably grouse, "I could get experience if someone would just hire me, but all the ads want me to have the experience already." Indianapolis also had a lot of foundries at the time, and one of them in 1969 was seeking trainees—and not experienced hands, but trainees.

Two years later, ads sought bulldozer scraper operator trainees, security guards, maintenance workers, food service workers, tradesmen, cashiers, cooks, and truck drivers. The *Recorder* also ran ads for jobs that required somewhat more skills but hardly extraordinary ones, such as an electrical construction apprenticeship program requiring a high school diploma and two years' math, advertising itself with the new designation of Equal Opportunity Employer, or a call for a plumbing apprentice, with high school diploma required—but also with instructions of how and where to get an application. Commonwealth Life and Accident offered careers in underwriting ("will train").

Where the ads indicated the location of the companies, few were out in the suburbs—many were on the east side of the city rather than the west side where most blacks lived, but this meant just a bus ride. Young blacks after the 1969 riot complained to the mayor about "unemployment," and would presumably have rolled their eyes if anyone had taken out a copy of the *Recorder*—the black community's local newspaper—and pointed to the want ads running in it every week, obviously aimed by white-run companies at blacks seeking jobs. We have to wonder just how the eye-rollers would have justified that if asked.

It is very hard not to sense that motivation played a part here. For example, in 1971 when those *Recorder* want ads were running, 13 percent of blacks were unemployed while only 5.1 percent of the population as a whole was. But was this because that was the best black Indy could do, or was something else going on—or not going on? In my research and interviews, for example, I have found no evidence that blacks in Indianapolis began petitioning the local transit company to start running routes more often to the nearby suburbs. Or, if factory relocation created the epidemic of poverty in inner-city Indianapolis, then wouldn't we expect that for at least several years, people there would have been in constant, agonized search for work, agitating publicly for it on a regular basis, and amply covered in their frustration by a journalistic establishment newly awakened, by the 1970s, to race issues? Sure, perhaps if this search bore no fruit in the wake of protest after protest, people would have given up after some years. But again, scholars, community activists, and residents themselves give not the slightest hint that there was any vocalized, indignant desperation like this in black Indianapolis. And then, what about the jobs that were indeed available to anyone willing to ride the buses?

The problem was the same twenty years later—the underclass core of black Indianapolis by the 1990s was not a people who gave the impression of being exactly *desperate* for work. Stephen Goldsmith, Indianapolis's mayor from 1992 to 2002, was deeply committed to improving conditions for poor blacks there. He spontaneously gave me a list of places where unskilled people could work by the 1980s that overlapped quite a bit with exactly the manufacturing companies readily visible on a map of the city today, some of which I have already listed briefly: UPS, GM, Stokley-Van Camp, International Harvester, Chevrolet Truck and Body, a clothing Call Center, and others. He said that although for many, manufacturing and low-level jobs were essentially all that were available to them, "anyone who wanted a job could work."

Just a clueless white man? Well, black commentators chime right in with him. The Indiana Commission on African American Males is no stranger to the blame game ("African-American males tend to be the target of most racist actions"). Yet, even its literature attributes the unemployment crisis not to work being too far away, but to the simple fact that "most black males are unaware of employment options and opportunities." Historian Lana Ruegamer similarly observes, despite a basically leftist perspective, "a contempt for work and school" among younger blacks in Indiana's cities by the 1990s reminiscent of that among Irish and Italian immigrants a century ago. Olgen Williams, black head of Christamore House, a facility helping poor blacks, casually notes that there came a point when inner-city blacks were not taking advantage of ready opportunities at plants like Ford.

Another example is Katherine Rosier's study of women on welfare in Indianapolis in 1990. Rosier's main point is to show that life was hardly easy for these women. But then the women also openly admit that the downward trajectory of their lives began with periods of substance abuse and sleeping around in the 1970s. In contrast to William Julius Wilson's Chicago interviewees who spontaneously mention factories having picked up stakes, none of these Indianapolis women speaks of "the factory jobs moving away"—because they hadn't.

Even the timing is mysteriously off if we suppose that factory moves left the ghetto to fall apart. By 1967, in Indianapolis, 43 percent of blue-collar jobs and 228 of 922 factories had moved to the suburbs. But that left 57 percent of the jobs available and 694 factories still in place—and yet this was essentially the employment situation when the Indiana Avenue riot happened just two years later. It's one thing to stipulate that a pot finally boiled over—but here it looks like it boiled over before anyone had even lit the flame.

Old Man Racism?

Finally, an appeal to racism will not help us. Discrimination was hardly unheard of in Indianapolis even after the 1960s. "In office after office not a black face can be seen," a black newspaper commentator observed in 1971. And a controversy over desegregating the schools through busing flared up in Indianapolis around this time just as it did in other cities. But the limits on black aspiration were falling away and fast. To compare this era with the days when the Klan ran the state and blacks were banished to the margins of society would be an insult to black Indianapolis, not to mention black people, period.

For example, in the early seventies there were even civic efforts to reduce what was already seen as a looming crisis among poor blacks. The Indiana Chamber of Commerce began affirmative action in hiring, with an additional call for businesses to sign a pledge to start on-the-job training programs for people with limited skills. The Indianapolis government signed an agreement with the Marion City Building Trades Council, stipulating that unions and contractors give hiring priority to the residents of neighborhoods where federally funded projects were being built.

Nor did residual racism hold back the large numbers of blacks who established thriving businesses starting in the 1970s. William G. Mays founded the Mays Chemical Company and later became president of the aforementioned Indiana Chamber of Commerce. Walter Blackburn's architectural firm specialized in building churches, schools, and low-income housing. Informed movers and shakers in Indianapolis, white and black, note the high degree of communication and cooperation between white and black community leaders over the past few decades.

When Work Disappears . . . People Move

And finally, if three miles is a little inconvenient, what about moving along with the factories? Once again, to paraphrase Shelby Steele, when work disappears, people move. The redlining of the old days receded after the 1960s across the United States, and in Indianapolis, it meant that *more* blacks moved to the suburbs than stayed behind in the inner city.

Now, it would be strange if even into the seventies Indianapolis was completely immune to the old-fashioned white neighborhood tribalism. As late as 1972, a test showed realtors steering black buyers away from homes readily shown to white ones or being quoted higher prices than white buyers. But as elsewhere, by this point this kind of thing was diluting into a *tendency*, rather than being an impregnable wall of the "Do you want a nigger for a neighbor?" variety. Blacks who were able to move out may have run up against some troglodytes in their search for houses—*but* then moved on to the next realtor and got what they were looking for.

There was even a neighborhood within the city, Butler-Tarkington, whose residents opened up to black buyers in 1956, creating the city's first deliberately integrated neighborhood—blacks went from 8 percent to 55 percent of its residents from 1950 to 1980. The whites here were transitional cases, yes—educated sorts affiliated with Butler University—and blacks tended to cluster in a particular quarter of the district. But this was a long, long way from grenades coming through the living room window. Indianapolis natives routinely note how vast the black middle-class exodus from the slums was. Racial discrimination had not expired completely in Indianapolis—but neither was it any longer a sentence to failure.

Then there is the issue of the commute. Lawrence Brookins's hour-long commute into central Indianapolis was neither unusual nor even extreme for blacks before the sixties. In Detroit, in the teens and twenties, black maids were riding an hour from Black Bottom to Grosse Pointe, while black men were riding *two* hours to the Ford River Rouge plant—and to thoroughly unfulfilling jobs with no real prospects for advancement.

We look at these people and think of their long commutes as normal—we think, "Times were hard, and they did what they had to do." But if this was so normal then, why do many of us have a certain sense that this would be too much to ask of poor young blacks today? We are taught that a two-leg bus commute is "too much," "too hard." And ideal it certainly is not. But when we think of a black man in a fedora jostling along on a ninety-minute bus trek on his way to wage work in 1925, we think that even if things should have been easier for him, he was putting food on the table. We do not see him as a "chump" who would have been better off staying home and either bootlegging or running the numbers.

Why, then, do we see the poor young black person doing the same thing eighty years later as surrendering to an evil system? Or if not quite that, why are we taught that today's black commuter is showing unusual pluck, while his brother who stays home, cadges off of his girlfriends, and sells crack is making an unsavory but "understandable" choice?

We see that black laborer in 1925 in black-and-white photographs, usually in static poses convenient to the camera technology of the period and consonant with a more formal era. He is wearing a hat, and likely a jacket and tie. But he was, after all, a living, breathing human being. Really think about him, feel him. In his time-travel classic *Time and Again*, Jack Finney has his protagonist note that for people in 1882, life was as vivid and particular as it is for us. This laborer lived life as vividly as the young black man today who is supposedly barred from working by the same kind of commute. The 1925 laborer laughed. Every now and then he cried. He knew irony and ambivalence. He probably smoked. He may have felt a little down on cloudy days. He belched sometimes. If unmarried, he probably wasn't a virgin. He had his own particular warm smell that his mother and the women who loved him adored. He saw movies. He cut himself shaving. He may have had a little niece who adored him and a cousin or two he just couldn't get himself to like. Just because he was more likely to be named Clarence than Jamal doesn't mean that he was a different subspecies of human being from the Jamal so familiar to us today.

And yet he went to work even when work was not close to home. Sixty years later, however, his equivalent in Chicago was telling William Julius Wilson things like, "The bus go out there but you don't want to catch the bus out there, going two hours each ways. If you have to be at work at eight that mean you have to leave for work at six, that mean you have to get up at five to be at work at eight. Then when wintertime come you be in trouble." This man was, not surprisingly, unemployed. The difference between him and the 1925 commuter in Detroit was not a matter of where work was, since work was just as far from the man in 1925. Clearly, the difference was in how interested the Chicago man was in working at all.

Thus, in American cities in general, tracing inner-city chaos and despair to people being unable to get to work is a nimble but hopeless argument. Even many top-ranking academics fail to see the link. Even leftist writers, trying to illustrate the link with neighborhood ethnographies, find themselves explaining away available jobs and their interviewees' inconvenient tendency to mention them. Any plausibility in the idea that long commutes to work are as unthinkable an expectation for poor blacks as asking them to skate there falls to pieces when we look at what the same people were doing in the same cities before the sixties.

So what did happen to black America in the sixties?

IF IT WASN'T THE FACTORIES . . . , PART ONE:
"DOWN WITH WHITEY"

Strip away jargon such as "residential nucleation" and "industrial disper-sion" and we are left with an argument that poor blacks in Indianapolis turned their neighborhoods into war zones because factory jobs moved up the road a piece. This is an unrealistic, condescending, and disempow-ering proposition, and black history deserves better.

A constructive black history must seek other factors that came into play in this same period and decide whether they offer a plausible expla-nation for the phenomenon at hand.

In that light, at the same time as Indianapolis was experiencing a moderate degree of "industrial dispersion," the reigning attitude in black Indianapolis was shifting toward the oppositional rhetoric now so famil-iar in the best-known black leaders of the last generation, focusing on, as a black YMCA director who saw the change described it, "what we are owed; what we are due."

The new idea was that America's racism rendered it unworthy of any self-regarding black person's embrace and that therefore blacks were ex-empt from mainstream standards of conduct and judgment. Certainly, only a few hotheads were walking around spouting this rhetoric explicitly at community centers and on the radio. But nowadays, rather than being curious loners, they were part of a new national sentiment that the younger, enlightened contingent of the white ruling class, a proto–Blue America, was thrilling to. A countercultural mood had become pervasive among young people across America, spurred mostly by two things: opposition to the Vietnam War and a commitment to civil rights for blacks sparked by the televised abuses that led to the Civil Rights and Voting Rights acts. That mood translated into a new bone-deep distrust of the Establishment, now no longer the province of especially politicized Old Left "eccentrics," but a mainstream commitment. Now it was the people who opted to side with their elders who were on the defensive. This meant that blacks who decided to go separatist now had a national mainstream movement be-hind them for support and role modelling, and hence, a new Zeitgeist in a new black America.

Certainly, this new orientation sat well with a people abused for so long and so indefensibly. It was, in its way, a race-wide cry of "Gimme a break!" The pot boiled over just now because whites, contemptuous of the ruling class in the wake of events in Vietnam, were newly interested in blacks' conditions, especially given the high visibility of the March on Washington, the Civil Rights legal victories, and Martin Luther King's subsequent assassination.

Thank God for that. But there were side effects. Acting up is an addictive drug. Its narcotic thrill has a way of spilling beyond the bounds of constructive intent. It is a kind of crack. Because it feels so damnably good, it can take over the body and soul and become the heart of one's existence, heedless of reality.

Gunshots from The Mountaintop, 1969

A symbolic tableau of the problem was another seemingly inconsequential wrinkle in the 1969 riot. As it happens, the rooftop the sniper had fired from was that of the Lockefield housing project. Students of urban sociology will immediately imagine the man on top of a tall, ugly tower reeking of urine and view him as protesting being forced to live there after his warm, cohesive black community was razed amid slum clearance.

But actually, Lockefield, Indianapolis's first housing project, was by any standard a lovely complex. Take a class addressing the inner city today, and when housing projects come up, you will be taught that the clusters of high towers typically built were mistakes in that they discouraged social contact, created entrances removed from the visibility of the sidewalk, and were constructed in ways that lent too many hidden spaces for criminals to take advantage of in circulating the grounds. The proper public housing will place low-rise buildings around common arenas, encouraging "community" interaction. Well, that is precisely how Lockefield had been built—lowish buildings surrounding a spacious mall. Windows were large, the buildings were amply cross-ventilated, and there were plenty of play spaces. Applicants clamored to live there. Nostalgia for their erstwhile "communities" was a low priority.

Just as some decry depictions of black communities like mine of early black Indianapolis as idealist, neglecting the ample "seedy" element, many of the same people will at the same time idealize those very same communities when decrying that they were razed for highway construction. In pre-Interstate Indianapolis, much of the housing available to blacks was overcrowded, substandard shacks, as the result of the virtual residential apartheid enforced since the 1920s. Many of the people in Indianapolis who rue the "dispersion" of poor blacks who were moved to housing projects would have to take a deep breath to even visit many homes in the ramshackle "communities" that legions of black people in

Indianapolis were forced to live in until the fifties. Black Indianapolis residents who got to move to Lockefield were often leaving homes with outhouses and outdoor wells.

And yet, gunshots from the roof—of what was almost a cartoon version of what analysts then and now advise as ideal housing projects. History again: Why not gunshots in 1940 from the tumbledown cold-water flats so many blacks were stuck in? Why did things like this only start happening when things were getting better? Attitude was playing as large a part in the new militance as realistic engagement with a changing society.

A New Conception of Dignity

Another symbolic tableau—literally. One of the booths at the Black Expo in 1971 was called "Dignity Unlimited," instructing black attendees with the uplifting image of a jail stockade in front of a painting of a black man and boy in chains. "The personification of blacks' new awareness," someone called it.

Awareness, hmm—but of what and for what? That exhibit in a time of such vast new opportunities for blacks would have baffled Attucks High School's black principal Russell Lane in 1934. John Wesley Hardrick, a local black portrait painter, was so heartened by the school's opening that he presented Lane with a painting of black laborers to hang in the school. Lane, however, refused to mount it in the lobby, for fear of discouraging his students' ambitions. One might marvel that people like Lane were less given to grimly sardonic gestures like "Dignity Unlimited." But in his era, it had not yet become, of all things, unfashionable to be constructive.

Older blacks after the Black Power era like retired schoolteacher Frances Linthecome were dismayed by the new oppositional culture. "I didn't feel this *was* my country before the 1960s. But after the Civil Rights movement and the laws changed, I was proud of America. It is hard for people to admit that they are wrong and to change, but that is what my country has done politically." But these days a lot of blacks thought people like Linthecome were missing some kind of higher wisdom. Mattie Coney's Citizen's Forum had been engaged in precisely the kind of uplift and spiritual bolstering that was considered *de rigueur* of the engaged black woman in Indianapolis back in the day. But by the 1970s, the new black vanguard looked on her call for mainstream standards as "inauthentic" and tarred her as an "Aunt Jemima" tool of the establishment.

The new ideology taught that dressing down whites for the sins of the past was a "blacker" thing to do than facing what needed to be done in the present. Under this new conception of "leadership skills," enter people like Mmoja Ajabu, who set up a branch of the New Black Panthers in Indianapolis in 1993. Ajabu hit the scene with a distinctly early-nineties brand of black militance, carrying on a tantrum aimed at enterprising inner-city Asians, of the kind that had helped spark the Rodney King riots the year before. He demanded that a Korean beauty supply store in a black neighborhood contribute $200 a month for neighborhood youth programs (they refused to cough up). He claimed to have gathered a "militia" to overthrow the government, warning: "We know we are talking about death and destruction and grief in a whole lot of people's families. But only then will they come to the negotiating table and talk candidly about getting something done." Chilling rhetoric from a serious brother, and Ajabu claimed 5,000 supporters. But only a dozen people had joined him in protesting the beauty shop, nor did many more join him in a few protest rallies or a failed call to boycott the city's public schools.

Ajabu mouthed a "program": economic development through employment and training, "empowerment," the idea that these things would allow blacks to keep and spend money among themselves, more black history and culture in schools, and more "sensitivity" to unruly black students. But histories of black Indianapolis in the future will not feature a turnaround forged by Mr. Ajabu's "program."

Oh, Ajabu "did some good things." There was a summer program for black youth—at least, for one summer in 1992. And no one would argue with his shepherding young black kids to paint houses for five bucks an hour—even if this was a once-off affair. And to the extent that he called for the police to be held more accountable for their actions, such efforts serve a purpose. Protests that police forces were unjustifiably injuring and even killing black men were at a high pitch in Indianapolis by the eighties as elsewhere in the country, and forging cooperation between the police and poor black communities is a key aspect of helping turn tough neighborhoods around.

But serious black leaders—or leaders of anyone or anything—do not get caught up in an arson episode and spend a year in jail for threats to a prosecutor. Especially when they are in their mid-forties and have a reliable job as a relay technician at an engineering company. Ajabu was a sadly familiar example of post-sixties black leaders acting out in the name of action.

The New Voice of God

The new thinking also infected the local black clergy. By the eighties and nineties a core of black pastors were monopolizing public attention in Indianapolis with rallies and media appearances spreading an anti-white gospel, calling indignantly for "payback" and insisting that contemporary black pathologies are legacies of slavery and segregation—a proposition that the self-reliant beginnings of black Indianapolis refute. These pastors hardly represent the face of the city's black clergy and do not even have large congregations. But true to the rule that you get the most face time by taking to the streets, one city official remembers, "You could have six moderate, smart young black ministers but not one of them would ever make it on TV. Talk about the military-industrial complex—I learned about a kind of teacher's union–Democrat-pastor complex."

Typical example: Seventy-five years after 6,500 Klansmen marched downtown in 1924 to enthusiastic throngs of 75,000, on a cold, dreary day in 1999 a ragtag crew of a mere thirteen Klansmen staged a rally on the statehouse steps, squawking through a faulty PA system. The highlight of the event: Reverend Lionel Rush of the Greater Harvest Institutional Church of God in Christ pressing against the barricades in dramatic protest. It made good press—Rush is well-known in Indianapolis as the local version of Al Sharpton. But just how this helped poor blacks in Indianapolis was an interesting question.

Olgen Williams is all too familiar with people like Rush who cherish histrionics over action. As Executive Director of Christamore House, he is dedicated to turning lives around for blacks in the inner-city Haughville neighborhood. Christamore House has established health clinics, libraries, and community policing programs, making use of government grants and, like Mattie Coney forty years ago, funds from corporations like E J Lilly. Williams had his "militant" phase in the early seventies but soon realized that "bringing things down and hating wasn't going to do it—what we needed was to build something up." Sad that this philosophy often leaves him feeling like a contrarian. The pastors most likely to get face time on local TV who could help him in his good works "never roll up their sleeves and tutor kids, help them with their math problems, help us give Christmas gifts—unless the cameras are around."

This sort of thing makes the era of Mattie Coney look sadly foreign. Her strategy for combatting racism was to urge the community to put its best foot forward. Her cleanup campaign began when she found out that realtors were using the condition of black neighborhoods as a justification for turning away white buyers. But the new conception of black authenticity tarred Coney's crusade as naïve treachery. "Real" black people growl that whites who steer people away from ugly black neighborhoods are evil for not understanding that blacks face racism. Black people more interested in teaching fellow blacks to do their best *despite* racism are not "real." They need to learn what's "real" from black people who wax indignant over thirteen Klansmen idiots bumbling around on the statehouse steps for an hour and a half.

Thus, the mood change in the late sixties was not just a matter of Afros, dashikis, slogans, and some things a few people said on TV. It was a permanent transformation of the group mind-set of the black community. A new meme took root, not among everyone, and to different degrees among those whom it did affect. But overall, it was powerful enough a factor that it changed the times. Black Indianapolis has never been the same.

We have a choice, then, between two factors explaining the descent of a previously dignified people into a violent, feckless underclass.

A: A new culture emerged of white-hot, unfocused animus against mainstream culture.

B: It got a little harder to get to work.

A black history that embraces B while dismissing A as beside the point substitutes therapy for common sense.

IF IT WASN'T THE FACTORIES . . . , PART TWO: WELFARE AS A LIFESTYLE

The other historical factor that had a conclusive effect on the fate of black Indianapolis was the vast expansion of Aid to Families with Dependent Children.

To many, saying things like that suggests an ideologue rather than someone sincerely interested in the facts of the matter. "But how can you call welfare a black problem?" one is often asked when criticizing the grand old open-ended welfare policies that reigned before the five-year time limit imposed in 1996. There are two factoids most often heard: Welfare was created for white widows, and there were often more whites on welfare than blacks.

Both are true, and I for one would be dismayed if America had no safety net of any kind for people down on their luck. But folks, there is more than those two factoids. Those nuggets of wisdom miss some crucial things about what happened to that widows' program in the 1960s. A series of relaxations turned welfare from a short-term charity program into an open-ended dole, available even if an able-bodied father was living with the mother and not working. Because this did not make headlines and emerged stepwise over several years, it was easy for the ordinary contemporary to miss and is today largely covered only in texts rarely read beyond academia. But it is nothing less than a lost chapter of black history—which it utterly perverted. In Chapter Four, I will return to the subject from a national perspective, but this chapter will lend a preview in terms of what happened in Indianapolis.

In Indiana, the transformation happened, as elsewhere in the late sixties, in large part appeasing rhetoric in the wake of the race riots sparked by the one in Watts in 1965. In 1967, Mattie Coney was asserting that "the idea of expecting a 'great white father' to hand one something for nothing has created a class of irresponsible welfare slaves. We must get rid of the idea that all one needs is to satisfy one's gullet, get drunk, have children, and throw them into the community to let someone else take care of them." But by 1970, there were more blacks on welfare in Indianapolis than ever before, concentrated strongly in the central district. In 1964, 12,171 people were on AFDC in Marion County; by 1972, 34,016 people were on it. This was not accompanied by a significant rise in the proportion of the black population in the county: It was 14.3 percent in 1960 and 17 percent in 1975. Nor did these percentages represent a larger number of actual people due to any general population explosion in the county: In 1960, the county's population was 697,567; by 1975 it was 782,139.

A Black Problem?

The data does, to be sure, leave a question, in that AFDC recipiency has never been tabulated in census statistics by race. It is well-known that nationwide, at many times there have been more whites on welfare than blacks. This has often been pointed out as indicating that focusing on welfare as a "black" issue is stereotyping—the "racialization of poverty," and so on. However, since whites vastly outnumber blacks in America and plenty of whites are poor, we should not be surprised that often a greater number of whites have been on welfare nationwide. While we must always check ourselves for stereotyping, the fact remains that the *proportion* of blacks on welfare nationwide, as opposed to sheer numbers, has often been a legitimate matter of concern.

After all, few have trouble understanding the issue of proportion when the issue is how many black men are in jail compared with the *proportion* that blacks constitute of the national population. With welfare, there was a similar discrepancy. Just as the *proportion* of black men in jail surpasses their representation in the general population, the *proportion* of blacks on welfare has not squared with their representation in the population. This means that all claims that any focus on blacks when discussing welfare is racist—whether levelled by a community activist, a polemicist like Ishmael Reed, or a rapper like Talib Kweli—are mistaken.

In this light, it is relevant that in the late 1960s there was a nationwide effort aimed at bringing not just poor people, but also poor *blacks* onto the welfare rolls. Even without race-based AFDC tallies, the statistics in Indiana make it clear that the rise in recipients was primarily among blacks. From 1964 to 1972, welfare recipiency rose in most of Indiana's ninety-two counties and dropped in some. It rose in counties to differing degrees, but to a striking degree only in certain counties—almost categorically, ones with significant numbers of blacks.

In 1972, only eighteen out of the ninety-two counties in Indiana had significant black populations (more than one thousand). In no fewer than ten of these eighteen, there were three times as many AFDC recipients in 1972 as in 1964, including Indianapolis's Marion County and Gary's Lake County. Crucially, statewide, rates only tripled in a single other county (Tippecanoe). That is, AFDC recipiency tripled in eleven of almost a hundred counties, and only a single one of these counties did not have a solid core of black people.

And even in counties with a heavy black presence where rates did not triple, the increase still tended strongly to be significant. For example, the city with the third most blacks after Indianapolis and Gary was South Bend, and rates doubled in its St. Joseph County (from 4,781 to 9,820).

Reasonably, we might suppose that poverty was most concentrated among blacks in Indiana, such that even if AFDC was aimed at blacks disproportionately, it was within a race-blind attack on poverty in general. But in fact there was no overlap between where welfare recipiency tripled in Indiana and where poverty was deepest. In 1969, 10 percent or more of residents were living below the poverty line in thirty of ninety-two counties in Indiana, but only in a mere three of these thirty counties did any blacks live at all. Moreover, in all three of these counties blacks numbered only in the hundreds; none was among the counties with healthy black populations. Crucially, none of these poverty-stricken Indiana counties was among the counties where welfare tripled.

Certainly, the AFDC rolls rose to varying degrees in most of these poor counties between 1964 and 1972—the welfare movement naturally did not affect only blacks with laser-beam precision. But only in heavily black counties did rates triple. Obviously enrollment efforts were aimed not at poverty per se, but at urban black poverty.

Did Welfare Pull Black Indianapolis Back from the Abyss?

We might also reasonably wonder whether the welfare explosion among blacks was a response to a drop in employment opportunities. But after World War II, the Fair Employment Practices Commission, which A. Philip Randolph had brought the Roosevelt Administration to its knees to create, gradually bore fruit for blacks in Indianapolis as elsewhere. Blacks were hired in increasing numbers in unskilled jobs especially as white workers were promoted, and blacks were gradually (albeit often amid hesitations and conflict) admitted to unions. By 1962, 751 of 3,200 workers for the city government were black, 334 of them (almost half) in skilled jobs. Just as in the old days, there was no unemployment crisis in black Indianapolis. In 1960—when this was still a segregated and openly bigoted nation—93 *percent* of black men were employed in Indianapolis. In shorthand, any able-bodied black man short of the occasional chucklehead or disabled person was working.

As a matter of fact, improvements in the employment situation were moving faster than ever just as the new oppositional rhetoric took hold and the welfare rolls started exploding. The FEPC rulings finally gained some teeth in the 1960s due in part to efforts by the local NAACP. The Indiana Civil Rights Act of 1963, forcing whites to hire blacks, was significantly strengthened in 1969—exactly the year of the Indiana Avenue riot—and again in 1971. Meanwhile, the national economy of the early sixties was flush, which led to increased job opportunities for blacks—and the economy even stayed that way in Indiana until 1971, longer than in many states.

Nevertheless, by 1976, while there had been little dramatic increase in AFDC enrollments in most Indiana counties, Indianapolis's Marion was an exception, where AFDC recipients went from 34,016 in 1972 to 42,208. It was soon clear that people were drifting onto the rolls even when there were clearly jobs to seek. Welfare hardly left one floating in cash, and in fact AFDC payments were on the low side in Indiana—no one was exactly sitting pretty from welfare checks. But they kept the wolf from the door—enough to dissuade countless people from seeking work.

One problem was that welfare, modest as its payments were, tended to pay more than entry-level work. Stephen Goldsmith worked in child support collection in Indianapolis in the 1980s and lost count of how many women on welfare readily said that welfare simply paid better than work. In 1993, welfare payments were the equivalent of $7.50 an hour when the typical beginning wage in an unskilled job began at $6.50.

And this returns us to the cultural issue. The idea of it being typical for black Indianapolis residents to casually live on the dole even when they could be making their own living would have stunned a hardworking black person in the city just a few decades earlier. Yet, welfare "as we knew it" seems so ordinary to us today that it can be hard to process a functioning black America without it. A last look at old black Indianapolis opens our eyes. Even when racism was naked and the black bourgeoisie was truly a sliver, black Indianapolis was so leery of government charity that it almost strains our belief, in light of what passes for progressive black ideology today.

Welfare in Old Black Indianapolis

In the first decades of the twentieth century, Indianapolis's black community took care of its own, through a range of charity organizations such as Alpha Home and Flanner House. Both of these got their starts with contributions from wealthy whites, but their leaders made every effort toward self-sufficiency after that, practically regarding their origins in white charity as a necessary evil.

White and black charity organizations were grouped under the umbrella of the Charity Organization Society, which was run not by the government but by local clergy. Blacks applying to charities for sustenance was hardly unheard of, but they did it only under uniquely pressing circumstances and generally sought immediate provisions in a pinch rather than open-ended support. For the first two decades that the Charity Organization Society existed, only one black family applied for help. Crucially, from 1894 to 1920, two-thirds of black applications to the COS came from two-parent families rather than from single mothers. Of the single black mothers who applied during this time, 90 percent cited illness as the reason, and a considerable number were widows or had been deserted by their husbands.

Nor did this last-ditch orientation toward charity come from a sense that black people were unlikely to get funds. A full 96 percent of black applicants from 1894 to 1920 saw their applications approved. The difference between this Indianapolis and the one after the 1960s was a Zeitgeist that stressed self-reliance as a guiding principle, with charity as a last resort.

The expansion of AFDC programs, then, was neither the only possible response to black poverty nor poor blacks' salvation from begging in the streets. On the contrary, the expansion of AFDC fills in a logical gap, explaining how an underclass began developing in Indianapolis just when employment opportunities were opening up to blacks as they never had before, and when factories were only just beginning to leave the center of town, and even then usually only relocating a few miles away.

The Lost Chapter in Black History

That is, the expansion of AFDC was the second of a one-two punch to black Indianapolis. It became possible to survive without working at the same time as the word on the street became the oppositional one, which we are so familiar with that we often think of it as one of the defining traits of genuine "blackness." Blacks who rejected mainstream norms were accepted as normal rather than as "characters" or layabouts. Naturally, in this new atmosphere, living on the dole lost much of the stigma it used to have. To some, initiative itself even became a sign of weakness, smacking of, say, Aunt Jemima in love with her white folks. Gone were the days when checking out was perhaps colorful but problematic. In came the days when for many, checking out was perhaps problematic but, in its way, no problem. For thousands of people, there was now no shame in open-ended dependence.

We must contrast black Indianapolis 1920 with a black man who former mayor Stephen Goldsmith talked to who bitterly complained about the paucity of jobs in Indianapolis, but refused work at McDonald's because they didn't pay enough, and even refused a $35,000 a year job driving a truck because he didn't like the hours. For those tempted to object that thirty-five grand is not enough "bling," I might note that in the mid-nineties I was making about that much as an assistant professor (in expensive New York State with its high tax rates) and thought of it as a thoroughly decent living. And, for those who may tell us that this was just one man, remember that black men refusing available work was epidemic in Indianapolis at that time—recall the statements of The Indiana

Commission on African American Males, Olgen Williams, and Lana Ruegamer. In the 1940s Bronzeville tenements in Chicago, there were lots of men sleeping in shifts in tiny flats, making the best of the fact that some men worked days and some worked nights. This seems almost other-worldly compared with inner-city Indianapolis in the nineties, and the reason had little or nothing to do with the want ads.

And even welfare's "beneficiaries" in Indianapolis knew this. An offi-cial who devoted several years to helping welfare recipients turn their lives around rues, "I encountered less resistance to changing welfare from the recipients than from many who claimed to speak for them." This included "concerned" white people, for whom hooking black people on the dole forever became a moral end in itself, saving an eternally piteous people from the evils of the capitalist machine. Bureaucratic self-preservation also played its hand: Stephen Goldsmith recounts welfare workers saying that they had been instructed to keep the rolls as high as possible.

Let's go back to assessing the deindustrialization hypothesis, then. To perform a thought experiment, we are asked to choose between two strategies for creating a violent underclass culture of lax parenting, casual violence, and widespread substance abuse.

One is to institute a program that leaves thousands of mothers with no reason to work and fathers with no reason to take responsibility for their offspring.

The other is to move factories with low-skill jobs a few miles away where the buses run less often than they do downtown.

I think that one could only accept the second strategy with an almost willful suspension of disbelief.

IMPLICATIONS FOR THE CONCERNED BLACK CITIZEN

Obviously, it would have been optimal for blacks if all of Indianapolis's factories had stayed in the city's center. But we must not be swayed by the seductive abstraction of terminology such as sociologist John Kasarda's of a "spatial mismatch" between uneducated men and low-skill jobs no longer just near their homes. Is this static, faceless analysis truly a useful characterization of human beings with basic resources of initiative and self-preservation? Surely we will at least ask immediately whether inner-city residents tried to do anything about the "spatial mismatch"—as we would expect they would—and if they did not, to find out just why.

Some will prefer to just stop at "racism"—but racism does not explain what happened in Indianapolis, given how many jobs were waiting for blacks to apply, and how very many blacks did make it out of the 'hood. This is why short of just throwing up our hands—which includes claiming that it was "complicated" in unspecified ways, which is usually code for saying that racism was the main problem—we must look to developments that dissuaded blacks from taking available employment. We look to these developments because they provide a key to an otherwise mysterious detour, and teach us what we must consider in moving beyond. In other words, we seek to make use of history to chart our future.

This proposition is not motivated by concerns local to "the culture wars," but by concerns focused on black American people's fates. This, and only this, is why I propose that what turned black Indianapolis down a wayward path was two things, and that the role of these two things is clear from the fact that they arose precisely when the turn happened, and were unknown in the city until just then. One was the rise of a hostile, anti-establishment ideology as mainstream opinion—"Dignity Unlimited," "Snooky" Hendricks, Mattie Coney tarred as an Aunt Jemima, Mmoja Ajabu considered important enough to get interviews with the *Indianapolis Star*. The other was the expansion of welfare such that it could provide a passable living indefinitely. The rest was history—ours.

If we could replay the history of Indianapolis but keep all factories just where they were in 1960, and then let loose Black Power ideology and the relaxation of welfare requirements, the central black district in Indianapolis would have undergone the same sad transformation. That is, black men would be idling on the streets at two in the afternoon watching young black women on welfare pushing baby carriages *while factories thrived just blocks away*, likely staffed by Latino migrants, Caribbeans, and Africans who had not fallen under the new cultural mind-set of waylaid poor native-born blacks.

It is not pleasant to contemplate such things. But I feel that we must look at them without blinking, and not just to score points in an abstract debate about morals, but to have any serious, constructive ways to help black people left behind. Really—we cannot help blacks left behind unless we truly understand what happened. "Learn your history"—yes. But not only about Emmett Till. We must also learn about what really happened to black communities in the late sixties—and what happened that should interest us is not racism.

If we understand what really happened in Indianapolis, then we will

not take a page from Deborah Mathis in her *Yet a Stranger* and spit on limiting welfare to five years as shoving helpless black women off of the rolls
"cold turkey"—especially when five years is hardly "cold turkey" and the
new program stresses job training. Welfare reform has not been perfect;
no doubt there could be better provisions for day care for the children
that spouseless victims (yes, victims) of thirty years of open-ended welfare
tend to have. But nevertheless, we will understand that any policy that un-
did serial generations of black women living on the dole was pro-black,
with fist raised à la Malcolm X.

Nor will we give in to the seductiveness of the plangent image of
young black men "spatially mismatched" from factories that move away.
To do so is to agree that the only humans in history incapable of adapting
to changing employment conditions were descendants of African slaves in
the United States. Or better, descendants of African slaves in the United
States only during the last three decades of the twentieth century—since
when "work disappeared" and life got too tough on black asses in the old
South, our great-grandparents, well, *moved.*

Instead, we have to understand that what created the deathscapes that
Tupac Shakur rapped about was a tragic cultural lurch into an identity
built around alienation from the Establishment, reinforced by government policies promoted at just that time that allowed poor blacks to
check out of working for a living forever.

Yes, blacks inherited the oppositional ideology from the countercultural movement of the 1960s. So in a way, genuine black history has a
place for the kind of black person who seeks to tar whitey at all costs.
Some blacks watched what whitey did to the mentality of black America
but made the best of themselves anyway and moved to the suburbs. But
among all races, some people are stronger than others, and the slings and
arrows of outrageous fortune waylay this person more than that person.
In that light, other blacks less self-directed or less lucky devolved into lifetimes of unemployment and sometimes even shooting one another dead
at public events.

Today, they are our underclass. What we must fix is the cultural orientation by which they have been waylaid—not *racism.* Blacks have been
here long enough that it is clear that racism alone cannot hold us down,
much less some factories moving away. Some of us got sideswiped by
something else forty years ago. Part of it was a sense that flipping the finger to whitey was the "blackest" thing we could do. But contrary to them,

to the extent that whites had anything to do with what happened to us, it was the "good" ones who were so good, so "understanding," so "hip," that they considered us exempt from reaching our highest potentials and coaxed us onto the permanent dole. And the most hideous thing is that we learned to believe them.

For those who insist that instead, "spatial mismatch" between cousin Dwayne and International Harvester was the key factor, the burden of proof is upon them to explain why these two factors—oppositional culture and open-ended welfare—would *not* have a profound historical impact on poor black communities. That is, they must be prepared to state that they would agree with the following proposition:

> When a community experiences a new charismatic oppositional ideology and links it to authentic race membership, and at the same time is encouraged by bureaucrats to sign up for open-ended welfare payments, this will have only marginal effect upon attitudes to employment, self-sufficiency, and adherence to mainstream behavior.

I know that some readers will feel able to actually agree with that proposition and maintain that factories moving three miles away was the cause of the SoulFest murders. But I am equally aware that more readers will see this as a curious underestimation of what human beings are made of, even with the worst of histories.

And having seen how hard it is to square the "deindustrialization" analysis with actual developments in a single city, in the next chapter we will see that it is equally difficult to see this analysis as useful counsel for black America on a national scale, whether the factories moved away or not.

CHAPTER THREE

The Birth of the Inner City, Part Two: The Saga

The factory idea is one part of a larger scenario that has become common wisdom about what happened to black America in the sixties. In the previous chapter, my aim was to open my presentation with the vivid and specific mise-en-scène of a single city. Because that city is particular in that manufacturing jobs did not leave it, Indianapolis was also useful in showing that this part of the general scenario does not hold water. Quite simply, if a black underclass developed even when factories did not move away, then a causal connection between availability of manufacturing jobs and social chaos is refuted.

But anyone who objects that addressing the factories alone oversimplifies social scientists' analysis of the development of the black underclass is correct.

There is, for example, the middle-class flight issue that William Julius Wilson stresses along with the factory point. Then, there are other assumptions that grow out of the factory analysis. Especially prominent is the idea that blacks did not follow the factories or move in pursuit of other work because even after the sixties, whites have only rarely allowed more than a few blacks to live anywhere but the ghetto. Meanwhile, there are mantras about the effects of housing project architecture and interstate highway construction on poor blacks, and finally, a common idea that the problem was that "drugs came in," as it is often put.

So one might assume that what created the inner cities was the combined impact of all of these factors. Actually, as I have noted, the factory explanation is held front and center so often that it is clear that many analysts consider it a kind of fulcrum (Thomas Sugrue opens his chronicle of black Detroit after World War II, *The Origins of the Urban Crisis: Race and Inequality in Postwar Detroit*, with a photo and description of the River

Rouge Ford plant that I mentioned black laborers commuting to in Chapter Two). But generally, the idea that underclass deathscapes were created by assorted manifestations of racism and neglect permeates the consciousness of countless people, from those in the Ivory Tower to those at cocktail parties to *New York Times* readers to lefty bloggers to rappers.

Michael Eric Dyson is typical of hip-hop fans in academia in his defense of the recordings of gangsta rappers like Tupac Shakur as a "critique of a society that produces the need for the thug persona." That is, the lyrics' celebration of acting up, and even their detour into reality as rappers so often fall afoul of the law, must be taken as a response to an America that leaves poor blacks with no choice but to slide into lives that are nasty, brutish, and short. It is not an accident that William Julius Wilson has been celebrated by the media as the go-to man on the underclass, or that Thomas Sugrue's book, based on the now traditional assumptions of how black neighborhoods went to ruin (and in itself, excellent) won the Bancroft Prize. I took a cooking class once where the partner I happened to be paired with was a very smart white woman in early middle age. Over the hours of preparing our dishes we naturally started talking about the issues of the day, and one of her observations was that it was criminal that the American government allows so many blacks to live in poverty.

Certainly many people, including ones reading this, hear that woman as speaking truth. This is encouraged in part by the fact that writings and even conversations about these issues are today couched in buzzwords that have accreted potent, emotional connotations over the past forty years, such as *segregation* and *opportunity*. The mere use of such words often makes works read like scripture that actually leave more questions than answers—scripture indeed, in that these words are now terms of preaching as much as explanation.

Thus, many people interested in black urban sociology consider a certain account to have been proven beyond any question. It has become a saga of sorts these days, often less presented as an argument than recited like *The Iliad*, the Icelandic *Edda*, or the Finnish *Kalevala*. Like all such sagas, it is composed of various stanzas—in this case, I count six—that each contain a savory drama, aiding memorization and narrative power.

All sagas reflect the concerns and worldview of the cultures they spring from. This underclass saga displays and reinforces a thinking American culture dedicated to protecting blacks from being blamed for problems that are assumed to actually trace to racial injustice. Books retelling the saga are praised by reviewers for exactly this reason and assigned by college professors who consider the saga a hallmark of broadened horizons. I was raised on this saga the way Alex Haley was raised listening to tales of Kunta Kinte. But after examining it as carefully as I am capable of, I have come to the conclusion that it is, like all sagas, a fiction.

What killed black neighborhoods was neither The Man nor economic forces, both of which black people had known all too well long before the late sixties. The key was what was new to the late sixties: a new way of thinking that infected blacks and whites alike. It effected a massive transformation in cultural attitudes that discouraged millions of blacks from doing their best, while at the exact same time teaching concerned whites that supporting blacks in this was a sign of moral sophistication.

To see what I mean, let's take the six stanzas of the grand old saga in turn.

FIRST STANZA:
LOW-SKILL FACTORY JOBS MOVED AWAY

This one is easy. Indianapolis developed a black underclass even when factories stayed in the city. This requires us to change our lens and adjust to realizing that even in cities where factories did move away, the emergence of a black underclass had *nothing to do with it*. William Julius Wilson's work is eloquent and sincere. But to defend his conclusions about low-skill manufacturing jobs while also being aware of what did *not* happen in Indianapolis is logically incoherent—like insisting that gravity is a hoax while watching pens and pencils fall to the floor whenever we drop them.

Even in cities where factories moved farther away, the idea that this ended up leaving millions of blacks unable to avoid sliding into useless, miserable lives just doesn't hold water. I am hardly alone in that judgment, nor are people who agree with me "conservatives" or professional moralizers. And this is because the notion simply does not square with what human beings are actually like.

Black Boston University economist Glenn Loury, for instance, agrees that William Julius Wilson's work on this subject never actually identifies a causal link between "deindustrialization" and multigenerational despair.

> Perhaps responsible men whose lives are already well organized are able to keep faith with both their employers and their families. Perhaps people who place a high value on being self-supporting are not deterred from a couple hours' commute on a bus. Perhaps women

who are energetic and disciplined can hold down jobs while sustaining the kinds of relationships with friends and relatives that make informal child care possible. The fact that most criminals are unemployed is not sufficient proof that unstable ghetto youths will prefer minimum-wage public employment to entry-level positions in the crack trade.

Meanwhile, even writers who subscribe to Wilson's thesis often give away an awareness that it is simply not true that work is unavailable to blacks in lousy neighborhoods. Elijah Anderson, for example, has it on the one hand that in the Philadelphia neighborhood he examines, "While some people may not want jobs, the overwhelming majority would work if they could find gainful employment." But then on the other hand, he later has it that "members of the Northton community have not been able to make an effective adjustment to these economic changes"—suggesting that the adjustment would indeed be possible. Of course, Anderson seems to think that for black people after the sixties, adjustment and self-direction were just too much to ask, such that he can admit, "Good jobs do exist in offices, hospitals, factories, and other larger institutions that provide not only good pay but also increasingly important health care and other benefits," but then in all seriousness he considers these to be beyond the reach of many blacks because "these jobs require training and are increasingly located in the suburbs."

This means that when writers like Anderson quote actual inner-city residents asserting that work is available, they dismiss them as uninformed. Anderson quotes a black minister and part-time cab driver: "There are jobs out there for people who want to work. It may not be just what they want, but there is work to be done if you want it bad enough. Honest and honorable work. Something has happened to our community." "A comfortable perspective," Anderson smirks, shaking his head at those in the area who "continue to believe in the infinite availability of work in the traditional sense." One of Katherine Newman's interviewees in *No Shame in My Game*, a black woman who used to live on welfare, tells her, "There's so much in this city. It's always hiring. It may not be what you want. It may not be the pay you want. But you will always get a job." Newman can't have this: "One imagines Patty would be tolerant of AFDC recipients. After all, she has been there. Not so." Newman actually calls views like Patty's "conservative," as if valuing working for a living is an ominous right-wing conceit!

Interesting, however, that when these interviewees claim discrimination, or attribute their problems to the way they were raised, writers of this kind receive their perceptions as truth with no questions asked, or at least let the observations float as "something to consider." But when the same people, who have spent their lives on streets the interviewer is making day visits to for a year or so, venture that for them, finding work is not the easiest thing in the world but feasible nonetheless, suddenly they are naifs, unable to perceive realities larger than themselves, too proud of having found work to understand that they were just lucky ducks. Scholarship and journalism this nakedly biased cannot be taken as authoritative counsel.

In fact, two academic evaluations of the deindustrialization thesis, based on statistical analysis of a wide range of American cities, have independently come to the same conclusion: that factory relocation was responsible for at most one-third of the rise in unemployment among poor, uneducated black men. That is, whatever effect the factory relocation had, for every man it left unemployed, there were two others for whom we must look to other factors. The authors of these studies are deeply concerned with inner-city employment problems and are more inclined to trace them to racism than I am. Yet, even their conclusions show that the schematic idea that because factories move, unemployment becomes a norm among poor inner-city blacks is a myth.

Make no mistake, however—naturally, factory closings could lead to higher unemployment at least for a time and even a rise in crime rates. But our topic is complete community breakdown, and what I consider refuted is that factory closings would lead to this specifically. Thus, Thomas Sugrue's demonstration that factory closings had already created a class of idling black "corner men" and a rise in crime in poor black Detroit neighborhoods by 1960 is well taken. But his main interest is in what led to Detroit's massive race riot in 1967, and his story largely ends there. Sugrue argues that unemployment was one of the main things that brought the young black men out into the streets—fine. But the self-sustaining black underclass that concerns us had not arisen in 1967, when even among poor blacks it was still common for people to marry if a woman got pregnant, there were no crack wars, and living on welfare was not yet a norm in poor black communities. And meanwhile, the same things happened starting in the seventies even in Indianapolis where the factories did *not* move away.

The carefully phrased assertions about "deindustrialization" from such chroniclers of single cities imply that they have examined dozens of cities nationwide and gleaned a universal process of cause and effect. But, in fact, each one draws conclusions from the city that happens to have been their focus and otherwise passingly cites studies about one or two other cities. Wilson, Sugrue, or any of the writers on these issues do not make the slightest mention of the Indianapolis story, nor do they indicate having considered whether similar stories might apply to cities other than the ones they happen to study. Instead, they refer constantly to a certain few Rust Belt cities like Chicago and Detroit, with an implication that the story was similar everywhere.

This means that even the most masterful writers and researchers on this subject are referring to an incomplete data set. As such, while Sugrue's book is a fantastic chronicle of how race, class, and politics operated in Detroit from the forties to the seventies (and he has a great eye for photographs), when he concludes

> The bleak landscapes and unremitting poverty of Detroit in the 1970s and 1980s are the legacies of the transformation of the city's economy in the wake of World War II, and of the politics and culture of race that have their origins in persistent housing and workplace discrimination of the postwar decades.

he has mistaken correlation as cause.

That means that if our saga has any value, it is the other stanzas that we must consider.

SECOND STANZA:
HOUSING DISCRIMINATION KEPT BLACKS FROM LEAVING INNER CITIES TO FOLLOW WORK

When work disappears, people move—right? Well, not when you're black, The Saga tells us. We are to assume that after low-skill manufacturing jobs left the inner-city areas, poor blacks were "penned in," unable to get away. The problem is supposedly that suburban whites enjoy not living near blacks, and realtors and banks preserve a sinister covenant to keep it that way.

Required reading for this idea is Douglas Massey's and Nancy Denton's *American Apartheid* of 1993 (what I would give to have some of these people's talent for titles!). This book makes a carefully argued case and has been especially influential. It is widely assigned in college courses, considered the kind of unassailable argument that renders nonsense any call for blacks to look on the bright side and forge ahead.

So if Gerald Reynolds, a black conservative who was appointed head of the United States Commission on Civil Rights by the Bush Administration in 2004, ventures

> Somebody can look at disparities in income and home ownership and conclude that it is due to discrimination, but before you can do that you have to perform an investigation because there are other factors that could explain these disparities. The disparities could be the result of discrimination or it could be the result of something else that has no relation to discriminatory conduct.

then we are to assume that he is missing a higher wisdom. The consensus among social scientists and beyond is that even after the Fair Housing Act of 1968, the old-time redlining policies keeping blacks out of decent areas have persisted under the table, to a degree that leaves an unofficial wall around the inner city. It is assumed that this has been proven via statistical analysis and survey research and that someone like Reynolds can only have missed this by not being privy to research on the topic—or being unwilling to engage it because it would interfere with his "right-wing agenda."

Redlining Lives On

It is not, it must be said, that redlining of a sort is unknown in modern America. One of the keystones of Massey's and Denton's argument is ample evidence that racist housing discrimination has continued to exist long after 1968. I cannot see that this data could be refuted and firmly believe that no serious address of race issues can gloss over such things.

So, in the mid-1980s, in 50 percent of their transactions, six real estate firms in Cincinnati and Memphis were showing whites homes only in white neighborhoods but showing blacks homes only in mixed neighborhoods. In 1991, Manufacturers Hanover Trust bank in New York rejected mortgage applications from 43 percent of high-income blacks but only 18 percent of high-income whites. Your local paper has likely documented similar things in your area, probably more than once.

Nor are such things a mere matter of tendencies in certain cities—the issue is national. In 1987, an analysis of no fewer than seventy-one local audit studies and more than two hundred local Fair Housing organizations showed that blacks had overall a 20 percent chance of experiencing discrimination in sales and 50 percent in rentals. A national survey by the *Atlanta Constitution* of ten million mortgage applications between 1983 and 1988 showed 11 percent rejection rates for whites but 24 percent for blacks—with even high-income blacks rejected more than low-income whites in thirty-five cities. Another national survey of the same period revealed housing shown more readily to whites in 45 percent of rentals and 34 percent of sales. Moreover, with the factor of financial assistance added in, blacks got the short end of the stick 53 percent of the time.

Clearly, something real has been going on here, and I am unaware of any study showing that these discrepancies can all, or even mostly, be reduced to issues of blacks' credit ratings or knowledge of how to work the system.

Stuck in the 'Hood?

However, the problem with Massey's and Denton's thesis is the implications they draw from it. They assert that because of these things, middle-class blacks who have made it out of the 'hood are hothouse cases. Reading *American Apartheid*, one would think that across America, quiet suburbs are almost exclusively white, while all but maybe about ten thousand blacks remain cowering in dump-water flats listening to bullets flying day and night, or at best, having made it to "inner ring" suburbs just outside the urban core, essentially new wings of the ghetto. "Seeing the cards so obviously stacked against them," Massey and Denton venture, "many otherwise qualified African Americans simply abandon their quest to purchase a home without really trying."

But many readers will see a certain disjunction between modern American reality and that portrait. There are millions of black people today who live in suburban areas far from the flying bullets. In 1970, only 3.6 million black people lived in the suburbs, but by 1995, the number was 10.6 million—when the entire black population was 33 million. Some respond to data of this kind by observing that in some cases, the suburb in question is one of those inner ring affairs. However, from 1980 to 1990, the number of blacks who lived in all-black areas overall—which includes these secondary ghettos—declined apace across the nation.

Massey and Denton, like many sociologists, nevertheless make much of statistics that show that quite large numbers of blacks continue to live in neighborhoods that are mostly black. They take this as evidence that slum life remains default for black people in America. But this interpretation rather mysteriously neglects that since the sixties, white suburbs have not been blacks' only alternatives to the ghetto. Middle-class black neighborhoods have sprouted and spread all over the United States (as a teen I lived in one in New Jersey). For example, if things were really as hideous as Massey and Denton imply, then one wonders just what Sheryll Cashin devoted her entire book *The Failures of Integration* to. Cashin—although subscribing just as wholeheartedly to The Saga as Massey and Denton—dwells at great length on middle-class black neighborhoods across the nation that she has studied. Were they just mirages? If not, then the implication Massey and Denton draw from the statistics is flawed: In our times, when black people live together, it is by no means always in slums.

Of course, this alone could be seen as addressing only part of the issue and a less urgent one. Massey and Denton could be wrong about the barriers that fortunate blacks faced, but correct about blacks without the money to buy pretty houses. But in fact, black middle-class areas have also come to offer housing to less fortunate blacks. One of Cashin's main observations is that across the nation, poorer blacks have moved into such neighborhoods, as a result of the kind of transitional stage between the terrorizing of the first black family on a city block typical in cities before the sixties and peacefully integrated communities like Philadelphia's West Mount Airy where I spent half of my childhood. Cashin recounts that many middle-class black suburbs trace to moneyed blacks having started moving into white suburbs, with whites then gradually moving away only after blacks reached a certain proportion. The result was that housing prices went down, upon which poorer blacks seeking to escape the ghetto moved in.

Cashin does not describe this in celebration, mind you. She is interested in the fact that the poorer blacks have often brought various social problems with them. But nevertheless, the process she documents also means that plenty of blacks of humble origins have been able to get out of the 'hood.

Tendency Versus Universal

So we have evidence of discriminatory housing policies on one hand, but equally ample—and intuitive—evidence that legions of blacks have moved out of the slums. One way to square the two is to note that the audit studies represent tendencies rather than universals.

Those tendencies are unforgivable, to be sure. But it would appear that blacks who encounter such things have gone to other realtors or

looked in other neighborhoods until the probabilities turned in their favor. That is, they exhibited the normal human persistence we would expect of people searching for something as central to existence as houses of
their own or even just apartments in places where their children's lives
won't be in danger. Moreover, this does not apply only to middle-class
blacks. Even for blacks with somewhat less money, statistics showing tendencies give no grounds for leaping to a conclusion that they were all but
barred from relocating.

Thus, we suspect that Massey's and Denton's notion that blacks who
could manage to get out of hideous neighborhoods "see the cards
stacked against them" and just decide to redecorate their shabby ghetto
walk-up and put an extra lock on the door is a fiction. It teaches us that
even blacks with the initiative to earn and save enough money to seek
peaceful surroundings are spineless, passive amoebas drifting about in
the current, whose only possible response to challenge is to move in the
other direction.

After all, let us recall how offended many blacks are when whites suppose that all blacks live in the ghetto. Immediately and indignantly we
talk up how many blacks have been strong and persistent enough to move
out. And we would be just as indignant if the white person objected that
these blacks were just random, lucky exceptions. Massey and Denton
(who are white) mean well, but what they have done nicely bolsters, with
numbers and buzzwords, the stereotype of blacks as ghetto folk.

The error in Massey's and Denton's portrait is clear not only from intuitive perception. Even the academic sociology literature indicates a different picture, especially after the seventies and eighties that Massey and
Denton addressed from the vantage point of the early nineties, since
which we have now come almost two decades further. About as much
time has now gone by since *American Apartheid*'s findings as had gone by
since the Fair Housing Act of 1968 when Massey and Denton were doing
their research. In that light, Paul Jargowsky reported in 1996 that economic segregation *between* blacks was increasing slowly but steadily (i.e.,
that middle-class blacks are living increasingly less among, or near, poorer
ones). Reynolds Farley and William Frey reported in 1994 that there are
many black middle-class communities emerging in the open spaces of the
South and West, in contrast to the long-saturated Northern and Midwest-
ern metropolises that Massey and Denton treat as a default situation.

Studies like these suggest that today, racist resistance to black neighbors is even less than it was in the seventies and eighties and that there are

increasing numbers of all-black neighborhoods available to inner-city people who have managed to amass enough money for a down payment or security deposit and have decent credit. Massey's and Denton's portrait of such blacks encountering so much racist stonewalling that they may as well not even consider leaving the slums appears that much more invalid.

No one is under any illusion that blacks today will never experience being steered to black or mixed neighborhoods, nor is there any reason to suppose that there do not exist some white communities with a quiet agreement not to let any blacks in at all. As it happens, the house I lived in as a teen in a middle-class all-black development in New Jersey directly abutted a golf course that was part of an adjacent white community (Tavistock), and it was well-known in my neighborhood that the golf course was closed to blacks.

So I know that the Civil Rights Act did not magically cleanse white America of racism. But the issue is one of degree. Since the seventies, discrimination has most certainly not made it all but impossible for black people to find housing outside of the ghetto. Black Harvard sociologist Orlando Patterson has concluded, "I am convinced by the sociological evidence, and from my own experience, that any Afro-American family that truly desires to live in an integrated, predominantly Euro-American neighborhood—which is not to say *any* predominantly Euro-American neighborhood—is capable of doing so." Apartheid this is not.

Yes, but . . . Part One: One Step Out of the 'Hood?

There are two objections that people of Massey's and Denton's orientation often come up with.

One is that even when blacks able to afford it move out of the 'hood proper, they still tend to live near it, and thus suffer from its sociological downsides such as crime. This is a major argument in *American Apartheid*, but once again, there is a certain nagging lack of fit with basic experience. Do most black middle-class people really live a few blocks from housing projects? Is being black and middle class *almost always* a matter of living on a special few "decent" blocks in an area that is generally a pit? Few who actually grew up black and middle class would find this intuitive, nor would anyone aware of how many quiet black middle-class suburbs there are in this country. And meanwhile, Massey and Denton do not illustrate their claim with on-the-ground descriptions; rather, they base the point on census tracts and income data.

And in that light, Sheryll Cashin's discussion of poorer blacks moving into affluent black neighborhoods provides a different perspective on the issue. Massey and Denton take the cold numbers and presume that it means middle-class blacks pressing their faces out against a glass wall around the slums are only able to get at best a census tract beyond them. However, the situation Cashin describes would yield exactly the quantitative configuration that Massey and Denton treat: neighborhoods where black people of high income live near black people with lower income. In deciding who is correct, we cannot help but see that Cashin trumps Massey and Denton: She refers to empirical, real-world evidence, while they are simply extrapolating from impersonal geographical statistics.

While I am also tempted to note that many blacks choose to live near blacks out of a sense of racial identification, I suppose I will refrain. I mention it only because when reading about how hard a time blacks may or may not have moving to white suburbs, I always think of how my mother actively sought for us to live with black people. She moved us from integrated West Mount Airy in Philadelphia to a new middle-class development in all-black Lawnside, New Jersey, because she wanted to live in a neighborhood that reminded her of the good things about her upbringing in segregated Atlanta. Was Mom really so odd in this? My personal experience makes me sense not, partly because being in that neighborhood I was surrounded by like-minded people for years, as well as others in Willingboro, New Jersey, whom we knew.

Yes, this was about true outer-ring suburbs rather than being near the ghetto. But then I have also known any number of middle-class blacks who actively seek neighborhoods that, while decent, are not too far from their "roots" in less fortunate areas. But I may be influenced by the fact that I now live in New York where there are so many blacks who feel that way about living in Harlem. In New York City the outrageous prices of homes in spotless neighborhoods have a way of making people especially open to this kind of "consciousness," and conditions were similar in Oakland where I lived previously.

But, these are just my personal impressions. An oft-discussed study in academia of whether blacks seek to live among their own is a 1976 survey in which nine out of ten blacks who would hypothetically prefer to live among blacks said this was because they feared how whites would receive them. The study only deals in the hypothetical and is also now pretty old. Short of concrete demonstrations that blacks often choose to live among their own out of cultural fellowship, rather than fear, I'll just leave this issue alone.

Yes, but . . . Part Two: White Flight

Then, Massey and Denton, like many analysts of race and housing, see great urgency in the fact that whites' tolerance of black neighbors tends to evaporate at a certain tipping point, upon which they begin picking up stakes and leaving the neighborhood all black.

Again, this phenomenon is real. The days are indeed past when it was common for whole blocks to turn tail when a single black family moved in down on the corner—a Gallup survey in 1997 showed fewer than two in ten whites saying that they would move if there were blacks "in great numbers," and only one percent said they would move if blacks moved in next door, and results like this are now standard across America.

But there is a limit. A study headed by Reynolds Farley found that whites in Detroit said that they would stay in a neighborhood that was only up to one-quarter black, and studies in several other cities have shown similar results.

But these facts, despite how frequently they are adduced (in part because of the memory-friendly nature of the rhyming term *white flight*) have nothing to do in the logical sense with our central question as to whether or not middle-class blacks are able to leave the ghetto. Rather, they just show that when blacks do leave the ghetto, they may encounter whites leaving, upon which the blacks have still left the ghetto.

The social science orthodoxy usually addresses this only as to the cases of less-than-affluent blacks moving, such that when whites leave the result is the spread of the same old ghetto. But this neglects that in other cases such as those that Cashin documents, the result of white flight has also often been new middle-class black neighborhoods. And then, as Cashin also documents, the empty houses whites leave there are often occupied not only by more middle-class blacks, but also by working-class ones taking advantage of the moderate prices that increased supply creates. To treat white flight as *inevitably* leaving a ghetto behind would seem to deny the economic diversity among blacks that is elsewhere considered so urgent to acknowledge, on the pain of revealing oneself as naïve at best or a racist at worst.

Thus, despite the injustice of white flight and the resonance of the term itself, it does not deep-six the basic claim that blacks who can are not barred in our times from leaving the ghetto on the basis of their skin color. We are treating not whether racism exists—big surprise, it does!— but whether it determines blacks' fates to the extent that our sociologists claim. And here, we have one more piece of evidence that it does not.

Detour: Segregation and the Ghetto

However, Massey and Denton have their reasons for covering the white flight issue despite its irrelevance to whether middle-class blacks are stuck in ghettos. The overarching assertion that they intend with *American Apartheid* is that while The Saga is legitimate, it is ultimately driven by the uniquely pernicious effects of a particular factor: segregation. Their idea is that when blacks, especially poor ones, end up living in all-black areas, a downturn in the economy will gradually and ineluctably turn the neighborhood into a festering slum full of layabouts, fatherless children, and people with needles in their arms.

I have chosen not to treat this idea as a separate stanza in The Saga, since the claim that the sheer concentration of black people in one place is a recipe for disaster is rather eccentric. It has not become the word on the street among thinking people outside of social scientists familiar with, in particular, Massey's academic articles. In fact, it smacks of being just a step away from the unsavory folk assertion, "You know what happens when you get a bunch of niggers together." If I were more given to pretending to see racism behind every tree, a part of me would be tempted to wonder whether Massey and Denton see black Americans as whole human beings.

However, it could be objected that in focusing on their arguments about whether racism pens blacks into the ghetto, I have failed to understand the larger lines of their argument. As such, I feel it necessary to take a detour and make clear that I have indeed digested their line of reasoning but find it flawed. It is, in fact, an object lesson in how seductive wording can disguise incoherence.

To see how treacherous words can be, let's take just one page in *American Apartheid*:

> What the black communities of the 1930s and the 1970s share is a high degree of segregation from the rest of society and a great deal of hardship stemming from larger economic upheavals.

Good—and indeed, black ghettos back in the day were no picnic. So the ghettos of the 1930s and the 1970s share something. But what made the *difference*?

> When a highly segregated group experiences a high or rising rate of poverty, geographically concentrated poverty is the inevitable result,

Okay, just like when you mix chicken with rice, the result is a dish with both chicken and rice in it . . . this statement is meaningless.

> and from this geographic concentration of poverty follow a variety of deleterious conditions.

"geographic concentration," "deleterious conditions"—beautiful music, but what causes the "deleterious conditions"?

> During times of recession, therefore, viable and economically stable black neighborhoods are rapidly transformed into areas of intense socioeconomic deprivation. Joblessness, welfare dependency, and single parenthood become the norm, and crime and disorder are inextricably woven into the fabric of daily life.

But why? Why is it that black neighborhoods must go to utter hell when conditions aren't ideal? Massey and Denton are presumably referring to modern inner-city hellholes. But as William Julius Wilson and so many others teach us, black ghettos have gotten vastly larger, meaner, and grimmer since the old days, which included the most vicious recession of the past one hundred years: The Great Depression. So—despite the pat wisdom that the words themselves imply, we have learned nothing of any value in understanding our history or plotting our future.

Certainly those sentences are not the whole of Massey's and Denton's argumentation on the role of segregation. However, nowhere else in the book (or Massey's academic article of 1990 on the same argument using similar data) do we get much closer to actual explanations. There is a running implication that the authors have proven the point with quantitative analysis. They make ample reference to statistical "predictions" that as the concentration of blacks rises, thus do rates of poverty, crime, welfare dependency, female-headed households, and so forth, based on what is termed "simulations." That term suggests a computer program fed assorted variables in poor people's lives, tabulating their interactions the way a computer processes meteorological data and yielding outputs based on sophisticated probabilistic algorithms applied to past events.

In such fashion, a computer can predict a hurricane, and Massey and Denton would have it that "simulations" can predict South Central. But if you wonder just how they could fashion a program that "predicts" poverty rates, or even things more particular like the number of boarded-up houses, on the basis of how many people in a neighborhood are of the same race, the answer is that they have done no such thing.

Rather, they have amassed data from a large number of cities in *modern* times, identified statistical correlations between assorted phenomena, and determined the general probability of those correlations on the basis of how they manifested themselves in the various cities. Then, they "ran the tape again" by seeing what happens if you create a kind of computer program primed with these statistical weightings based on *modern* conditions—including high segregation—and fed it data such as welfare recipiency, boarded-up windows, crime rates, and income levels.

But their analysis is based on an assumption that we can pronounce on what happened to black America without addressing, of all things, *history*. If the simulation is primed only with the reality of, say, 1975, then how can we treat it as modelling human behavior in American cities writ large when it has no historical component? Do Massey and Denton suppose that this is of no relevance because life has always been tough for poor blacks, period? It has, yes—but again, degree, degree. Yes, poor black communities in 1930 knew suffering just as ones in 1970 did. But then, in 1960, one in five black children were born out of wedlock, whereas by 1994, over three-quarters were. (Yes, those numbers for whites were 2 percent and 25 percent, but there is a stark difference in sheer proportion.) Or, recall that in just twelve short years from 1964 to 1976, AFDC recipiency almost quadrupled in Indianapolis. Massey's and Denton's "simulations" address "welfare recipiency" as a changeless factor as if white liberal consensus were urging poor blacks onto the rolls in 1940 just as it was in the late sixties. But it wasn't.

Yet, what Massey's and Denton's "simulation" has to offer is roughly the likes of "Segregation in Indianapolis in 1980 was to x degree, and crime was at the rate of a, while segregation in Cincinnati in 1980 was to y degree, and crime was at the rate of b. On the basis of this, our simulation shows that if segregation in a hypothetical city was to z degree, then crime would be at rate c. Hence, we conclude that segregation is a crucial determinant in social problems in poor black neighborhoods."

Which cannot help but lead us to ask what kind of "simulation" implies that black people came to America in roughly 1970. What was going on in poor black neighborhoods last week is most certainly not what was going on in them remotely as much in 1935. To pretend this isn't true requires letting go of any nostalgia or admiration for, say, Harlem in the 1920s, which old-timers articulately saw as a safer, more dignified period in the neighborhood's history, and this principle applies to any black district across our nation. A valid, constructive, and usable black sociology must attend closely and obsessively to *history*. How, after all, can anyone purport to point the way to our salvation while shoving under the rug our *history*? What about the *history* of welfare legislation? What about the *history* of conventional wisdom among influential thinkers on social policy? Say that these things are difficult to quantify—and it still leaves the question as to how valid an analysis can be that pretends that such factors did not exist. To designate such things as challenging does not eliminate their existence as crucial factors in black American social history.

Massey and Denton, for all of their good intentions, slip here. Shelby Steele has assailed the scholar who "is not giving us the results of objective research. He is offering an ideological and predetermined arrangement of causality, one that is designed to support a demand for interventions from the larger society." Steele actually aims this at William Julius Wilson. But despite my being in eternal awe of Steele as someone whose writing helped wake me up to thinking for myself about race, my reading of Wilson leaves me disinclined to parse him that way. But unfortunately, Massey's and Denton's disregard of history leads me to see Steele's analysis as appropriate for them. To assume that such an abstractly isolated factor as "segregation" alone is the *cause* of the sociological problems of the inner city is but one of several analyses one might readily propose—as witnessed by how few people on any level have fashioned such an argument.

But what we do know is that as a word, *segregation* has the potency of Spanish Fly. For example, Massey and Denton do not write in their statistical tables "Concentration of blacks," which would rightfully lead many to question the book's implications for black resilience and common sense. They write "racial segregation," making us think of an abstract evil most readily associated with things like signs on water fountains in the Old South and little black girls escorted into schools under armed guard as white onlookers threw rocks. No, Massey and Denton are not cynically utilizing the term to advance their careers. But their spontaneous attraction to such a counterintuitive, and marginally insulting, notion is due not to engagement with human reality, but to a deeply felt imperative to toe a certain line that makes white people feel like they've got the racism thing covered.

The segregation conceit is equally weak elsewhere in the book. Massey and Denton introduce us to the Mexican neighborhood Little Village in Chicago, which is stable today despite factory closings and recessions. Little Village "continues to house a variety of supermarkets, banks, restaurants, bakeries, travel agents, butchers, auto shops, hardware stores, and other retail outlets," while black North Lawndale right next door is a typical violent slum.

As part of their segregation fetish, Massey and Denton attribute the difference to the fact that Little Village is not *all* Mexican. Our authors want us to believe that the difference was because—really!—Little Village was only 75 percent Mexican while North Lawndale was, you see, 98 percent black. So this means that if three in four people are brown, then you get a thriving working-class enclave, but if everybody is *black*, then you get a degraded war zone. Am I the only person who gets a little itchy reading things like this and watching it be received as Solomonic insight?

To wit: Would Massey and Denton concur that if black ghettos were only three-quarters black, then factory relocation would have had no effect? Or—imagine presenting them with a typical black inner-city horror show, in which it turned out that three out of four people there were black instead of 98 percent. Would they scratch their heads wondering why it wasn't a peaceful working-class enclave like Little Village?

Where is their explanation of just what the difference is between 75 percent and 98 percent? Where is the tipping point? And what causes it? Just why is it that when black people live only among their own instead of hanging out with the occasional Latino, white senior citizen, or Arab immigrant—that is, one person among four—they must inevitably lapse into lives on the dole?

And finally, how would Massey and Denton explain neighborhoods where poor blacks and poor Latinos live mixed together in classic underclass conditions? Whether it is 75 percent this or 98 percent that—these sterile statistical metrics of "segregation" lose all application here. In 2000, to be "Straight Outta" Compton, Los Angeles, was to come from a place that was 40 percent black and 57 percent Latino. That same year, the Watts that TV's *Sanford and Son* had been set in was 38 percent black and 61 percent Latino. Yes, these communities once had larger black populations; the Latinos came in later. But Compton's blacks, though now constituting a mere 40 percent that Massey and Denton surely would not consider enough to "tip" a black community, have the same problems they did when they were predominant. This means that *cultural factors have persisted regardless of external conditions*. To decide that in these areas, "segregation" takes in both blacks and Latinos en masse as one "colored" group is arbitrary and would seem to disrespect the "diversity" of culture and experience that social scientists consider it so urgent for us to attend to.

In sum, I find Massey's and Denton's rather arbitrary isolation of segregation as the key to underclass ills to be a mistake.

Conclusion About Stanza Two

Massey and Denton look at polls where whites say that they do not want their neighborhoods to become mostly black and look at all-black inner cities. Then, they assume a cause from a correlation: that blacks are concentrated in inner cities because whites wouldn't let them move out.

But data both intuitive and academic speak against the idea that after 1970, white racism remained so decisive that blacks had little or no hope of finding housing beyond the slums.

Nothing makes sociologists quake in their boots more than the idea of anyone looking at a *tendency* in a group's behavior and basing a *generalization* on it. Exhibit A would be frequent warnings against thinking of welfare as a "black" problem. But then, Massey and Denton show that it is not uncommon for blacks to be steered away from the nicest neighborhoods when they go to a realtor looking for a house and expect us to take that *tendency* and concur with a *generalization* that none but a lucky sliver of black people ever has any hope of getting out of the slums or just a step beyond them. We are to subscribe to this generalization even in the face of a burgeoning black suburban middle class whose presence is all but inescapable to anyone other than a mountain hermit and whose flowering the same sociologists even elsewhere celebrate as a justification for racial preference policies.

I'm sorry, but no matter how good the intentions are, we are faced here with ideology rather than logical engagement.

Sheer logic dictates that we consider that factors other than residual housing discrimination have left so many blacks in inner cities. Massey and Denton can keep grasping at straws with observations such as that underclass pathologies are most concentrated among precisely the two groups who are most segregated in neighborhoods, blacks and Latinos. But again, this is correlation, not cause. Peel away the magic words, and listen to these authors telling us basically that, "If underclass behavior is most common in black and Latino neighborhoods it must be because they're all in there living together." Question that and listen to Massey's and Denton's ilk object that we are leaving out the boom-and-bust economy. Upon which we will ask, "What about Little Village? And precisely what is the difference between 75 percent and 98 percent? And why do blacks in neighborhoods where they have long been a numerical minority have the same problems that blacks have in neighborhoods where they constitute 98 percent?"

We are taught so insistently about how diverse we are, about how America is composed of distinct cultures of people. But is it really true that all cultural traits are positive ones? Or, is it really true that the only group with any negative traits worthy of mention is evil, Wonder-Bread, supremacist white America? Could it not be that all of us, alongside our positive cultural hallmarks, have some counterproductive cultural baggage that we need to deal with? And if so, then might we open ourselves up to considering that the reason poor blacks are concentrated so strongly into inner-city districts is this kind of baggage?

Could it not be that an awful lot of blacks have idled in neighborhoods that one would expect to have become ghost districts decades ago because a new oppositional consensus deprived them of norms of dignity that once held sway in poor black neighborhoods? Once, people like this were a private underbelly of such communities, treated by most residents as car wrecks. Today, they are the heart of those communities and are sung of as heroes by an entire music industry.

They are also pitied as powerless pawns of capitalism and racist bias by an academic and journalistic establishment. Orlando Patterson has these last as "committed to the 'two-nations' and 'racism forever' view of America" because "they are intellectually terrorized by the fear that any report of a decline in racism exposes them to the charge of racism or of being a 'Tom'." I wouldn't go that far—most of these people genuinely believe what they are saying. But their neurons are firing that way not in response to reality, but to the same meme of self-affirming alienation that has waylaid the blacks they write about.

THIRD STANZA:
WHEN MIDDLE-CLASS BLACKS MOVED AWAY, THE POOR HAD NO ROLE MODELS

Informally, this one is usually put as something like, "There used to be doctors and lawyers living on the same street as the poor folks. Once they moved out, the poor didn't have anybody to show them how to act."

More formally, one generally reads something along the lines of

Their departure has diminished an extremely important source of moral and social leadership within the black community. In pursuit of status and employment, and out of genuine concern for their own survival, the black middle class and those who aspire to it increasingly leave the ghetto behind. In their wake, unemployment, crime, drug use, family disorganization, and antisocial behavior have become powerful social forces.

William Julius Wilson has it that middle-class blacks were "social buffers" for poorer ones.

Once again, the word choices tempt like a Siren—"social buffer," "role model," poor blacks suffering from "concentration effects." At one point, Wilson deftly gives an almost cinematic shot of "the perceptive ghetto youngster" looking around him and learning from what he sees. Massey and Denton tell us, "The out-migration of middle-class families from ghetto areas left behind a destitute community lacking the institutions, resources, and values necessary for success in post-industrial society."

But what these people are telling us, in clear language, is that poor black people are incapable of behaving by themselves.

This is the only way that we can interpret the idea, since it is by no means a human universal that when poor people live in large numbers in one place, social chaos results. It can happen—but just as often does not.

When Role Models Disappear: Beyond Blacks

For example, if when middle-class people leave, poor ones must sink into oblivion, then we would expect that this happened to poor Jews on the Lower East Side in New York as fortunate Jews moved away to nicer neighborhoods. But no such thing happened.

This is not to say that the streets were models of harmony and tranquility. Ishmael Reed notes a *New York Times* editorial from 1883 that describes Lower East Side immigrants throwing rocks, fish, and "vile and indecent epithets" at a truck driver trying to get through a street packed with pushcarts. But Reed's idea that this indicated a nineteenth-century white underclass equivalent to today's black one is way off. Boisterous behavior filtered through the lens of the naked classist contempt typical of 1883 is one thing. But mackerel is decidedly not what the grandmother in a violent black housing project is afraid might come through her living-room window.

Perhaps we think that what made the difference with the Jews was a strong religion that held the community together. But then, black Americans are a deeply Christian people. Churches have traditionally been their community anchors, and even some of the most violent gangsta rappers thank God in their liner notes. What's the difference, then?

Which returns us to the question as to why apparently only poor blacks go to rack and ruin when no one in the neighborhood went to college. Massey and Denton describe poor blacks as lacking institutions and resources—but wouldn't that also apply to people who had only come to this country a few years ago? And in any case, by the 1960s, black people had been free of slavery in America for a hundred years! And for those ready to sing of the "legacies" of slavery living on, we will refer them to the endless lists of lodges and churches and charity groups that were the norm in black communities nationwide from Reconstruction until, precisely, the 1960s.

In the 1959 film *Imitation of Life*, one of the most striking scenes is when Lana Turner's black maid Juanita Moore, striking a tone masterfully poised between the deference required in the era and pointed self-assertion, informs Turner of her rich personal life, which includes "several lodges." Hall's character is just a maid—the social network she belonged to was by no means a cocktail-sipping black-bourgeoisie world, and she was not the type on her way to moving to a split-level in the 'burbs.

And that character reflected a reality. Black people without a lot of money did tend to belong to lodges and church groups in those days. Any black person can possibly confirm this in a quick conversation with their grandparents, and can get scholarly confirmation of it in any number of accounts of black communities in the first half of the twentieth century, in which tabulations of dutiful black organizations of all kinds and for all classes become almost monotonous. This was, exactly, the sense of "community" that black old-timers recall before the sixties.

And where, in Wilson's or Massey's and Denton's characterizations, is this? Where is the Black Culture that we celebrate? To read their description and nod is to give up an adherence to the idea that blacks are a strong people, much less beautiful.

In deciding whether Stanza Three is valid, we must ask ourselves a simple question: What other group of poor people besides black Americans has been depicted as going to hell because middle-class ones were not around?

Job Information

Wilson suggests that the problem was that without middle-class neighbors, poor blacks had less access to job tips and other crucial information from the wider world. Massey and Denton couch the same idea in the Siren language: "Given the social isolation enforced by segregation, black men are not well connected to employers in the larger economy."

But doesn't this sound as if these were people living in a society that had missed the invention of writing? There were newspapers. And then even word of mouth based on that. We see it as natural that the *Chicago Defender* played a major role in bringing Southern blacks north—despite the fact that a great many of the migrants were by no means heavy readers and likely learned of the opportunities announced in the *Defender* from others sharing the information with them by word of mouth. Apparently, that was "well connected" enough for countless millions of black people then. What was the difference later?

For example, the struggling cases that Katherine Newman covers in her *No Shame in My Game* tend to have relatives who have done better in life than them, and they are by no means as cut off from the larger world as Jews corralled into their ghettos were in Europe, a comparison that the work of most writers on the black underclass literally invites. Newman notes, "Survey research is a particularly weak method for picking up on the nuances of social relations, especially those that are as calibrated as the connections between Kyesha and her grandmother, or Nadine and her uncle. It is likely to underestimate the diversity of ties that ghetto dwellers have to the outside world."

Massey and Denton are again drawing dramatic implications from census data indicating high segregation rather than considering the reality of actual human interactions; Wilson, meanwhile, seems largely to be guessing.

So again, what made the difference? Could it possibly be that the sharecroppers felt more urgency to move than their children in the cities did? And if so, why? (As for the idea that blacks are all but "penned" into ghettos, see Stanza Two.)

How Good Is the Guess?

It is important to remember that the black middle-class exodus idea is just a guess. And we must note that the guess finds no support on the ground. Poor blacks at the time did not watch luckier ones' moving vans pull away and say, "Gee, who am I going to have to show me the way now?" I seriously doubt that poor black mothers looked out the window and wondered how their kids were going to grow up okay now that there were no more insurance salesmen and school principals on their blocks.

Even academics can have a hard time making the guess work. An article by sociologists Gary LaFree and Kriss A. Drass shows that the presence of affluent blacks not only has little influence on the behaviors of poor blacks, but also has *much less* influence than the presence of affluent whites has on the behaviors of poor whites.

LaFree and Drass are perplexed by that finding, but I think it points to my basic contention in this book. Alienation and dismissal of mainstream norms took hold of poor black communities in the sixties in a way they had not before and have since thrived independently of external conditions, as memes often do. Thus, the difference between poor blacks and poor whites that LaFree and Drass found is predictable—and as we would expect of a meme, it holds on regardless of whether well-heeled, quiet-living role models are living nearby.

Of course one might surmise that even if the meme drives poor black behavior today and numbs people to influence from traditional strivers, that if the strivers hadn't left the neighborhoods in the first place then the meme wouldn't have set in. But that brings us back to the Lower East Side. Why do only poor black people require a vigilant bourgeoisie to hold them back from social disaster?

Empiricism or Politics?

The middle-class exodus idea has gotten around so much partly because it nurtures a part of the modern black American soul. Namely, there will always be black Americans who think that "real" black people are what one writer has termed: "the grass-roots folks, the masses, the sho-nuff niggers—in short, all those black folks who do not aspire to white-middle-class-American-standards." Black people of that opinion were around before the late sixties (Billie Holiday was one of them). But today that orientation is a norm, magnified by influence from the white counterculture, elevated by Black Power separatism, and now thriving as a legacy of the era. Ironically, this view has a strong hold on black academics and journalists despite their middle-class status.

Thus, the gangbanger is an antihero, but the middle-class couple leaving the 'hood for the 'burbs in 1972 are suspicious characters. Just think how odd it is that *the thinking class of a race that has suffered so much recalls its first escapees from the slums less with joy than with ambivalence.* Clearly an ideological factor is filtering common sense.

So we have to be vigilant as to whether our acceptance of the middle-class exodus stanza is based on gut biases rather than logical reasoning. Applying the latter, we cannot avoid the conclusion that linking the emergence of the black underclass to Dr. Bryant and his lovely wife moving away implies that there is something uniquely weak about black Americans. That is not only unfair and unrealistic, but also unnecessary. The middle-class black exodus idea makes no sense and must be disincluded from serious addresses of what happened in the inner cities and what to do about it.

FOURTH STANZA:
HOUSING PROJECTS MADE SOCIAL CHAOS INEVITABLE
FOR POOR BLACKS

Writers on race and urban development are often given to implying that underclass behavior is an outgrowth of poor blacks being relocated into public housing in the fifties and sixties. More musically, it is typically phrased along the lines of "the demolishing of low-rent housing through slum clearance and replacement of these units with massive high-rise public housing projects sited exclusively in black residential districts."

Does Dispersal Drive a People Berserk?

There is no doubt that the first step of this process, when poor black neighborhoods were razed to make room for commercial buildings, uprooted and dispersed what had been close-knit areas. From 1949 to 1973 no fewer than 2,500 neighborhoods were bulldozed in almost a thousand cities. Also, provisions for blacks who were relocated were vastly inadequate. The number of units destroyed dwarfed the number of public housing units built: By 1967, the ratio was ten to one in Detroit, about seven to one in New Haven, and so on.

But the question is whether these hard knocks, which they surely were, really made inevitable single women raising too many children by different men in the projects, many of the men shooting one another over drugs outside of the housing projects, and almost no one in the housing projects having a job or even thinking about getting one.

Mindy Fullilove thinks so, analyzing blacks from the bulldozed communities as undergoing a psychological "root shock" trauma that "destroys the working model of the world that had existed in the individual's head." She even hypothesizes (perhaps anticipating someone noticing that the generation that underwent the shock are now grandparents) that the root shock trauma has lasted across generations and explains why gangsta rap music is so angry.

Fullilove even thinks that the Civil Rights movement and "the strength of the ghetto communities" (how striking to see a black person with a PhD use that phrase!) could have gotten poor blacks by despite manufacturing jobs pulling out—if it only hadn't been for urban renewal. Sheryll Cashin assumes in passing: "We don't have to imagine the effect on a neighborhood of plopping down massive buildings in which at least 90 percent of the occupants are extremely poor."

Or don't we?

Very Tall Buildings

It sits easily in the mind, this notion—it's whitey's fault again. But let's stop and think about what this account is actually saying. Poor blacks uprooted from their homes and moving into tall, crowded buildings must slip into chaos. Hmm. But this means, quite simply, that we would expect that throughout history, whenever poor people left home and moved into buildings crowded tall, there would be similar results.

Which means that the Eastern European Jews in *Fiddler on the Roof*, hounded by pogroms from their shtetls and fleeing to tall, crowded tenements in urban American ghettos, ended up at one another's throats on the Lower East Side. But they did not, as I have noted already. If Fullilove sees a difference between the "root shock" of blacks in the 1950s and that of people leaving their continent and language forever, I would be interested to know what it was. It was not that the Europeans were voluntary immigrants, since they would much rather have stayed where they were born and came to the United States in anguished flight from persecution and grinding poverty. Meanwhile, Jacob Riis's photos make it painfully clear what pits the tenements were, and at the turn of the century, the people there didn't even have radios or television to begin to ease the experience, and forget air-conditioning or electric fans.

Yet, these tenements were not nearly as violent as the projects later would be, and while substance abuse (then, mostly alcoholism), unemployment, and fatherless childrearing were hardly unknown, they were not *norms*. There was no drug crisis on the Lower East Side that Riis depicted. People worked for their keep—miserably, but still. And if you knocked somebody up you married them, even if you didn't particularly like them. So, why was it different for black Americans in the 1960s?

However, the guiding idea is actually that what drove poor blacks over the abyss was *very* tall buildings. This thesis is based on work in the 1970s by Oscar Newman, who argued that buildings high enough that most residents could not watch the outside common areas from their windows encouraged crime, exacerbated by ample concealed spaces such as side stairwells, apartments mostly situated in a row along a single hallway instead of facing one another, and entrances displaced from the visibility of the street. The arrangement of living spaces discouraged a communal vigilance over the common spaces; the residents tended to "experience the space outside their apartment unit as public."

Oscar Newman's argument is, in itself, unassailable, showing for example that crime increases proportionally with the height of housing project buildings nationwide. Reading his closer demonstration that crime was higher in 1970 in the Van Dyke high-rises in Brooklyn than in the Brownsville low-rise project right across the street despite both projects containing the same number of people with the same demographic profile, one encounters one of the best pieces of sociological work ever composed.

But—Newman's thesis in no way allows us to trace the specific horror of the *Boyz n the Hood* world to building height.

For one, Newman addresses a particular problem: crime. He does not argue, and few of us would, that the architectural factors he treats make women have multiple children by multiple men without being able to take care of them, or that building height makes children disidentify from school at previously unknown rates, or makes drug addiction more enticing, or makes people start using high-powered firearms against one another for petty reasons so regularly that it no longer even comes as a surprise. Clearly, there was more at work than architecture to create this change in mood, as opposed to rates of crime alone.

And one thing that makes this clear is that when the high-rises were first constructed, while crime rates were higher than average, as we would expect given the realities of poverty, they did not yet render the projects war zones. Carol Steele, a black woman who had lived her whole life in the Cabrini-Green projects in Chicago, says that in the fifties

> Cabrini-Green was a small city unto itself, filled with working families in which both parents lived at home. Children walked to the nearby elementary school. They played hopscotch along the open hallways that led to the apartments. In the afternoons, neighbors gossiped while they weeded vegetable gardens between the towers.

"I want that world back," Steele says today. Now, we can be sure that life wasn't perfect in Cabrini-Green back then—surely, for example, a lot of that gossip was about pregnancy out of wedlock. This and more were well established in poor black communities before the late sixties, as I will discuss in Chapter Five. But there was still a qualitative difference, one that Steele wants back—in the same tall, ugly buildings today considered an architectural condemnation to violence and ennui.

So even Newman's thesis leaves the question as to why high-rise projects went so very wrong in terms of not just crime but also so much else *only in the late sixties*. Also important to keep in mind is that the same thing happened in the low-rises; crime alone lagged behind the high-rise rate somewhat, but hardly enough to disqualify the low-rises as, overall, awful places to live as well. Why just in the late sixties? Say that it was some kind of frenzied rage against the machine—but then you must explain why this happened specifically starting *in the 1960s*. "The pot boiled over," "blacks had had enough," yes—but even in 1920, blacks had endured grinding racism for almost sixty years after Emancipation. The brief ray of sunshine of Reconstruction could even be seen as fueling black fury after it proved not to bear fruit. Lynching was normal, and even outside the South, any black person who was not sweeping was lucky. Why no revolt *then*?

Oscar Newman actually addressed this, although few seem to have paid much heed to this part of his exposition. He notes that in 1965, the federal standards for admission to the buildings were relaxed, such that many more families on welfare could move in. This was crucial to the difference between Cabrini-Green 1955 and Cabrini-Green 1995. For example, in the Rosen Apartments project in Philadelphia, in the early 1950s, two-parent working families were typical, and only 28 percent of the families were on welfare. Rosen mixes low-rise and high-rise buildings, and at that time, crime rates in the high-rises were only 10 percent more than in the low-rises. But twenty years later, about two in three families there were on welfare, and the crime rates in the high-rises were horrific.

Thus, Newman is successful in showing that the architectural nature of housing project buildings did not make being poor any easier. But he also shows that there was a major "bump" in the texture of these residences starting in, as we see again and again, the late sixties, that cannot be traced to building height. When writers claim that the problem was simply putting poor people in tall buildings, they are vastly oversimplifying, encouraged in this partly by the memory-friendly, schematic nature of the idea and the fact that the buildings are so painfully ugly. They have not engaged with the actual writings of Oscar Newman, and thus have not had occasion to see that he addressed solely a rise in criminal activity, rather than a seismic shift in broader cultural norms. All casual references to the effects of tall buildings on poor blacks neglect that the crucial factor that distinguished 1960 from 1970 was not architectural, but cultural.

"You Know What Happens When a Bunch of . . ." Revisited

In any case, the building height issue is usually treated as fuel added to a fire that was set by "segregation" in general, and in this, the lurch downward in the projects is often linked to the departure of stable families, a variation on the middle-class suburban exodus idea. The journalist interviewing Carol Steele slides right into this gospel: "Cabrini-Green's decline began in the late 1960s after riots and racial tension began driving away working families." The article quotes Columbia sociologist Sudhir Venkatesh as saying, "The people who remained were the people who couldn't afford to leave." Now, the nature of journalistic quotation is such that Venkatesh could have meant many things by that. But typically, sociologists make comments like that in reference to the Massey and Denton paradigm: Put lots of poor blacks together, and they can only end up shooting one another in the face. This is certainly what the article intends the quote to imply, and Venkatesh is a protégé of none other than William Julius Wilson.

But then we must recall the Mexican Chicago neighborhood Little Village, where poor people live together and get by. Massey and Denton want us to think that this is because the area is only 75 percent Mexican, but again, they give no reason why black neighborhoods would be okay if they were only 75 percent black and do not even address the black-Latino melange of South Central Los Angeles.

A common response is that Mexicans are "plucky immigrants" unfair as a comparison with black "involuntary immigrants." Most important, Massey and Denton do not take this tack; for them, it's all about the good old numbers. But still—so what about poor black sharecropper communities in the late 1800s and early 1900s, when the vast majority of blacks were rural rather than urban people? Here, there was no black middle class with fancy degrees living among the barefoot folk: They had mostly moved to the cities amid the slow flow of ambitious Americans of all races in that direction at the time. Basically, everybody in these communities was poor. For a cinematic mental image, think of *Sounder*, or where Celie grew up in the film of *The Color Purple*, or John Singleton's *Rosewood*, or the childhood scenes in *Ray*. Was there some illegitimacy? You bet. Did men pop knives late at night when they had had a few too many? Not uncommonly. But were these communities anywhere near as nihilistically violent as modern black inner cities? No—no account even begins to suggest so, and, in fact, a certain strain of black historiography celebrates the cultural coherence of such counties and towns. It is not inevitable that poor black people all living in one place go to hell.

Yes, these sharecropper communities had no high-rises. But again, the underclass problem is hardly restricted to the higher buildings, and in any case, again Oscar Newman treated crime, just one of an array of issues that face us. Newman's work allows that even in low-rise buildings, not only a goodly amount of crime, but also any number of other unsavory things we would cluck our tongues at were going on. We can be sure such things were hardly news in poor black sharecropper communities—and we can be just as sure these things existed there to nowhere near the extent that has been accepted as normal in, say, South Central over the past twenty years.

We must search for other factors that created a new black America at this time. Two were the expansion of oppositional identity from a personality trait to a badge of racial authenticity and the expansion of welfare with poor blacks in mind. Both of these things happened in the late 1960s. Is there any coherent way of fashioning a claim that the fact that housing projects fell apart completely at the same time was an accident?

Slum Clearance as Racism?

In addition, the idea that slum clearance in itself was a naked injustice is based on sloppy history. How can we depict a "howl of amputation" among displaced blacks whose parents had left the South with empty pockets? Or—urban renewal critics have a way of glamorizing old-time black "communities" that were, for all of the social connectedness, overcrowded, tumbledown slums. Someone who grew up in Pittsburgh's Hill District gives a description that nicely captures the good and the bad.

> The buildings were old, the streets were cobblestone and old, there were many small alleyways and people lived in those alleyways. The houses were very close together. There were small walkways that ran in between the alleyways that was really a playground. So, the physical condition of the buildings helped to create a sense of community.

We all lived in similar conditions and had similar complaints about the wind whipping through the gaps between the frame and the window, and the holes in the walls and the leaking and the toilet fixtures that work sometimes and don't work sometimes. But that kind of common condition bound us together as a community. I knew everybody on my block, and they knew me.

We might wish the government had paid to fix these houses instead of bulldozing them, but this would not have addressed the overcrowding, and as chroniclers of various cities' early black ghettos note, the houses tended to be made of wood and were overall beyond real repair anyway. There is a tour one can take on the Lower East Side in New York City of tenement apartments preserved as they were in the first few decades of the twentieth century. They reproduce living spaces exactly akin to what blacks had to put up with in the cramped ghettos they lived in before urban renewal. I dare anyone to take the New York tenement tour, ducking into dimly lit, claustrophobic two-room flats with bathrooms in the hall, and recalling that the people who lived in them year in and year out had neither air-conditioning nor television, and come out feeling nostalgic for the "warmth" of old-time black urban slums.

Thus, the fault we might ascribe to the government is that they did not build *enough* public housing. The layout of the high-rises was not optimal by any means, but this did not make the difference between housing project 1960—a grungy place where not everybody worked for a living, best avoided after dark—into housing project 1990—the bloody "PJs" where most people did not work, best avoided at all times of day. The key here was breakdown in earlier senses of propriety, that occurred in these projects and beyond throughout the sixties, as studies from the era clearly show (recall Chapter One).

Have you ever, somewhere far back in your mind, felt just a little twinge when someone was mouthing the idea that poor blacks cannot be expected to live productive lives in tall, crowded buildings? I mean, a little twinge of the sort that we are trained, on the subject of race, to let pass? Well, attention must be paid to that twinge; go with it. Insisting that what created violent, smelly black housing projects was "concentration," "density," or even "root shock" is just shy of racism for whites, and in a black writer, suggests internalized feelings of racial inferiority.

FIFTH STANZA:
HIGHWAY CONSTRUCTION BROKE DOWN POOR BLACKS'
SENSE OF COMMUNITY

We also hear that when interstate highways were built through poor black neighborhoods, this "fragmented" communities. Physically, it did. Indianapolis residents regularly mention that the construction of Highway 65 through what were once flatland black slums broke up and dispersed the communities. In Detroit, the construction of the Lodge Freeway required clearing away 2,222 buildings.

But the question is whether the path from this kind of "dispersion" to, for example, the South Bronx by 1975 was so inevitable. Do any of us feel that twinge again?

Okay, people separated by a highway will likely have less casual contact with one another than they once did. But as always, blacks are portrayed as bizarrely lacking human resilience. Just what makes it implausible that blacks would forge new or stronger ties with people on their side of the highway? Where is it stipulated that when a black community is divided in half, that the halves alone are not large enough to become new communities of their own? Precisely how large a Village does it take?

Picture a black neighborhood in 1955—we're looking at it from a low-flying plane. Now we watch a nasty highway laid down through the middle of the neighborhood. And now—do we spontaneously fear that the people down on the ground are ripe for becoming wards of the state for shooting one another? I think many of us have to work a bit to even imagine that the highway is going to have, really, much of anything at all to do with crime, sex, or drugs.

Yet, many of us have a conditioned reflex to suppose that highways might be dangerous in this way for black people in particular. And black people are a special case because, well, they are descendants of slaves. And because they endured segregation after that. Yes—but now we have to specify precisely what that history, tragic though it is, has to do with what happens when a large road is built through a neighborhood. Some might try to, but the answer will likely be suspiciously lengthy and vague— leaving us time to seriously wonder whether this highway idea is really worth our attention.

The idea that highways were part of why black communities took such a bad turn was imprinted in part by Robert Caro's vivid and wrenching description in his awesome 1974 biography of Robert Moses, *The*

Power Broker, of how Moses tore expressways through neighborhoods like Brooklyn's Sunset Park and the Bronx's East Tremont and destroyed what had once been thriving, comfortable working-class enclaves. However, the destruction that he described did not entail the residents suddenly turning to depravity because they were no longer "close-knit." Rather, with the loss of social connection and the destruction of businesses that the highway required, the residents gradually moved away. What turned the neighborhoods into slums was that when real estate values went down, apartments were cheap enough for the poorest of the poor to move in—by the middle of the twentieth century, blacks and Latinos—and vacant buildings gave shelter to winos, pimps, and drug addicts.

But this does not stand as an explanation for how the black underclass arose. The people Caro describes who turned, for example, East Tremont from a peaceful working-class Jewish enclave into a violent black and brown disaster area were a particular segment of brown communities that had always existed—as I noted in Chapter One, there has indeed always been an underclass *segment* of American society (and it bears mentioning that it has never been all brown). The question is why what began as one more place where the unluckiest people happened to gather went on to become black slums of a massiveness never known in America before, with hitherto unthinkable degrees of violence, family breakdown, and substance addiction.

Of course, the usual suspects tell us that it was the inevitable result of poor blacks being concentrated in one place. But again, why didn't this happen in poor black communities before? Why hadn't the East Tremont Jews, who had grown up in the miasmic slums of the Lower East Side, devolved into the same kind of misery down there instead of moving to the Bronx, since they surely knew contempt and alienation just as Caro describes the black and Latino people as knowing? Why—precisely, why?— couldn't the poor blacks who moved into East Tremont have remained a small, tragic community, just like myriad others that had always existed on the outskirts of black quarters? What made their lifestyles become so widespread as to become a black norm, instead of the underbelly it had once been? Massey and Denton will remind us of "segregation"—which brings us back to Mexican Little Village. For a very long time, blacks who moved into East Tremont constituted nowhere near even the 75 percent of the population that Massey and Denton consider a magic number keeping Little Village from "tipping"—Jews hung on for a long time. And there were a decent number of working-class and middle-class blacks in East Tremont as well—"role models"? Right?

Like the "concentration" analysis of housing projects, this is a fragile notion cooked up a few decades ago to prop up the idea that anything bad that happens to black people is white America's fault. That was the fashion back then, but in our moment, more of us are prepared for a more realistic and constructive approach to racial disrepancies in America. Isn't it time to let these house-of-cards canards fall down?

SIXTH STANZA:
"DRUGS CAME IN"

When asked what went wrong in their neighborhoods, the response that longtime residents of black inner-city communities tend to give is not that factories moved away, that housing projects were too tall, or that the darned highway was the beginning of the end, but rather that "drugs came in." Which makes perfect sense, as the violence of the drug trade and the widespread addiction it encouraged is the most immediate damage any person in the neighborhood would notice. People not working, or men abandoning their children, are less immediately processible issues year to year, and alone would hardly be processible as a crisis threatening the very lives of neighborhood residents.

But if we simply leave it at that drugs "came in," it sounds as if we mean that drugs were somehow imposed on black communities and that poor blacks were inherently incapable of resisting overusing them and basing their lives on selling them. A reasonable-sounding way of putting this might be something like, "When a powerful narcotic is widely available for affordable prices, and offers massive financial reward to its vendors because of legal proscription, it is predictable that its use and sale will become a bedrock of the local economy in communities of poor people, faced with limited opportunities for employment beyond subsistence level and vulnerable to the temptations of temporary relief from a grinding existence. It is to be expected that competition between vendors will occasion violent turf wars that will rend the fabric of the communities."

In which case we would expect that poor black communities in the 1920s under Prohibition, when the sale of alcohol was illegal, would have devolved into the same chaos we are familiar with in today's inner cities. There were, after all, plenty of black bootleggers—why would there not be? And they made much better money than was available in low-level factory and service jobs.

But those communities did not become underclass havens in which sale of, say, bootleg gin or beer became the economic anchor. Nor were drugs remotely unknown in poor black communities before the crack wars. Claude Brown's *Manchild in the Promised Land* recalls how heroin, aka "horse," was hardly unknown in Harlem in the 1940s, where so many people had so little to hope for. Yet, someone living in much of Harlem as it was by the 1980s would have given quite a bit to live in the Harlem of forty years before then that Brown described.

This was because drugs did not become the food and money of black neighborhoods until the eighties. Recall, again, Chapter One, where we saw that in studies of poor black communities in the early and mid-sixties, the drug problem is present but by no means a scourge, with the main manifestation of substance abuse being "winos" hovering around the edges of things.

On the seventies sitcom *Good Times* set in a Chicago housing project, the "wino" was regularly mentioned, generally in passing derision, as a marginal problem rather than a neighborhood-wide scourge. (Recall also Aunt Esther's staggering drinker husband Woodrow on *Sanford and Son*, played for laughs.) There was indeed one two-part episode of *Good Times* in which J. J.'s new girlfriend turned out to be a heroin addict (played by Debbie Allen). But despite the show's attempts at some socially conscious honesty about black poverty, drug addiction and sale were not presented as dominating the building or the neighborhood. This was because to the extent that by the mid-seventies this very thing was becoming a reality in real-life black ghettos, it was a new development.

And as always, we cannot begin to say that blacks in the seventies were in a more miserable state than their grandparents had been in the twenties and thirties. In fact, employment opportunities for blacks picked up nationwide in the sixties, and racism, at least of the overt kind that barred almost all blacks from decent employment or housing, was outlawed and quickly receding.

So our question must be just why drugs "came in" and took such a vicious hold on poor blacks just when they did. I know that some are inclined to the theory that the CIA funneled cocaine into South Central Los Angeles (and presumably, across the nation). But even there, the question is why poor blacks were so *open* to resorting to using and selling it instead of getting respectable jobs. Yes, crack cocaine was invented, and is uniquely potent and addictive. Yes, raw cocaine became somewhat cheaper in the early eighties. Regularly, authors cite the invention of crack as the reason black communities went to pieces—but if it were that simple, then why didn't we see at least something like this happening even out in the white suburbs? After all, as typical black spokesmen so often remind us in their eternal quest to protect blacks from "stereotyping," white kids in Pleasantville are no strangers to all kinds of drugs. So where has been the crack "scourge" in Scarsdale? Or to bring it back home, why wasn't half of Harlem doing heroin in about 1950? Why didn't ethnographers in the sixties like Rainwater and Hannerz find poor blacks strung out block after block the way journalists would find them twenty years later?

"Because crack is so cheap," wise folk say. But is crack *that* cheap? Cheaper than powder, yes, but what exactly do we mean by cheap? Clearly, crack remains enough of an investment that its addicts end up unable to pay for much else except the next hit—crack costs a lot more than a pack of Now-and-Laters. And meanwhile, heroin in the 1940s was also "cheap" enough that, for example, Claude Brown hardly depicts it as something as pricey and precious as gold dust. In those days, heroin was by no means a drug of the elite: Ordinary, downwardly mobile folks could get their hands on it regularly enough to become addicts and stay that way. After all, if it cost much more, then it could not have developed such a presence among blacks with modest resources. Anyone who claims that drug use was not one of the issues facing poor black America in, say, the 1940s simply hasn't had occasion to read enough of the relevant sources or talk to people who were there. Recall the musicians in the biopic *Ray* who were addicted to shooting up, anticipating their modest earnings from gigs so they could buy more of the poison.

Crack in 1985 was cheap enough, but still cost enough to ruin a life; heroin in 1945 cost a lot more than bubble gum, but not so much more that anyone interested could not get some on a regular basis. That is— poor blacks knew drugs "coming in" long, long before the early 1980s. The question is why drugs "coming in" hooked every second person in poor black communities *only after the sixties*.

Black leftist music critic Nelson George is typical in how he drops a stitch when addressing the "drugs came in" issue. As to the question as to "why heroin flowed so intensely into black neighborhoods," after a quick doff of the cap to good old factory hypothesis, George offers only the government conspiracy theories. He is sensible enough to accept them only with a certain ambivalence: "African-American belief in government duplicity toward them is deep-seated and even sometimes overly paranoid"—but too short on other explanations to avoid concluding that history lends these theories "real credibility." Even "credibility" leaves uncertainty, but after this George can only move on.

It seems that many are comfortable with the idea that poor blacks are so vulnerable, so devoid of any human agency, that all one has to do is wave a crack pipe in front of them and about every second one of them will leap at it like a dog grabbing a pork chop. Not only does this make me uncomfortable, but also more to the point, it doesn't make sense. Poor blacks did not, *as a rule*, leap at drink or drugs this way *in such great numbers* in the old days.

They only did so to such a ruinous extent after the sixties. This was because they were now living in a period when the levels of basic shame in doing so were lower than they had ever been in American history. This was sparked initially by the countercultural revolution among whites, when drug use went mainstream. But where poor blacks took this ball and ran with it in the uniquely destructive way in which they did, the issue was a new culture of alienation, under which becoming a drug seller or chronic user was not only okay, but also even a mark of strength. Or at least, just okay.

Take it easy, we were told. And the white stockbroker did a few lines after work and sold a little blow to a friend or two in the foyer after a party. Fuck authority. *Bright Lights, Big City.*

But the same Zeitgeist meant something different for the black man in 1978 who grew up poor. Fuck authority. Why should I salute The System and work for "chump change" for years without being sure it will pay off? Especially when the po-lice are knocking niggers' heads together? So off he went to the corner to take his place as one more black man making a *living* selling blow—and eventually he went to jail. *New Jack City.*

Not because of the po-lice, who had been vicious for decades before 1978, during which young black men such as himself had nevertheless continued to work respectable jobs. Not because factories moved away, since even in Indianapolis brothas were drifting down the same path with factory jobs just down the road. And not because he didn't grow up with the role models of buttoned-up "Negroes" who shunned drugs, who

made him slightly sick anyway because they "thought they were white."
He went to jail because a new culture decided how he related to the world
he knew. That culture did not exist until about 1966.

WHAT HAPPENED AT TEN O'CLOCK?

The aim of this chapter has not been an old and useless argument that underclass blacks are simply amoral refuse of society. I, for one, am utterly
incapable of seeing such people and dismissing their plight as simply
"their fault." I cringe when whites assume such a thing, or when they pretend not to, but rather clearly do in their heart of hearts. I looked at North
Philly out of the car window as a kid and wondered not, "What's wrong
with those people?" but, "What made them that way?" And I was quite
open to the idea that societal inequity was at fault—only to find over the
years that the explanations just did not seem to describe actual human beings, even poor ones, and even poor ones with black people's history, and
even their present.

We are told of a "lack of hope," but I have always been nagged by a
more stepwise, historical question about the problem. This lack of hope
did not bear such hideous fruit even in poor black communities until
about forty years ago—just the final tenth of the entire period during
which black people have lived in this country: at ten o'clock p.m., as I put
it in the Introduction.

It's clear what happened to today's underclass—they never knew anything but that world. But what led to this kind of lifestyle for the vanguard
generation who created this underclass society at a particular time?

And in that light, I cannot help but see a connection between the fact
that poor blacks took their bad turn exactly when a new sociopolitical
consensus took over the country as a whole, including new government
policies that encouraged poor blacks to build lives around it. Poor blacks
drank in a new orientation toward traditional assumptions of what was
normal. We know this partly because underclass culture began deepening
and spreading even when external economic conditions did not make it
predictable. Indianapolis is a key example of this slippage between behavior and circumstance. Another is the Jeffrey Manor neighborhood in
Chicago in the early seventies. In his *American Dream*, Jason DeParle
quotes a former welfare mother who grew up there who notes that at that
time "everybody started losing they damn mind!" and has no explanation
for it. The social scientist hits the census data expecting the usual glum

discrepancies, but in fact only 10 percent of the woman's census tract were poor at the time, nine in ten families owned their homes, 73 percent of adults worked, the average household income was a third *above* the city average, and only one house in ten was living on welfare. DeParle mentions Mary Pattillo-McCoy's argument in her widely read *Black Picket Fences* that poor blacks have known a situation where they teeter ever on the brink of going the bad way: "You could go any way any day," McCoy quotes such a person as saying. But the question is why so very many people started going in one particular way only during a particular few decades in a four-hundred-year stretch of black history.

DeParle's interviewee gets at the answer in her way: There was something in the air. There was something about the times. Norms changed. There was now no longer anything *shameful* in the community about things that had been shameful before. There was a new conception of what was *ordinary*—contrasting with what things were like, as the St. Louis girl in the projects had it, "before 1960." These are ways of saying that the issue was cultural.

Thus, it is a vast oversimplification to assert one more time that the underclass are "demoralized by racism and the wall of social resistance facing them," as Elijah Anderson has it. Even he seems to know that the obstacles facing such people are not exactly insurmountable, as he says that they "lose perspective and lack an outlook and sensibility that would allow them to negotiate the wider system of employment and society in general." In other words, there *is* employment to "negotiate." What made these people lose perspective, outlook, sensibility, and negotiating skills to such a striking degree at a certain time was not The Man—it was a new way of dealing with The Man. A cultural orientation sets in and can thrive independently of surrounding conditions.

Christopher Jencks put it well: "Such differences can, of course, be seen as part of racism's appalling historical legacy. But if all whites were suddenly struck color-blind, we would not expect these differences to disappear overnight—indeed, they would probably persist for several generations. That is what it means to invoke 'culture' as an explanation of such differences." Jencks makes the sober observation that for authority figures in such communities before they fall apart, "Censoriousness and blame are their principal weapons in this struggle: blame for teenaged boys who steal from their neighbors, blame for drunken men who beat up their wives, blame for young women who have babies they cannot offer a 'decent home,' blame for young men who say a four-dollar-an-hour job is not worth the bother, blame for everyone who acts as if society owes them more than they owe society."

Jencks's point is not to be taken as suggesting that our solution today is just to "blame" underclass blacks for living by the only patterns they ever knew in a real way. It would not only be unfair, but also would help nothing. The blame issue here is important, however, in the historical sense. Jencks is correct that "blame," when coming from loving, concerned mothers and tongue-clucking church elders and back-porch gossip, served a function. Writers like Michael Eric Dyson have their right not to see anything in that old consensus but "bourgeois" snobbery that held blacks back from acting out against the inequities of the Establishment. But such a position is clearly more a certain variety of politics than basic moral truth, and I doubt it has, or will ever have, many adherents.

My argument, then, unabashedly assumes that there is such a thing as a culture of poverty. We must be under no illusion that this book only "implies" this or that it is "dressing up" the culture of poverty argument in new clothes. *My explicit aim is to argue that poor blacks indeed have been waylaid by a culture of poverty.* I unhesitatingly agree with all those before me who have analyzed poor blacks post-1970 in that way. The only "new clothes" I intend is in my attempt to get at just what led poor blacks to fall into this culture of poverty so deeply at a particular time. *This book is, most definitely, one more in the line of arguments that poor blacks' problems are primarily due to culture rather than economics.* Its argument stands or falls on whether my particular argument is effective.

I am well aware that the culture of poverty argument has often been dismissed as "blaming the victim." But even the writers most notoriously associated with the culture of poverty argument, such as Oscar Lewis, Daniel Patrick Moynihan, and Edward Banfield, were quite aware that the culture was the creation of larger forces. I am as well, but I question whether in the case of poor blacks after the late sixties, the relevant larger forces were institutional inequities. Another larger force that can determine the history of a people is a cultural orientation, established in response to societal inequities of a particular moment, but then riding on normal psychological weak spots and going on to guide choices and attitudes indefinitely, independently of what would benefit the subject most in the society they know.

For example, take that idea that poor black people somehow do not know how to find work. In fact, quite a few have shown themselves to be perfectly capable of honing in on and even following work—under certain conditions. In Wisconsin in 1991, half of the AFDC recipients had moved in from other states, one in five in just the past three months. What was so attractive about chilly Wisconsin?

Answer: It happened to give higher welfare payments than most states. One of the black women Jason DeParle covers in *American Dream* openly tells him, "We came up here because the aid in Chicago wasn't nowhere as much as it was up here. We were figuring out how we were gonna pay our bills." "Socially isolated" though they were, and as distant a relationship as they had with the printed page, and even years before the Internet, these three women showed normal human orientation toward survival as optimal as possible.

Unfortunately, however, their America detoured their efforts of self-preservational into the sinkhole of the permanent dole, and this brings us to the next chapter. Open-ended welfare—white America's expression of therapeutic alienation—did much more to bring down poor black America than we often learn. Yet, resistance to this truth has been so common, and in its way so articulate, that we must take a good look at the issue before proceeding.

CHAPTER FOUR

Why Are You Talking About *Blacks* on Welfare?

Because of the way the intersection of welfare and race has been framed for so very long, I so far have left myself open to the charge that my emphasis on what welfare's expansion did to black America is either veiled racism or just plain bad history. In this chapter I would like to correct that possible misimpression.

One senses that many think that living open-endedly on welfare was already the norm even in the early black ghettos. In other words, one might think that in 1940, about every second woman in Harlem or Bronzeville was living on welfare, had grown up on it, and was going to see her daughters join the rolls somewhere in her late teens.

It's not hard to see why. For one thing, in our times, even for people of about sixty, by the time they came of age, welfare was already a norm in poor black communities. The people who came of age in the early black ghettos when welfare was not yet a norm are now in their eighties or older, so we hear from them less. Meanwhile, the transformation of welfare into an easily available and open-ended program took place in stepwise procedural developments unlikely to make newspaper headlines, especially in an era when black poverty was less on the radar screen than it became later.

Finally, the evolution of welfare is mostly described in academic books, often as just one part of a broader discussion on topics like social insurance, politics, and urban planning. These tomes, sitting on university library shelves and barely known beyond the academic and think tank worlds, are not sources that someone interested in black history is likely to come across. Rather, in the late sixties and early seventies, their attention is drawn to the assassinations of Martin Luther King Jr. and Malcolm X and school desegregation, with the Black Power movement briefly flagged as a passing fashion statement that helped alert whites to blacks' plight.

As such, many may find my focus on welfare suspicious. Some will think of Ronald Reagan's "welfare queen" line of claiming that people lived high on the hog on their checks, deliberately having babies to get more compensation. But no one got rich on welfare, and I am aware of no evidence that women regularly got themselves knocked up to have more free food in the fridge. Those arguments will be of no interest to us.

Then, some will recall Charles Murray's *Losing Ground* of 1984 and suspect that I will merely recap that book's argument. But Murray's focus on whether or not welfare scooched blacks a few steps beyond poverty and whether couples avoided marriage to come out a little better at the end of each month have no bearing on my argument, which is about larger cultural changes. I will not repeat Murray's case here.

Yet, the expansion of welfare in the late sixties was a much more crucial factor in black history than Afros, Nixon's Southern Strategy, or King's death. To understand what really happened to poor blacks at this time, we need to understand a chapter not found in John Hope Franklin's *From Slavery to Freedom*, Kwame Anthony Appiah and Henry Louis Gates Jr.'s *Africana* encyclopedia, or a great many other fine sources on the black experience. That chapter is about how what is intended as an instrument of social improvement can cut a people off at their knees.

WELFARE IN THE LATE SIXTIES: NOT JUST FOR WHITE WIDOWS ANYMORE

A standard objection to people who decry a black "welfare culture" is that welfare began as a program for white widows, that there have always been more whites on welfare than blacks, and that criticizing blacks on welfare is therefore racist. Only the first part of that objection is true.

Welfare Before the Sixties

Welfare indeed began in 1935 as a small program intended for widows and old people without other means of support. Until the sixties, what was often called "home relief" conjured up an image not of a poor young black woman, but of a destitute aging white widow. There were black people on welfare, but they were often subject to tighter eligibility requirements and lower payments than whites, especially in the South where, for example, Georgia's program had a black quota. This continued a long tradition of restricting blacks' access to public assistance: No fewer than 96 percent of the people receiving "Mothers' Pensions" before the creation of Aid to Dependent Children (ADC) had been white.

Therefore, when you peruse the photos of poor blacks in Bronzeville in the 1940s in Richard Wright's *12 Million Black Voices*, few of the women were depending on welfare in open-ended fashion. Wright noted that "for every five white mothers who must leave their children unattended at home in order to work, twenty-five of our black mothers must leave their children unattended at home in order to work," pointing at the low wages that black men earned and how tragically hard their women had to work to compensate for it. This was brutally unfair, but we must also note that Wright did not say that most black women were on welfare—because they weren't. The tendency was that women went on "relief" if they could find neither work nor a man to help support them, and this was by no means the regular situation. The Harlem James Baldwin wrote of growing up in was not one where welfare was women's main source of money. In these times, women often scraped by as domestics while the men did grunt work in restaurants, hotels, and factories.

Welfare in those days was a mean little business meant to get people by in a pinch. Women had to let social workers do a home check to see if their lifestyles were "suitable" and make sure there was not a man living with them who could work. If they qualified, then payments were scanty—hardly anything to even begin to found a lifetime upon. As late as the early sixties, Lee Rainwater in his study of the Pruitt-Igoe housing project in St. Louis makes only brief, passing references to welfare: Even in the worst black communities it had not yet become a norm.

Welfare as We Knew It

The "welfare as we know it" that Bill Clinton promised to mend developed only in the sixties, when the number of people on the rolls increased by 169 percent, and then by 30 percent more from 1970 to 1975. In New York City, by 1972 almost one in six residents were on welfare.

Indeed, these numbers included whites. But the factoid that more whites were on welfare tends to imply that the proportion of blacks on welfare was basically their proportion of the population. This is mistaken.

Even in 1961, 43 percent of welfare recipients were black, even though at the time only about one in ten Americans were black, fewer than half of them were poor, and 13 percent of whites were poor themselves. Just nine years later in 1970, in New York City, 47 percent of the people on AFDC were black, whereas 13 percent were white and 40 percent were Puerto Rican—but by now, the American economy had boomed throughout the sixties, opening up opportunities to work for a living that blacks in 1961 would have envied. And after this, in many other cities, blacks outright outnumbered whites on the rolls. By the 1990s there were surely people insisting "there are more whites on welfare than blacks" in Milwaukee, but in fact by the 1990s seven in ten long-term AFDC recipients there were black.

Now, one interpretation of the disproportionate number of blacks who were on the rolls by the early seventies would be that poverty in black America was on the increase or even just sitting static. We might suppose that the problem was a new employment crisis in black America, such as that low-skill manufacturing jobs had moved away. Urban political expert Fred Siegel gets this just right.

> Talk to intelligent urbanites in New York, Los Angeles, or Washington about welfare, and almost the first thing they'll tell you is that people are on welfare because of an absence of jobs. When you point out that the welfare explosion in America not only began in New York but also coincided with the great economic and jobs boom of the 1960s when black unemployment in the city was running at 4 percent, about half the national average for minorities, they look puzzled and tend to change the subject.

That is precisely my experience, but in this chapter, the print medium inherently prevents changing the subject.

Ironically, at the very time that long-term welfare dependency was becoming a norm rather than a stopgap in black communities, black poverty and unemployment were decreasing, and not just in minor degrees. In 1940, almost 90 percent of black Americans were poor—that is, for all intents and purposes, all of them. By 1960, a little less than half were. Unemployment among black men decreased by almost 50 percent from 1960 to 1970 (from 7.8 to 4.2 percent). Thus, welfare was not expanded to arrest a downward trend in blacks' progress.

The welfare explosion in the sixties, then, was a black issue: It affected black America much more than white America. And this was not just because racism had left a greater proportion of blacks poor than whites, as that problem was lessening significantly by the 1960s. Welfare became a staple means of living in poor black America because of a deliberate effort to lasso onto the rolls blacks who had previously been under the impression that they were doing the right thing by working for a living.

America Wakes Up

This had its roots in a new interest in poverty in a race-neutral sense, among thinking people and government officials starting in the early sixties.

Before this, one could sit at a forum addressing poverty and hear from smart, concerned people that poverty was just "one of a constellation of social defects, to be found in the individual and his immediate community." That was, for instance, 1956. But ten years later, a new way of thinking had deemed it backward to think of poverty as a cultural issue. The new consensus was that poverty was not due simply to laziness or bad luck, but to self-perpetuating aspects of the capitalist system.

So far, so good. Here was America getting past a primitive, moralistic judgment of poor people as simply not being able to cut the mustard. And this was the context that Daniel Patrick Moynihan's report *The Negro Family: The Case for National Action* folded into in 1965. Moynihan's identification of a crisis in poor black communities where mainstream norms of marriage and childrearing were impotent was received by many as racist. Assorted writers chugged out a stream of arguments that for blacks, broken families were a healthy coping strategy minted in the times when slavers broke up black families, and still proactive for a people disproportionately mired in poverty. But this work was celebrated largely in the academy and among scattered "militant" advocates. It was consigned to the archives once black inner cities drifted into rampant violence and drug addiction that not even the most ardent black nationalist could prop up as legacies of the plantation or as constructive countercultural approaches to living.

Meanwhile, others were more receptive to what Moynihan had intended as a sincere alarm, his purpose being to call for public policy to improve the quality of life for poor blacks. They were so receptive that by 1970, the impulse we now know so well to think first of black people when poverty is mentioned was set. Only in our times do we need a new concept of "the working poor" to remind us that plenty of white people are scraping by on the bottom as well. "The Other America" that Michael Harrington had grabbed us by the collar to tell us about in 1962 was largely a race-neutral concept. But now it was not only the poor, but also the black poor, who were seen as an especially urgent problem.

Which they were, in terms of the proportion they made up of the black race. Clearly, the American Dream was not working very well for a particular ethnic group in our nation, and the new concern about them was, on its face, progressive and humane. It shows up a certain hollowness at the heart of the New Deal, in its lack of interest in the disproportionate injustice that poor blacks were suffering. Franklin D. Roosevelt never really gave a whit about black people and was typical of his times. The thirties' concern with "The Forgotten Man" was focused on white people; black Civil Rights leaders had to be contented with politely tugging sleeves. Here in the late sixties was a new Enlightenment.

The question, however, was just how to address black poverty.

Job training?

Educational subsidies?

No—how about teaching black people to sign up for welfare even when they were getting by without it?

White Radicals, Black Dependence

In 1966, that was exactly what happened. The new idea was that we were not to teach blacks how to deal with the System, but to teach them to check out of it.

That year, a task force report from the Advisory Council on Public Welfare, *Having the Power, We Have the Duty*, took as a given that poverty is permanent and that the only solution was a combination of redistribution of wealth and guaranteed income: "Most public welfare recipients . . . cannot realistically be expected to become self-sustaining." But at least that was only about people already on welfare at the time. Things really got going when well-intended whites decided to apply that ideology to what we now call the working poor, deciding that they would be better off refraining from supporting themselves.

In New York in 1966, the Mobilization for Youth was set up to encourage poor people to apply for welfare. The organization trained its workers to tap an applicant's "inner victim," in language that suggests a dim view of the applicant's mental sophistication: "In dealing with low-income people who rarely have the experience or the education of thinking in conceptual terms, in terms of where the system is at fault, it's the immediate thing like the Jewish landlord, the Irish cop on the beat, the Italian grocery-store owner, the lousy teachers, or the welfare investigator . . . if you try to tone this down at the very beginning, you're running the danger, through your own intellectual and professional goal-setting methods, of alienating yourself from the people you want to organize." Black historical chronicles tell us that at this time figures like Stokely

Carmichael were shaking whites into a commitment to addressing the legacies of racism in American society. But they leave out that too often, what those whites learned was that the victims of four centuries of injustice were exotic simpletons.

Especially effective was the National Welfare Rights Organization led by former chemist George Wiley and Columbia University social work professors Frances Fox Piven and Richard Cloward, guiding troops of activists who were mostly black women. Rarely in American history have people with such an openly radical, and even destructive, agenda had such power over the daily lives of innocent people.

They openly encouraged as many people as possible to be given AFDC payments, hoping that this would bankrupt the government and force a complete overhaul of our distribution of income. It wasn't that they thought there was no work for blacks—just that it was beneath blacks' dignity to start at the bottom. Piven's and Cloward's lefty journalist ally Richard Elman was dismayed that blacks were expected "to go the hard route, to be . . . taxi drivers, restaurant employees . . . and factory hands." The National Welfare Rights Organization became well known for disrupting government meetings and held rallies in forty cities calling for people to be allowed to enroll in the AFDC program. While the manifesto nominally addressed the poor in general, in practice the call was mainly focused on blacks. By the fall of 1968, the organization was staging more than two hundred protests a month, sometimes assisted by the Black Panthers. A core idea at this time was that welfare was a "Civil Right," as argued in an influential law review article by Charles Reich.

Here was one of those intermediate moments, as even traditional Civil Rights leaders were not with the program here. Piven has recalled, "We met with Whitney Young [executive director of the National Urban League] . . . and he gave us a long speech about how it was more important to get one black woman into a job as an airline stewardess than it was to get fifty poor black families onto welfare. We went to Bayard Rustin [coordinator of the March on Washington], but he said, 'if you have an idea that takes two hours to explain, then you don't have an idea.' " Imagine a time when heroes of The Struggle couldn't quite wrap their heads around the idea of teaching people to quit their jobs and go on the dole!

But before long, they wouldn't have to wrap their heads around something that was right before their eyes every day. When Piven and Cloward published a manifesto article in *The Nation* in 1966, there were thirty thousand reprint requests, and their National Welfare Rights Organization changed black America. One thousand neighborhood service centers were established nationwide to encourage people to go on welfare who would not have done so otherwise. In New York, welfare commissioner Mitchell "come-and-get-it" Ginsberg, who had been Cloward's colleague at Columbia, pushed caseworkers to recruit people and abolished not only the requirement that applicants be screened by interview, but also that an investigator visit their homes. This was typical of a national pattern.

The first crack in the dam had been in 1961. Until then, the sheer existence of an identified father of her children disqualified a woman from welfare, under the assumption that the father of the child could work to support his progeny. But after 1961, as long as the father was unemployed, welfare was available. But the decisive relaxations started in 1967. As of that year, women on welfare were allowed to keep much more of their earnings on the side. By 1968, a woman could collect welfare even if the unemployed man lived with her. From then on, typically efforts to check that the man was seeking work, or to help him find it, were minimal to nonexistent. Then in 1969, the old one-year state residency requirement was dropped to allow people who moved in from a less generous state to sign right up. Thus, it became possible for welfare recipients to do what Jason DeParle's interviewees did: move to another state to seek higher payments.

These incremental procedural changes, each in themselves seeming so dull and insignificant, created "welfare as we knew it," the program that meant that a young woman who got pregnant in her teens had available to her a lifelong check from the government, regardless of whether the father or fathers of her children worked for a living, and could keep picking up that check wherever and whenever she moved within the United States. No one black or white in the thirties, forties, or fifties had known welfare of this kind. Welfare 1940 and welfare 1990 were as different as a three-minute 78 record that wore out after twenty-five playings and a seventy-five-minute CD that will play perfectly until the sun consumes the earth.

Welfare had once been a low-profile affair, offering a temporary safety net to people who found themselves in dire straits. Notice, for instance, how small a role welfare plays in most narratives and chronicles of black American life in the thirties, forties, and fifties, despite widespread black poverty. But now, "welfare" referred to a well-publicized bureaucracy eagerly courting even people who had been getting by on their own, and after it got people onto the rolls, unconcerned with when or even whether they left. This new version of welfare quickly took over poor black communities and became one of their defining traits. The nation's welfare rolls increased by 107 percent from 1960 to 1970—in contrast to only 17 percent from 1950 to 1960.

And then there was that these relaxations of the requirements were handy for the ambitious local pol. The expansion of AFDC acquired a new use, just as what were once hairs on reptiles evolved into a new use as feathers on birds. For liberal white officials, AFDC became less about political philosophy, which echoed weakly beyond the halls of Columbia University where Piven and Cloward were based, than being one part expiation for past sins against blacks and one part riot insurance. Meanwhile, as overt racism ebbed, the stage was set for a new crop of black municipal officials. For them, welfare benefits were handy patronage in a quest for power and votes, just like job assignments had been for white urban machine kingpins in the recent past.

Mix political cynicism and a new cultural imperative to give blacks what would later be termed reparations, and you get the bloated, self-perpetuating AFDC bureaucracies after the sixties, where over the years, workers were compensated more for signing people up than for ever getting them back to work. In New York, caseworkers began priding themselves on jimmying the requirements to get applicants the best deal. Former Indianapolis mayor Stephen Goldsmith found that in that city, welfare caseworkers stressed that their job was to determine eligibility with the fewest errors, that the system had no penalty for not finding people jobs, and that it did not distinguish between people who wanted to work and those who didn't. Could there be a more perfect way of hooking legions of innocent people on the dole?

These changes had a crucial effect. It used to be that you could only get welfare if you provided a certain level of home life for your children and if the children's father(s) were AWOL, and social workers were always on the watch waiting for justifications to get you back into the workforce. Many will recall the noisome, snippy white social worker characters in old plays and movies about people down on their luck—*Street Scene* is a relevant play still performed occasionally these days, and others may recall Brooke Allen's character in Spike Lee's film *Malcolm X*—and will note that this character is an anachronism by the seventies. Before then, the culture of welfare administration held a ticking clock before recipients: Welfare was a pit stop, not a living. That is, welfare went largely to women who were widows or might as well have been, who were trying their best and did not expect to be on "home relief" for long.

But after 1966, it was possible for a woman to go on welfare regardless of the quality of home life that she provided her children, even when the children's father lived with her without having or seeking work. After 1966, her city's government had no interest in whether she ever worked again, and in fact valued her as a notch in their bedpost of how many black women had been seduced onto the rolls by a new informed white consensus that saw this as a victory. That, ladies and gentlemen, was open-ended welfare—the Welfare as We Knew It that, until 1996, was as ordinary as Kool-Aid in poor black communities.

The impact was massive, almost counterintuitively so. In 1966, 4,666,000 people were on AFDC nationwide. Just four years later, 9,660,000 were. In the sixties, a third of the people whose incomes made them eligible for AFDC were on the rolls. By 1971, 90 percent were.

A New Consensus

Quickly it became politically incorrect to suggest that welfare recipients train for work in the future. In 1967, House Ways and Means Committee chairman Wilbur Mills ventured a quiet proposal that welfare recipients either work or train for payments—but *only* if they were able and *only* if states provided child care. Yet, he was received as if he had suggested that poor blacks should, say, sprint to work. Before long, a mother on welfare was shouting at New York City mayor John Lindsay, "I've got six kids and each one of them has a different daddy. It's my job to have kids, and your job, Mr. Mayor, to take care of them."

There was a certain theatricality in that statement, and who knows what sociopolitical justifications were operating in this person's mind—but what is important is that she would even say it, compared with, for example, the chariness of charity among blacks in Indianapolis in the early twentieth century. One would look long and hard searching for documentation of a black person saying anything like this in a public forum before the 1960s—and come up with nothing. The times had changed.

In 1970, Richard Nixon, of all people, proposed to replace AFDC with a Family Assistance Plan, which would have recipients work, but with the government making up the difference between their salary and the poverty line. The idea was that the government would stop making up the difference once that line was passed, under the assumption that welfare was intended to allow people to get by until they could start working themselves beyond poverty of a degree all would consider dire. But it became what Moynihan described as "almost a talisman of advanced liberalism" to condemn the proposal as "an attack on the poor," insisting that the payment ceiling be set far above the poverty line.

But even AFDC itself had not lifted people out of poverty, which revealed the new consensus. Welfare advocates wanted not the old school "home relief" safety net, but an open-ended program committed to compensating people whom fate had left out of the middle class because of the pitfalls of capitalism. At hearings that Senator Eugene McCarthy held on behalf of the black poor, one mother said, "We only want the kind of jobs that will pay $10,000 or $20,000 . . . we aren't going to do anybody's laundry or babysitting except for ourselves." To lend a sense of what those figures meant at the time, leftist welfare advocates were standing pat at just $5,500 as the minimal point at which the Family Assistance Plan should stop payments, which was itself far above the $3,721 poverty line for a family of four in 1969. Another woman said, "You can't force me to work! You'd better give me something better than I'm getting on welfare. I ain't taking it." This woman was, for the record, none other than the Vice Chairman of the National Welfare Rights Organization.

Even though open-ended welfare was especially dangerous to the black community at this time, we must be under no illusion that what happened was somehow inherent to black people. Welfare policies are always and everywhere subject to exploitation. In the late nineteenth century, Republicans held the White House for a forty-year stretch broken only by Grover Cleveland. As such, the distribution of Civil War pensions was almost always in Republicans' hands, and to court votes, they drummed up wider awareness of the pension programs and loosened their eligibility restrictions. One result was widespread fraud in the system. Just as with AFDC a century later, pension rolls expanded independently of need. If pensions had been going to those who needed them, then they would have been distributed evenly across the states. Instead, pensioners were concentrated in heavily Republican states, and most so where competition with Democrats was fiercest, which egged on the use of pensions to attract votes and tip close contests.

Thus, black America was placed in the line of fire of a policy ripe for exploitation, of a sort that only pushed blacks further into dependence over subsistence. All it took was one generation before it looked perfectly normal for healthy black people to live as dependents on monthly checks from the government generation after generation, with only old heads and historians aware that this was not the only possible version of black America, even among its poor.

Which brings us to the concerned black person circa 1990 snapping, "Why are you talking about *blacks* on welfare?"

WELFARE EXPANSION: THE AFTERMATH

But the reason so many were treating welfare as a black problem by the seventies was because after its expansion, in inner-city slums across the nation successive generations of black children barely knew their fathers and were raised by single unemployed mothers stuck in terminal poverty living on modest checks from Uncle Sam, year after year, even when the economy was flush. This was the first time in black American history that dependency had been a *norm* in its poorer communities across the nation, even in times when opportunities were sparser and lesser than blacks today under eighty have ever known.

And the result was not only that more poor black women lived on AFDC but also that their lives proceeded just as they had before. After welfare expansion, poor black women's lives changed considerably.

Work Disappears?

Between 1964 and 1976, the number of black children born to single mothers doubled, to 50 percent, and by 1995 the percentage was more than three-quarters. In 1935, 85 percent of the women receiving what was then called Aid to Dependent Children were widows. By the 1960s, 93 percent of the women receiving what was by then called Aid to Families with Dependent Children had either never lived with the father of their children or had been left by him.

Nor can we humanely just chalk this up to a "You go, girl!" overthrow of old assumptions that a woman needs a man, by ladies who went on take care of themselves just fine, thank you very much, as, say, dental assistants and municipal workers. These single women were not exactly living large. Poverty rates for two-parent black families plunged over this time and beyond. In 1959, in two-parent black families 61 percent of children were poor—unpardonable—but by 1995, that problem was vastly lesser: Just 13 percent of black kids in two-parent families were poor. But by that same year, among black children raised by single women, poverty was almost five times that rate—62 percent.

In other words, after welfare was expanded with poor blacks in mind, poor black fathers rarely helped rear their children, while mothers typically raised the children alone and in poverty, getting by on eagerly anticipated monthly checks from the government instead of working for a living. And the upshot was a new poor black world where children grew up watching an adult realm where work was optional, which too often determined the choices they made as they came of age having internalized this.

The young black man who missed developing a native sense of work and career as an identity is that much more likely to be open to choosing extralegal activity as a source of income. He lacks any sense that going in this direction compromises his legitimacy as a human being. And then add the ideology he drinks in from the oppositional orthodoxy, teaching him that white America is not worth his allegiance anyway, also preached to him almost nonstop today by leading hip-hoppers who provide him with a new kind of folk music.

William Julius Wilson sees this "perceptive ghetto youngster" as going the wrong way because he can't watch Judge Jenkins's son studying for the bar exam. But what Wilson neglects is that this youngster, if in, for example, Detroit in 1925, also saw poor black men taking the bus to Ford's River Rouge plant every day and their wives—not girlfriends—on the same buses going to work as domestics. If welfare had not eliminated such working couples from his "perceptive" eye, then even after Judge Jenkins moved away he would still have grown up, quite simply, in a world where even poor black people worked for a living—because it was the only way to eat. But the expansion of welfare did make those "working poor" black couples exceptions by the 1970s, and hence the perceptive ghetto youngster "perceived" men on the corner selling drugs, and women on the stoop feeding their kids with food they did not go to work to buy. As often as not, his perception led him to drift to the corner.

No? Well. In the strict sense, the expansion of welfare and the onset of this new black community norm is a mere correlation: One came after the other. But both basic logic and sheer compassion require at least considering that the relationship is not only correlative but also causal. What I mean is this.

SOME CONSERVATIVE RHETORIC

Before the five-year time limit imposed in 1996, welfare recipients from the seventies on consisted of three main groups of roughly equal size. About a third were people temporarily down on their luck—abused wives with children, new immigrants—who typically used welfare as a stopgap measure to survive while getting back on their feet. Another third were so addled by drugs, violent upbringings, and other pathologies that they are unfit for work forever.

But then there was another third who were essentially taking a free ride—not because they were evil, but because open-ended welfare catered to the lesser instincts of human nature. We don't like to talk about those people, but anyone with any experience with this side of black American life—such as relatives that most middle-class blacks have—knows that the core of the welfare world pre-1996 was women who gave birth in their teens for no particular reason other than having grown up in an environment where this was the norm. As often as not, such women continued having children afterward because, with open-ended welfare standing always at the ready, there was no reason not to, and with their previous kids already barring them from getting much of anywhere, another child would be one more source of unconditional love, as well as, ultimately, something to do.

Star Parker is president of the Coalition on Urban Renewal and Education, which works with the inner-city poor. Parker was once a (black) mother on welfare and reminisces about how the old system did not exactly stimulate someone who already had a child to try to live by working.

> "Let me make sure I understand you correctly," I inquired of the welfare caseworker as I presented her with my pregnancy confirmation note from a doctor. "All I have to do for you to send me $465 a month, $176 worth of food stamps, and 100 percent free medical and dental assistance is keep this baby. As long as I don't have a bank account, find a job, or get married I qualify for aid? Where do I sign up?"

Of course, individual experiences varied, and by no means all long-term welfare recipients in the inner city made calculations this deliberate, or cheerily said, even to themselves, "Where do I sign up?" But the main point is the effect of an environment in which individuals' choices so often converged on living permanently on government checks, in part because this had become easier than ever before in American history. Before the late sixties, *the program Star Parker found available did not exist.*

Early experience leaves a powerful imprint—it is not surprising that so many people growing up in this culture took this route. However, my point is that this third of the typical welfare caseload were neither temporarily down on their luck nor either psychically or physically incapable of work. The men who created these children felt free to abandon their mates for the exact same reason—welfare ensured that the children would eat in any case, and thus marriage became beside the point.

I do not mean to "bash" these people—I view them as done in by white society's misguided brand of benevolence. Welfare culture was the product of a system white leftists created that allowed blacks to realize the worst of *human* nature, in discouraging individual responsibility, the one thing that pushes most people to make the best of themselves. We praise the white middle-class mother for providing for her children, but the fact is that the woman had no choice—either she provided for them or they died (or were taken from her). Open-ended welfare, presenting the option of not working to provide for one's children, meant a culture of people where more than a few of whom did not. Certainly, this was only reinforced by the fact that a person growing up in the parochiality of the inner city, hobbled by a substandard education, is unlikely to spontaneously imagine a career for themselves in the outside world. But if there were no way to have children and support them without working, then these women would have been much less inclined to do so—as they were not until welfare was expanded— and would have been more open to thinking about venturing into that wider world.

The multigenerational welfare culture developed on the simple basis of *human*, not "black," nature. The same phenomenon is often reported on Native American reservations, where open-ended welfare policies have similarly tended to create cultures of indolence, dependence, and substance abuse long after white racism receded as a significant obstacle to advancement. Worldwide, for each person who strives to be the best that they can be, there is another one who, given the opportunity, will seek the most gain for the least effort. That is Aesop, the Bible, and common sense, and still, not a pretty thought—which makes it even sadder how directly open-ended welfare made blacks face it so regularly for thirty years. As Shelby Steele has written, "Inertia is the common response to situations like welfare, where just enough basic needs are met to undercut motivation and risk taking."

We might even be able to save a bit of Massey's and Denton's "segregation" argument here. In an America where vast numbers of poor blacks lived together in neighborhoods and a program was instituted that allowed its women to live on the dole forever if they had kids, a "geographical concentration" of mothers who took that option unsurprisingly meant that the children they raised were unlikely to spontaneously see another way of living. Massey and Denton think that crunching numbers from modern black inner cities shows that "concentration" alone was why things went wrong, as if things would have come out the same way even if open-ended welfare were not created in the late sixties. But their "simulations" do not include that crucial variable. Their work includes, for example, no engagement with Drake's and Cayton's classic profile of black Chicago between the Wars, *Black Metropolis*, in which welfare hovers at the margins.

A simulation that included this and took history into mind would show that without open-ended welfare, poor blacks maintained the close-knit, work-centered communities that even sociologists like Massey and Denton celebrate, ruing that highway construction "dispersed" them. But contrary to Massey's and Denton's fetishization of "segregation" as a modern problem, "segregation" was not exactly unknown to blacks before housing projects. The problem was not "segregation," but what federal policy allowed blacks to do about it. After and only after 1966, one choice was to become a ward of the state forever and leave your kids thinking of that as normal.

On the Ground

Even the most sympathetic accounts of women on welfare make it painfully clear that AFDC did not save people from a System that refused them work, but allowed them to circumvent supporting themselves on work that was readily available.

Welfare was hardly bounteous, but for one, it tended to pay more than entry-level work. Stephen Goldsmith spent twelve years working as a prosecutor locating fathers who had abandoned women on welfare with whom they had made children. He notes, "welfare did not make work unnecessary—it made work irrational. What kind of mother, at any income level, would take a job if it meant her children would be worse off?"

And then, nationwide, most women on AFDC also worked under the table. For example, one study of fifty mothers in Chicago on welfare showed that all of them made money on the side, and Jason DeParle deftly observes of his interviewee Angie: "The fact that work and welfare were contrasting ways of life—a given of the public debate—was nonsensical to her." We certainly cannot begrudge these women the extra money—more food for the kids and even a little more fun for them in lives that often lacked much of it. But this still only made it even less likely that someone would let go of the AFDC checks and try to survive on work alone. Angie took a job at a nursing home but only lasted eight days because she didn't like the work ("I don't want to find no dead person!")—and could go back on welfare. She takes a post office job and lets it go for vague reasons, but hits upon clarity in admitting, "I knew if I left the post office, I could still have money."

DeParle is a *New York Times* writer who self-avowedly began as an opponent of welfare reform, and even though he has reconsidered upon seeing its benefits, he is a very sympathetic chronicler of these women, not a right-wing crusader against "welfare queens." Yet, his book overflows with anecdotes like these making it painfully clear that Welfare as We Knew It was hindering people from doing their best. Angie again, on why she and her friends moved to Milwaukee, makes it clear that getting off of welfare was not exactly a high priority: "You think we just had to live in Milwaukee? So many opportunities for us here in Milwaukee? We got a nice job in Milwaukee! Nice home! We didn't come here because of that shit!" Angie was a product of a system that kept her from knowing, wanting, or *needing* to do better than this.

"Know Your History"

DeParle brings himself to toy with the notion that *just maybe* AFDC "played an enabling role" in his interviewees' having children out of wedlock so casually. But for we who seek truth, "why" is only the second-best word; the best one is "because." History, as always, lends some useful light for getting from "why?" to "because."

Nationwide, the rate of childbearing went down during the Great Depression. This suggests that people with limited opportunity can refrain from having children. Clearly, black inner cities are places of low opportunity—I assume that no one of any political stripe could even begin to disagree there. So—why all the kids?

The usual line here is that lack of opportunity makes young women have kids because they see no other future for themselves. But what kind of future did financially desperate people in 1932 see for themselves? After all, they did not know as we now do that the Depression would be over by the end of the decade.

A crucial difference between 1932 and 1992 was that in 1992, the government offered a program under which a woman could take care of a baby she had out of wedlock without working. There is no need to tar her as having the baby to get a check. Just as easily, as DeParle has it, the availability of the check "enabled" her having the baby. Women of this kind are given to saying that their incentive was not the check, but to belong to what they perceive as "the baby club"—that is, all they ever know is that women around sixteen give birth. Yes, but—crucially, there was no "baby club" for poor young women (of any color) in 1932, because the government offered no way to take care of such babies without working very,

very hard; the only other choice was leaving the child at the orphanage. So—fewer babies.

For example, it was considered a problem in Bronzeville of the twenties that among poor black women, just 15 percent of births were out of wedlock! Then, once the Depression hit, the number went *down* to less than one in twelve. A survey like Drake's and Cayton's of black Chicago at this time makes it painfully clear that these women had little sense of "hope" or "self-definition." And yet, out-of-wedlock birth rates then considered extraordinary were so low that today they would barely occasion notice, and the woman who had several children by different men was a marginal type. So, what made the difference in poor black women's "choices"?

There is a wrenching moment in Elliot Liebow's survey of the DC ghetto in the early sixties, where a young black woman cries to a man who is leaving her, "Where can I go? To my mother's grave? . . . You know I'm all alone, so where can I go? Nobody wants a woman with three babies." But the vignette is a period piece, in that a few years later she wouldn't have such a problem. She would no longer need a man to want her as a marriage partner or even to take care of her financially because the government would take care of her and her babies until they were grown, and then allow them in turn to have babies that the government would also take care of. It is hardly unlikely that this is exactly what happened to the woman Liebow describes and her children.

So one imagines plenty of people who thought of themselves as Doing the Right Thing to salute Richard Elman dismissing the idea of black people settling for being taxi drivers and restaurant employees. But the result was that foreign immigrants have taken exactly those jobs and put their children on the way to middle-class lives, while blacks whose ancestors have been in this country for more than three hundred years marched to Elman's tune and wound up living in hell.

An alternate black America is so easy to imagine. While cabdrivers without foreign accents are rare in New York, in DC, black American cabdrivers happen to be quite common. Why couldn't black men nationwide who didn't feel like hiking out to the factories take jobs driving cabs right within the city?

And soul food restaurants could easily be as common as Indian or Thai ones. Most people like fried chicken and greens; if you ask me, they're a damned sight better than burritos or General Tso's chicken and give Samosas and pad thai a run for their money. I wonder how many people could say that anything they have had in all but the best Ethiopian restaurants can even hold a candle to barbecue at the humblest black American takeout joint. But instead, in New York, one largely samples barbecue at the occasional spot that whites usually open. In Oakland, some blacks sell it, but on the margins—the hipper little papers have to remind people how good the food is every couple of years or so, and the places tend to be shoestring outfits, such that soul food home delivery is all but nonexistent. Soul food could, and should, be a delivery staple alongside Chinese, Thai, and Indian nationwide. The reason people of all races nationwide are not ordering it over the phone weekly is not deindustrialization. The reason is, ultimately, Frances Fox Piven and Richard Cloward and the ideology that they infected black America with, teaching us that if "the business of America is business," we are exceptions—even if this is the only homeland we will ever know.

The Detractors

There have been assorted arguments that seek to disconnect the expansion of welfare from the development of the black underclass, but they strike me as hair-splitting confections that almost willfully ignore basic human realities.

For one, if poor blacks were a hair or two less poor after welfare's expansion, then this may not be great news for Charles Murray's assertion that welfare did not alleviate poverty, and it may even have been good news, in itself, for poor blacks. But only to a negligible degree. They were still poor, and an underclass still developed. Our question is why this was.

In the same vein, back in the day economist Robert Greenstein wrestled with Murray over his hypothetical scenarios in which poor black couples methodically decided whether or not to marry on the basis of whether taking welfare would mean more money for the woman and child. This is irrelevant here. For whatever it's worth, there is no concrete evidence that people were making "choices" this deliberate. But whatever the truth is, what is important is not trying to kick the legs out from under Murray's specific claims, but to answer why at a particular time so many poor black people refrained from work and never sought it again until a time limit was placed on welfare in 1996. Sitting down at a table and doing calculations may not be the only way that human beings come to do things, but haggling over details on this subject has little to do with addressing the urgent plight of poor black people in the real world, beyond academics and think tank wonks dueling over niggling numerical wiggles.

More to the point are arguments that underclass developments do not correlate perfectly with changes in AFDC. Christopher Jencks, for example, is fully aware of the role of culture in the plight of the black underclass, and I am a great admirer of his work. But even he notes that AFDC payments stopped increasing in real value after 1973 and yet out-of-wedlock childbearing continued to increase, and further that there is no correlation between the number of such births and payment levels in particular states. Jencks states, "Since making welfare less attractive did not discourage single parenthood after 1973, it no longer seems likely that raising benefits encouraged it before 1973." In a similar vein he also notes that black male unemployment, after falling in the late 1960s, actually rose somewhat in the seventies for a while just as AFDC payments were decreasing in real value.

William Julius Wilson makes similar claims. But then one must also take into account a certain ideological beef of his. When authors are given to writing in a measured tone, they often give away what really fuels their fire at a single moment when they step away from quiet prose for just a second and let fly with something. In Wilson's two main books, this moment is page 178 in *When Work Disappears* when after recounting various sharp criticisms of "welfare culture" he writes, "One has the urge to shout, 'Enough is enough!'"

I can only agree with Wilson in being uncomfortable to see poor black people discussed as if they cheerfully decided to live pathetic lives and threaten us with violence. However, where Wilson sees the reason for their behavior as manufacturing plants no longer being downtown and there no longer being doctors and lawyers to imitate, I see it as the result of a new cultural imperative that was enabled by welfare programs that went from safety net to lifestyle.

And in this, I find it unrealistic, and almost disingenuous, of learned social scientists to pretend a lockstep between social behavior by real human beings and the abstract details of annual economic conditions. Enough is enough here as well. If the entire field of economics has become increasingly aware that treating humans as entirely "rational actors" is faulty science, then we must ask all social scientists to consider this in their analysis of, yes, even poor old black America. Don't worry—the sky will *not* fall in. And that means keeping in mind that cultural patterns can set in because of a stimulus at a particular time but then go on to thrive even when that stimulus is taken away, regardless of subsequent conditions.

Forty years ago, countercultural behaviors and attitudes arose among whites in specific response to government officials hoodwinking the American public about the motivations, actions, and progress of the war in Vietnam. Did those behaviors and attitudes stop after the Vietnam War ended? Of course not—an attitudinal meme was set, which continued because there was little reason for it not to, and in fact conferred a sense of belonging and higher wisdom in its inherents. Hence, David Brooks's *Bobos in Paradise*, a dead-on portrait of today's *Harper's* crowd, sticking their middle finger up to The Man in what they listen to on their iPods, how they dress, and how they felt about George W. Bush's election to a second term, while still seeking choice real estate and squeezing the most possible out of their mutual funds fed by the same stock market that they despise when it comes to its role in encouraging globalization.

The same would apply to inner-city mothers on welfare in the seventies: Childbearing out of wedlock was now "normal." There is no reason to think this would change simply because welfare payments went down somewhat. Obviously, for one, it did not change—rather, such women typically supplemented their welfare payments with under-the-table earnings. Go beyond sociological studies of urban blacks and learn that all humans are couched deeply in cultural hallmarks, each group preserving these over vast spans of time regardless of historical changes. Well, what's good for the Maori tribesman, or the Jew in the shtetl in *Fiddler on the Roof*, is good for the black American in Detroit. Right? Cultural patterns persist because they are all a generation has seen. I presume we are not proposing that black Americans are not human beings.

In Katherine Newman's *No Shame in My Game*, we see young blacks jeering at their peers trying to work for a living, something one hardly needs a book to notice in such settings and now goes on regardless of the state of the GNP, as an entrenched suspicion of "chump change." The issue here is not the amount of the Earned Income Tax Credit in one year versus another, but a cultural difference, distinguishing these kids from, for example, the men sleeping in shifts in Bronzeville tenements working whatever jobs they could find. These kids are products of a post-sixties AFDC *culture* in which work was optional. Black Americans are subject to the operations of entrenched *culture* just like other people. As to dutiful pretenses otherwise by people too smart and learned not to know better, indeed, "Enough is enough!"

WELFARE CONTRACTION: THE SOLUTION

As I write, there is no better argument that open-ended welfare was doing more harm than good than the simple fact that the limitation of the program to a five-year time limit in 1996 has already diminished black poverty. There has been no magic, to be sure. Women off welfare are not driving Volvos in the suburbs, but have joined the ranks of the "working poor." There remains a serious deficit of child care programs to help them do their best. And it is clear that some people have been left incapable of ever fending for themselves.

But nevertheless, the predictions so common in 1996 that poor blacks would be starving on the streets have shown themselves dead wrong. For years, the statistic that more than 40 percent of black children were born in poverty was commonly heard as implying that racism remained eternal in America. As such, it should relieve a great many people that the figure was just 30 percent by 2002, and the fall from 44 percent in 1993 was sharpest after—you guessed it—1996.

There is even evidence that leaving the welfare rolls is being driven as much by a new Zeitgeist as by sheer issues of payment levels, the economy, and incentives. The rolls have fallen even in states where the government has not dedicated major effort to getting people off of the rolls, such as Texas and Illinois. Seven states where the economy has been especially weak since 1996 have nevertheless cut the rolls by three-quarters, such as West Virginia. "Message effects," social scientists call it. Here on the ground, we say that the culture is changing.

Post-AFDC, when DeParle's Angie's car breaks down, she has to get up at 4:00 A.M. and catch two buses to a 6:30 shift until she finds a job closer to home. Suddenly, she sounds like the black commuter in Detroit in 1925, and even she knows that the new policy is why. She tried at one point to go back on the rolls, but under the new system this required taking classes and accepting a truly lousy makeshift job. Angie's verdict: "They just did what they supposed to do. If they probably would a gave me AFDC—who knows?—maybe I'd be on there now."

There are still plenty of kinks to work out, and women after welfare rarely rise to the middle class. But since 1996, we have learned a simple lesson: When open-ended welfare disappears, people work.

"BUT THEY'RE STILL NOT MIDDLE CLASS!"
THE NEW WORKING POOR

Yet, many thinkers see little to no value in that lesson. Their verdict on welfare reform is that as long as its former recipients are not now in the middle class, or on their way to it, then something is very wrong.

To these people, the main thing is that these women have joined the ranks of what is lately termed "the working poor," depicted as having almost no realistic chances of ever managing anything better than a virtual subsistence lifestyle, despite going to work every day. Especially prominent has been journalist Barbara Ehrenreich's *Nickel and Dimed*, now given free to freshmen at several universities. Editorialist David Shipler's *The Working Poor* helped to establish its title as a general term.

There is no doubt that the lives of such people ought be widely known to responsible, thinking Americans. It is indeed very hard for people with little education and narrow horizons to work their way to tony suburbs, even when their limitations are not their fault. Serious illness will threaten financial ruin; vacations will be infrequent; career satisfaction will be an irrelevance. The grand old American Dream is much harder to achieve for some people than others; more to the point, for quite a few, the American Dream is unreachable.

But regarding modern black history, our question is just why we would have expected people with little education and fitful work experience to be living in starter homes just a few years after getting off of the welfare rolls—or, frankly, if ever. The expectation otherwise implies that former welfare mothers are a unique case deserving special compensation that no one argues should be given to the trailer park people in books like Ehrenreich's and Shipler's. It would seem that many suppose that the reason these women were on welfare in the first place, and the reason that they are working poor now, is because there has been no place for them in the economy.

But this requires some rather odd cart-before-the-horse argumentation, in which writers very carefully pretend that black Americans (and the occasional Latino) are the world's only people for whom hardship can never be traced to personal life choices in any serious way.

Welfare expansion's harm to black communities did not end in 1996. Rather, the gloomy existences that journalists so eagerly depict former welfare recipients leading are a direct result of life "choices" made under a system that enabled the worst in people. My point is not to condemn people who usually were doing all they ever saw around them and later have tried to make the best of themselves with varying success. My point, rather, is to make clear what an odious legacy the supposedly enlightened white Establishment left us with.

Babies

Perhaps some may still hear echoes of Bill Bennett. Well, let's curl up with Katherine Newman's thoroughly PC *No Shame in My Game*. Newman diligently tries to convince us that poor blacks in New York trying to get beyond welfare are stuck in an economy with no place for them. But, in fact, the book ends up being an almost uncannily articulate argument that the interviewees are heirs of a cultural context that they did not ask to be born in, but which marked them deeply from an early age and ruined their lives. I leave Newman's book almost perplexed that she intended it as an argument from the left.

For example, typical in Newman's book is a person like Latoya. She lives with her common-law husband Jason, who is a carpenter. She had her first child at sixteen, another during a brief marriage, and then another with Jason, despite that her relationship with him is extremely unstable. "I gotta find me a job where I can just work, you know, a certain amount of hours, then spend some time with the kids, and then take my days off and go to school. That's what I'm looking for," she says. And she will not find a job like that, we all know.

Newman wants us to curse the work world that has no place for a woman taking care of three children with little education and no skills. But like many writers about women in Latoya's world, Newman leaves unmentioned a certain elephant sitting in the middle of the room—namely, why did Latoya have to have the kids at all?

Newman operates according to a certain school of thought that "respects" Latoya's "choices" and is extremely wary of saying or writing anything that could even imply a question as to poor black people's "right to reproduce." That may preserve the sensibilities of, well, mostly academics and Newman herself, since poor blacks themselves are often more honest about situations like Latoya's. One would almost think from work like Newman's that Latoya had been forced to have those babies by some kind of governmental edict. But, in fact, Latoya had those babies quite casually when she knew that she did not have any way to provide them with more than a subsistence existence, nor did their fathers.

And in this, she and the men contrast with poor black people before the late sixties. Even in 1960, 67 percent of black children were born to two-parent families. Of course few of them lived shiny, happy Parkay lives. But in that era, black people who made children typically lived together even if they were poor or at least tried to for a spell. Only in Latoya's time has an orthodoxy settled in that we almost take as a given—that if two black people make a child, then if they are poor they will not raise it together. Sure, the job situation does not offer Latoya any convenient options now that she has the kids. But we are not immoral ideologues to note that the reason Latoya is stuck facing an economy that cannot accommodate her responsibilities for her kids is a cultural shift she grew up in the wake of. That cultural shift left Latoya unconcerned with squaring her reproductive "choices" with economic reality.

We see this kind of thing again and again in Newman's book. Danielle has five kids and her husband left her; she got off welfare and supports herself with a job at "Burger Barn" (Newman's generic term for various fast food outlets), but can't get training to become a nurse or teacher because she has to take care of the kids. But again, why the kids? And especially, why *five*???

One answer to why Danielle had all those kids is that black people, particularly because of Christian convictions, tend to disapprove of abortion, and more conclusively than most middle-class educated white women. In *American Dream* Jason DeParle recounts one woman's story about having one of her children, where she heard about what abortion entails and says, "Are you telling me I have to have my baby in order to kill my baby? That's murder for real!"

But the answer then is not abstinence (I for one wouldn't wish that on anybody) but contraception. Especially over the past thirty years or so, it is highly unlikely that any urban black teen is naïve about how babies are made. Today, they can learn most of the facts just listening to the tracks on hip-hop albums that don't get radio play because of their explicitness. Indeed, ghetto men (and not just black ones) often resist using condoms. But it's not 1930—the Pill today is cheaper (and with fewer side effects) than it's ever been.

"When they get pregnant," a sixteen-year-old black girl from the DC ghetto has said, "none of that is an accident. Every teenage girl knows about birth control pills. Even when they twelve, they know what it is." Some see statements like that and question the girl's familiarity with, well, the world she has spent her whole life in. Yet, most of them would take her word as gospel if she said that there were no decent jobs available in that same world. How many of us really think that a young black woman in Bed-Stuy doesn't know "where babies come from"?

Not that Latoya is at fault here in a moral sense. One senses that she was not thinking terribly hard about cause and effect when she was a teen, likely because no one around her was. How could she have helped it, really? But this simply brings us to my cultural argument. It shows that the days had passed when community norms would have probably held her in line or at best seen her go the wrong way and tsk-tsked at her as a "loose" woman, discouraging many young women from risking such opprobrium. In Latoya's world, the very term "loose" is obsolete, as almost every girl she grew up with was a "loose" woman according to the taxonomy that ruled before the late sixties (and almost every boy was a "loose" man).

Here, a brie-and-Zinfandel orthodoxy grabs our heads and forces us to look at the economy. But we might gently take those hands off of our heads and ask what factory jobs moving away (Stanza One) had to do with whether Latoya went on the pill or asked her lovers to use condoms. Or is it that Latoya had all those kids because there were no middle-class blacks to consult with about the elementary basics of birth control (Stanza Two)? You could assign a squadron of graduate students to scan every bit of the literature on urban black poverty—the books, the articles, the conference handouts, a Google trawl, a LexisNexis trawl—and they would turn up maybe two accounts of a ghetto black girl since 1970 saying, "I didn't know I would get pregnant if I had sex." And if anyone wants to say that Latoya had all those kids because of "residential segregation," (Stanza Three) then we will hear them saying that Latoya had three kids she had no way of taking care of beyond subsistence level because she lived among her own people. And we will move on.

A Terrible Thing to Waste

There is actually another elephant that Newman keeps stepping around: education.

We read again and again that it is hard to find a low-skill job—as if it is somehow evident that after all, poor black people simply could not, of all things, go beyond a high school education. Sure, Princeton and Dartmouth would be unlikely possibilities—but they are hardly the only avenues to self-sufficiency available. To wit, if jobs today often require more than a high school diploma, then why would poor blacks not have begun getting A.A. degrees at community colleges or some vocational training, of the sort advertised on billboards and placards on buses and trains and benches and on television? Those ads, after all, are not aimed at people seeking BAs at Ivy schools.

Do we perhaps sense that this would be an unrealistic expectation for poor blacks beaten down by racism and segregation? Understandable, from what we have known in the short time-spans of our own lives. But the hunger for education among people a step beyond, of all things, plantation slavery should teach us something.

In 1866, a white man remarked upon two ex-slaves who had "commenced to learn themselves, had gathered 150 pupils, all quite orderly and hard at study." Around the same time, contributing to the construction of a school in Autauga County, Alabama, "children without shoes on their feet gave from fifty cents to one dollar and old men and old women, whose costumes represented several years of wear, gave from one to five dollars" while "colored men offered to pawn their cows and calves for the money." Such people were giving their lifeblood for black schools even though they had already paid taxes for the construction of white schools! And it worked: In 1860, 95 percent of black Americans could not read—that is, basically, black America was illiterate. By 1910, only 30 percent of black Americans could not read—that is, black Americans were a literate people concerned with a lower-class third lagging behind.

So, "Learn your history" does not mean only slave ships and Bull Connor. None of us could even begin to dismiss those ex-slaves as "inauthentic." They were every bit as real as, say, "real" black people like Latoya. Let's just imagine telling one of those black people in overalls who grew up in shacks as chattel that they were "not really black." They differed from Latoya in their orientation to education *despite* obstacles, which if we are so strong, we cannot present as responsible for our present-day problems.

Attitude, then, plays a big part here. Contrast those ex-slaves in Alabama to Latoya's reminiscence: "You know, when my mother told me (to get an education), I was like, 'Yeah, whatever'." Newman just threads things like this into a text intended to convince us that Latoya's problems are the fault of the suits. But couldn't Latoya's "whatever" have something to do with her current plight? One thing clear is that Latoya's attitude to education was never comparable with that of blacks who had known an oppression that Latoya never knew to the remotest extent.

Yes, it's hard to go to school when you are raising children alone. But that brings us back to why Latoya had to have so many kids so early in life anyway, instead of spending some time getting some skills. There was a time in her life when Latoya could have had exactly the sex life she wanted but used some birth control, meanwhile preparing herself to live a decent life. But instead she got knocked up a few years after puberty and has taken it from there since. Call that "conservative" or "judgmental" and note that countless blacks from all walks of life in America today would readily say the exact same thing, including utterly "authentic" blacks in the 'hood—whom social scientists would line up to use in their surveys—who happened not to make Latoya's "choices."

Latoya is not a "strumpet." She went the way she did because it was all she ever saw anyone else doing. But why? Because the culture had changed. That's what it means to note that it was all she saw, as opposed to struggling black women before the late sixties, who usually—not always, but still, indisputably, *usually*—saw something different.

When Work Disinclines

Finally, Newman would like us to go away with a mental picture of poor blacks desperately clambering for work only to find that there are too few jobs for too little pay. But one actually leaves the book with a mental picture of poor blacks who often have a distinctly ambivalent attitude toward working at all, torn always between doing the right thing and doing what the word on the street considers cool—which is acting up and fashioning oneself as an independent actor—that is, the meme that has detoured black America.

For example, people who take jobs at "Burger Barn" deal with serious mocking from their peers, who consider entry-level work of this kind as "chump" jobs. This is a problem well-known to anyone familiar with the inner city, emerging in one account after another. One of Newman's interviewees says,

> To go there and work for Burger Barn, that was one of those real cloak-and-dagger kinds of things. You'll be coming out—'Yo, where you going?' You be, 'I'm going, don't worry about where I'm going.' And you see your friends coming and see you working there and now you be, 'No, the whole Project gonna know I work in Burger Barn.' It's not something I personally proclaim with pride and stuff.

The problem is so bad in New York that Burger Barn managers prefer to hire from other poor neighborhoods because locals are pressured by their friends from the neighborhood to give out free food and goof off. (The restaurant managers are rarely, say, middle-age white men "stereotyping" the black workers; they tend to be ethnics of the surrounding community themselves.) Thus Newman quotes one girl as saying that *she is not ashamed to have a job*—a statement that clearly indicates a community where attitudes to employment are not precisely those of, say, pre-1960 black Indianapolis.

The people mocking their working peers as earning "chump change" do not present what would be a better option. Or perhaps they do so via omission: One should sell drugs or go on welfare because the only work we niggaz can get won't take us no place nohow. But elsewhere even Newman has to admit that these same "perceptive ghetto youngsters," in Wilson's terminology, could do better than this. She admits that they have plenty of relatives doing perfectly well in stable working-class existences: "Of course, the erosion of job opportunities does not explain the whole picture, for there are people in Kyesha's own generation who have done far better than she has: half sisters who have jobs as transit cops or housing cops, for example. Education matters; skills matter."

It is almost strange when Newman comes up with, "To my knowledge, we have no compelling explanations of why the same family produces such divergent pathways in life," as if the obvious explanation were not that some people are more susceptible to what's in the air—cultural directives—than others. One person tries his or her best despite the bullshit. The other person, perhaps even a sibling of the previous one, drifts with the tide. Who among us, including white Katherine Newman, hasn't seen this in our own families? It's not a black issue, but a human one. Some people know that "chump change" today will be the salary of a transit cop—or Burger Barn manager—tomorrow. Others thrill to the seductive "'tude" of peer culture, drift here and there, and end up as interview subjects in books like Newman's.

Newman only explores why so many "perceptive ghetto youngsters" go the latter way in her loving coverage of ones who don't work out because they are constitutionally incapable of being polite to customers, especially testy ones. The defensive, tripwire demeanor that underclass life tends to value and encourage conflicts with the requirements of customer service jobs in the real world.

Newman reveals herself as caught in a passing ideology of her times in that she not only documents, but also legitimates this. She actually considers it unfair to expect professionally edgy black kids to smile at McDonald's. One senses that Newman is put off by the idea of anything adding to the burdens that struggling black folk put up with already. I can see where she is coming from, but the issue is *why* these people have to put up with so much, and why "going off" and even violence have become so central to how they interface with the world.

Newman would say The System. I would say that what created the underclass demeanor was a cultural shift that occurred independently of anything The Man was doing—that is, it was not about the factories, middle-class blacks moving away, or redlining. It was a new Zeitgeist that elevated alienation as the trump card of the race. As such, while this does not mean that the cocky demeanor these kids have a hard time shaking is their "fault," it isn't whitey's fault either. It is the "fault" of an unusual set of social circumstances in the 1960s, in which whites were open to letting blacks act out and blacks were newly open to doing so, as centuries of racism left them with little else to base an identity on.

David Shipler's *The Working Poor* shows similar issues of culture that hold back working poor people. As to black ones, Christie has several kids by several men; she decided not to finish college, while her brother is an accountant and her sister is a loan officer. Debra had a kid at eighteen; she gets a job in a factory but can't adjust to showing up on time and other procedures, and assumes that the boss likes Hispanics better. Debra even has that apparently vanishing species, the Factory Job—but it's attitude that is holding her back more than anything else. Caroline works at Wal-Mart and is angry that she isn't being promoted—but also for some reason smells very bad, and so on.

These cases are examples of the fact that attitude clearly plays a part in a great many poor blacks' employment histories, reminiscent of how there was never any fevered quest for employment among Indianapolis blacks as the sixties became the seventies. When a slum renovation project in heavily poor black Newark, New Jersey, seeks local workers at five to six dollars an hour in the early nineties only to find almost no takers and ends up bringing in workers from the suburbs, advocates of the working poor respond that the people did not want to take "dead-end" work. But here, they were not being offered jobs stocking shelves at Kmart—this work could have given them both skills and contacts. But they opted out.

Which means that, at least, they were getting by. We presume first that they were not starving, and second, that unemployment was rampant among them—as we learn from even the sociologists and journalists most empathetic with the plight of ghetto blacks. It is therefore reasonable to suppose that most of them were getting by either selling drugs or relying on welfare payments through one channel or another. That so many of them felt these "choices" as natural as opposed to taking decent work says something about poor black culture by this time.

Stereotyping Versus Reality

All of this also casts a certain light on the claim that inner-city blacks are barred from work because employers have "stereotypes" about them. And there is clear evidence that they do. In one article, Joleen Kirschenman and Kathryn M. Neckerman document countless employers in Chicago saying of inner-city blacks things like, "They don't want to work" and, "They've got an attitude problem," and William Julius Wilson records the same. But we must be cautious about assuming that these preconceptions have no basis in fact.

The first question is: Beyond all of the particularities involved with the inner-city black issue, is it *logically impossible* that if employers consider a certain group unpromising as workers, that their judgment is based on fact? Most would say that it is not *logically impossible*, even though we must always watch for stereotyping. But then we bring in inner-city blacks and ask: Is it *logically impossible* that if employers consider inner-city black Americans unpromising as workers, that their judgment is based on fact? Some may immediately suppose that because blacks have been subject to racist stereotyping of an unforgivable nature for so very long, that it *could not possibly be* that employers' preconceptions are based on fact. But in the logical sense, we can only conclude this after examining whether employers have no reason for their bias other than preconceptions passed along independently of empirical experience. After all, it is *logically possible* that a white employer might have no bias against blacks in general, but resist hiring inner-city blacks because of actual experience.

The closest Kirschenman and Neckerman come to addressing this is a brief guess that the poor quality of many urban schools in Chicago may render inner-city blacks less prepared for jobs, and a study cited equally widely by Jomills H. Braddock and James M. McPartland ventures a similar idea. But issues of formal qualification skirt the attitudinal factors so consistently adduced by employer interviewees, and both of these studies leave the implication that racism is the main problem in the end.

But these employers clearly say that their judgment is based not on a racist orthodoxy teaching them from childhood that niggers are no good, but on concrete experience with inner-city black hires. One of Kirschenman and Neckerman's interviewees says, "I think one of the reasons, in all honesty, is because we've had bad experience in that sector, and believe me, I've tried. . . . We've had more bad black employees over the years than we had good." This is but one of a great many such statements they present, and Wilson's survey is full of similar ones, including ones where whites clearly say that they know that the reason for the behavior in question is societal inequity.

While some might dismiss this as employers seeing the behavior that racism subliminally conditions them to see, other writers, albeit as sympathetic to inner-city blacks as writers like Kirschenman, Neckerman, Braddock, McPartland, and William Julius Wilson take the employers' experience as valid. Wilson comes right out and says of inner-city black men that "their attitudes and actions, combined with erratic work histories in high-turnover jobs, create the widely shared perception that they are undesirable workers." That is, Wilson tells us that *being* undesirable workers feeds a perception that they are undesirable workers.

And this brings us back to history, as always. Amid all of the problems poor blacks had with employment before you-know-when, whites saying that they were undependable or had a chip on their shoulder was not one of them. In the days when uneducated blacks could easily get glum but solid assembly-line jobs, they showed up on time and did their best. Indeed blacks in the old days were endlessly parodied as lazy in the larger popular culture. But when it comes to their performance in blue-collar urban jobs blacks felt fortunate to have, I have seen not a single book, article, or memoir *before the sixties* in which white employers complained that blacks "don't want to work" or "have an attitude." Nor does any work I have consulted on this problem as it exists today observe that employers' views today merely continue an old tradition—and we can be sure if such evidence existed, these writers would anxiously document it in a quest to show the Racist Roots of American Society.

Walter Jenkins working at the River Rouge plant in Detroit in 1925 wasn't exactly happy in his work, but he didn't have an attitude problem there. It's Dwayne Williams in 1995 showing up late at the Staples warehouse in Los Angeles and telling his boss that she is a racist for calling him on it who has an attitude problem—and that scene is not a "stereotype," as Wilson and others amply document situations like this. The preconceptions that our studies document today are a post-sixties phenomenon. And we must ask why.

Wilson would say that the reason is, as always, larger socioeconomic currents buffeting poor blacks about in the current. He notes a particular preconception that blacks are unwilling to start at the bottom, and looks sadly on employers' tendencies to prefer desperate Latino immigrants to fill such positions. For Wilson, this means that the new influx of foreigners after the Immigration Act of 1965 was one more burden for poor blacks to bear. But what about the fact that blacks once readily started at the bottom even when such immigrants posed no competition, and even when blacks had few opportunities to rise above the bottom at all? What about the endless chronicles of the Pullman Porters? This was lousy work, but these were in no sense lazy men, and there is no record of them reviling themselves as working for "chump change," *nor did other blacks mock them as such*. Which brings us back to today's urban black kids *ashamed* to be seen working.

The difference today is, obviously, a drug trade that offers a much better income. But then, that only happened—once again—after the sixties. And if Wilson, one of our best-regarded sociologists, acknowledges that this trade makes inner-city black men less amenable to the realities of holding a job, then how can we assail employers who start leaning toward Latino immigrants as racists?

Even allowing the leftist perspective on this the most leeway possible, we can only conclude that the situation is much more complicated than a mere matter of white employers being bigots. And in the end, I think it is clear that a cultural transformation in the sixties has rendered inner-city black people less dependable workers than poor blacks were before.

Note, for example, an underacknowledged kink in Wilson's argumentation. Why couldn't it be that poor blacks today seek and hold low-level jobs as diligently as they did in the past, such that Latino advocates ended up complaining that poor blacks' hold on low-level jobs impeded the advancement of immigrants from Mexico, Puerto Rico, and the Dominican Republic? Why is that scenario so unthinkable? Why does the "chump change" orientation become a general problem only starting in the late sixties? What has happened is not only changes in the realms of labor and the economy—despite how training and politics tend to draw scholars to those factors—but also in culture.

Culture, Not the System

The American Dream of a house in the burbs, a two-car garage, and kids in fine schools is not available to everyone. But even the most dedicated portraits of the world of what we now term the working poor show clearly that The System alone is not why a disproportionate number of black people *have wound up in this kind of situation in the first place,* such as the women now facing the five-year limit on welfare. To present a single black man or woman with no kids having trouble getting ahead is one thing. But people like Newman give us single men and women who started having children in their teens and now have trouble getting ahead, tell us that their frustration is the fault of The System, and pretend that these people's "reproductive choices" were as unremarkable as someone else's deciding to hold off having kids until they earn job qualifications of some kind.

And in a way, their past life "choices" and their current attitudinal orientations are thoroughly unremarkable in a sense: understandable results of the worlds they grew up in. But all the same, they play a crucial part in their current plight. Those choices and orientations were hardly unknown among blacks before the sixties. But when such choices became *normal and unquestioned* in black communities across the nation, it meant that a great many more black people got stuck in the "working poor" situation than would have otherwise.

CONCLUSION

This brings us back to the issue of the oppositional fashion. It was this new bone-deep animus against The System that taught whites to aggressively usher so many blacks into eternal dependence. That a fashion that took effect at a particular time was the factor is clear from the simple fact that whites did not aim such efforts at blacks before this time. White activists for racial justice were hardly unknown before the mid-1960s. And yet among their legions of efforts on our behalf—including the founding of the NAACP—none included a nationwide drive to stop poor black people from working. That only happened when the ideological sentiments of the times made such efforts acceptable to a decisive number of people. Those sentiments—the countercultural revolution—made a better America in many ways, including for the black middle class. But they had, unintentionally but decisively, a much grimmer impact on less fortunate blacks.

Namely, in expanding welfare into an open-ended benefit, they taught poor blacks to extend the new oppositional mood from hairstyles and rhetoric into a lifestyle separated from mainstream American culture—not to mention black history before the mid-sixties. One is correct to subject to question the idea that something so difficult to quantify as a "mood" was the key factor here. But then one must also recall how black leaders in post-Victorian Indianapolis were almost embarrassed to call upon whites for charity, under a sense that this would imply that blacks were not "worthy" enough to make their own way and that blacks only applied for charity in desperate conditions. Mood is real. Mood does affect history, and profoundly—regardless of how difficult it is to capture it with cold, hard figures. The figures are not, despite social scientists' insistence, the whole story.

Now, hindsight makes many of us feel that these proud Victorian black people in high collars, leaders and toilers, failed to understand that the combination of capitalism and racism made it unrealistic to expect that more than a lucky few blacks could rise above sweeping floors and burping white babies in the America they knew. Might we feel that poor blacks then would have been lucky to have open-ended welfare programs to apply to? In other words, could it be that the oppositional mood that taught black men to refrain from legal work and black women to live on "home relief" for decades was good news for poor blacks?

Well, we must ask: Was what happened once such programs were available good news? Could we tell struggling blacks in Indianapolis in 1915 that generations of poor black women never knowing work, with their female children casually having children and going on the dole at sixteen, and their male children so alien to the work ethic that selling drugs with "gats" in their pockets felt ordinary, and all of this being a black community *norm*, was progress? If we told them that one thing that "enabled" all of this was the invention of a cheap yet powerful narcotic, crack, then do we imagine that they, in their suits, gowns, and shiny shoes, would just say, "Oh, well, then that's okay" and give us a high-five for "contesting the hegemonic tropes of a superordinate class that essentialize the subaltern?"

They would not. They would wonder *why* so many people drifted into centering their lives on crack instead of making the best of themselves as most early black Indianapolis residents did. *Most* of them, not all—leftists need not worry that I am leaving out from the Black History diorama the noble thugs they cherish. But still, *most*; black Indianapolis in 1915 was not "New Jack Indy" by a long shot, and anyone who claims otherwise better come armed with trunks full of books, periodicals, and microfilm on early twentieth-century Indianapolis. And post-Victorian blacks in Indianapolis lived in a city where fifty years later factories did *not* move beyond where anyone who wanted to work could do so—which means that we would be that much more challenged in explaining to them why it was inevitable that SoulFest would become a setting for gangland slayings.

And finally, since the reform of welfare in 1996 we have seen poor black women who once lived by welfare working for a living. They are not having a great time by any means. Their lives mirror, in many ways, those of their grandmothers and great-grandmothers who toiled for a living year by year in thankless jobs as sharecroppers or maids. Not great. But—*would Welfare as We Knew It be preferable?*

I suspect that only scattered radicals would think so, and even Piven and Cloward only encouraged this as a temporary situation, assuming that it would spark a hard-disk crash in Washington that would lead to a new America where everybody was given the means to be middle class. But the disk-crash never came to be—and so what about Welfare as We Knew It as it lived on for the next thirty years *sans* revolution? For most of us, what Stevie Wonder sang of as working hard "just enough for the cit-ay" is a much more vibrant rendition of Black Pride.

It's better for a person to work for their living. We all know it. We all also know that slave ships and *Plessy v. Ferguson* and lynching and segregated water fountains were hideous. But then we still know that even for descendants of people who suffered these things—and even for people who experienced them—it's better for a person to work for their living.

Which only shows that where white radicals taught us to take a page from their new animus against The Suits and thumb our noses at The System and go on welfare because whitey wasn't devoted to us getting ahead, they sent us to hell.

FACING IT

I once appeared on a television talk show with a man, white as it happened, who had been active in the Civil Rights movement in the sixties. At one point I said that an unintentional by-product of the sixties was a tendency for more than a few blacks to exaggerate victimhood for emotional reasons rather than out of constructive intent.

The man responded with a description of the segregation of pre-Civil Rights Act America, how complaint and resistance had freed blacks and changed the country, and that therefore airing one's victimhood was a right that blacks had "earned."

I didn't quite understand his response at first. I wasn't talking about airing genuine victimhood—who would have an argument against that? But how do a people "earn" the "right" to cry wolf, and why would we consider that a good thing?

But the misunderstanding was an example of how difficult it can be to grasp the nature of the post–Civil Rights brand of black resentment I was referring to, and how common and self-destructive it is. This man, despite being a richly informed media commentator and a seasoned witness of modern American history, genuinely did not understand what I was referring to.

But it is as important to understand therapeutic alienation as it is to understand the nature of systemic racism.

A number of thinkers and journalists, black and white, disagree. They want us to think about things like Black Middle Class Rage and "American Apartheid." Many of them know a lot about statistics.

But they are also utopianists. Is this what black America needs?

CHAPTER FIVE

The Meme of Therapeutic Alienation: Defined by Defiance

The guiding idea of this book can be illustrated by, of all things, jugs in Cyprus. There is a village there where potters always add two blobs of clay to jugs. They don't know why; they just do it because that's the way it's always been done. But jugs excavated in the area from 500 BC are modelled on the female form and always include two breasts. Over time, the connection with the female body was lost to history, and modern potters just add the blobs as a meaningless gesture.

Of course, the blobs have a certain aesthetic appeal. Not knowing about their origin as breasts, one might even think that at some point modern potters decided to add the blobs themselves because of a certain balance they lend the jugs.

Why did early cars have running boards when there was no need for them in vehicles slung just a foot off of the ground? Because carriages, mounted a yard above the ground, had had them. Early car designers felt it natural to include running boards in what were thought of at first as "horseless carriages." Of course the running boards could lend some minor use here and there—one might rest the foot on them to tie a shoe. But if carriages had never existed, carmakers would never have thought to create running boards, nor would anyone have ever called for them.

ACTION VERSUS GESTURE

In these cases, something began as a purposeful *action*, but devolved into a reflexive *gesture*. The gesture lived on because it hurt nothing, and even lent marginal benefits, although not the ones that the original action was intended for. This process has been called *skeuomorphy*, and it determines a great deal of our lives—much more than we are often aware of.

For example, it has decisively shaped black American identity since the sixties.

This chapter will examine how in black America, what began as concrete *activism* aimed at getting justice devolved into abstract *gestures* unconcerned with justice. The vestigial gestures live on because they serve a psychological function: They assuage personal insecurities that are legacies of our station in American life until very recently. Many today genuinely think that the gestures *are* activism. So much time has gone by, and ever fewer were mature in the era of genuine Civil Rights activism. Unsurprisingly, a great many are unaware that these gestures are expressions of a way of thinking that permeated black America in the late sixties and has lived on ever since, a *skeuomorphic* dissolution of the sincere and proactive work of early Civil Rights leaders.

Our problems, then, have not been the eclipse of the manufacturing economy, overly ambitious middle-class blacks, drugs "coming in," structural racism, or any of the things commonly adduced. Under ordinary conditions, black America could have stood up to all of these things. But conditions have not been ordinary since the late sixties. The burden of legalized segregation and disenfranchisement was immediately replaced with another one: a sense that black Americans are defined by defiance.

Only rarely does this create a gun-toting rebel spouting revolutionary rhetoric. More commonly it just programs one with a general sense that the rules are different for us. Things considered ordinary requirements of others are "too much" for us—or at least, most of us. Choices considered inappropriate by others are "understandable" for us—or at least, most of us. Allowing that racism plays no significant part in our lives would be disloyal for us. Even if some of us are okay, it must always and forever be that most of us are much less okay, and this could only be whites' faults. To be authentically black is to maintain a wary sense of white America—whatever that is—as eternally "on the hook."

The most crucial and damaging aspect of this way of thinking is that it is passed on from person to person and generation to generation because it sits well on the soul, but *regardless of societal conditions*. For this reason, this ideology has hindered black America from adapting to changing economic conditions. It has rendered black America overly susceptible to the temptations of open-ended dependence and criminality. It has discouraged black American leaders from innovative responses to community problems.

Yet over the years I have learned that my take on this is an eccentric one. Some are aware that posturing is not unknown on the black sociopolitical scene. But few are aware that it is the decisive factor on that scene today.

In this chapter I will try to get my conception across.

SEA CHANGES

See It Then

In 1957, Marian Anderson was the subject of a *See It Now* documentary on CBS, covering her tour of Asia. As it happened, the Little Rock schoolhouse episode occurred during the tour: Governor Orval Faubus ordered the National Guard to block nine black children from entering Central High. The special incorporated the contrast between this event and Anderson's tour, including a brief interview with her on the subject.

A concerned black citizen sent a letter in response to the special, complaining that it mentioned Little Rock and the Lincoln Memorial but nothing about "the many of our race who are on top."

A letter like that would be much, much less likely today. We are all taught that it is more urgent for whites and blacks alike to see the many who are on the bottom. The many who are on the top are considered a distraction from this, threatening to lull blacks into complacency and to distract whites from realizing that they still remain on their "hook." For many more than a few today, "Uncle Tom" and "sellout" come to mind reading a letter like that.

The difference in mood here tipped in the late sixties. That letter would have been perfectly ordinary as late as 1963 when Oxford-accented A. Philip Randolph was one of the top leaders of the March on Washington, and out of step as early as six years later, by which time Stokely Carmichael was the head of the Student Nonviolent Coordinating Committee. Some may wonder what the point is of looking at the glass as half empty. The answer is that the meme of therapeutic alienation puts opposition and alienation first, regardless of external conditions. Naturally, it creates a sense that the best PR for blacks is glum and accusatory.

This is the change I am referring to: what on the ground felt like a change in "the mood." That mood change was not a mere passing fashion—that mood was permanent, even if its initial surface expressions in clothing, rhetoric, hairstyles, and art had passed away by the late seventies.

Root Causes

An early episode of *All in the Family* had two black crooks hold up the Bunkers, Mike, and Gloria in their home. Bleeding-heart liberal Mike, steeped in the Root Causes paradigm that had become entrenched in the sixties, pardons their crime to their faces on the basis of the conditions they grew up in. The crooks find high comedy in this and have a grand old time slipping into the speech patterns and mannerisms of ignorant "Negros" who are passive victims of circumstance, gaily outlining an exaggerated vision of the poverty they grew up in. (The crooks were played by Demond Wilson, just before being cast as Lamont in *Sanford and Son*, and Cleavon Little.)

In this, the episode is very much not only of its time, but of its year. The year 1971 was about the very last moment that one could discuss the Root Causes explanation as a question rather than as a truism in polite society. Ten years later, the perspective had been preached as truth in universities and schools of journalism across the land for so long that if Norman Lear had black characters making fun of it again, he would have been savaged by an avalanche of protest.

Back in the day, even race activists insisted on treating blacks as individuals responsible for their fates. The idea was, "Let us show what we are made of." The new ideology, committed to alienation for its own sake, cannot help but sweep under the rug this basic human desire to excel, because it is a tricky business to do one's best while also nurturing a sense that one is only enlightened or "real" in eternally assailing The Man for making the playing field less than level. The new ideology is more compatible with placing blacks as done in by massive, abstract injustices, and because that position assuages a damaged soul, those kinds of politics are encouraged.

Under the new regime, then, the black crooks would become romantic figures—and big surprise, around the very time this *All in the Family* episode was being written, Melvin Van Peebles's *Sweet Sweetback's Baadasssss Song* was hitting the movie houses, portraying a black criminal as a hero and touching off a years-long series of like-minded blaxploitation films.

Mo Better?

In 1966, the Detroit branch of the National Urban League tried to help prepare young black people for success on the job market by having them perform playlets. One of them had a character named "Mo Humphrey," given to saying "Uh huh" and "Naw, man" and dressed sloppily. "Mo" cleaned up his act by speaking standard English and dressing neatly and got the job.

Contrast this with today. Many black educators cherish black folk speech as "Ebonics" and would shudder to see a young black person taught to "correct" it into standard English, as opposed to carefully teaching them that they speak two equal "languages," one being Ebonics and the other an alien, white-oriented standard English that they must switch into as a necessity. These people are correct that Black English is a different kind of English rather than a degraded one. But their perspective on standard English as the menacing tongue of what they call "the gatekeepers" was a direct outgrowth of black nationalist politics; it did not exist before the late sixties.

Also, while consensus still requires anyone seeking a serious job to dress conservatively, we are taught that for a Mo, shedding what would today be his "hip-hop" fashions is an imposition, under which a black young man is forced to shed an expression of his "culture," in favor of donning the uniform of the alien mainstream world. The Mo of 1966 just dressed too casually. The Mo of 2006 dresses against The Man. Even if later, white kids started imitating him, Mo got there first.

Fun with Slogans

In the 1960s, Civil Rights leader Bayard Rustin was dismayed by a new breed of separatist black leaders. They shunned proactive lobbying and careful rhetorical suasion, instead preferring high-profile altercations, preferably involving getting arrested. In 1963, Rustin counseled the increasingly radicalized Student Nonviolent Coordinating Committee (SNCC) that "the ability to go to jail should not be substituted for an overall social reform program." In Rustin's eyes, these scenes were ultimately, as he put it, "gimmicks." The typical demonstration often had "no relation to the fundamental question of how to get rid of discrimination" and was just "an end in itself." In other words, Rustin was watching activism devolve into mere gesture. A. Philip Randolph, who had founded the Brotherhood of Sleeping Car Porters and spurred the founding of the Fair Employment Practices Commission, saw the same thing. "Black Power is neither a program nor a philosophy. It is, like white supremacy, a slogan."

But slogans are powerful things, and old-school leaders like Rustin and Randolph would soon be edged aside by a new mood, in which slogans were considered activism in themselves while programs and philosophies were considered beside the point. But it would have been self-evident to any leading black organization before this time that being arrested on camera without a specific constructive goal in mind was mere playacting. Therapeutic alienation was taking over.

Rustin's speech didn't go over well with the SNCC that night in 1963, and a few years later its chairman would be Stokely Carmichael, openly advocating violence and popularizing the "Black Power" term that Randolph criticized.

Carmichael was brought in to replace John Lewis. Lewis was devoted to nonviolence. But he was enough on fire to have the original draft of his speech at the March on Washington nervously edited for white consumption and to have been beaten in Selma on "Bloody Sunday." Lewis went on to found the Voter Education Project, registering voters throughout the South and getting black politicians elected. Carmichael, on the other hand, moved to Africa after a few years, and spent the rest of his life making speeches about imperialism, pan-Africanism, and socialism, which had a rather diagonal impact upon the lives of the people he had purported to be so concerned about in his Black Power days. Lewis was, and remained, an activist, whose efforts helped create today's black leadership. Carmichael, changing his name to Kwame Toure, was, and remained, a performer. One tries today to identify something that Carmichael left behind for his own people, and comes up with nothing except newsreels in which he says some colorful things.

For a time, the mind-set had more of a hold on activists and intellectuals than on the black general public. In 1967, H. Rap Brown, having replaced Carmichael as SNCC chairman, was making a typical speech to blacks in Jacksonville, Florida, chanting "get yourself some guns." Governor Claude Kirk walked onto the stage, welcomed Brown to Florida, and said, "I don't want any talk about guns." The audience quickly gathered around Kirk telling him their concerns, while Brown ended up standing alone.

But the ideology spread fast, among a people left so susceptible to it by a hideous past, and before long, black "leaders" committed to acting up over action were accepted as normal on the black political scene. Al Sharpton rose to prominence in the 1980s refusing to recant his support of an arrantly mendacious rape accusation by a teenage black woman seeking an alibi for time spent with a boyfriend. The idea of this as progressive is senseless unless we see that theatrics was the point. Sharpton has since done nothing to indicate otherwise: He has spearheaded no leg-islation and given no sign of wanting to, and his National Action Network has made only *gestures* toward its stated goal of registering black voters. Yet, there has been no nationally influential body of black leadership di-rectly and sustainedly decrying Sharpton's tactics and freezing him out of all substantial discussion of blacks' plight.

Sure, black editorialists tell the truth here and there. But the heads of the NAACP and the National Urban League have not seen it as urgent to clearly and decisively dismiss Sharpton as a representative of the race. By the late 1990s, leading black intellectual Cornel West was standing be-hind Sharpton's posings as a politician, and by 2004, Sharpton was "run-ning for president," guesting on *Saturday Night Live*, signing a contract for a television show of his own, and being repeatedly called on to debate Jerry Falwell on morality, of all things, on television.

The point is not that Sharpton has hurt black America in any serious way; a people are not done in by someone making speeches. Sharpton is crucial to my point solely in that he has even been allowed a place at the table, when as late as 1960 he would have registered at best as a local char-acter. Sharpton appeared, basically, "normal" by the 1980s because of the filter that the meme of therapeutic alienation places on the mind. For some, it meant outright cheering for Sharpton. For most, it simply meant not minding him—but even this reveals a frame of mind that many fewer blacks could have even let pass before the sixties, and certainly not blacks' national leaders.

THE ORIGINS OF THERAPEUTIC ALIENATION: WHITES TOSS OUT THE BALL

My claim is not that therapeutic alienation is a tic that somehow emerged only among black people. Not only does it occur in plenty of other peo-ple, but also black people inherited it from others: specifically, whites dur-ing the countercultural revolution.

Whites' alienation from the Establishment began, of course, as a gen-uine and concrete opposition to the Vietnam War, as well as racism. The countercultural movement effected profound transformations in Ameri-can society, which all of us are thankful for today. However, there was, amid the constructive efforts, always a certain gut-level thrill in the sheer rebelliousness in itself. As such, it was not surprising that after the smoke cleared, a mood was left in the air, finding pleasure in rebellion for its own sake. Action devolved into gesture, as the Cheshire Cat in *Alice in Wonderland* disappeared and left just his smile.

That legacy lives on in mainstream American culture today, in the form of a spontaneous embrace of anti-Establishment sentiment in a great many people, expected in particular of the educated and/or thinking person. Certainly plenty of active, committed political activism remains. But there is also a general psychological legacy that expresses itself not in outright rejection of the Establishment or concentrated efforts to change it, but in quiet attitudes now taken as normal that would throw most people brought to our America from as recently as 1960. David Brooks's *Bobos in Paradise* captures this perfectly: people living lives intimately tied to grand old middle-class Establishment values and concerns who go to great lengths to ensure that their kids perform well enough on tests to get into top schools, but who decorate their lives on the edges with genuflections to the counterculture in terms of artistic taste, dress style, food, and voting choices.

In the film *School of Rock*, Jack Black's protagonist teaches affluent, well-behaved schoolchildren that the essence of rock music is rebellion against "The Man," although the character's life has given him little reason to rebel against such a Man and the students' lives even less so. It's funny in the film, but the joke wouldn't make sense to someone from, say, 1950 when mainstream pop music had yet to incorporate this alienated strain. Since the 1960s, oppositional attitude has been so central to most rock music that it is commonly assumed that the music young people embrace will be a vehicle for setting themselves off from the previous generation, resentment set to music. And that assumption has been true—but for only about the past forty years. In 1955, older people considered early rock transgressive because of its volume and the sex-miming dance moves that it encouraged. But the lyrics of Buddy Holly or Elvis Presley were nothing approaching the angry, tortured lyrics of Kurt Cobain. Cobain was a product of a new cultural mood that has a special affection for popular art that channels the insecurities and gripes inside of all of us.

In 1972, Hanna-Barbera ventured a flat little animated sitcom called *Wait Till Your Father Gets Home*, portraying the "generation gap" between a tubby suburban dad and his "wacky" family, including a plucky layabout "hippie" son and a wife who sweetly sided with him and their smart-mouthed daughter. "Kids today like to have their own way and what Dad doesn't know won't hurt him," the wife cheeped in the theme song, which was the only good thing about the show, and catchy enough that I had always recalled it and was once moved to download it (the Web is truly amazing . . .). I played it for someone too young to have seen the show who said, "Why did they sing it in those tinny voices?" I had never thought about that. The song was sung in decidedly raggedy style, sounding just like any old people from anywhere rendering the tune. This did contrast with the smooth, professional vocals that had been typical of shows until then— think of the lush harmonies in the theme songs to shows like *The Patty Duke Show*. But that deliberately sloppy rendition was a sign of the era, in which the unadorned and unpracticed was elevated as "real," and thus warm, something producers would use to entice viewers to embrace a show. To hell with you who insist on singing that takes effort and training—take a hit of the human voice as it comes out naturally. That was, and is, the times.

So the theme, so to speak, of rejecting Establishment mores began as a white "thang." Poet Philip Larkin memorialized the change from the other side of the Atlantic, where the change had had a similar impact ("Oh, be-have!!!") in his famous lines from "Annus Mirabilis": "Sexual intercourse began / In nineteen sixty-three / (Which was rather late for me)." Later in the poem Larkin notes that the new attitude was "A quite unlosable game"—get that, a game—and critic and essayist Clive James parses this as suggesting that "the new liberty was merely license." That is, the *action* of seeking political liberty fades away and leaves an indulgence of *gesture*. James elsewhere has noted, "One gets the sense, after a while, that living philosophical insights curve away from history to re-enter it later on as psychodrama, posturings and myth."

Philosophical writer Lee Harris recalls a friend who joined a disruptive protest against the Vietnam War involving laying down in front of cars crossing a bridge. The friend was openly unconcerned with whether it would help lead to America's withdrawing from the conflict, participating instead because it would be "good for his soul":

He had no interest in changing the minds of these commuters, no concern over whether they became angry at the protesters or not. They were merely there as props, as so many supernumeraries in his private political psychodrama. The protest for him was not politics, but theater; the significance of his role lay not in the political ends his actions might achieve but rather in their symbolic value as ritual.

This will recall for many the Black Panthers, Jesse Jackson, and many black student college campus protests. White people like Harris's friend heartily approved of blacks' aping them in this kind of display in the late sixties; we saw in Chapter Four how such whites even shunted this approval into legislation aimed at blacks. Today, the white American version of therapeutic alienation continues to determine mainstream perceptions of black actions and artistic contributions. For example, as Elijah Wald teaches us, the current mania over rough bluesman Robert Johnson contrasts with his relative obscurity among blacks when he was alive. Black audiences then preferred slicker, louder acts, who languish in obscurity today, neglected by most white fans of old bluesmen. Their preference of unadorned, societally marginal Johnson with his obscure, glum biography reflects a kind of taste that became mainstream in the late sixties. Johnson evokes an upturned finger, an indictment of those men talking on their cell phones outside that studio in New York several decades later. The other bluesmen were a little too, well, fancy—they seemed like they wouldn't have minded being able to dress up nice and talk on a cell phone.

THE ORIGINS OF THERAPEUTIC ALIENATION: BLACKS TAKE THE BALL AND RUN WITH IT

This brings us to why black Americans drank in therapeutic alienation so readily once whites presented it as a model, in their own politics and in celebrating it as the essence of true blackness. In investigating what happened from the perspective of the historian, we seek causes. For example, why could it not have been that therapeutic alienation stayed a "white thing," that blacks looked upon as a luxury unavailable to a people with such serious work to do on concrete problems? We ask that not rhetorically, but as an actual query. In an era when meaningful social contact between whites and blacks was slight and the line between the races was so much more sharply drawn than today, why did the "hippie" ethos jump that line so easily and turn black America upside down?

The reason was that this sea of change gave black America something that it wanted, even if it ended up being poison more often than not. The stage had been set with concrete action: when blacks wrested the victories of the Civil Rights Act of 1964 and the Voting Rights Act of 1965 from a racist America. But there had always been a theatrical thrill inherent to the marches, the protests, the talk show appearances, the speeches, the cheering crowds. It felt good—and not only because it had helped black America as a whole, but also because it helped black people participating in it to *feel* whole.

Fixing a Hole

And in the late sixties, black America needed not only legislation, but also to feel whole. Communally, sure—but also individually, deep down, after the parade was over, when you were all alone, after dark, just you. After centuries of degradation, there was a hole in the black American soul. How could a people feel truly good about themselves when they had been told that they were animals by the Establishment forever and were too far removed from their ancestral roots in Africa to feel the true wholeness of its indigenous cultures in any real way? When Eddie Murphy did his "happy African" characterization in *Coming to America*, he captured a real difference that we see between African immigrants and black Americans. Africans often have a genuine pride, as products of countries where people on all levels of society are black, that contrasts with a wary "don't tread on me" air that history has left on black America.

Naturally, then, the Bayard Rustins and A. Philip Randolphs and Whitney Youngs would see a new generation of blacks falling into calling themselves activists while indulging in what were actually gestures, like Lee Harris's protester friend laying in front of apolitical commuters' cars and pretending this was meaningful participation in the antiwar movement. For blacks this kind of thing was, literally, therapeutic. It was not political, but psychological—compelling as a quest to heal the wounds of centuries of degradation.

As such, where for whites therapeutic alienation took its place as an add-on, for blacks it took its place as a racial identity: an entire psychological conception of one's place in the national fabric. Here was where the idea settled in that for blacks, defiance is not only one of many personality types, but also the soul of authenticity. This happened because deep down, blacks *hurt* inside.

Debra Dickerson observes that when black students took over a building at Cornell University in 1969 demanding a Black Studies department, even after the administration created one, many of the students remained heatedly opposed to the university's leadership as racist, condemning more constructive black students as insufficiently "militant." Militancy had become an end in itself because "what they actually wanted was beyond the white man's power to bestow." At the end of the day, history had stuck these students with a sense that "without their oppression they are no one special," such that they come to feel that "the only way to matter is to create and prolong turmoil." As sad as this is, the grim reality is that it is also, as Dickerson perfectly puts it, "Kabuki. It's a stylized acting out of unresolved trauma and revenge fantasies."

Certainly not all blacks fell under this influence. Older blacks, for example, tended to miss it. But a great many younger ones did not, enough that a new tone was set, and new developments were channeled by the new frame of mind. For example, alone, the shift from integrationism to separatism *just as racism began receding* seems odd—unless we realize that it was natural under a mood that cherished defiance as authentic because of its therapeutic effect on damaged souls. Or, the Black Power rebels were so long on noise and so short on action because as products of their era, they were more interested in the noise than the action in the first place—understandably so, for people who were moved more by a psychological scar than the less immediate abstractions of societal problems. Hence, in the Hollywood blaxploitation depictions of like-minded black rebels, there was lip service to political *action*, but the films were actually about the *gestures* of gun-waving and recreational sex.

The Challenge of Being an Individual

The roots of black America's therapeutic alienation in inner pain ties in to the teachings of Eric Hoffer in his classic monograph *The True Believer*. Hoffer wrote in 1951. He only knew the old-time Civil Rights movement and did not even address it; he had no way of knowing the problems of black leadership that we would face today. Yet, in his take on the nature of mass movements, Hoffer captured the essence of what is so confusing about black sociopolitical orthodoxy in our moment.

Hoffer was interested in why individuals, originally as self-directed and idiosyncratic as all humans are, so often subsume themselves into ideological movements based on idealized visions of the past and contemptuous caricature of the present, with proposals for the future oddly light on practical programs. Hoffer's points of reference were movements like Nazism, Fascism, and Southern white supremacy, and he surely would have classed militant Islamic fundamentalism similarly. But much of his analysis illuminates today's Politically Correct black orthodoxy eerily well.

"Militant" black ideology, even when diluted into quieter convictions among ordinary people, looks to an idealized African past, insists that the present is still, as Ishmael Reed has it, a matter of endless days "at the front," and proposes a "Black Nationalist" future of hazily described multi-class black "communities" difficult to imagine in an increasingly miscegenated and multicultural nation.

Hoffer argues that such movements are parasitic upon the emergence of civilization itself. The agricultural revolution pushed humans beyond our initial condition as members of small bands of people tightly bound by ancient communal imperatives, which served to maintain arrangements in which all participated directly in finding food and caring for children. Original man had few "choices"—individuality was a marginal concept. Maybe this one was a good whittler and that one sang well, but in the end, everybody in the village was in it together. But the development of larger societies left classes above the menial with leisure time, choices of specialized occupation—that is, more room for nurturing one's individuality.

Hoffer's thesis is that this very individuality is an unnatural condition, lending a sense of existential disconnection, so much so that it is almost intolerably threatening to many people. This makes membership in collective ideological movements spiritually attractive, in absolving them of the discomfiting responsibility of making their way as unbounded independent actors.

Hence, they embrace movements whose manifestos require elisions of empiricism and logic that appear bizarre to the outside observer, based on visceral sentiment disconnected from concrete reality. The Nazi sings of a mythical Aryan utopia in the past and singles out Jews as obstacles to the rebirth of that utopia. The Southern bigot fashions a plantation paradise and constructs an unempirical stereotype of blacks as rapacious animals. We look at Leni Riefenstahl's *The Triumph of the Will* and wonder how so very many ordinary people could be marching in step to Hitler's mythological rantings, not understanding that the root of the allegiance was more a desperate self-erasure than constructive progress.

Black Power as a Hofferite Mass Movement

Black Power ideology has, obviously, inspired nothing remotely as hideous as Hitler or Mussolini. But the hold that this way of thinking has exerted upon so many is due to the same inner quest for self-abnegation that Hoffer described. Freed from overt segregation and discrimination after the sixties, black Americans were faced for the first time in their history with true choice, with opportunities to succeed—or, crucially, perhaps fail. In other words, the new legislation at last gave blacks their place in civilization, as it were, such that they could play their part on the American stage as individuals. But as Hoffer noted, being an individual can be challenging. The challenge was especially intimidating for a people who had had so little opportunity to prepare themselves for the task.

Naturally, then, for many the response was a new hypersensitivity to the obstacles, a new fetishization of The Man, not right in front of you but *there*, all around you, like oxygen or God, holding you back, cutting you down. It's not about me—(that is, I'm not sure how I feel about me)—it's about him. As such, today's black American meme of therapeutic alienation, albeit occupying not the battlefield but the university classroom, the kitchen table, the black call-in radio show, the blogsite, and the hip-hop CD is a product of the same tendencies in mass movements that Hoffer describes in other times and places.

Hoffer notes that under this kind of movement, "to rely on the evidence of the senses and of reason is heresy and treason," since the guiding imperative is to march in lockstep to an ideology whose core motivation is opposition to the present at all costs. Thus, a core of black scholars of Black English insisted in 1996 that black students require tutelage in "Ebonics," despite reams of studies in contradiction and millions of successful blacks showing that such techniques are unnecessary. Those who questioned the orthodoxy were tarred as morally unfit, regardless of the facts they brought to bear on the issue. The key was simply whether you were with us or against us.

Because reality is always complex, an ideology so compelling as to seduce an individual into marching in step with thousands of others must be based on ideas that address the gut rather than the brain. But because the real world is complex, these ideas can never withstand careful analysis, such that as Hoffer put it, "a doctrine that is understood is shorn of its strength." Thus, it is pretended that race issues are uniquely "complex," their mystical underpinnings proposed as justifying assumptions such as that unequal outcomes always mean unequal opportunity. To get down to cases is to be accused of "not getting it," with little attempt at logical elucidation necessary. Predictably, adherents value what Hoffer pegged as "impassioned double-talk and sonorous refrains" more than "precise words joined together with faultless logic," and, hence, black scholars like Cornel West rocking black audiences with Latinate words delivered in the cadences of the church and the street, with the content of what they are saying considered a background concern. I have watched black fans of West start mm-hmming to his cadences and angular gestures even when what he was saying was either too arcane for any but one or two scholars in attendance to know whether it was true or too ordinary to merit such vigorous consent on its face alone. The theatrics alone are the message.

For those uncomfortable to see this ideology likened to Hitler and Mussolini, we might heed thinkers like Erik Erikson, who wrote that in moments of rapid social change, "youth feels endangered, individually and collectively, whereupon it becomes ready to support doctrines offering a total immersion in a synthetic identity (extreme nationalism, racism, or class consciousness) and a collective condemnation of a totally stereotyped enemy of the new identity." It is hard not to see post–Civil Rights black America in that description, and Erikson meant exactly what Hoffer did.

We Must Be Clear

My argumentation so far could possibly be misinterpreted as implying that racism alone was what created therapeutic alienation. However, racism had been a reality forever: It must be understood that this response to racism was in turn enabled by a particularity of the moment: whites' new interest in the black condition amid the commitments of the counterculture. This allowed a new vent for a spiritual insecurity among blacks that had existed for centuries with whites uninterested in paying it attention. After all, there are all kinds of human responses to insecurity, and black Americans had previously manifested many of them.

Insecurity can make you work harder, which meant that blacks back in the day openly said, "If you're black you have to try twice as hard." I have lost count of how many times I have heard black people on radio call-in shows I participate in ask why that adage has fallen away. It's because of a new mantra that says, perhaps, "If you're black you have to complain twice as much."

Insecurity can make you withdraw into yourself and have as little contact with The Man as possible. That was Bronzeville, Tulsa, the Shaw district in DC, Central Avenue in Cleveland, Indiana Avenue in Indianapolis, Auburn Avenue in Atlanta, and so on.

Insecurity can make you just give up and while away your days in idle misery. That was black sharecroppers mired in debt and poverty, with not a hint of a sense of posterity or hope. They lived, they worked too hard, they had too many kids, and they died, staring at us vacantly in the one photo they may have had taken of them the day they married or a second one that a photojournalist may have come through and taken.

Or—insecurity might make you dutifully protest when a white woman uses the word *nigger* in condemning it. But that will only happen with the precondition of an Establishment newly receptive to such a "message."

Only in the late sixties, for example, could William H. Grier and Price M. Cobbs's *Black Rage* become a best seller, introducing the idea that blacks' problem was not only discrimination but also whites' deep-seated psychological feelings of bias against blacks. This helped usher in a keystone of therapeutic alienation, that our interest is in whether all whites esteem us in their heart of hearts.

That seems so ordinary now but is, in fact, a rather eccentric fetish of ours. Blacks before the late sixties assumed that whites did not like us, and thought that sheer opportunity was what their people needed. But starting in the late sixties, endless investigations and condemnations of whites' psychological biases against blacks took center stage—even though blacks' regularly saying that they thought whites would always be racist meant that the goal was less to fix something than to dwell in it indefinitely. As historian Elizabeth Lasch-Quinn has it,

> The desired goal was no longer civic equality and participation, but individual psychic well-being. This psychological state was much more nebulous, open to interpretation, difficult to achieve, and controversial than the universal guarantees of political equality sought by the early civil rights movement.

We cannot say that blacks had spent a long period of time after the Civil Rights Act of 1964 supposing that this alone gave them the opportunity to succeed, had eventually learned that it did not, and for that reason started looking to whites' personal biases. *Black Rage* was published just four years after the Civil Rights Act and was being planned and written years before, basically *concurrently with* the Civil Rights Act. The new focus on psychological issues emerged, then, *just as* discrimination was outlawed and white consensus on blacks shifted from dismissal to professional guilt. And it emerged despite that earlier blacks had no particular interest in cleansing whites' psychologies, largely because it never seemed remotely promising as a project.

Nevertheless, Cobbs pioneered encounter groups in which blacks dressed down whites for their subliminal racism, a trope familiar to any number of people who have sat through corporate diversity "seminars" since. This kind of thing has only been possible in an America where two conditions reigned. One was that blacks gained a sense of comfort in assailing whites, with only faintly constructive purpose, as a coping strategy for feelings of insecurity. But if that were the only condition, then certainly somebody would have started convening encounter groups in, say, the late forties when the basic tenets of psychology penetrated the American Zeitgeist to an extent they had not before. There was another necessary condition: Whites were newly open to pretending to like being yelled at and that has only been the case since the sixties.

Therapeutic alienation, then, was spurred not only by "racism," but also by a particular congruence of sociopolitical factors at a particular time. If the new ideology of the sixties were a response simply to "oppression" writ large, or blacks being finally "fed up," then we might try some thought experiments.

> After Republicans dismissed Reconstruction in 1876, blacks, mostly stuck in thankless sharecropper existences, were outraged and revolted across the South. A culture of the gun took hold among young black vigilantes terrorizing whites. A new musical genre called "rag-hop" developed, with lyrics calling for freedom chanted over fierce drum beats and banjo strummings. Over the next twenty years, blacks' demands for equal participation had exerted such a pull upon the national consciousness that when *Plessy v. Ferguson* was brought before the Supreme Court in 1896, an eight-to-one majority ruled in Homer Plessy's favor.

or:

> In 1919, black men returned from serving in the Great War only to find themselves and their families terrorized by race riots, corralled into slum quarters, and denied all but token political representation. Black laborers in Detroit, inspired by charismatically indignant community leaders, took to downtown streets and destroyed millions of dollars of property. Blacks across the nation did the same, such that the government devoted itself to the "Colored Problem" on the pain of further destruction and bloodshed. *The Crisis* editor W.E.B. Du Bois thundered, "At her peril does America ignore the roiling power of her millions of dark-skinned denizens here in this land, thirsty for the fundamental human rights so long denied them." In 1924, President Coolidge broke his trademark contempt for activism with a policy titled "Positive Commitment," seeking to "foster participation

on the part of colored peoples in the realms of commerce and scholarly pursuit according to the proportion that they represent in the American populace."

or:

In 1947, as blacks saw that even after their participation in World War II, the government had only given them reluctant and minor concessions, they realized that open revolt was their only path to justice. Philadelphia burned in July, followed quickly by Boston, Los Angeles, Detroit, and Atlanta, with smaller riots such as in Indianapolis. A new "Black Power" ideology took root among blacks denied equality for much too long. The deliberation and restraint of earlier Civil Rights leaders fell out of fashion, with new ringleaders taking up weapons and often operating on the margins of the law. NAACP lawyers arguing *Brown v. the Board of Education* proudly wore their hair "natural" and gave press conferences in dashikis, signalling a new allegiance to their African roots.

Well, why not? There is not a thing in any of these hypothetical accounts that would seem at all illogical in John Hope Franklin's keystone black history text *From Slavery to Freedom*—except for the fact that, we immediately think, if blacks had tried such things in those times, whitey would have crushed us like a bug. Which is true. The angry, theatrical separatism now so often treated as genuine and progressive was impossible until whites were poised to give it the floor. And this means one thing: The privileging of alienation over action so familiar to us is not an inevitable response to being given a really bad hand. If it was, it would have ruled black America, really, starting in the early 1600s. It is one of many responses possible. The one we know is only so common because in the sixties it became *possible*—and only then.

Path Dependence

Therapeutic alienation's birth under particular conditions and its persistence long after they pass away has a model not only in the meme concept but also in social science, where it exemplifies what is termed *path dependence*. Path dependence refers to the fact that often, something that seems normal or inevitable today began with a choice that made sense at a particular time, but has survived despite the eclipse of the justification for that choice, because once established, external factors discouraged going into reverse to try other alternatives.

The paradigm example is the seemingly illogical arrangement of letters on typewriter keyboards. Why not just have the letters in alphabetical order? Or why not arrange the letters so that the most frequently occurring ones are under the strongest fingers? In fact, the first typewriter tended to jam when typed on too quickly, so its inventor deliberately concocted an arrangement that, for example, put A under the ungainly little finger. In addition, the first row was provided with all of the letters in the word *typewriter* so that salesmen, new to typing, could wangle typing the word using just one row.

Quickly, however, mechanical improvements made faster typing possible, and new keyboards placing letters according to frequency were presented. But it was too late: There was no going back. By the 1890s, typists across America were used to QWERTY keyboards, having learned to zip away on new versions of them that did not stick so easily, and retraining them would have been expensive and, ultimately, unnecessary. So QWERTY was passed down the generations, and even today we use the queer QWERTY configuration on computer keyboards where jamming is a mechanical impossibility.

Similarly, therapeutic alienation set in initially as the direct result of certain conditions. First, blacks had been bedeviled by racism for centuries. Second, they were abruptly freed from official segregation and disenfranchisement, leaving them subject to the kind of dislocation that Hoffer and Erikson described. Third, at this time a cultural consensus was setting in among whites that conditioned them to listen to blacks' complaints and respond to them as best they could. Without this factor, there would have been no room for therapeutic alienation to set in. Rather, blacks would have dealt with their insecurity in other ways, and ironically, they may have made for a better black America: Imagine an alternate-universe black America, 1970, on fire with a commitment to overcompensating! But alas.

Crucially, once this new ideology had set in, it stayed in place, passed down generations of blacks even when the conditions that sparked it receded. There was no going back. One of path dependence's seminal treatments notes that one thing that encourages it is "collective memories and rituals," and this is true of therapeutic alienation: We are often taught that striking a battle pose is an homage to the Civil Rights struggle in the past, Malcolm X's upturned fist in the iconic photo of him on so many T-shirts and posters being a kind of summation of black racial identification. But equally powerful in keeping therapeutic alienation alive is that although the Bull Connors are long gone, blacks retain another reason to stick up that fist in ritual fashion: the nagging sense that we are not quite okay. Therapeutic alienation parasitized that sense and has been riding it ever since.

Social scientists are not completely unaware that the basic nature of path dependence has something to do with, for example, inner-city blacks' problems. Even William Julius Wilson notes "accidental or nonconscious cultural transmission" or "transmission by precept"—"whereby a person's exposure to certain attitudes and actions is so frequent that they become part of his or her own outlook and therefore do not, in many cases, involve selective application to a given situation." In other words, people can do things just because they have never known anything but people around them doing them, even if they end up doing so in conditions unlike the ones that made their models do them, and even if doing so causes harm. However, such thinkers only flag this kind of analysis in the margins, deeply wary of any hint of locating culture as the problem. For them, at best they allow that "there's some of that," but what they want us to really pay attention to is factories, racism, role models, redlining, and urban renewal.

I submit, however, that "accidental or nonconscious cultural transmission" is nothing less than central to what created modern inner cities, as well as a great deal of black sociopolitical ideology beyond the inner cities, including even that of academics and journalists who speak for them. That is, in fact, the central thesis of this book.

Therapeutic Alienation as Meme

Many readers will have already noticed that what I am referring to is the concept of the *meme*. Memes, as analyzed by Richard Dawkins, Daniel Dennett, Susan Blackmore, and others, are thought patterns that become entrenched in society via self-replication from mind to mind, along the lines of genes in organisms. Wariness of cholesterol is a meme. Awareness of concepts such as the subconscious is a meme. The children's tune "nyah nyah-nyah NYAH nyah" is a meme. No one taught it to you; you just picked it up in the air.

Especially useful for our purposes are memes like claims of alien abduction. A great many Americans are soberly convinced that they were taken into flying saucers and intrusively probed by extraterrestrial beings. Yet, the scenario of flying saucers and odd human-like creatures inside them is a product of science fiction novels and films that have only existed since the late nineteenth century. No one in 1650 was claiming that aliens came down in flying saucers and stuck things in them—because they had no models in popular culture upon which to base such ideas. Yet, there is no reason to suppose that the aliens only invented their saucers, or started coming to earth, exactly when writers on this planet happened to start fantasizing about them. Clearly, today's abduction claims take a page from books and Hollywood. The first claimants were copied by subsequent ones, such that now there are thousands of people nurturing this fantasy. If the claims were real, then they would have been as common in China in AD 900 as they are today in the United States. History makes it painfully clear that the claims are a modern meme, and in this case, the meme thrives unconnected from reality. Memes can do that.

Therapeutic alienation is this kind of meme. We are told that the alienated worldview of so many blacks is a response to a lack of hope, recognition, and sense of empowerment. But this view neglects history. In black America before the late sixties, naked racism all but deprived quite a few blacks of hope, recognition, and empowerment. Yet, at that time, the claim that racism left black people with no chances of making their lives better was not common wisdom, but one of many ideologies in the air. Unlike today, that claim was especially rare among blacks who had college educations, made decent salaries, and circulated regularly in white company. Blacks knew their racism quite well, thank you very much, and individual blacks were known to preach despair. But they were not elevated to major positions of leadership; they did not set the national tone. The guiding idea was to make the best of the obstacles, not fetishize them. A black writer might get some attention with victim-focused messages, but would encounter legions of other blacks who deplored him for it as discouraging progress, while whites would largely nod and move on. Progress was thought to mean forging ahead, not identifying what made doing so futile.

On the surface it looks as if we can just say that "the mood was different then." But the problem is that in that era, it would seem that today's mood would have made more sense than it does now. To be sure, blacks before the sixties protested against discrimination year after year. But separatism and oppositionalism as identity, as syllabus, as a mainstay of music, as spiritual authenticity, was not yet fashionable. Whites and blacks mature in the sixties were well aware of a mood change, typically perceiving a new black identity based on anger. But here is the paradox: Certainly, racism is not worse now, and yet only in our times has anger acquired such influence, rather than in, say, 1884. Less hyperbolically, why was it common coin in black America a hundred years later in 1984? The reason is because whites' new interest in blacks' bad hand gave entrée to a new meme, attractive to souls damaged by a vicious history, that channeled our response to obstacles differently from what our own people thought of as natural before the mid-sixties. And that meme today has no connection to modern reality. It is a tic, a fashion, a reflex.

Historical contrasts between Civil Rights activism then and now often only make sense as determined by the therapeutic alienation meme. In 2003, the chairman of the NAACP was condoning a witch hunt against a white person who used the word *nigger* in a sentence criticizing its use, while an AIDS crisis festered among blacks nationwide and struggling inner-city blacks were starving for advice on how to open small businesses. But in 1923, Julian Bond's NAACP equivalent would not have given a second's thought to urging a white person's "repentance" for having done nothing wrong. James Weldon Johnson was more interested in that blacks were virtually barred from anything but menial employment and were being lynched regularly. In fact, he famously wrote, "I will not allow one prejudiced person or one million or one hundred million to blight my life. I will not let prejudice or any of its attendant humiliations and injustices bear me down to spiritual defeat. My inner life is mine, and I will defend and maintain its integrity against the forces of hell."

To which Bond would presumably nod—but why, then, would what that white supervisor said strike him as worthy of even the slightest notice? Why hasn't Bond, chairing the NAACP of all things, been more interested in the actual on-the-ground problems that the less fortunate of his people face? Because Bond is under the influence of a meme born in the sixties that elevates the thrill of shaking a fist at whitey, so seductive that it can distract one from less thrilling but more urgent work that actually improves people's daily existences. James Weldon Johnson lived too early to be influenced by that meme.

This meme only appears to constitute natural behavior when we restrict our view to the present. It is, in fact, quite unnatural. It is propagated not by reality, but by the same psychological comfort that professional martyrdom has lent isolated personality types since our species arose.

The meme idea captures what has been going on especially well in terms of explaining the past and present. It is time to spell out more precisely my grounds for classifying the problem in this way.

TRAIT ONE:
MEMES CAN THRIVE INDEPENDENTLY
OF EXTERNAL CONDITIONS

Therapeutic alienation often does harm. If a person refrains from seeking available work out of alienation from The Man and The System, then this lowers the quality of life of children they might have, as well as of their own lives if they drift into seeking money by illegal means. If a person decides that doing well in school is "white," then their earning power may suffer later. If a person attacks a white person as racist on flimsy grounds, it tends to encourage whites in a sense that blacks just can't be dealt with constructively. If a person has a deep-seated sense of whites as sinister based largely on abstract ideological leanings, books claiming that the Greeks stole hallmarks of civilization from Africans, and the like, then even if they achieve enough to get a job at a law firm, their air of social distance may prevent them from being made partner.

Memes as Parasites

Why, then, does this frame of mind persist? After all, it is not, in the present day, a response to external conditions. Certainly, a black person unfortunate enough to experience an unusual degree of clearly racist abuse will develop a deep-seated antipathy to whites. But under the mood since the sixties, a black person can just as easily develop such an antipathy when whites have neither stood between them and anything they wanted nor insulted them socially. The answer is that the therapeutic alienation meme thrives not because of external reality but because of internal reality. It gives vent to the insecurity that bedevils all of us—especially attractive to members of a race left terminally self-doubting because of centuries of contempt and dismissal, and especially available in a post-sixties mainstream culture intent on censuring itself for possible racism.

In this, therapeutic alienation displays something typical of the meme as generally analyzed: its parasitic nature. Like parasites and viruses, memes can latch onto aspects of our psychology and persist even if they do harm otherwise.

Robert Wright notes that brains tend to sort out memes that are not good for them, such as the meme that leads some people to kill themselves in the name of a religion like the Heaven's Gate cult in 1997, which as Wright puts it "doesn't seem to be catching on." In fact, if sincere decrying of personal injury were the basis of episodes like the one at the

University of Virginia, or the belligerent alienation in much hip-hop music, then it would be downright counterintuitive in terms of what we know about human psychology. Namely, ordinarily the human brain discourages fetishizing downsides and setbacks, since they are harmful to the functioning of the self. Many studies have shown that individuals tend to live in a kind of denial about how much oppressive tendencies affect them as opposed to other members of their group; psychologists even have a name for it, minimization. For example, one study showed that women in a sample were fully aware of sexism and wage discrimination in their workplace, but tended to be unaware that they themselves were suffering from it just as the other women were.

This is, in a way, not even surprising. On some level we all suppose that part of coping with the realities of life is looking on the bright side, getting up and brushing ourselves off. What, then, drives so many black people to stress the bad, to an extent that leaves many puzzled? What brought us to the point where so many people think that progressive thought for black people means endlessly rehashing the past, with labored claims that the legacies of the past render striving in the present futile?

If therapeutic alienation is a meme, then there is no longer a question. Daniel Dennett describes religious faith, for example, as based on memes "parasitically exploiting proclivities they have 'discovered' in the human cognitive-immune system." With therapeutic alienation, the proclivity in question is the need for a hole in one's soul to be assuaged, independently of whether one encounters significant amounts of racism or discrimination. A virus thrives by supporting itself on a host in a way that does not kill that host. A closer analogy would be that many animals live in symbiotic relationships in which one member benefits massively while the other one benefits in a minor way, that it would survive perfectly well without. Clownfish like Nemo live among anemones's tentacles because it provides perfect protection from predators, but the only benefit they provide the anemone is nibbling away debris from its tentacles—a kind of dust-off that anemones without clownfish boarders do quite well without.

But being that clean must be nice. As is having a way to feel like you matter, when a small voice is always telling you that being black means that you don't. Elsewhere Dennett notes that "there is no *necessary* connection between a meme's replicative power, its 'fitness' from *its* point of view, and its contribution to *our* fitness." Therapeutic alienation thrives because it gives a sense of security—even though it also has a way of encouraging dissension, planting new seeds of insecurity, and even dissuading people from trying their best.

The Meme as Self

In thriving on the basis of the subjective despite being proposed as a political position, therapeutic alienation demonstrates another aspect of the meme as argued by one of its most prominent analysts, Susan Blackmore. The meme lives on the basis of the personally felt, the viscera, the gut. That is, the meme is a part of one's essence. A song is as powerfully evocative as a smell. A gesture local to a culture and passed around as a meme is a marker of the vitality of personhood—witness young Americans making a W sign with their fingers and putting the signage in front of their forehead to express "Whatever . . . ," a deeply subjective evaluation of a person, statement, or situation, and the badge of a young generation. For Blackmore, the "self" is, in fact, nothing but a conglomeration of memes.

In the same way, the idea that black America is bedeviled by the operations of The Man is based on the subjective, internal, emotional terrain of individual feelings. It is not a faceless, sterile proposition like, "Insects constitute the greatest proportion of the world's faunal biomass," and thus not an empirical, outwardly oriented parsing of the state of black America, founded on constant and careful reference to demographic developments. The idea that being black remains hell for all of us is argued with an indignant fierceness that reveals the operations of the gut, even more so in the ritual in which a white person who seeks explanation too precise is dismissed as "not getting it."

Imagine: A black fan of racial preferences in university admissions says that black students often go to schools where textbooks are old. A white person ventures, "Have French irregular verbs or photosynthesis changed over the years?" Now, there might be reasonable responses to that question—suppose someone said, for example, that newer textbooks present information in ways best suited to prepare students for advanced placement classes or standardized tests. I don't know whether that is true or not, but at least it would be an answer. But just as likely, that white questioner would be greeted with eye rolls and clicks of the tongue, and perhaps one or two black people fleeing the room in tears, with any black professor in attendance taking the black people's side. This is about feelings, not reasoning. What started as Civil Rights for black America became "How I Feel" regardless of whether we got our Civil Rights. The political is personal, as it were.

This is what humans do. It even happens in how languages change. In Old English, the word *since* could only refer to one thing happening after another one: *I have been sad since my uncle died.* Even the form of the word then conveyed this literally: *siththan* was a combination of *sith* "after" and *than* "that"—"after that." But if you think about it, in that sentence, *since* could also be taken to mean that your sadness was *caused* by the death of your uncle: that is, *since* could mean *because—I have been sad because my uncle died.* This is because as often as not, what happened before something is what caused it: It rained, and afterward the grass grew—because of it having rained.

But when you use *since* to mean *because* in a sentence like *I have been sad since my uncle died,* you are telling us of what was going on inside you, instead of just spelling out that one thing happened after another. You are getting personal. *Since* did not even imply that meaning in Old English. But over time, because people are inherently so personal, that is exactly what *since* started meaning. Today, we can use *since* in sentences like *Since you don't like oysters, we won't go to that restaurant.* Here, the "because" meaning is the only one possible—the sentence does not mean that we aren't going to that restaurant *after* your not liking oysters. Any language is full of words that started as neutral concepts about the exterior world that drifted into becoming personally felt concepts about our internal experience.

As a meme, therapeutic alienation recruited something outwardly oriented, political activism, and transformed it into something inwardly oriented, healing the soul. The late sixties welfare activism we saw in Chapter Four showed this, as Gareth Davies chronicles:

> For many of the professionals who had designed the community action concept under the auspices of the Ford Foundation and President Kennedy's juvenile delinquency commission, the mere act of confronting local political establishments was therapeutic. For all the ostensible threat it posed to traditional structures, and for all its wild demands, this was essentially a vehicle for personal growth and individual transformation.

Davies goes on to record the NACCP's Norman Hill as complaining that activists had decided about poor blacks that: "They needed not money, but identity; not jobs, but self-respect; not decent homes, but a sense of community; and finally not better schools with more funds to make education effective, but control over their destiny." It was now all about the self, the personal, the *me*. It behaved like a good meme does.

TRAIT TWO:
MEMES CAN CONDITION A RESISTANCE
TO EMPIRICAL EVIDENCE

The analyses of Dickerson, Hoffer, and Erikson zero in on a key factor: a sense of affront expressed in neglect of basic lines of reasoning. Some see this and suppose that it is "complex," others think it cynical, and others quietly wonder whether black people really *might* have a few less IQ points on average than other groups. None of these surmises is necessary. This imperviousness to logic is a hallmark of memes, which can lead a thoroughly rational and moral person to rank the benefit they draw from the meme over logic.

For example, claims of alien abduction are rooted in terror people feel because of sleep paralysis, which commonly includes hearing humming, feeling vibrations, seeing lights, and sensing someone else in the room. Predictably, there is evidence that people making such claims suffer sleep paralysis more than most. They channel their terror through the particularities of a flying-saucer scenario that Hollywood has placed in the air, and once that interpretation has set in, they tend to resist the idea that sleep paralysis was what happened to them, with an elaborate web of specifications: There are no photos because the aliens have the power to be unphotographable; no evidence of break-in because they can walk through walls; one's memory of the event is hazy because the aliens erase your memory; and so forth. What is crucial to them is a balm for their terror, so crucial that reality takes a backseat.

In the same way, therapeutic alienation responds to psychological distress, but is then channeled through a particular sociopolitical rhetoric inherited from a mainstream cultural ideology of the 1960s. But that meme has limited actual material to feed itself with because in 2006 most blacks encounter overt, in-the-face racism very seldom. But the sense of protection that the meme offers is so soothing that for many, the result is to fashion oneself as bedeviled by racism independently of actual facts or experience or at least to vastly exaggerate these. To someone under the effects of the meme, the conflict with reality is a background cognitive dissonance, well worth the sense of place and legitimacy that the meme lends.

Racism at Yale

This tolerated dissonance generates countless racial controversies that otherwise look like something out of Samuel Beckett. In the mid-1990s, some black Yale law students claimed that the reason so few black students were traditionally chosen to work on the *Law Review* journal was racism. But the application process is based on blind tests. The black students' answer was that there must be a "black" writing style that was being dismissed. But they never explained what that style is; it is plain that no such style exists, and they would have burned in effigy any white student or professor who claimed that one did.

None of this made a whit of sense. I don't mean that it was "crazy" or inappropriate or unwise—I mean that this does not sound like a discussion carried on by reasoning members of our species. Or—it only does if we realize that the black students' responses were perfectly coherent as products of insecurity about their full worth as black Americans. Under that analysis, these students gained an internal sense of place, a "way to matter," by being defiant against a proposed racism always in the air. This assuaged the uncertainty inside of them, and especially for young people, this can be more important in the end even than making sense.

This point is important and will need a couple of more extended illustrations.

Renting a Negro

A rich example of this disconnect from reality is, of all things, a Web site called rent-a-negro, created by black artist Damali Ayo when she was about thirty years old. The Web site satirically presents a service offering black people for rent by whites, the idea being that mainstream America only sees blacks as simian exotics to parade at social gatherings to suggest social sophistication, as in the 1920s when wealthy white New Yorkers had black artists perform at their parties while their equivalents in Paris fetishized Josephine Baker shaking her bananas.

In mock testimonials, Ayo has whites exclaiming things like, "Having a black person at my next party would certainly liven things up!" Blacks are available even for "Drop-in / Appearance," eliciting blather like, "My friends would think I was so cool if we *just happened* to run into a black friend of mine when we were shopping or eating lunch at our favorite restaurant!"

Certainly Ayo intends this as parody—indicated in particular by the fact that so many of the "testimonials" are, like the ones I quoted, comments that a potential customer would presumably make *before* using the site. They are ultimately intended as portraits of how whites think regardless of whether they have actually rented a negro. Rather, the idea would seem to be that whites would, on some level, *like* to be able to rent us in this way.

Nevertheless, the testimonials and the rest of the Web site are a dead-on parody of white America—in about 1970. Indeed, the whole thing reads like something from that year when Tom Wolfe skewered just this kind of thinking in *Radical Chic*, in which Leonard Bernstein and his set entertain Black Panthers in just the frame of mind Ayo depicts. But it is hard to see what whites like this have to do with 2003, when Ayo put up the site. Her whites are the dopey foils that Norman Lear sitcoms used to trot out to be put in their place as unwittingly "prejudiced," as it was put back then, by the Jeffersons and Maude. Okay, racism in subtler forms is still around—but are we Pollyannas to admit that most whites have gotten past this kind of especially naked ignorance and condescension over the last four decades? Sheer embarrassment discourages all but a sliver of isolated, backward whites from wearing racism on their sleeves like this in modern America. I thought that now, the order of the day was calling whites out on their *hidden* bigotry despite their having learned to hide it.

For the record, Ayo was born in 1972, and thus did not even know the era when whites like this were still commonly encountered in the prime of their lives. She passed puberty in the mid-eighties, and entered college in 1990. Is she referring to such an anachronistic portrait of race relations in America because her personal experience shows that things haven't changed since then as much as we think? Or is she recruiting that era because it lends itself to the self-righteous thrills of pretending to be indignant? Listening to Ayo herself making her case in a radio interview, the answer to that question becomes clear.

It would be one thing if Ayo restricted her complaint to strangers touching her hair, or even being asked if she is an affirmative action product—both depart from any conception of civility. But in the interview, and on the site, it is clear that Ayo's main problem is being asked about aspects of being black at all. Her idea is that any such questions are intrusive and objectifying, and that in even deigning to respond to them she is lending a societal service. The Web site is founded on the joke of her actually charging for such questions.

What, however, does Ayo expect instead? Let's listen to her directly, in a radio interview after a white caller gently asks whether such questions might be a matter of benign curiosity rather than racism.

> I live in a country where black people have been a part of this society for hundreds of years, and it seems to me that people should know more about each other at this level in our development . . . people are always asking me how I wash my hair, and I say, well, 'How do you wash anything?', like let's think about this, let's think more as a community . . . I think there's some mental work and some growing that can be done in this country that just hasn't happened.

This questioning about her hair is what Ayo focuses on in the interview, rather than affirmative action or people actually touching her hair unbidden.

When the white caller suggests, "Should they not just ask?" Ayo answers, "Learn what you can on your own; there are some great resources out there." The (white) host, despite solidly liberal politics (this is NPR), reframes the caller's question, since it hits on such an obvious curiosity in Ayo's point. Ayo answers, "What I'm really asking people to do in this piece, which is a piece of conceptual art work, let's not forget that, I'm asking them to pause. . . . I don't have to make an effort to learn about white people; that's taught to me on a daily basis . . . it's imbalanced."

One question is Ayo's offense at the hair washing question. It is not racist to see a tightly elaborate hairdo and simply want to know what the washing methods are for it.

But the main problem is her call for whites to, apparently, use Web sites and books and magazines to find the answers to their questions about blacks. Wouldn't this, really, pave the way for blacks encountering no questions to complain that whites are not interested in them, do not see them as full human beings, and/or have the gall to learn about blacks from books and Web crawling instead of from actual human beings? One can hear it now: "Whites only want to encounter blacks at a safe remove," and so on. Ayo gives her counsel in full cognizance of the fact that it is so counterintuitive that it will never be a norm. Whites, told by the post–Civil Rights ethos to be interested in blacks, will always now ask blacks questions in an effort to "acknowledge" and "engage" us—but Ayo wants it that even then, they encounter blacks glumly offended at being exoticized. And as to the very obvious question whether it would really be optimal for whites to learn about blacks from Web sites, Ayo has no answer. Why? Because rent-a-negro.com is dedicated not to racial healing at all, but to a smaller goal: perpetuating indignation regardless of reality or common sense. Ayo *wants* to feel indignant, and one could only do that in 2003 by disengaging with reality.

Ayo gives away again and again that indignation is her main objective, with progress or even common sense beside the point. First, there is the language. We are dealing with "white privilege," for example, a buzzword concept referring to a kind of "new racism," in which whites, although increasingly hard to peg as overtly bigoted, remain abusive to blacks in being the ones whom history and the power of numbers have left more likely to call the shots. But we cannot change that whites got here first, or that they outnumber blacks. And even if not a single black person were poor and blacks occupied places of power in the exact proportion that they represent in the population, whites, in total, would still have "more power." Thus, the complaint about "white privilege" is aimless defeatism, which a person only comes up with when what they really want to do is complain for its own sake.

Or phraseology such as, "I live in a country where black people have been part of this country for . . ."—yeah, yeah: that is, "in a country" *with a history of slavery and segregation* where "black people have been a part" *in being the mules of the Southern economy and helping to build our cities and no one acknowledges this*. But we cannot change that history, and if the fact that blacks helped build the Capitol was skywritten on the hour seven days a week in every American city and whites were given tax breaks to discuss it in living rooms nationwide each night, it would do not a thing for blacks living in poverty or even for black lawyers not making partner. So why even bring it up? Especially when Ayo is, as a matter of fact, offended if a white person asks her whether her great-grandparents were slaves! These particular ways of putting such things are today established jargon from the victimspeak manual, and big surprise—the Web site gestures toward reparations in a joke about retroactive payments.

Then there is one of those logical contradictions. On her site, she quotes "G.B., University President" as saying of a negro he has rented, "I'm delighted to show her off!" So Ayo means that college administrators' interest in blacks is really just good old tokenism à la 1970 when evil whites on TV were shown sticking blacks into jobs "to lend the place a little color—heh, heh, heh . . . (fade out before commercial)." I would agree with her here. But then, I will put my neck on the line and venture, based on her general politics as evinced in the Web site and the interview, that

Ayo just may not exactly disapprove of racial preferences and does not quite see Ward Connerly as a hero. It is beyond me to make any A-to-B logical sense of that other than to suppose that Ayo is dedicated primarily to indignation wherever she can squeeze out a basis for it. White administrators claiming interest in "diversity" are making blacks into objects, but then white and black people who are against preferences that put color first and qualifications third do not understand the travails that black people have endured in trying to "be a part" "of this country."

This is someone seeking alienation independently of reality. And in this, she is a sign of our times.

Racism Forever

We also see this disconnect from reality in summations about how far we have come on race in America overall, where some blacks let alienation trump engagement. In 2000, the *New York Times* solicited opinions for one of those Conversations on Race, in which black psychologist Beverly Daniel Tatum (best known for *Why Are All the Black Kids Sitting Together in the Cafeteria?*) intoned, "A cultural system is operating to reinforce cultural stereotypes, limit opportunities and foster a climate in which bigotry can be expressed." And the solution is "a structured dialogue about race relations." Let's take this apart.

"Reinforce cultural stereotypes": that is, *Spider-Man* movies carefully have almost all street criminals be white in New York, while journalistic etiquette has long refrained from noting criminals' race until absolutely necessary. In the meantime, black people themselves cherish black hip-hop stars gleefully teaching millions of black young people that being a "thug" is cool, as black "hip-hop academics" cheer on the sidelines that these people are giving America a "message." And yet Tatum, pretending that America has not budged from a state that forged her opinions in about 1972, asserts that it is white America that is still teaching us that blacks are lowlifes.

"Limit opportunities": In 2000 especially, this was code for the assault on admitting black students into elite universities with lowered standards that was being led by Ward Connerly and supported by the conservative press. That is, an assault on exactly what was called tokenism in the sixties and seventies, including by people of Tatum's politics.

"Foster a climate in which bigotry can be expressed," says Tatum in a country where for most whites, being called a racist is as hideous a prospect as being deemed a pederast. That is, however we feel about covert racism, America today is a place where when bigotry is overtly "expressed" it is vehemently—and, one would think, blessedly—condemned. Now, there is no question that bigotry can be expressed below board. But where exactly is the "cultural system" that clearly "fosters" the open expression of bigotry? What modern reality is Tatum referring to?

"Structured dialogue"—what, exactly, would the "structure" be? I venture that any "structure" imposed upon the black participants in this "dialogue" will be slight. Surely people oppressed by an America in which "a cultural system is operating to reinforce cultural stereotypes, limit opportunities and foster a climate in which bigotry can be expressed" will be allowed to "turn it out" in whatever fashion they desire. The "structure"—or, perhaps, stricture—will be imposed upon the whites. That is, the "structure" will be one in which Tatum gets what she wants: People like her get to decry with no obligation to make sense, while whites have a choice between nodding sympathetically or being tarred as racists. Anything other than this will not satisfy her because her guiding principle is to satisfy a personal itch.

Logic does not allow that Tatum requires this out of a genuine sense that it will achieve anything for black America. After all, people like her have been foisting this kind of "structured dialogue" upon white America for forty years, and yet remain aggrieved that a debt remains unpaid to black people, that the day has not yet come when whites across our nation get down on their knees and "understand," and forthwith somehow render all blacks backyard-barbecuing middle-class *Cosby Show* homeowners. Tatum has seen no evidence that this kind of "dialogue" has any concrete effect—but continues to call for it in prominent venues.

This is because what really drives her is personal. When one feels inferior to whites deep down, one is uncomfortable presenting oneself as a self-directed individual. That individual wouldn't be good enough. So one seeks a tribal identity, hiding oneself within a multitude living for an abstract ideology larger than any one person. That ideology is one lending a substitute identity, one seductively easy to fall into and soothing to the soul for someone whom history divested of anything more connected with reality. That is an identity based on being the noble underdog battling an evil machine—regardless of what is actually happening in the land that one's ancestors turned upside down to make one's life and career possible.

Sam Harris artfully says, "We have names for people who have many beliefs for which there is no rational justification. When their beliefs are extremely common we call them 'religious'; otherwise, they are likely to be called 'mad,' 'psychotic,' or 'delusional.' "

Those latter three diagnoses are strong words, and luckily we do not need to consider them, since the therapeutic alienation I refer to is indeed "extremely common" among blacks (and also has its place among other people). Rather, what we are faced with is something very much akin to religious faith. Harris notes "Faith is what credulity becomes when it finally achieves escape velocity from the constraints of terrestrial discourse—constraints like reasonableness, internal coherence, civility, and candor." This is a sadly apt summation of episodes like the University of Virginia one, of rent-a-negro.com, and so much else.

TRAIT THREE:
MEMES PROLIFERATE BY COPYING FROM ONE PERSON TO ANOTHER

Therapeutic alienation also reveals itself as a meme in that so often, its expressions are clearly modelled on manifestations in the past, even when current conditions would not motivate that kind of manifestation.

A Different Kind of Role Model

After the Columbine High School murders in Colorado, there was a string of cases across the country where alienated high school teens were discovered to be plotting similar massacres, in some cases even bringing them to fruition (although thankfully, with fewer deaths). Being socially ostracized in high school has been a sadly typical experience for countless teens since time immemorial, but bringing guns to school and firing away is hardly an immediately attractive notion. That was the tragically specific response of Eric Harris and Dylan Klebold, but in their wake, teens across the nation seeing them on television picked up the idea and aped it regardless of the fact that otherwise, they would have been vanishingly unlikely to choose that method of addressing what was hurting them.

But this copycatting aspect of memes hardly needs result in murder. In Malaysia and Indonesia, women are associated with a syndrome called *latah*, in which upon being startled, a woman starts shouting obscenities and performing sexual gestures, and in extreme cases submits herself to performing whatever action someone demands, all of this to general amusement. Sometimes *latah* can last for hours. Afterward, the woman apologizes and claims that she does not remember what she did. The practice is most typical of lower-class, middle-age, rather reticent women who have recently undergone a personal tragedy such as the loss of a spouse.

To people of these cultures, *latah* is considered a natural trait, latent in all people. But the fact remains that *latah* is unknown among Zulus, Latvians, Aboriginal Australians, Koreans, Mennonites, black people in Detroit, or, in fact, any humans but women of a highly particular social and biographical profile in precisely these Southeast Asian regions. *Latah*, then, is not a mental disorder natural to Homo sapiens under certain conditions. Despite the women's claims that they have no control over their behavior, *latah* is a meme. Women copy it from one another. The women in these cultures would not do this if they had not seen other women they knew doing it. This means that at heart, *latah* is a show. One observer has even noted, "It is often difficult to separate the genuine cases from those which are basically histrionic and exhibitionist in nature."

Like all memes, *latah* survives because it confers a psychological benefit. It is a therapeutic way of letting off steam in highly hierarchical cultures that place great value upon decorum and reserve. But we cannot therefore treat it as an inevitable response to stress and misfortune. Japanese culture is also based deeply in hierarchy and reserve, and yet no *latah* there, nor among, say, the Amish. *Latah* is a chance local development that happens to have taken root via imitation down the generations.

Takeover, 1989 at Stanford

I saw a perfect demonstration of the copycatting aspect of the therapeutic alienation meme many years ago at Stanford University. On a spring day in May 1989, sixty Stanford students took over the university president's building and were arrested. The idea was that in not acceding to certain demands regarding minority issues, the administration had revealed itself to be racist, such that forceful, disruptive action of this kind was necessary.

Interesting, though, what the "demands" were. There was already a Black Studies program, so the students couldn't recapitulate the grievance of black students who had waged similar protests twenty years before, most famously at Cornell. Rather, the main demands were for a Native American Studies department and professor, an Asian American Studies department, and a full-time assistant dean for Chicano affairs. For the black students—who had an academic program, a student association, and a theme house—the grievance was more abstract. There was just a racism "in the air" on campus. At the time, the most ready reference point was that the fall before, two drunken white students had colored in black

Beethoven's face on a flyer hanging in the black theme house advertising a talk exploring whether or not Beethoven had African ancestry. It was a clumsy joke, but hardly a matter of scrawling or uttering a bad word, leaving someone a threatening note, or the like.

Yet, most black students surveyed afterward decreed Stanford a racist campus—although only 30 percent of the students referred to direct experience, and even then, almost none of them referred to, for example, white frat boys driving by throwing bottles at them, teachers dismissing their abilities, or being called "nigger." All but a few just contributed that this "racism" was "hard to explain," "subtle," and the like. There was also talk of a black professor saying that he was on the verge of quitting for lack of "support" (this professor, in fact, still teaches at Stanford seventeen years later and not long after the protest created a popular course on black hairstyles, an "assertion" of "blackness" if ever there was one). And then many also thought there weren't enough black professors. If black professors are not 13 percent of the faculty when black people are 13 percent of the American population, then you know what *that's* all about, of course.

I was a graduate student at Stanford that spring. I watched the arrests, as police buses and clumps of officers clashed with the usual early evening calm of the Quad. But that aesthetic incompatibility was not the only one I noticed. Overall, some things just didn't quite jell about this protest.

For one, I had always been a little perplexed reading and hearing about the demands. There are times when persistent injustice requires making noise and a lot of it. An episode called the Civil Rights movement comes to mind. But it was hard to miss a certain difference between what a Bayard Rustin had wanted and what these students wanted.

Because there is no department of Native American Studies devoted to an infinitesimal component of the student population, we *take over a building and get arrested*? There is an Asian dormitory and student association, but no Asian Studies department means *taking over a building and getting arrested*? Does one *take over a building* because there is no *assistant dean* of Chicano affairs, planning the event partly at meetings of a university-funded Latino student association? Black students had a dormitory, an academic program (a healthy one), a theatre group, and a student association—and soon two, when the following year I cofounded one for graduate students, encountering no resistance whatsoever to a nice bit of funding. And yet an administration that has funded all of this without question is still so "racist," so appallingly dismissive of black people, that we *take over a building and ride down to the station house*?

One approached the list of demands anticipating backward lapses of racial awareness, only to find rather bland matters of administrative detail, dwarfed by a general and obvious commitment to nurturing students' quests for ethnic identity. It seemed as if the protesters were looking for things to object to.

The other thing that didn't add up about "Takeover 1989" was a matter of demeanor. Watching the protesters rounded up and driven away to be arrested, something that struck me powerfully was a simple but highly indicative thing about the students: their sheer *joy.* I will never forget it— faces beaming through the bus windows, many students even brandishing exuberant "nyah-nyah" gestures and postures as they were loaded onto the buses.

There is a crucial contrast here: Grins are sparse in footage of the Birmingham protests or the Selma march. Occasionally someone flashes a smile at the novelty of the camera focusing on them, but overall there is no schoolyard "nyah-nyah" smugness. What were the students in the Stanford protest so *happy* about? Remember, the administration had yet to make any concessions that evening. All the students knew was that the police had come to arrest them and that they were on the evening news. Which means that the students were simply happy about acting up and getting attention.

In other words, "Takeover 1989" was, at heart, a show, based like any good show on a preexisting script carefully followed like old footstep patterns given out in schools of dance. It was a theatrical gesture, modelled on sincere Civil Rights activism in the past, but only on the basis of its superficial attractions when viewed on film, read about, and recounted by charismatic veterans: the noise, giving the finger to the authorities, *showing* oneself to vibrate to a higher moral awareness rather than being initially aroused by the awareness itself. Whether the "protest" actually led to the hiring of an assistant dean of Chicano affairs was beside the point. They were imitating protests elsewhere, doing a *show.*

Of course, there are times when imitation drives truly sincere activism. There is no reason to accuse the sit-in protesters in the early sixties, taking their cue from previous examples, as just putting on shows for the thrill of it. These people were responding to genuine discrimination they encountered every day, and put their physical well-being on the line in doing so. But "Takeover 1989" was a different kind of imitation. For example, even the Cornell protesters in 1969 stormed Willard Straight Hall when it was full of not only workers, but also parents sleeping there during Parents' Weekend, and they forcibly evicted all of them. But the Stanford protesters took over president Donald Kennedy's office before eight A.M. when no one had come to work yet. That is, they weren't sincerely aggrieved enough to venture confronting actual people at their desks, as for example, the sixty militants in Tehran did when they took over the American embassy in 1979 and bound and blindfolded sixty people. Deep down the undergraduate protesters at Stanford couldn't stomach bursting in on Kennedy and physically ousting him from his chair because there was no assistant dean of Chicano affairs. Rather, they had just enough pepper to pose themselves in the building at dawn to be encountered later. They were setting a scene, as it were, for a daylong imitation of a protest: a *show*.

To stick your tongue out of a bus window is *showing* it to the suits; the message is "gotcha—I can disrupt your workday and tar you as a racist in the media. Nyah on you." The message of Civil Rights protesters was not, however, "gotcha," but a deeply inflamed demand for equal participation in society. People who participated in sit-ins and got hauled off to prison were not having a good time. They did not stick their tongues out—a juvenile gesture associated with trivial interactions between children, driven by small, personal explorations of sandbox pecking order.

"Takeover 1989," then, was a mere copy of the Civil Rights protests, and a highly faded one, rather like a fifteenth-generation cassette duplicate. It was an expression of a meme, sparked by past movements motivated by sincere aggrievement, but later settling into the consciousness of generations of undergraduate protesters on the basis of the psychological comfort it lends. As with memes like claims of alien abduction, it settled in even without substantial connection to reality. It lives on because it feels good. It provides a balm for the insecurities of the young, in giving them something to feel morally superior to—as well as assuaging survivor's guilt among privileged black college students who want to shield themselves from any charge of being unconcerned with the people of their race less fortunate than them.

NECESSARY CLARIFICATION

Personality Quirk Versus Cultural Hallmark

It is crucial to understand that the fact that therapeutic alienation did not come into existence in 1967 is not counterevidence to my particular point. Certainly there have always been individuals of this profile. The eternal martyr is a personality type, likely known even in the first hunter-gatherer bands of our species in Africa. My interest is in the fact that this kind of thinking now occupies such a central place in black American culture. It is condoned, encouraged. It is presented as a model for black college students to emulate. It is given a place at the table in discussions of race and let pass as "deep" or "one way of looking at things." It anchors discussion on many black radio call-in shows across the country. Hip-hoppers set it to catchy beats and are celebrated from the dance floor to the Ivory Tower as political philosophers.

There is rarely anything completely new under the sun—but certain things at certain times become entrenched in ways that they were not before. An example is the now widespread practice of carrying around plastic bottles of water. Before about ten years ago, this was common among people engaged in some athletic activity like biking, but ordinary people did not carry bottles of water in their handbags. Riding in someone's car in 1975, one was not regularly offered a swig of bottled water. You wetted your whistle at water fountains.

It was a marketing consensus that made these bottles staples of our lives, and now they are a norm. In response to a remark that water bottles are now ubiquitous, we do not respond, "Well, my uncle Bill was carrying around a flask of water in his suit pocket back in the 1940s." Clearly, he was marching to the beat of his own drummer then, whereas today, we all march in step armed with our bottles of Poland Spring. Uncle Bill's hydrophilia does not refute that our national relationship to portable water is vastly different than in his day.

In the same way, even if great-aunt Mattie was a drama queen about race in 1940, therapeutic alienation has since acquired a cultural legitimacy that it did not have in 1940, when Mattie was received as an oddball.

A Form of Sophistication?

Then, some may say that therapeutic alienation serves some kind of universally advisable human purpose. We might say, for example, that there is something advanced in blowing the whistle even when the offense is "societal" rather than individual and that our sensitivity to this is a sign of progress.

But then we must recall that the UVA protest was not aimed at what most of us would identify as societal racism, but at racism that did not even exist. This is the particular kind of alienation that interests me. Keeping that in mind, we must then remember that while new traditions often take hold because they serve a purpose useful to society (e.g., the decrease in smoking), they can also take hold without having any constructive purpose at all.

Take the water bottles again. They are typically considered a method of keeping "hydrated." But if a Martian came to Earth and listened to us telling him that these bottles lent us vital defense against going dry, he might suppose that people had been carrying such bottles around since time immemorial. He would assume that humans require that their whistles be seriously wet 24-7, just as fish require submersion in the same water.

But again, the likes of Dasani only became default in America in the late 1990s. People in 1950 had the same biological needs for water as we do, and yet they just waited until they were near spigots or water fountains to take drinks. The Ricardos and the Mertzes had no portable water. Yet, we do not hear of earlier Americans being bedevilled by dehydration crises.

We do not "need" to sip water all day long at fifteen-minute intervals any more than Ethel Mertz did when out shopping for dresses with Lucy. Rather, marketing has made the bottles available everywhere and moderately priced, and it was a natural next step to, after finishing a bottle, continually refill it from taps to always have water on one's person. The step was natural because while it isn't *necessary* to have a water bottle always on hand, it is kind of nice. It feels good to wrap your lips around that bottle now and then. Portable bottled water is basically the new cigarette.

Thus, the water bottle has become so default that many of us might wonder how we ever did without it, like e-mail. In thirty years, younger people directing plays and movies taking place in the 1980s and earlier will occasionally slip up by having characters pulling out bottles of water, assuming that Americans always carried water around for no particular reason. But the reason we drink that water is due not to necessity, but to marketing smarts having taken advantage of a natural human oral fixation.

In the same way, it is neither inevitable nor enlightened to respond to the social imperfections in America by insisting that whites are bent on asserting their "privilege" over blacks, or by checking out of mainstream societal norms out of a sense that the White Man doesn't like you and teaching twelve-year-olds to sell crack, or by developing the most nakedly misogynist popular music humankind has ever known. Notice, for instance, that blacks produced no music remotely as nihilistic as gangsta rap even when black men were regularly being hanged from trees.

Alienation as fetish is a chance tradition of our times, like bottled water. Americans under the Eisenhower Administration hardly thought of themselves as deprived in not having portable water because it wasn't any more necessary then than it is now. It thrives today not because it is necessary but because it is pleasurable.

Therapeutic alienation thrives today for the same reason: satisfaction rather than urgency. When Julian Bond puts his energies into asking a woman to apologize for nothing, logic does not allow that he is seeking justice, any more than logic allows that someone turning on an air conditioner is seeking to hear a symphony. Bond's goal was the self-indulgent joy of being indignant against an enemy, regardless of whether the person deemed an enemy meant or even caused any harm. Therapeutic alienation allows people to please themselves like a cat with a ball of yarn.

Whites Do It Too, But . . .

As I have noted, blacks inherited therapeutic alienation from an ideology in the wake of the countercultural movement. What began as sincere and targeted opposition to genuine problems devolved into an attitude, which among many white hard leftists parallels the black therapeutic alienation meme precisely. Marc Cooper gets this just right in noting that since George W. Bush's second victory in 2004, the Michael Moore/Moveon.org wing of the Democratic party has often shirked practical attempts at coalition-building for "thinly disguised self-affirming psychotherapy and aesthetically gratifying rebel poses." "It's much easier nowadays," writes Cooper, "to fancy yourself a member of a persecuted minority, bravely shielding the flickering flame of enlightenment from the increasing Christo-Republican darkness, than it is to figure out how you're actually going to win an election."

Naturally some will ask why, then, I am focusing on this frame of mind in black people. The reason is that it occupies a more prominent part of the psychology of too many black Americans. For whites, it is a matter of one's politics; but for blacks, it tends to be a matter of one's whole sense of identity in this nation. Politics is, for most, just one part of an identity. The kind of person Cooper describes may claim to feel frightened about Republicans' purported desire to rape the environment, leave the poor to starve in the streets, and persecute Jews and Muslims, but the fright in question is usually a rather abstract and studied one—precious few such people act on this fright and follow through on that notion of moving to Canada, for example. But for blacks, therapeutic alienation proposes a more concrete and pervasive threat—the whites and their operations that we encounter 24-7, the whole fabric of our existence.

CONCLUSION

My argument, then, is that a great deal of black thought today has its roots in a distinct change in the late 1960s that rendered the then sharply different from the now. If you have ever been perplexed by statements and positions by people posing themselves as expressing the authentically black viewpoint, wondering just how what they say is pointing the way ahead when it sounds more like wallowing in the past, then the answer is that they are under the influence of the meme I have attempted to identify in this chapter.

This is why the NAACP rakes George W. Bush over the coals at their annual meetings and pretends to wonder why Bush refrains from speaking before them and dutifully tars his administration as racist. Circular? Yes. Strange? No—predictable.

This is why when it turns out that Strom Thurmond had a love child with a black servant, various black columnists tell us that Thurmond with his pants down during the Coolidge Administration is somehow something we must "acknowledge" eighty years later when there are more middle-class blacks than poor ones, two black Americans are in top positions in the Bush cabinet, marriages between blacks and whites are ever on the rise, and black-white dating is unremarkable among people under approximately forty in Blue America and many places beyond. What would the "acknowledgment" accomplish? The question is not rhetorical. It would accomplish the alienation for its own sake that many blacks have been taught to rely on to feel like they deserve to live.

This is why cosmopolitan black intellectuals listen to hip-hoppers celebrating sociopathy and violent sexism and sing of it as a constructive "message" we all need to hear. Young black men brandishing spiky anti-authoritarian attitude is ambrosia to people accustomed to founding their sense of place in America upon hating whitey, since history has deprived them of something more individual and coherent to use as their spiritual bedrock.

The upshot of realizing that black ideology has been driven by a meme is that we must resist a misimpression that black people's oppositional statements and positions are always driven by current conditions. As often as not, black "victimology" is not a logical response to experience, but the manifestation of a cultural tic that a post-1960s Zeitgeist encourages us to misconceive as an expression of wisdom. The tic persists because black self-hatred persists—but self-hatred and sincere political activism are not the same thing.

It also persists to the extent that it does because of technological developments. Memes spread more easily today because of population density and improvements in transportation and communications. The last includes radio, television, the Internet, and, especially, portable music, such that one can be medicated daily in therapeutic alienation by listening to the edgy strophes of hip-hop getting dressed, on the way to work, cooking that evening, and in after-hours nightclubs.

The result of this is that society can plant a way of thinking in a people that engages only fitfully with reality or progress but lives on for decades because it soothes the soul. Let's have Ralph Ellison, who nailed what I mean better than I could myself, bring us to an end.

> Grounding our sense of identity in such primary and affect-charged symbols, we seek to avoid the mysteries and pathologies of the democratic process. But that process was designed to overcome the dominance of tradition by promoting an open society in which the individual could achieve his potential unhindered by his ties to the past.
>
> However, in undertaking such transformations he opts for that psychic uncertainty which is a condition of his achieving his potential, a state he yearns to avoid. So despite any self-assurance he might achieve in dealing with his familiars, he is nevertheless (and by the nature of his indefinite relationship to the fluid social hierarchy) a lonely individual who must find his own way within a crowd of other lonely individuals.
>
> Here the security offered by his familiar symbols of identity is equivocal. And an overdependence on them as points of orientation leads him to become bemused, gazing backward at a swiftly receding—if not quasi-mythical—past, while stumbling headlong into a predescribed but unknown future.

Too many of us have been living out for way too long what Ellison described. What ought to be a proud ethnic identity is instead a twelve-step program. We can do better than this.

However, some black Americans, learned and influential, would object that my delineation of a then and a now in black America is evidence that I am one misled brother, and that the alienation I refer to is indeed based on ongoing injury in the here and now. I think particularly of two groups. One argues that even affluent blacks continue to suffer racist insult on a near-daily basis; they refer mainly to anecdotes, but I believe these to be worthy of address. The second group is the social science orthodoxy, who see their statistical surveys as proving that segregation and bigotry continue to determine the black experience.

A responsible address of race in America, whatever its perspectives, cannot proceed as if these people's arguments do not exist and have not swayed countless concerned people. We must hear these people out, and in the next two chapters we will.

CHAPTER SIX

What About Black Middle-Class Rage?

I have argued that today, a cultural tic has settled into the black community, of claiming grievance related to racism that far bypasses current reality. Specifically, I argue that this tic is explicable only as the product of a psychological filter, given the obvious present-day reality.

But many would contest the very claim that we live in a new reality, such that for them my whole argumentation falls to pieces right there. These are the people who claim that even though legalized discrimination is in the past, racism continues to dominate the American landscape in less formalized ways. Nor, they argue, is this limited to encounters between whites and lower-class blacks, such that we might, as some do, argue that discrimination is now based largely on class. These people claim that even for middle-class and affluent blacks, life remains an ongoing obstacle course of racist encounters—in department stores, in school settings, on the street, in passing conversations, and, as most discussed, with the police.

To people like this, all calls for blacks to stop dwelling in the past are out of court, since the past is not yet past at all. Naturally, they see no value in the black conservative literature: "How can he say blacks can do whatever they want to," they ask, "when I hear car doors locking as I walk down the street on my way from class?" "He can talk all he wants to about how times have changed," they say, "but once when I was working at a store a white woman who thought I had shortchanged her called me a nigger!"

Few books and articles stepping away from the leftist orthodoxy on race issues acknowledge people of this frame of mind to any serious extent. Yet, there are quite a few blacks who think this way—and, most important, I think that my argument stands up despite their perspective. This is partly because these people can exaggerate. But they could not all be lying. The more useful point is that the things they complain about do not belie that, still, times have changed deeply, including for them. At the end of the day, the way they choose—or have been led—to process remnants of racist bias is a mark of the meme I discuss in this book.

BLOWS TO THE SOUL

The most prominent exposition of this school of thought has been Ellis Cose's *The Rage of a Privileged Class*, widely discussed when it was published and still in print almost fifteen years after its debut. For Cose, middle-class blacks endure "repeated blows to the soul," such that "hurtful and seemingly trivial encounters of daily existence are in the end most of what life is."

Cose refers not to the statistical differences between whites and middle-class blacks such as higher degrees of "residential segregation," slightly lesser acceptance rates for car loans, or discrepancies in health care. These things would be shaky cases for an existential "rage" in any case, given that they tend to be subject to many interpretations beyond the ones that pop up briefly on newspaper front pages. Even Cose allows that "in the real world such statistics are almost irrelevant, for rage does not flow from dry numerical analyses of discrimination or from professional prospects projected on a statistician's screen."

Cose is concerned with immediate, everyday occurrences. The black law firm associates who watch lesser-qualified whites making partner. The high-powered black corporate lawyer who goes to work early one morning and gets off of the elevator with a young white associate who doesn't know him, and starts to key himself into his office only to have the white man block him not once but twice asking, "May I help you?"—assuming that this black man must be some kind of criminal. The woman who arms herself with a Bally bag in high-end stores to keep clerks from assuming she can't afford the merchandise or doesn't belong there. Black people trailed in stores by clerks assuming they may be shoplifters. The black professor asked by a white student what qualifies her to be teaching the class. The *New York Times* bureau chief running for a rental car shuttle bus at the airport, suddenly flanked by DEA officers who join her on the bus and interrogate her in front of the passengers, trying to find out if she is carrying drugs.

Cose paints his picture mainly from interviews with people, most of whom are acquaintances. He has occasionally been criticized for building the case on mere "anecdotes," but often, people who level this charge at a book are indulging in a cheap trick. It is true that black people Cose is close to and comfortable with are perhaps especially likely to harbor the alienated psyche that he does. One cannot help thinking that generally, black people who did not vibrate to this sensibility would not be ones that Cose would, as a matter of course, be likely to hang out with. Presumably, when he was preparing to write the book, Cose put out feelers to at least some black people who ended up not having much to offer a book about black middle-class "rage," and as such, they did not make it into the book. Perhaps their absence renders Cose's sample less than ideally representative.

But then, he could not get his point across resonantly without giving us real people talking. Unless proposing the occasional uniquely gripping tinderbox of a thesis, books that essentially set statistics in prose are rarely read in any real way beyond the Ivory Tower and think tanks (even by journalists), and thus usually have no impact on public discussion. Besides, Cose makes ample reference to surveys in which black people of similar occupations and station say that they have experienced discrimination in the workplace, even if it has not kept them from advancing.

A VOICE FROM THE GALLERY?

Although I try to argue on the basis of evidence from as many corners as I can find, I cannot even begin to claim that my writing on race is not founded, at heart, upon my personal experience. But because of this, I find Cose's book, and other sources painting a similar picture of middle-class black experience, uniquely challenging to grapple with. This includes Ishmael Reed's views on race, founded upon a basic perception that even today, and even for middle-class blacks, every day is "Another Day at the Front," as he has titled one of his books. Deborah Mathis's *Yet a Stranger* and Lena Williams's *It's the Little Things* are similar examples, in which it is assumed that all middle-class blacks live lives in which snubs, glares, and open condescension from whites are routine. For Reed and Mathis, in particular, their assumption that all successful blacks experience incessant racist abuse naturally leads them to sharply condemn black writers who stray from the victim line—to them, this victimhood is indisputable, and thus the accusations of "sell out," and the like.

The Life I Lead

The problem for me is that in my four decades as a middle-class black man in America, I simply have not experienced the endless procession of racist slights and barriers that Cose describes. The life I have led as a middle-class black person makes the "rage" of Cose's interviewees look, frankly, foreign and peculiar to me.

For example, Cose documents that after the Los Angeles riots in 1992, 78 percent of blacks in a poll agreed that "blacks cannot get justice in this country," and I well remember that line resonating among even comfortable, assimilated middle-class blacks at that time. I was aware of racial profiling—I grew up in Philadelphia where the naked racism of the police force under Mayor Frank Rizzo in the seventies was something even a kid couldn't miss hearing about regularly. I was even aware that if circumstances were just so, it was possible that I myself could have a nasty run-in with the police influenced by my color. Yet, I considered this an abstract and unlikely possibility, hardly tincturing my daily existence with a sense of imminent threat the way lynching did for all black men in the old South. And I presume that even Cose would not see this as the naïvete of a pampered soul, since he notes that "as awful as Rodney King's treatment may have been, most middle-class blacks know that they are not very likely to find themselves on the wrong side of a policeman's baton."

The nut was that I just couldn't see the King video as a symbol of my personal experience with white America, as "a glaring reminder that being black in America means that you operate under a different set of rules," as one of Cose's interviewees has it. In fact, the black response to the Los Angeles riots was the first of several race episodes in the nineties that frustrated me to the point that I was eventually moved to step outside of my linguist career to write on race.

Since then, one of the trickiest aspects of my second career is that I must work constructively with the fact that legions of middle-class blacks like me harbor a bone-deep sense of constant abuse from whites that I, to the best of my knowledge, have not experienced. Some have told me that this is because I am "clean-cut" but that is irrelevant; the idea is that these things happen to reserved, cultured blacks in expensive suits and cars, not just baggy-pants teens.

Nevertheless, here is my life.

I have no problems with the police. I have never been pulled aside for a drug search or even touched by an officer. Actually, I have found it pretty easy to talk my way out of several moving violations, and the only time a police officer has stopped me for anything besides those was a black officer in Oakland who turned out to want to tell me how much he liked *Losing the Race*!

Only once do I recall ever being tailed in a store, and since so many blacks complain about this tailing, I have always watched for it. And my experience was that when I was about sixteen, a black friend and I dropped into a tiny Slavic bookstore in Philadelphia because I, as a language freak, was just intrigued by the place. The woman behind the register, a probably Polish-born middle-aged woman, was obviously terrified, and the store was so tiny that her displeasure was overwhelmingly present to us, to the point that we left the store. But that was not quite what most blacks complain of. After all, it was likely extremely rare that young black men entered that store, and what's more, it was just on the edge of a sketchy black neighborhood, such that we might suppose that the woman assumed that since aging books in Polish are rarely of interest to young black men (or most Americans), we might have been in there to rob her. I know I am supposed to simply decry her as "stereotyping" but I cannot. She was just human, reacting to a highly unexpected presence in a store located in a bad neighborhood, and as a foreigner from a country where blacks are virtually nonexistent, unlikely to be attuned to the factors of dress and demeanor distinguishing class among blacks.

Nor have I ever gotten the sense that a clerk considered me too poor to afford higher-end items—rather, I have the typical mainstream experience of having to ward clerks off from trying to get me to buy more expensive merchandise to up their commissions—that is, the same experience whites have. And despite my occasional television appearances, I have nothing approaching the public recognizability that would make such clerks think of me as a celebrity, and besides, I didn't have such experiences even long before I had ever been on television. No cashier has ever, to my recollection, asked me for an extra form of ID.

Not once has any white person questioned me to my face as to my credentials for engaging in an activity or profession. The barriers to promotion that many blacks report in corporate life and law firms have been unknown to me in academia. There, black faces are so "welcome" that on the contrary, being black often makes it easier rather than harder to get tenure. Possibly racist bias makes it harder to advance in some other fields, but definitely in linguistics during my experiences, being black has been nothing less than an advantage in employment and promotion. No whites in my earshot have said anything suggesting that they were "impressed" that I did something despite being black, despite Cose's interviewees regularly reporting such experiences. Indeed, I have occasionally felt that when I did a talk that was merely bread-and-butter, I got praise a little beyond what I deserved, and that this was definitely based in a quiet sense that it was great that I had been up there with my black face, showing that linguistics is an equal-opportunity realm. But I cannot see this as damning my existence or worthy of "rage," especially since I have never experienced this to a degree that could be considered outright condescension.

A Harvard Law School grad whom Cose interviews when she has advanced to a teaching position "feels ambushed whenever she hears a cutting racial remark," but my personal experience in almost two decades of life in academia gives me, in all sincerity, no idea what she is referring to. No one in academia has ever said anything like, "There goes that black stuff again" or "It's great to see a black person do a good job like you're doing" when I could hear it. I have recounted elsewhere that the one person who ever called me "nigger" was a drunken laborer reduced to mumbling it as I went back into my apartment after I had bested him in an argument, which I could only see as a desperate belch from a bested opponent whose life no one would envy and that mine had already soundly surpassed. I suppose I might also recall a little guy at a day camp when I was about nine who called me "blackey" once or twice, but in clumsy jest, and I am afraid that this experience in 1974 did not arouse in me any "rage," especially not of a sort that I would still harbor thirty years later.

I also feel it necessary to note that I consider my life's experience a conclusive case against the idea that to be black and middle class is to live with white abuse as an everyday threat. The nature of the issue is such that there is no survey necessary: I'm black, have been for a very long time, am not nearly light-skinned enough to look anything but, and these things simply do not happen to me. I am even told that I tend to look rather "serious" when walking down the street (I tend to be outlining and writing paragraphs in my head)—my default demeanor is not a smiley, gentle-looking one. Again, it doesn't matter that I don't look or talk "street" because the Cose idea is that the nastiness falls upon blacks of all "profiles." My life has taken place in Philadelphia, New York, Oakland, and San Francisco, all fertile breeding grounds for the Cose perspective. I also lived for years in Palo Alto, as a graduate student at Stanford, when I made extra money playing cocktail piano in wealthy white homes in surrounding towns. I therefore was often driving around those enclaves in a beat-up old car late at night—but was never once stopped as a suspicious figure (and officers could not have seen how "clean-cut" I was just seeing me through the car window, nor could they hear my tragically "proper" speaking voice). Also, I am a night owl and no stranger to bars; my favorite one in New York is in an area where late at night, "streety" young blacks congregate selling drugs and making a lot of noise. On countless nights I have made my way home from that bar in the wee hours, but never once have been bothered by an officer. If Ellis Cose had for some reason sought me out to fill out the anecdotes in his book, I would have come up with nothing to support the idea that white people bedevil me constantly with racist actions. This means something.

I Am Not Alone

And I might also add that my life lends me my own "anecdotal" collection of "interviewees" who would concur with me. I know about eight black Americans—some friends, others long-term acquaintances—who readily agree with me that the middle-class black life of constant racist abuse that Cose and his friends depict is not theirs. No, they are not lower-class or blue-collar people; predictably, I tend to be closest to people with histories and lifestyles similar to my own. Nor, however, are any of them scions of the black elite, nor are most of them light-skinned, nor do all of them even have college degrees or significant bank accounts. But then, again, these things technically shouldn't even matter, as we are told that this abuse is aimed at any black person between about ten and sixty, regardless of demeanor, class, or accomplishment. And I can honestly attest that "whitey" just does not torment these people, or me, in the ways that Cose describes. *The Rage of a Privileged Class* got around quite a bit among reading blacks in the mid-nineties. I have no statistics to offer, but I have lost count of how many times I have asked middle-class black people, "Is what that book describes your experience?" and had them answer, "Well, no." Everybody has a story or two—or three. But "most of what life is"?

However, as noted, it's not that my friends and I have not experienced racism. It's there indeed. For example, I know my racism when I see it and am not possessed of a fragile sort of pride that makes me reluctant to admit when racism has been imposed upon me (i.e., I have no quiet sense that racism is only something that should happen to, you know, *those* kinds of black people).

When I got my BA at Rutgers in the early eighties, a great many of the white students were products of lower-middle-class New Jersey families, their parents being products of pre–Civil Rights Act America. Even at that time, overt expressions of racism were taboo on campus, but it was impossible not to suspect that a lot of those kids did not have the most savory feelings about "the blacks." I recall a late-night debate with a white guy from Paterson, New Jersey, hardly a hotbed of racial progressiveness, in which it became clear that he considered blacks' overrepresentation in the ghetto to be due to their mental and even biological inferiority. I talked him into a logical corner in which he had to quietly but testily admit this in a word or two, and I just let the exchange stop there.

Or, I will never forget being at a deathlessly WASP wedding at an Oyster Bay country club, when the otherwise all-white male entourage and I retired to the bar. One of the club's members, not in the wedding, was a guy intoxicated like a cartoon character, staggering around approaching strangers and making lame, back-slapping jokes. As I started following the other men into the bar, he grabbed me and said, "I gotta let ya know— there're a lotta white women in there . . . HA, HA, HA, HA!!!!" But what did that mean? Clearly the fact that a nigger was going in there—and one better poised to attract said white women than he was—rattled him a bit. Ha, ha indeed—a little *Birth of a Nation* in 1995.

Or on women, back to Rutgers—a white woman I had become friends with told her white female roommate that she was enjoying hanging out with me, and the roommate interpreted her (mistakenly) as being interested in me romantically. My friend told me that the roommate said, "How could you? I could never be with a black guy." That was 1984, and the vignette resonates with Cose's depiction of a smiling white world roiling with subtle racist rot underneath, in that the roommate was always quite friendly toward me. She never knew that I was aware of what she had said (and I had better things to do with my time than confront her about it). The fact was that if I had by chance been inclined to try to date dear June (yes, that really was her name in all of its Cleaver-esque resonance), I would have run up against a "No Coloreds" sign. Although, of course, she wouldn't have said so—leaving me unsure as to whether the problem was with me or something larger.

Another one was when I encountered something blacks often describe: an assumption that there is a potential romantic attraction between all black men and all black women, as if we do not have the same idiosyncratic issues of personal tastes and preferences that other people do. Some years back, Condoleezza Rice gave an address to the Manhattan Institute think tank. One attendee hinted to me in all seriousness that he hoped that I would have the occasion to talk to Ms. Rice while she was visiting since *she and I would make a good couple*. I see: the National Security Advisor to the President of the United States, a richly accomplished figure on the world stage, slips her phone number to a slightly prominent linguist and writer a decade-plus younger than she whom she has likely never heard of until that night. The Elephant Man I am not, but I am also no Denzel, and so one would not expect me to pull this off by brunt of sheer hottitude. And make Rice and me white equivalents of our respective selves and no one would ever even begin to imagine such a thing: Imagine, say, an unmarried Diane Sawyer and even a writer light-years more prominent than me such as Jonathan Franzen. The idea was based on a sense that for Rice and me, blackness alone is so overwhelmingly definitive that a romantic attachment would be immediately imaginable even between people so vastly different in terms of place in the world, past experience, and even age. That is, there is a sense here that blacks are a different species: *Homo niger*, perhaps.

So, yes, things happen, and those are far from the only cases I could recount. But when a retired black psychologist intones to interviewers that "We live lives of quiet desperation generated by a litany of *daily* large and small events that whether or not by design, remind us of our 'place' in American society," I'm sorry, but I just don't feel it. For me, these things have been occasional episodes, extraordinary happenings, rather like, say, getting caught in a brief hailstorm—something a little odd and a little annoying that happens every once in a while. Hail does not set the tone of a lifetime.

REALITY CHECK

In that light, while I cannot even venture that the people Cose interviews are lying, I must admit that I can't help thinking that it is possible that they are misinterpreting at least some of their experiences. Too often in my own life I have seen blacks level charges like these in situations where the whites in question have a thoroughly convincing alternate interpretation, and in Cose's book, we do not hear from the whites. Cose can't help that—we can't expect him to have travelled the country smoking out every participant in every story he was told. But the problem remains.

The Rashomon Factor

Even Cose and his interviewees admit that such misinterpretations are possible. They would attribute it to rawness left behind by the indisputable instances, while I suspect that our cultural meme also plays a significant part, but no matter. The fact is that sometimes, the clerk "trailing" one in a store is trying to nudge his way in to make suggestions and make a sale. This has been done to me (sometimes successfully) by black and Latino salesmen at stores like Circuit City and Good Guys, for example, who were also doing it to everyone else in the store because it was their job (the computer I am typing on was shown to me by an African who "trailed" me—black-on-black racism, I suppose). If I went to a Circuit City in a white suburb early in the morning when I was the only customer, and white salesman, Todd, shadowed me from speaker to speaker, I could easily decide to righteously claim that I was being trailed.

In a book covering similar ground to Cose's, *Living With Racism: The Black Middle-Class Experience*, Joe Feagin and Melvin Sikes quote a black college dean who says,

> When you're in a restaurant and . . . you notice that blacks get seated near the kitchen. You notice that if it's a hotel, your room is near the elevator, or your room is always way down in a corner somewhere. You find that you are getting the undesirable rooms. And you come there early in the day and you don't see very many cars on the lot and they'll tell you this is all we've got. Or you get the room that's got a bad television set. You know that you're being discriminated against.

I'm sorry, but no—this particular example is one of paranoia. I dare anyone to do a study—formal or informal—and find even a tendency in restaurants in any city that the people seated near the kitchen are mostly black. Restaurants need to fill all of their seats, and some of them are closer to the kitchen than others. All people sometimes get put there as the good seats get taken up, and that includes black people. White readers will surely recall getting the short end of the stick in countless hotels—it's part of what most Americans call the hell of travelling, so often satirized in movies, on television, and in humor columns nationwide. Even early in the day, both businesspeople and travellers tend to be away from the hotel engaging in whatever activity they came to the town to engage in. Get up early in a hotel and the buffet is usually bustling by seven a.m. with people on their way to their workdays outside the hotel. Stay in a hotel whose lobby and bar were full of people the night before and notice at eleven a.m. the next morning that the parking lot has about seven cars in it, but that by about six p.m., you can barely find a space and the lobby and bar are full of many of the same people from the night before.

Certainly we hear of occasional cases where white idiots at, say, Denny's turn out to be giving black patrons substandard treatment. These people must be punished. But in 2006, these are *exceptional* cases, which is why they attract so much attention. Black people in 2006 do not have to confer with one another as to whether a place they want to go "serves blacks"—one encounters a troglodyte Denny's outlet as a surprise. Any black person who compares these once-off holdouts with what was normal life for blacks until the mid-sixties is disrespecting their ancestors.

Then there are cases where it's tough to call, but that are extremely hard to classify as what I have since 1993 informally in my head called "an Ellis Cose story."

For example, when I was looking for an apartment in New York, I settled on a very particular spread of blocks in a neighborhood that appealed to me because the layout reminded me of the Philadelphia neighborhood in which I grew up. In New York, most apartments are only viewable through broker agencies, so I signed up with one and made my desires clear. Yet, on the first day, the broker agent kept showing me apartments in areas of the neighborhood a couple avenues over or a few blocks above what I had specified. The neighborhood is one where these distances often make the difference between treesy serenity and noisy semi-shabbiness.

After that first day, however, I explicitly told him that whatever the charms of these "vibrant" blocks, I was interested in exactly the spread I had said, and that it was pointless for us to "look at" apartments anywhere else because I would have no interest in living in them. Whereupon he promptly showed me an apartment where I desired, and as it happened, the very first one he brought me to was the keeper.

I know that according to a certain script, I am supposed to recall this as my experience of "steering," where a white agent was trying to nudge me into living on blocks where, perhaps, there were more of "my own kind." But I'm not sure—there were too many factors at work.

For one, the chance that the white people on the block I took an apartment on are quietly opposed to a black "presence" are vanishingly slight, given that the neighborhood is populated by just the kinds of whites who are least likely to harbor feelings of this kind—highly educated Democrats, many even married to brown people. In fact, there are quite a few "coloreds" on my block and elsewhere in my cherished spread. These are the kinds of whites who Sheryll Cashin in *The Failures of Integration* admits are exceptions to the resistance that most whites have to sharing their neighborhoods with more than a few black people.

Besides, suppose it was just that at that time, the agent happened to have more apartments to show in the other sections and the vacancies had been sitting for awhile, and for the mundane reason of wanting to cap a sale on a block that was less than easy to sell, he was trying to see if

I would fall in love with a place not far from what I thought I wanted. After all, clients take apartments they didn't expect to all the time—many readers will have had such experiences; I know I have in the past. Not to mention that all of this took place over only two days: Maybe on the next day he would have shown me places exactly where I wanted on his own accord.

Or just maybe he *was* sitting on scads of vacancies in my spread. But as it happens, I will never know because the first place he showed me there when I clarified things ended up meeting all of my specifications. If this is "racism," as far as I'm concerned, bring on more. I have better things to do with my time on this earth than sit around *wondering whether* someone has discriminated against me and nurturing *possible hurt* over it. There are indeed real cases of steering, such as ones where whites are readily shown apartments one day that blacks are not on the next day (as I covered in Chapter Three). But it is also possible—as, again, even Cose admits—that at least some of the stories Cose has elicited were not as cut-and-dried in reality as they sound in the telling. One cannot help getting this sense from more than a few of the stories in Cose's book.

Books Get Old Fast

There is one more thing that I suspect gives more reason for hope than these "Ellis Cose stories" imply. A fair amount of time has passed since Cose's book was published in 1993, based largely on recollections of the eighties and even seventies. I suspect that the terrain has—thankfully—changed at least somewhat since then.

Cose describes black Harvard product Mark Whitaker interning for *Newsweek* in the late 1970s aiming to become the editor of the magazine, saying that he was not going to let race hold him back. Cose frames this as poignant naïveté by a young black man unaware of what he was going to run up against, rejoining him in the late eighties when he is just assistant managing editor, now laughing at his "ignorance and arrogance" in supposing that a black man could ever become editor of *Newsweek*. But five years after Cose's book was published, Whitaker indeed became *Newsweek*'s editor in chief.

Cose recounts a successful black person noticing that on trains, they are always among the last people whites sit next to as the car fills up. I had the same experience for years riding the commuter train between Philadelphia and New Jersey in the late seventies and early eighties. But today, it no longer happens to me on trains or planes. Now and then I find that I am, by chance, one of the *first* people a white person sits next to, and I look now pretty much like how I looked in 1980. I happen to be one of those people who is often told by old acquaintances that I look just like I looked twenty years ago, and although it is not precisely true, I suspect that the good old "black don't crack" phenomenon plays some role here. If anything I looked *less* "threatening" as a teen, since I wore glasses, giving me an especially nerdy appearance. Granted, even today many whites might be warier of sitting next to a young black man with a certain "'hood" appearance. But however one feels about that, it's a different issue—Cose and his friends are aggrieved about what happens to middle-class black people.

Cose mentions, as blacks fifteen years ago routinely did and many still do now, that black men have a hard time getting cabs in New York, again, regardless of class or appearance. I can't speak for the eighties and nineties, but at this writing I have lived in New York for three years and take cabs often. And I can honestly say that not a single time have I been bypassed by a cab, even though I have been highly attuned to the possibility, given how much one hears about it. When I put my hand in the air, a cab stops in front of me on a dime, just like for everyone else, day or night, wherever I am going. Sometimes I find the cabs almost overzealous, with two competing for my patronage or one stopping for me just because I stepped off of the curb on my way across the street—that is, the same experiences white New Yorkers have. I assume that the problem was real in years past. But since the practice was publicized, decried, and made fineable some years ago, it would appear that one more remnant of old-fashioned racism has fallen down. If every month or so I was standing in the rain watching empty cabs pass me by to scoot to a stop to pick up a white woman down on the next block, I might well start feeling some "rage"—but in three whole years it hasn't happened to me. That is quite long enough to confirm that the problem no longer exists.

REALITY BITES

Yet, while there are grounds for tempering Cose's portrait, we must accept that middle-class black people do experience enough slights of this kind to motivate books like Cose's, as well as other books and articles. Clearly these people are not making all of these things up out of thin air.

Promotion Time

There are, in fact, types of "Ellis Cose story" whose corners cannot be rounded off. One is the glass ceiling that a great many blacks experience in the corporate world.

My own observations, as well as Cose's considered opinion, suggest that the issue here is less racist bias than a "birds of a feather" phenomenon. There is very vexing tension here between assimilation and identity preservation. The "black-identified" sales representative or lawyer may cross every *t* and dot every *i* in terms of their formal responsibilities—and yet, if they have a sense that only with blacks do they feel truly "comfortable," do not really share in the office jokes, and only hang out after work occasionally, then when it comes time for promotions, they may be at a disadvantage for the simple reason that the white partners "got in" socially more than they did—with this often even figuring in how effective a person might be in bringing business in.

Few can criticize this person for nurturing a racial identity, but the sad truth is that there is a downside of this because since humanity began, popularity has played as large a part in getting ahead as ability. Certainly this is not always the reason blacks fail to rise but so high up career ladders, but it is a very common problem. Cose's conclusion that the resulting discrepancies justify affirmative action in the business world is one I can barely argue with, and efforts to give young blacks advice about making their way in the corporate world and finding mentors are important. More to the point, while "racism" is not the culprit here, we can see how a middle-class black person who has done everything right and watches white people they are just as qualified as, or even more so, get promoted over them will start getting nagged by a sense that, as they say, race matters.

Blacks and the Police

Then there is, of course, the po-lice. Far beyond the interactional slights that the Cose school call attention to, blacks' main reference point for the idea that racism continues to define life as a black American is negative, violent, and even deadly encounters with police officers. Police profiling is a genuine and serious problem, in terms of both reality and perception.

To be sure, statistical study has at times refuted specific allegations of bias against blacks in stops and arrests, such as one that showed that traffic stops were close to equal between blacks and whites in Oakland whether it was light or dark outside, darkness being crucial in that police cannot see the color of the driver. Then there are times when the "street" version of cases where the police kill a black man diverges significantly from a still tragic but race-neutral reality, as was true of the Amadou Diallo case. Quite a few black police officers are involved in activities deemed "profiling" and are as baffled and irritated at the charge as white ones.

But still, even though there are increasing rapprochements between police forces and poor black communities lately, over the decades there have been far too many clear revelations of racist officers and racist squads to say that poor blacks have had no grounds for fearing the police.

However, our topic is not poor black men being frisked for drugs, but trench-coated, middle-class black people, who recount as well ugly encounters with police officers, as well as the public's assumption that they are criminals, where we cannot assume that their color had nothing to do with what happened.

Take what a middle-class black university student of modest build told a sociologist about his walks to his apartment in a white neighborhood.

> I've seen white couples and individuals dart in front of cars to not be on the same side of the street. Just the other day, I was walking down the street, and this white female with a child, I saw her pass a young white male about 20 yards ahead. When she saw me, she quickly dragged the child and herself across the busy street. What is so funny is that this area has had an unknown white rapist in the area for about four years . . . white men tighten their grip around their women. I've seen people turn around and seem like they're going to take blows from me. The police constantly make circles around me as I walk home, you know, for blocks. I'll walk, and they'll turn a block. And they'll come around me just to make sure, to find where I'm going.

This man also mentions white men hurling beer cans and calling him names. The sociologist (Joe Feagin, author of the abovementioned *Living With Racism*) notes that "Everyday street travel for young black middle-class males does not mean one isolated incident every few years." Feagin is overgeneralizing; I might note that it has never meant anything like this for this one black middle-class male or many I have known. But accounts like this one are too common to be dismissed as fringe occurrences.

Let's look at another one, from a man less low-key than Feagin's interviewee. In 1999, Bryonn Bain, a black Harvard Law School student, was leaving a nightclub in New York at Ninety-sixth and Broadway when he was mistaken as the person committing a crime nearby, arrested, and held overnight in jail. Throughout he was treated with searing, dismissive contempt, including having one of those little metal Metropolitan Museum of Art clips taken from him with, "We can't have you slitting somebody's wrist in there!" He wrote a piece for his class on Critical Perspectives on the Law, and the professor of the class, Lani Guinier, encouraged him to submit a version of it to the *Village Voice*. The format of the *Voice* piece was what Bain titled a "Bill of Rights for Black Men." This Bill of Rights demands recitation if we are to understand the community sentiment that faces us.

Congress can make no law altering the established fact that a black man is a nigger.

The right of any white person to apprehend a nigger will not be infringed.

No nigger shall, at any time, fail to obey any public authority figures—even when beyond the jurisdiction of their authority.

The fact that a Black man is a nigger is sufficient probable cause for him to be searched and seized.

Any nigger accused of a crime is to be punished without any due process whatsoever.

In all prosecutions of niggers, their accuser shall enjoy the right of a speedy apprehension. While the accused nigger shall enjoy a dehumanizing and humiliating arrest.

Niggers must remain within the confines of their own neighborhoods. Those who do not are clearly looking for trouble.

Wherever niggers are causing trouble, arresting any nigger at the scene of the crime is just as good as arresting the one actually guilty of the crime in question.

Niggers will never be treated like full citizens in America—no matter how hard they work to improve their circumstances.

A nigger who has no arrest record just hasn't been caught yet.

We must dwell on this a bit longer. Bain was not received as a lone martyr, but as a fellow sufferer. Here are three reader responses from the avalanche of letters that the *Voice* received.

Bravo, Bryonn Bain. As a journalist in Miami, I know firsthand what you are talking about. A nigger is a nigger is a nigger to the police. You have no idea how many times I have to pull out my I.D. before people actually believe I am a reporter. And even then, they want to inspect the plastic card.

Adrienne Samuels
Education Reporter, *The Miami Herald*

I want to thank *The Village Voice* for having the courage to print the story "Walking While Black." Would that it were it could be mandatory reading for the Ward Connerlys of the world who think racism is passé.

Martha Estes
Downingtown, Pennsylvania

I am a Yale graduate who recently learned that several of my classmates were harassed by New York police after they were stopped in a BMW (which clearly had to be stolen, since the driver and the passengers were people of color). Like Bryonn Bain, I always felt that my prestigious background was some sort of shield—that going to private schools and Ivy League universities somehow made you immune to racism. Incidents like this are a wake-up call for me. The question is, what is the next step?

Mali Locke
Bronx

We can only imagine Bryonn Bain and the people who wrote these letters shaking their heads when anyone, especially a black person, says that the Civil Rights revolution is over, or that racism is no longer a problem.

THE CONUNDRUM

So—

A. Some "Ellis Cose stories" may be exaggerated to some degree, and stories like this probably decrease by the decade.
B. Yet, it is unequivocal that stories of this kind are a part of life as a middle-class black person here and now.

C. And yet again, the fact remains that the middle-class black life that many think of as default, where these snubs, slights, and even promotions denied and overly aggressive policemen are less very occasional episodes than the fabric of life, sounds like an alternate universe to me and many black people I know.

We must grapple with the fact that both B and C are correct.

Engaging B, we will not dismiss countless black people as liars.

Nor, however, will we, engaging C, dismiss me and my friends as functioning adults mysteriously blind to reality.

One interpretation might be that for some reason, these things happen weekly to some black people but only every three years for others. But I see no reason why this would be. I suspect that another interpretation works better.

My life brings me into contact with a pretty wide range of black people—wider than many might suppose given what I do for a living and my decidedly un-"street" demeanor. And from what I know, black people who think of these things as "most of what life is," as Cose puts it, are a type. One meets these people, but just as often does not—I would venture that these people are a minority, a certain kind of black person sometimes described as "really into that kind of stuff." Specifically, I think what we are seeing is a difference in how blacks perceive and deal with the inevitable imperfections of a racial landscape just a few decades past a time when blacks couldn't try on shoes at Sears—in Philadelphia.

Degree is the key issue here. Yes, there are the "slights." Yes, whites may still occasionally stand guard at a door or two here and there for reasons traceable to what color we are. But as often as not, we are free to enter through one of about ten other doors.

Yes, there are the encounters with the police. But the issue is how one processes it. It's unfair. It's frightening. It feels, I suspect from reports of it, a lot like being raped. But does Bryonn Bain really take from what happened to him that whites *in general* despise black people *in general*, and that his entire life is a battle against white supremacy? Is Bryonn Bain incapable of drawing distinctions, delineating the specific from the general? Is Bryonn Bain not, in a word, *human*, rather than, roughly, a cat who learns to fear all people because of one ugly run-in with one person as a kitten? How could Bryonn Bain square any sense of black strength or black pride with interpreting what happened to him as evidence that he should walk in petulant fear of White America forever based on one awful thing that happened to him when he had already lived long enough to be an adult? Does he really think that his Bill of Rights for Black Men has anything to do with the legions of whites he has grown up knowing, such as at Harvard Law School? Isn't that Bill of Rights something of a performance? Indicatively, he has been active on the Spoken Word poetry scene.

Could the reason he can assert black pride while allowing one hideous night long past his formative years to set his entire sense of life in America be that he has fashioned an identity that asserts itself through assailing white perfidy, rather than asserting itself through his own accomplishments and his comfort with himself?

THE THERAPEUTIC ALIENATION OF A PRIVILEGED CLASS

For blacks in today's America, to propose that whites' evaluation of us, if imperfect, determines the spiritual contours of our existence suggests that we have some kind of problem with ourselves. It would be one thing if we were still living in a segregated America where it was plain that most whites thought of us as exotics at best and cattle at worst. It would be another thing even if it were about 1975 and most of us had vivid recollections of that time and whites minted then were still in the primes of their lives. But in 2006? It has gotten to the point where the "rage" that Ellis Cose and like-minded blacks feel is based on an expectation of perfection that few human beings of any color ever experience. I can understand passing annoyance. But "rage"? "Blows to the soul"? "Most of what life is"? James Weldon Johnson again

> I will not allow one prejudiced person or one million or one hundred million to blight my life. I will not let prejudice or any of its attendant humiliations and injustices bear me down to spiritual defeat. My inner life is mine, and I will defend and maintain its integrity against the forces of hell.

To swell to this and still read *The Rage of a Privileged Class* and nod sagely is utterly incoherent—unless alienation is the guiding impulse, a therapeutic alienation serving to soothe a hurt that being tailed in a store now and then could not have created. The hurt was created long, long ago and lives on in people decades removed from the America that levelled it.

That is, any black middle-class person in our moment who feels that any of the things that Cose describes show that racism defines their lives hates themself deep down. I mean that precisely, and yes, that includes the encounters with the police. I am sincere in saying that I would write the exact same thing if by chance I had my head cracked in by the police for no reason one night—if it ever happens, just try me. The police might make a dent in my head, but never could they make the slightest dent in how I feel about my life as an individual human being in this imperfect but promising nation.

MIDDLE-CLASS BLACK PRIDE

I am aware that what I just wrote is the kind of thing that gets me labelled a "contrarian." But I do not write that out of some strange joy in getting people angry. I write it because to me it is self-evident truth, deeply and spontaneously felt since childhood. In this, I do not consider myself a person of any unusual "fortitude," nor am I making a simplistic call for people to "get real"—what does that even mean, after all? I am intrigued that all black people do not feel the same way I do—for the simple reason that I know so very many who do. As I have tried to show, it is not that I am unaware of racism or never experience it. The issue is how I process it as I go through life. Here are two examples.

When I became a college professor of linguistics, one of the classes I taught was a big survey class. I was, again, well aware of that certain stereotype hanging in the air. And I didn't like it. No one was lobbing it in my face—the PC atmosphere of a college campus makes such things almost unknown. But a black guy standing up there when the students are used to white professors? And teaching a strange, wonky subject like linguistics rather than black literature or art, or a racially relevant topic like sociology? I knew that deep down at least some of those kids, whether they were aware of it or not, harbored some quiet little doubts.

My response to this was not to spend the semester musing over it and sharing it with friends over drinks. My response was to do the most concrete thing I could to disabuse the students of any doubt that I was qualified to teach the class—that is, to *prove* it. So, my first lecture for that class, then and for the next several years, was a survey of the languages of the world, in which I deliberately threw onto the board sentences from as many languages as I could fit into the ninety minutes, pronouncing them, and making sure to always write them out from memory.

The idea was not to be intimidating; the lecture was full of anecdotes and fun factoids, and so forth. And crucially, I did not spend the rest of the semester overcompensating like this. The first lecture was the only "show-off" one. I needed only that first lecture for the crucial purpose of letting those kids know that I knew a lot more than they did, just like their other professors—i.e., that I was *normal*. It worked—comments I always got after that lecture let me know that it taught the students that they were in good hands. And I felt like I was Doing the Right Thing. I thoroughly enjoyed playing one small part in showing the students that black people are not incompetents, not by just saying that we aren't and daring them to say otherwise, but by showing them. Concretely.

Some would say that I shouldn't have had to prove myself to this degree. And technically they are right: In an ideal world, I would not have. But there is nothing sadder than the fact that in our times, some would see me having a craven need to show off for white folks, as if I were a member of the old-time black bourgeoisie having cotillions and learning Greek to "show the race at its best," scorning rough-hewn black migrants for messing up the tableau. Today, we know that nothing those old-time blacks did could dissuade most whites from thinking of them as tailored apes. But we live in different times, and that first lecture did not leave the students thinking of me as an idiot savant or as a cute mimic of white ways—it left them thinking of me as qualified to lead them through a semester.

To just pretend not to mind students' possibly wondering about my competence, or to carefully restrict my sense of competence to how black people feel about me, would be to elevate being alienated over trying to do something about what alienates me. And if I did that, I would be craven indeed, cowardly, that is—afraid to take my place as a self-directed individual instead of hiding behind the facile, petulant manifestos of a tribe.

Then there is the acute injury that Cose and others feel when a white person shows that they do not understand that racism still exists. But if racism bars you from nothing you want, and does not define your existence (back to James Weldon Johnson—can any of us say that we know anything like the racism he did, switching trains at the Mason-Dixon line?), then why is it so vital that whites be so consummately informed about the issue?

I do know the blind spot Cose finds in some whites. In the early nineties I was in a play at Stanford, and throughout the four-week rehearsal period had made two passing jokes referring to my being black. One was to the makeup person, when she asked what I was going to need by way of hair care before performances and I jokingly said something about my hair not needing to be "done" before each performance as opposed to, especially, the white women's hair. The other one was when a woman in the cast I had become friends with (Chicana, for the record) said she was feeling under the weather and I said, "Sounds like you need some tea . . . something warm and brown—like me! [ha ha]" (Yes, she was hot.)

But generally, I did not represent myself as a "racial" person in the production; rather, I was known, if anything, as something more specific and race-neutral, the resident show music encyclopedia. But I had indeed made those passing comments, and one day as the large cast was on its way back to the dressing rooms, amid the general clamor I uttered a third one to somebody (I forget what it was, but something as inconsequential as the other two). One white woman, about twenty and from the California suburbs, who had by chance been present when I had tossed off the first two remarks, snapped, "You're really into that stuff, aren't you?" and went on about her business.

Clearly, to her, black people needed to just knock off the race stuff, and to her, my bringing up race even in jest was evidence of something that I needed to just let go. As far as she was concerned, it wasn't 1962 and so "get over it." She had probably been quietly wearied of the diversity workshops that Stanford put freshmen through, as well as the aggrieved discussions about "racism" on the campus in the wake of the building takeover I described in Chapter Six. She was also a thoroughly "white" lady, by no means the type of white undergraduate who finds herself vibrating in tune with the black "thang" during her college years, and certainly knowing nothing of the work of people like Ellis Cose and Ishmael Reed. She knew what she knew; Stanford's attempt to nuance her sociopolitical judgments had failed. She was not even, really, very nice in general.

And so—first of all, why should I have cared how she felt about my sense of humor or anything else? And as to the idea that I was to view her as a stand-in for white America, I do not need white America to love or "understand" me. Most whites probably do not and never will "get it" to the extent that we might prefer. But to me it's more important that they "get it" so much more than they did forty years ago, especially since at this point they "get it" enough that, to the extent that anything is barring black people from making the best of themselves, it is no longer that white people think they are monkeys and leave them no door to enter.

I assume that we black Americans like ourselves enough for this little girl—and what she represents—to be irrelevant to our psychological well-being. That is—I have never been able to understand how I could on the one hand truly subscribe to the notion of black strength, but then at the same time hear this woman's little comment and run crying to Stanford's diversity coordinator about how white people just don't "see it," wondering when, oh when, that great day will come—but actually having less interest in this as a question than as a performative statement of grievance. When pricked, I bleed indeed—but only when slings and arrows assail me in ways much more trenchant than transparently uninformed and backward static from people like that girl. If I know she is behind the curve, whence my sense of "injury"?

In this, I present no "paradox." There is nothing "deep" here. "She hurt me" is a great way of parsing oneself as besieged by "racism." The emotional kick is clear. But after the smoke clears, the fact remains that "She hurt me" is logically incommensurate with "I am strong." And yet, few blacks would agree with a white person who told them that they are not strong. The only way to wrest sense out of this is to understand that for blacks who shout to the heavens after little episodes like that—or even years later recount to interviewers like Ellis Cose how deeply the remark "injured" them—being alienated is itself the driving impulse. Being strong in the true sense is considered—and here is the tragedy of our times—beside the point.

Therefore, my verdict on the rage of the black middle class is that it is a product of the meme of therapeutic alienation. This is not because the complaints have no basis in reality, but because under ordinary conditions, these episodes would not occasion anything like lasting, life-defining "rage" in people without a deep-set psychological wound. When Gerald Reynolds was appointed head of the United States Commission on Civil Rights in 2004, replacing hard-leftist Mary Frances Berry, the *New York Times* featured him as a "conservative" figure, quoting the following:

> I just assume somewhere in my life some knucklehead has looked at me and my brown self and said that they have given me less or denied me an opportunity. But the bottom line is, and my wife will attest to this, I am so insensitive that I probably didn't notice it. This is about how I feel; *it's not that these things aren't around, but that they are so minor that they cannot color one's sense of existence.*

The italics are mine.

If it were 1914, 1944, or even 1964, Reynolds would be so blind to reality as to be clinically insane. But in 2004, Reynolds's attitude was not conservative, but common sense.

It must be clear that my point is not a bromidic call for black people to "buck up" against what Cose describes, reaching deep into themselves to shield their senses of dignity instead of giving in. I am not preaching in this chapter: I am making an observation. That observation is that a great many black people have never even thought of Ellis Cose stories as something that required dipping into their special reserves of endurance, and that those who do are bringing something extra to the table. To wit, the statement, "We live lives of quiet desperation generated by a litany of *daily* large and small events that whether or not by design, remind us of our 'place' in American society," is not an accurate one of black America. It describes only black Americans of a certain psychological stripe.

Surely, Cose was saluted by countless black people after he published his book as "telling it like it is." Just as surely, there are blacks whose response to my denial that Cose described *the* black experience will be that it is theirs as well as that of most of the blacks they are friends with. But they are most likely to become close to black people of their frame of mind, and least likely to become close to black people less alienated from whites. The fact remains that they and their friends are just one segment of black America.

There were legions of blacks who read Cose's book or interviews with him who did not see their lives in what he presented, and they were less likely to contact him. They are the ones I tend to know, they include me, and we are not rare. I recall a party where the people I spoke most to were a group of blacks in their late twenties and early thirties, ordinary upwardly mobile New Yorkers. Eventually the discussion turned to little episodes we had had with whites who didn't "get it" in various ways, such as stereotyping. I had just finished the first draft of this chapter, and could not help tossing out what was, certainly, a leading question in terms of my argument here, but useful to making my point nevertheless. I asked, "Do you think of things like that as setting the tone of your life?" I should note that none of them knew of my work on race, so they were not filtering their responses according to the possibility that they would wind up in a book like this.

They all immediately shook their heads, and not in noble resistance, but with an air that indicated almost a perplexity that anyone would think of such things as "most of what life is." They were living active lives as young adults and having a great time at it. Throughout the evening they had amply shown in the jolly conversation that to them, the "Ellis Cose stories" were occasional static, too trivial to qualify as the substrate of their existences, and usually even funny. If anything, these episodes only left them thinking of the whites as the inferiors, and as such, were almost self-affirming rather than defeating.

This is, quite simply, a normal response to "Ellis Cose stories." It is normal because it is a norm: The black people at the party were not strangely proud or "strong," and I have met countless blacks like them— surely many blacks reading this are of this group as well. Perhaps blacks who think like Ellis Cose are another norm: But they are hardly the only ones, nor even, from what I have known of middle-class blacks for forty years, a majority.

BLACK MIDDLE-CLASS RAGE DISRESPECTS
OUR ANCESTORS

Cose is aggrieved by Senator Daniel Patrick Moynihan's judgment in an interview with him that the black middle class are "caught with the legacy of grievance which is inappropriate to their condition." But Moynihan had it perfectly right. It's not that there are no grievances to air, but the fever pitch that Cose harbors, depicts, and encourages is indeed disproportionate to what it would arouse in healthy people who truly like themselves.

"Learn your history," I am told. And I have, obsessively, for my whole life. I am well aware of what kind of real racism blacks not long before my birth in 1965 suffered.

The important issue is degree: In 1957, for $20 a year a black family could join the "Tourist Motor Club," which gave a list of hotels and restaurants where blacks were allowed, and a guarantee of $500 bond money if they were arrested for making the wrong choice. "What would you do if you were involved in a highway accident in a hostile town—far away from home. You could lose your life savings—you could be kept in jail without adequate reason. You could lose your entire vacation fighting unjust prejudice."

Because I am a fan of vintage pop entertainment, the examples especially ingrained in my mind are often ones that bygone black celebrities underwent. That is, black figures of national prominence were not immune to brutal indications that white America thought of them as mascots at best.

I think of Bert Williams, a highlight year after year in the teens in the *Ziegfeld Follies*. He was a national megastar, but when he made his first splash in the *Follies* in 1910, not some but most of the white cast urged Florenz Ziegfeld to fire him because they didn't want him around. The lore is that Ziegfeld insisted on keeping him because: "I can replace every one of you, except the man you want me to fire." So obviously Williams had a certain Element X, such that some two-bit black "coon" singer with less of that Element X would not have had the same clout.

Yet, even as a crossover megastar, Williams still wasn't a human being. Nine years later in the fall of 1919, Broadway actors, many newly affiliated with the Actor's Equity union, rebelled against brutal working conditions and walked out of shows up and down Broadway. The historiography of the strike resonates with tales of stars, chorus members, and stagehands marching while glittering productions closed down on a moment's notice. We moderns can barely help but assume that everyone knew what was up at any given time from day to day. After all, wasn't it on the Web—well, no, of course not, but maybe on the evening news on TV? But then again, no—not in 1919, but what about on radio? No again—radio only knit America together ten years later. In 1919, no one but the occasional techie sort knew from "radio transmission." In 1919, however "modern" people already felt, word got around in the thick of the moment only by telephone. You had to call someone up. Which means you had to care about them.

Which means that Bert Williams one night went to the theatre to black up in cork makeup and dress for that night's performance of the *Ziegfeld Follies of 1919*. And then he went out to find the stage dark. And only then did he realize that there would be no show that night, upon which he had to assume that the strike had happened. Although he was a top star on Broadway, *no one had seen fit to call him on the telephone and tell him!* Not one person! That is—despite performing with the whole cast night after night after night after night in a small space, not a single person in the whole cast *or crew* was moved to call him on the telephone and tell him that there would be no show that night! Not even the stage manager! "You see, I just didn't belong," he said. And he did not.

I don't think of Bert Williams as a figure in a stilted black-and-white photo. I think of him as a real, breathing human being, in color, even though we have no color pictures of him since he died in 1922 (actually, he was quite close to *my* color). I have not heard only those scratchy three-minute recordings of him squawking songs like his signature "Nobody" in primitive sound, seeming about as human as someone in a medieval painting (sorry, but I do not process those ancient 78s as vividly as Williams fans today claim to; the technology was too paltry). No, I have seen surviving *film* footage of him, silent, but still showing a moving, subtle, roiling, nuanced human being. That is where one gleans the true Bert Williams, who, clown though he was, would have been 1) shocked that Broadway would ever see serious black dramas and 2) appalled at the likes of "Diddy"—rich from a career of foisting blackface caricatures on America of the kind that Williams and his friends only did with their noses held because it was the only way to make a living in their era—playing the lead in a black Broadway drama, as he did in *Raisin in the Sun* in 2004. Williams is *real* to me. He had a way about him; he was a *person*. He was *alive*—right here on the island I happen to live on as I write this, eating food and leaving plates to be washed, scraping the pavement with his shoes, having sex, coaxing a stray eyelash from his eye now and then. And still, no one even deigned to call this human being that night in 1919. It sickens me. And it also leaves me acutely conscious of the fact that the like would never happen *to me* because despite the claims of certain folk, New York 1919 is indisputably hugely different from New York 2006.

I think of Ethel Waters, singing a song depicting a black woman bemoaning her husband being lynched in a 1933 Broadway musical, *As Thousands Cheer*. More than a few have urged that the song be cut as too "serious," in an era three decades before white liberal sensibilities had permeated the theatre to the extent with which we are now familiar. But the number stayed in and became a signature moment in musical theatre history. Yet, despite Waters making this "statement" in the show, and despite that she has even shared the stage with white stars in another skit, there is a flap before the premiere when some of those same white stars approach the producers and refuse to take curtain calls with Waters because she is a colored person.

They were rebuffed, but still. Those stars included Marilyn Miller, *Ziegfeld Follies* sensation whose place in the era was roughly that of a pirouetting Julia Roberts; Clifton Webb, an elegant dancer who went on to make an immortal mark as a soignée upper-crust figure in films like *Laura*, and Helen Broderick, a wry dame of a certain age who is a delight as Ginger Rogers's pal in *Top Hat*. And yet the way they treated Waters shows that they, typically of whites of their time, were out-and-out bigots who would view me as just above a chimpanzee. Seventy years ago Ethel Waters was in the same building as them every night, watching them gaily interacting with other whites while treating her with distant politeness, asking for her not to be allowed to take a bow and yet, after being denied their request, likely still greeting Waters formally backstage as if they had not had that grisly conversation with the producer, of which Waters knew.

And the show went on to run a *year*. Ethel Waters—a black woman who, as anyone who has read her autobiography knows, sensed herself very much as, in a sense that our modern race essentialists could readily relate to, a white-wary black "*waw*-man"—shared a theatre with those motherfuckers for a *year*.

I think of similar episodes more recent, running right up against when my own lifetime began. In 1964, Sammy Davis Jr. starred in the musical *Golden Boy*, in which he not only romanced but also kissed a white woman. During the Detroit tryout, at the kiss the balcony exploded in fury and the performance was shut down, the police shepherding the cast out of the theatre. That happened the year after the March on Washington.

In assessing black middle-class rage of the Cose variety, as always, we have to compare then with now. The "rage" in question would be completely understandable—inevitable, even—in the era of Williams, Waters, and Davis. Whites' treatment deeply imprinted the psychologies of all three: W. C. Fields described Williams as the saddest man he ever knew; Waters retreated into professional testiness and even paranoia; Davis spent his life openly wishing he were white and only went "hip" in the seventies, including making a loveless marriage with a black woman, when it became clear that he would lose his black following otherwise.

In comparison, nothing I have ever experienced in the eighties and nineties and beyond could remotely compare with what Williams or Waters or Davis experienced. I would choke to even venture that anything that has happened to me is evidence that "racism" defines my life, in view of the debt that I owe to people like Williams, Waters, Davis, and even my own ancestors. Frankly, I would sense proposing myself as a fellow traveller with them as a kind of self-indulgence. Encountering the occasional moron behind some counter makes our lives tragedies, when eighty years ago quiet middle-class blacks with the same values as their white equivalents were chased out of white neighborhoods with rocks and guns? When forty years ago in 1966, white demonstrators protested the integration of a housing development in Chicago, in which city two years later,

Sammy Davis Jr. came through in a touring production of *Golden Boy* to experience white audience members applauding at a point in the script where the white woman refused him?

Life is perfect for no one, white or other, and not even the slave ships, sharecropping, or lynchings in the past make this different for black Americans. All we have is the present. The past is always just that, the past. Even if it has implications for the present, anyone who tells you that what we are going to do in the present is settle scores from the past is blowing smoke. Never since 1965 has white America come to its knees for blacks, and even then the genuflection was only halfway and often laced with pragmatism (Lyndon Johnson knew that the Voting Rights Act would solidify a dependable black voting base for the Democrats, for instance). What we do in the present is forge ahead. Beyond the occasional commemorative exhibit or stone memorial, no humans have ever moved on by getting back. Getting back—say, at whitey—interests people with the narrow goal of medicating themselves, rather than thinking about moving ahead the people who need help. In the real world, we will "get back" to moving them and ourselves ahead, and the very fact that getting ahead in any realm is a challenge indicates that it always entails dealing with imperfections and inconveniences.

It is unclear to me that this is counterintuitive or even a "conservative" message. One could feel this way as someone who votes Democratic and celebrates Kwanzaa—there is ample "black strength" in this orientation. Which brings us back to the question why Ellis Cose and his comrades can find so many successful black Americans today who harbor the same sense of racial aggrievement as Bert Williams, Ethel Waters, and Sammy Davis Jr.

I believe that the reason for this lack of fit is not that Ellis Cose and his comrades live lives as brutally stamped by racist dismissal as their grandparents did, but that Ellis Cose and his comrades are brutally stamped by the same meme of therapeutic alienation that has had such a tragic impact on black America as a whole. They feel that their skin color delegitimizes them as human beings; they have a hole inside of them. They fill it by exaggerating how much racism affects them psychologically because it gives them a socially potent way of feeling like a player, like someone with a purpose. It's not that the episodes they recount are fictions, but that in them, these episodes foster a self-conception that suggests a block on the normal human tendency to place a barrier between one's self-regard and the occasional potshots that threaten it.

Recall, for instance, the *minimization* tendency that psychologists have identified that I mentioned in the previous chapter—under normal conditions people have a way of denying the extent to which they are affected by negative social forces, even if aware of their broader manifestations. The black middle-class rage phenomenon flouts that tendency, and the reason is that in terms of racial self-image, these people are psychologically damaged. Fundamental self-love means that passing injury leaves a dent, which one can hammer out with a bit of healthy denial— the minimization effect. But without self-love, passing injury leaves a wound. One way of healing it is to seek a sense of legitimacy in being the noble victim of the injury. That alone can be an identity in itself, a substitute sense of self. Since the sixties, adopting that identity has guaranteed a certain audience offering not only sympathy and attention, but also warm plaudits that one is keeping the flame of The Struggle alive. You matter. You have a place. And most likely, that place is where you stay. After a while, you know no other way to be. It has become your way of being human.

CONCLUSION

So we might hear that my previous chapters are invalidated because since racism continues to deeply scar black lives, it is incorrect to claim that a psychological meme has made black Americans found their self-conceptions upon alienation from whites to an extent that does not fit modern reality. I consider this chapter to refute that judgment.

Racism continues to affect black lives—but in an intermittent fashion that we cannot see as explaining millions of black people checking out of the job force forever, abandoning their children, letting a violent drug trade become the economic foundation of their communities, or even claiming in diversity seminars and classrooms and on op-ed pages that their lives are defined by endless encounters with bigotry. When black men were hanging from trees, poor blacks tended to keep their heads up to an extent that makes black Indianapolis in 1920 look like Beverly Hills compared with black Indianapolis in 1990. When black men were hanging from trees, blacks lucky enough to reach quiet middle-class existences tended to even downplay the extent to which racism affected their lives— there was no equivalent to Ellis Cose's book in 1940, and if anyone had written one then fortunate blacks would have condemned it as defeatist. This means that racism is not the reason for the Ellis Cose sensibility starting in the late sixties and early seventies. Other factors had a decisive effect, upon which the previous chapter is useful.

But journalists like Cose and the citizens he interviews are not the only people who burn with the news that racism is still everything for black Americans. We also hear this view from academics who devote careers to trumpeting the same thing. Do they have things to share with us that make a more conclusive case than the rage of corner office executives and Harvard Law School graduates? Let's see.

CHAPTER SEVEN

What About the View from the Ivory Tower?

Where do I get off anyway? Whatever I think about black history and memes and the rest, people who have devoted their academic careers to studying the black American condition almost never come to the kinds of conclusions that I do. Aren't they the authorities? They have the numbers, they go to the conferences, they *know*, don't they?

Myself, I wonder. I think it has been clear in this book so far that I try to look at as many sources from our authorities as I can before coming to my conclusions. But even so, could it be that the academic literature on the plight of blacks contains a wisdom or counsel that I am missing?

From what I have seen, I think not. Most academics pronouncing upon the condition of black America paint a picture that contrasts so starkly with the range of actual experience that we are dealing with not wisdom but a kind of religion, which is a different thing entirely. In this chapter I will explain.

SCHOLARLY WORK ON BLACKS PRETENDS THAT WE ARE THE WORLD'S ONLY PEOPLE WHOSE CULTURE HAS NO NEGATIVE TRAITS

For one, among academics studying black America, there is a studious commitment to tracing black communities' problems to the operations of larger forces. Of course, in some cases that analysis is correct. But in others, it is not unreasonable to suppose that there are entrenched patterns of behavior that do not correspond meaningfully to present-day conditions. This is another way of saying that there are sometimes cultural problems. Certainly, those problems usually trace, ultimately, to the operations of racism in the past. But they have a way of sticking around after the conditions that created them have faded into history or marginality, in the way of memes as I described in Chapter Six.

But academics have an institutional antipathy to cultural explanations of black issues. The problem is that this flies in the face of basic empirical engagement, of a kind that is considered unexceptional regarding seemingly anyone but black Americans.

For example, Katherine Newman, author of *No Shame in My Game*, is a top-ranked anthropologist, who has taught and researched at Columbia and Harvard. Yet, her book is devoted to a thesis that the problems of poor blacks in New York are due to a System that won't allow them to get ahead. I have already remarked in Chapter Four on how the actual facts of her subjects' lives repeatedly strain that analysis. Yes, the System does not exactly lay out a red carpet for them. But then, their early life "choices" had a lot to do with this, and those choices are hard to trace to deindustrialization and the like.

Newman knows this on some level. She writes, "Family trees among the working poor display a curious pattern of working siblings and jailed ones, of men and women who have made it to maturity alongside brothers who have died young. Tiffany has worked since she was fourteen, but her older brother has been a drug dealer and in and out of jail since his own teen years." But all Newman can come up with is, "To my knowledge, we have no compelling explanations of why the same family produces such divergent pathways in life."

But don't we? Anthropologists are hardly unfamiliar with the simple fact that cultural patterns can channel behavior independently of modern stimulus, and often in ways that are harmful. An extreme example would be the blood feuds that Albanians still carry out today in a modern world where they serve no purpose. Another would be the example that Jared Diamond chronicles in his book *Collapse*, when Norse settlers in Greenland ended up perishing because they had a cultural aversion to eating fish, such that when the agricultural practices they brought from Norway led to a famine in Greenland where the soil could not support it, they could not get through it by using a food source that the seas around them were teeming with. As for why some people in Tiffany's family fail while others do fine, is it really such a stretch to remember that cultural traits express themselves to differing extents in individuals? Surely anthropologists, cherishing diversity and individuality, do not have a hard time wrapping their heads around this. Some Albanian men are more given to feuding than others; probably at least a Norse settler or two ventured to go fishing instead of starve.

But when it comes to her struggling black interviewees, Newman somehow leaves all of this common sense aside. At one point she even lapses into outright scholarly dishonesty, so convinced that to allow that black people have negative as well as positive cultural traits would be "blaming the victim." She cites a study as saying that poor black women have children so early due to "the fear that postponing childbearing to later years is risky since older black women tend to develop health conditions that can impair fertility." But are inner-city black teenagers really consciously aware of medical statistics of this kind? It seemed so counterintuitive to me to imagine young black women expressing this particular "fear" to interviewers that I checked the source Newman footnotes, and in fact it says no such thing. It refers to academic research on the health tendencies, but not young black women actually being aware of them and their effect on their life choices, unsurprisingly given that obviously, inner-city teens have no exposure to obscure academic treatises (just as few people of any kind outside of academia do).

Newman's perspective kicks in hard among academic analysts of race problems right in the late sixties. Ulf Hannerz in *Soulside* in 1969 is an eloquent example, in his tortured take on the concept of a "culture of poverty" despite his book having quite vibrantly depicted one. Hannerz expresses the usual worry about "blaming the victim," writing, "If promiscuity, births out of wedlock, alcoholism, conspicuous consumption, and unemployment (defined as voluntary) are parts of a cultural heritage, it could be held that the culture of poverty causes poverty, rather than the other way around."

Okay, but the question is still: *Does* the culture of poverty cause poverty? The very soul of academic training is supposed to be teaching the scholar what it means to assess the world with true objectivity. So the question is, however one's analysis of the poor might be interpreted or misinterpreted, is it true that a culture of poverty ends up fostering behaviors on its own steam? Even Hannerz cannot ignore that the idea is hardly counterintuitive: "Of course, we cannot easily exclude the possibility that it has some partial validity."

But then he must say, "This idea, if given an emphasis it probably does not deserve, certainly has profound implications for American social policy." But what's that "probably"? He hasn't given any demonstration that the idea does not deserve emphasis. What really worries him is, again:

"If nothing helps, why bother with a war on poverty?" But who said that admitting that there is a such thing as a culture of poverty automatically means turning our backs on the poor? Is it such a logical leap to imagine addressing the culture of poverty itself?

Hannerz knows this, too: "Obviously, this point need not only be a part of a coldly contemptuous view of the life of the poor." But he can only come back to the following:

> Yet one may feel somewhat uneasy with the orientation of this term as well, both because it may lead to the belief that such programmed acculturation really takes place in a cultural vacuum and because it focuses attention on changing the poor as individuals rather than on changing that system where they have been assigned places as poor.

In other words, we must focus on The System at all costs. But these days, black leaders nationwide are doing marvelous things in, indeed, changing the poor as individuals. What, after all, is so ominous about that? It only seems ominous if we assume that poor blacks are driven only by external forces. And this is nothing less than a dehumanization of black Americans. Haven't we dealt with enough of that?

What invalidates perspectives like Hannerz's and Newman's is that they are implausible of actual human beings. Pretending that all black problems are due to The Man seems well-meaning but actually verges on exactly the kind of condescension from which social scientists devote their careers to shielding blacks. In *An American Dilemma*, even Gunnar Myrdal claims, "The Negro's entire life and, consequently, also his opinions on the Negro problem are, in the main, to be considered as secondary reactions to more primary pressures from the side of the dominant white majority." Ralph Ellison famously responded, "Can a people (its faith in an idealized American Creed notwithstanding) live and develop for over three hundred years simply by *reacting*?" Ellison went on: "Men have made a way of life in caves and upon cliffs; why cannot Negroes have made a life upon the horns of the white man's dilemma?"

Ellison's observation need not be taken as meaning that there should not have been a Civil Rights movement. Nor, however, need it be taken as meaning simply that black Americans have a culture only in the sense of the blues, playing the dozens, and the like. To fully understand that black Americans are human entails the challenge of facing straight on that black culture has imperfections because all cultures do. One has not learned the lesson that blacks are the equals of whites until one allows that they are not perfect, since after all, whites certainly aren't.

Likely, many sociologists would object that they indeed do know that culture can have negative effects for black people too. But then ask them, "So, in what ways?" and note that there will be a certain pause. That pause alone shows that they actually have never had occasion to even think much about the issue before. At the very least, they are so uncomfortable talking about it that whatever they come up with to tell you, you can be sure in their minds, the issue is marginal. Do they think black culture is imperfect in any facets significant enough to, say, devote an article or book to or deliver a conference presentation on? If not, they bear out my argument. To help black people, social scientists would have to do this, compassionately but honestly and clearly, on a regular basis. They do not, and as such, they do not help black people.

George Orwell once wrote the following:

> We are all capable of believing things which we *know* to be untrue, and then, when we are finally proved wrong, impudently twisting the facts so as to show that we were right. Intellectually, it is possible to carry on this process for an indefinite time: the only check on it is that sooner or later a false belief bumps up against a solid reality, usually on a battlefield.

In this case, the reality was not a war, but, for example, the results of welfare reform, which have shown that poor black women did not end up begging on sidewalk grates once they could no longer spend their entire lives dependent on the government.

Social scientists' elevation of systemic explanations in the face of obvious counterevidence is what Orwell described. In their heart of hearts, these people are well aware of the simple fact that in human groups, patterns have a way of sticking, and that there is no reason that this reality is suddenly suspended only among poor black descendants of slaves in the United States. However, an ideological filter prevents them from acknowledging the truth in their public statements and writings and likely even in their own minds.

There is plenty that is great about us. But it is sheer fantasy to suppose that beyond this, we are just marionettes jerking around with rises and falls in the GNP. Work on blacks that marginalizes something as basic to human nature as negative aspects of culture is, at best, an abbreviated description of a people who need better and is therefore of limited use.

SCHOLARLY WORK ON BLACKS IS AMBIVALENT
ABOUT BLACK PROGRESS

Intellection is supposed to enlighten us. But too often scholarly writers on blacks consider it enlightening to teach us that there is something sinister and small about the millions of us who moved away from the ghetto. Technically, what these writers wish had happened was that luckier blacks stayed in the ghetto and helped to uplift poorer ones, the result being thriving multi-class black communities. Never mind that this suggests a kind of permanent, wary racial balkanization that would impede "getting past race" in any meaningful way.

The main problem is that this seems to be founded in a bone-deep suspicion of blacks who had the gumption to seek the beyond. At times, this kind of work sounds almost as if it were written by old-time bigoted Southerners who wanted the darkies to know their "place." Examples of this include Elijah Anderson's *Streetwise* and Sheryll Cashin's *The Failures of Integration*. While writers like Anderson and Cashin see conservative views on race as unfeeling, their quietly contemptuous take on middle-class blacks moving to the suburbs is, when we strip away the gloss of educated prose style and terminology, rather mean itself.

I think most middle-class blacks who have worked hard to get the good things for themselves would be outright offended if they took a gander at the way they are parsed in books like *Streetwise*, *The Failures of Integration*, and *American Apartheid*. But besides being mean, this strain departs from the very mission of humanistic inquiry. What kind of authority can we see in work that calls for self-directed human beings raising children and seeking to realize the best of themselves to live in or near crummy, and even dangerous, neighborhoods? What kind of sense can we see in it? I can only see sense in it as based on seeking alienation at all costs—alienation from whites and alienation from blacks who dare to suggest, in their actions, that the economy and racism are not the only reasons that the ones in the inner city are still there.

The Black Middle Class as Milquetoasts

Contempt for middle-class blacks runs throughout Anderson's *Streetwise*. For middle-class blacks who left, "Ostensibly they are motivated by concern about crime, drugs, poor public schools, run-down and crowded housing, and social status . . . but for many there may be a deep emotional desire to get as far as possible from poorer blacks." Does Anderson by chance mean that these uppity negroes just don't like their own kind? But why is Anderson apparently unconvinced that crime, drugs, bad schools, and crowds are enough to make someone want to leave a neighborhood? How is his quick jump to an "uppity" analysis he would condemn from a white writer a levelheaded analysis of human beings? Why does he describe middle-class blacks as "aspiring" to the middle class, as if it were not the soul of humanity to "aspire," and as if blacks somehow never actually make it to being middle class?

Cashin snorts more than once about affluent blacks' homes as "trophy palaces," which she says "remind me of funeral homes, the size and pretense to stately grandeur are so overwhelming." Anderson grouses that among middle-class blacks, "For some there is an almost ritualistic concern with propriety and decorum," as if the "raucous behavior, including cursing and loud talk and play" that he describes among poorer blacks is somehow preferable—more "authentic," perhaps?

Anderson's primum mobile comes through in one of those William Julius Wilson "Enough is enough" moments, of the kind that occurs in Cashin's book with her "some black conservative" line. Anderson has a description of a ghetto black man playing his radio way up loud, as was common in the eighties among people of that demographic. This was, briefly put, a major pain in the ass. I wonder how many among us who were there can smile recalling sitting in a train and having to put up with someone like this playing his boom box at top volume, usually with a sullen glare daring anyone to call him on it. But to Anderson, these guys were heroes.

> They walk confidently, heads up and gazes straight. Spontaneous and boisterous, they play their radios as loud as they please, telling everyone within earshot that this is their turf, like it or not. It may be that this is one of the few arenas where they can assert themselves and be taken seriously, and perhaps this is why they are so insistent.

"Boisterous"! Anderson's heart swelled at the sight. Okay, this was partly because he saw the man as done in by Society, and thus enjoying his one possible moment in the sun. But even with that ideology, one could still see Society as *driving the man to be a public nuisance.* But Anderson thought he was *cool!* To Anderson, sticking it to The Man is everything. I have read that passage of his so many times I have it memorized; it is, to me, horrific, to an extent that helps make one write a book.

The Black Middle Class as Traitors: Scholarship or Partisanship?

Let's take away, for example, the sonorous buzzwords that the middle-class exodus argument is usually couched in, such as escape, fear, resources, striving. That is, "escape" from lowly blacks one considers oneself above and wishes whites didn't associate one with; "fear" of scowling young black men whose demeanor is actually a healthy response to racism; "resources" that the blacks who stay behind lack that you have; "striving" to live in a quiet community with good schools, in a quest to live one's life in a setting traditionally associated with white people, implying glum questions as to one's comfort with black identity.

Instead, let's just lay out what people like Anderson and Cashin are saying in plain language, which also leaves out words that have taken on distracting connotations: Middle-class blacks who moved to the suburbs should have stayed in the ghetto to serve as role models for poor blacks, and the fact that they didn't do this reveals them as morally dim.

And now, let's assess this judgment on the basis of an actual black couple. We will put aside for now the statistics, the bird's-eye views of census tracts, the broad, pregnant pronouncements about class(ism). Instead of flying over Prince George's County or Chicago, we will start our descent—fasten your seat belts—and alight in a front yard on a crumbling black block in Philadelphia in 1967. The McWhorters and their two-year-old son are watching the last pieces of their furniture put in a truck and are moving that day to quiet, clean, integrated West Mount Airy.

I once asked my mother why we moved to Mount Airy instead of staying in that neighborhood, and she said, "Because it was turning into a ghetto." And it was—today that neighborhood is indeed even more a 'hood, and is in fact exactly one of the areas that Mom used to drive me and my sister through to let us know how lucky we were. That is, Mom did not leave that neighborhood out of a naïve, heartless view of poor blacks, and in fact was on her way to becoming a social work professor beloved by her (mostly black) students at Temple University for teaching them about the operations of systemic racism and inequity. She grew up in segregated Atlanta, participated in sit-ins, swooned over Julian Bond, and even lit into me when I was ten when I said I wanted to be a paleontologist because it wouldn't make a contribution to "The Struggle."

Yet, she lit into me in, yes, a nice duplex with a pretty lawn, in a neighborhood where no one was getting shot, the public schools were solid, and the streets were wide and well-paved. She and my father worked hard to allow me and my sister to grow up there and were happy that conditions in America were now such that we could.

Yet, Elijah Anderson would see my parents as culpable. For him, Shelli and John Sr. were bourgeois negroes who "fled" black antiheroes like the admirably "boisterous" boom-box carriers. He would have counseled Mom and Dad to stay in the neighborhood they left. Never mind that this would mean that my mother may well have had to cut up her refrigerator box and put it out in the trash in little pieces week by week, as he reports of a woman in another degraded Philadelphia neighborhood. Never mind that it could have been Dad who had his head busted in by a crazed crackhead and left with seizures, as per another episode Anderson notes in his "Northton." That is, Dad who was no scion of the black bourgeoisie, but a working-class South Philly product without a college degree, who had made himself a solid career as a photographer for the city government and would a few years later earn his BA and MA in education.

Cashin seems to even explicitly feel that my parents shouldn't have had any qualms about exposing themselves to such things, quoting a white woman who chose to raise her family in a dicey black neighborhood as saying, "There are worse things than getting shot. I don't want my kids to grow up being afraid of black people." (Did Cashin's editor not at least query her on this bizarre passage?) I suppose it is rather small of me that I would consider the number of things worse than being shot to be very few and am relieved that I didn't grow up in a neighborhood where I had to endure such indignities. But apparently my parents should have chosen a life so glum that having one's flesh ripped through by a bullet is a mere inconvenience—with, I suppose, the fact that the bullet didn't hit a vital organ being a lucky bonus, a sign that God was on one's side that day. I'm sorry, but I cannot picture my mother getting shot in the arm and see it as better than her, me, her husband, and her infant daughter living peacefully in our house on Marion Lane in Mount Airy.

I am aware that Mount Airy apparently fell short in not lending my mother the character-building experience of gunshot wounds in the service of being a "model" for the blacks in the neighborhood who were disinclined to gunplay. And certainly, my parents chose a lifestyle that Cashin's interviewee considers "soulless, impoverished." Now, if I wanted to split hairs, I would mention that the neighbors across the yard were black, as were the people in about every second house in our cul-de-sac or every third one across the driveway out back, including the parents of my two best friends at the time. But then, I suppose, all of these people, too, were "soulless" black folk because they opted out of North Philly. I cannot resist noting that Anderson and Cashin would run up against a wall in designating the Burrises (across the yard) and the Chappells and the Whites (parents of my best friends) as "soulless" on any level; all of these couples were quite "black" enough to pass muster with the Soul Patrol. But for our purposes, let's stick with my parents, and assume that Shelli and John, barbecuing in their yard instead of ducking bullets, were impoverished souls.

But those are personal qualities. What about the issue of their responsibility to their own people, whether or not they were sorts inclined to, if we may, bust a move, in the name of, well, "soul"? Even as "soulless" people, wouldn't their starchy ways have been useful as a "model" for poor blacks back in the hood? The question remains: Were my parents morally culpable in busting a move to Mount Airy? Escape, fear, resources, striving—got it. But now: Could Elijah Anderson sit before my parents, look them in the eye, and tell them that they made a mistake in moving to a nice neighborhood?

Let's imagine that Anderson supposes that Mom and Dad should have "known" in 1967 that the departure of people like them was going to leave their former neighbors without role models and plunge them into inner-city pathology. Never mind that this analysis is, in my view, mistaken: I think that what created the inner cities we are familiar with was a cultural shift and the relaxation of welfare policies in its wake, as I have argued in Chapter Four. That means that even if middle-class blacks had stayed behind, if new welfare policies had still hooked most of a neighborhood's poor blacks on welfare just as a new oppositional mood was becoming common coin, then the result would have been middle-class blacks cowering in their living rooms.

But let's even give people like Anderson maximal breathing room and posit that it is possible, formally, that these factors would have had less of an effect if middle-class blacks had stayed in the ghetto. We have no test case in America to confirm this, since there are no cities where large numbers of middle-class blacks resisted their oh, so self-involved, classist impulse to move to nice neighborhoods when they were able to. But Anderson's condemnation remains incoherent nevertheless: How could my parents have known in 1967 that the inner-city degradation we are familiar with was even a possibility?

The idea that the middle-class exodus created the inner city only became common coin decades later. In 1967, what my parents knew was that minority families who saved some money typically moved out of the ghetto, and that eventually the ghetto ceased to exist, such as what happened—or did not—with Jews on the Lower East Side in New York. My parents were also presumably aware of the massive and well-publicized War on Poverty at the time, promising to uplift even the poorer blacks less fortunate than them. In 1967, they could not have imagined New Jack City or Elijah Anderson's "Northton," since such deathscapes were unheard of in America until long after they moved. And as such, my parents had saved up some money, saw that they could afford a house in a nice neighborhood, and moved into it. Do they deserve condemnation—or even smug clicks of the tongue?

Or—could Anderson really tell my parents that they should have known that with factory jobs receding, their departure was going to leave their poor neighbors "uniquely vulnerable" to social pathology? Here, the conclusive error in the analysis is especially clear, since Indianapolis shows that even when factory jobs stayed nearby, the same inner-city developments occurred.

But that is something that we only know now, almost forty years later. Let's say that in 1967 the verdict was still out on the effect of deindustrialization. Still, just as the middle-class black exodus analysis only emerged decades later, the idea that factory closings would (supposedly) leave blacks idle and violent was unknown in 1967. There were, at best, a few obscure academic articles worrying that factory relocation would make it harder for poor blacks to get jobs. But even these writers gave no sign of supposing that young black men were on their way to devolving into making their neighborhoods war zones in which fatherlessness and crack addiction were norms. The question, then, is how my parents could have, at that time, applied factory closings to their decision to move—even if we saddle them with the responsibility of keeping up subscriptions to arcane academic journals alongside ones to *Ebony* and *Jet*.

Never mind that the closing of the factories, to the extent that any John Q. Public at the time could have seen it as a menacing development, was a gradual affair. Only about ten years after 1967—at the earliest—could anyone on the ground have readily perceived that factory jobs were no longer abundant enough to support a community. Certainly, we do not expect my parents to have been obsessively tabulating factory closings in North and West Philly in 1967. They were living their lives, buying groceries, paying bills, and striving—sorry—for the best life they could imagine within their means. And as black people who came of age in the middle of the twentieth century, they were achingly aware of the fact that their people had been barred from the best for centuries and that a Civil Rights revolution had recently opened up opportunities for them to get the best—or at least, pretty darned good. Elijah Anderson would have it that they should have refrained from seeking even pretty darned good, refraining from such out of a predictive analysis of broad sociological developments that no individual at the time was likely to perceive living day to day. What kind of counsel, what kind of judgment, is this from our learned class?

One thing this counsel lacks is empathy. Anderson surely understands that a black couple in 1967 sought a nice house not only to escape poor blacks but also out of simple human desires to have the most pleasant lifestyle possible. But he cannot join them in their pride, even though they were doing exactly what their ancestors had fought for. Anderson's empathy, his love, goes to the street corner thug, despite his surly conduct and loud radio. Interesting—Anderson wants us to love the thug as the product of sociological currents beyond his control, but somehow, the fact that middle-class black homeowners were subject to similar perceptions beyond their control does not excuse them from his contempt. The thug must be understood; the suburban homeowner must be tarred as a black Babbitt. The thug's pride in 2007 is noble, but my parents' pride in 1967 was parochial, classist ignorance. What enforces the difference in judgment? Alienation *über alles*. This is a distortion of intelligent leftist politics into sandbox pettiness. One must love the rebel and distrust the conformist, regardless of the lapses in logic and compassion necessary to maintain this perspective.

The Black Middle Class's Just Deserts?

Cashin has a take on the black middle class that is, in itself, stimulating, although in the end it is, like Anderson's view, deeply bound in oppositional identity rather than practical progressivism. Cashin notes that when blacks move to suburban enclaves in large numbers hoping to form black versions of tony white suburbs, after blacks become a perceptible presence, whites flee. This depresses housing prices such that poorer blacks can start moving in as well, increasing the crime rate and lowering the quality of the schools. Cashin notes that there exists not a single black suburb where this "element" has not become part of the mix over time. As such, she concludes that blacks seek sepia versions of the *Leave It To Beaver* neighborhood in vain.

What is key is Cashin's solution to this: She advises middle-class blacks to move back to the inner city to make them back into the cross-class communities they once were. In other words, Cashin thinks that middle-class suburban blacks should move to the slums!

There are two problems here. One is that it is painfully obvious that this will never happen. Surely, even Cashin would agree that buttoned-up barbecue-grill blacks are not going to pack up their "palaces" and move into ugly neighborhoods where they will fear for their children's safety. Why suggest this, then? Because it is a handy way of having someone to condemn as morally beneath you.

And typically of an idea borne of the alienation meme rather than sincere intent, it squarely contradicts an earlier statement Cashin makes. At another point in the book she says that expecting middle-class blacks to roll up their sleeves and try to uplift poorer blacks in their suburbs, or to keep their kids who are failing in schools because of the challenge of educating lesser-prepared students, would be to impose too much of a burden on people with enough on their plates. But why, then, is it not a burden to expect successful people to *relocate to a slum*?

Then there is another problem with Cashin's argument that qualifies, most politely, as a "paradox." On the one hand, people of her leanings swoon at the thought of inner-city "communities" where blacks of all classes live side by side, such that the middle-class black exodus qualifies as a betrayal. But—if working-class blacks have since followed the affluent ones to the suburbs, then why can't we see *this* as a reincarnation of the cross-class black Valhallas that people like Cashin see as so vital to black uplift? Really—if affluent blacks have been joined by less fortunate ones in Prince George's County, Virginia, then doesn't this bring us back to Black Ghetto 1952? Wouldn't we expect Cashin and Anderson to be writing books about the New Black Outer Cities? Shouldn't we be seeing places like this as promising sites for middle-class blacks to resume their function as role models for the downtrodden?

Apparently not. Instead, throughout Cashin's discussion of the lesser-class incursions into wealthy black enclaves runs a certain tone: a smug tsk-tsk aimed at striver blacks who hoped they could get away from the niggers only to find them moving in two blocks away ten years later. She structures her entire section on this issue by presenting a series of assumptions affluent blacks make about how nice their new neighborhoods will be, and systematically showing that these dreams will not be borne out as poorer blacks follow them and ruin the schools, raise the crime rate, and so on. The general air is one of "gotcha!" and that tone gives away what she, and like-minded writers, are truly about.

The guiding impulse is not that blacks of all classes must live together—that is just a smoke screen masking something more particular. The real commitment is based on a sense that, simply, the barbecue-grill black family with the lawn in a quiet neighborhood has to go. No, blacks in the 'burbs will not try to work things out with their poorer neighbors because even though this would recreate the cross-class black community of yore, it would also allow the "strivers" to continue to "escape" living dead in the heart of the ghetto, with no "palace" to retreat to, thereby stepping aside from fully "facing," 24-7, the plight of people living in the 'hood. Rather, blacks must move into that inner city and embrace the residents there in all of their violent, crumbling "reality." That way, no more black people deigning to live in palaces as the inner cities fester.

Thus, middle-class blacks must offer a helping hand not in quiet neighborhoods, but while enduring an ugly, dangerous environment. Just deserts, after all, for their traitorous exit in the seventies. In other words, Cashin has a bone to pick with middle-class black suburbanites. She is arguing on the basis of personally felt alienation founded in score-settling, rooted in a visceral commitment to class warfare from below. If she were arguing solely on the basis of constructive intent toward helping blacks left behind, she would see the New Outer Cities as potential sites of black uplift, rather than as presenting middle-class blacks there as faced with a local "burden" of unachievable uplift that she mysteriously fails to see in asking the same people to move to a war zone.

Then there is another thing that Cashin leaves out. Presumably, after middle-class blacks left their palaces to go "soulful" and live in the 'hood, poorer blacks would remain in the suburbs who did not have the money to move back to the 'hood they left. Never mind that we suspect that Cashin would not even begin to try to convince these poorer blacks to move back to the 'hood—because they clearly already know "who they are," they are exempt from the lesson that middle-class blacks need to subject themselves to. But wait—we all know what happens when—Lord forbid!!—too many poor blacks live in one place and most of the jobs available are service ones. Watch out—certainly, we would expect new destitute, violent "outer cities" where barely a child knows his or her father, replicating what had happened in the inner cities. At least that is what the PC version of modern black history stipulates, and I would be interested to see how people like Anderson and Cashin would manage, decades later, to trace even these new suburban slums to something whites or uppity blacks did.

The Black Middle Class as Archaic Caricature

In general, peeking out from behind the sober prose of Anderson and Cashin is a sense that middle-class blacks are the light-skinned, tea-sipping "Black Bourgeoisie" criticized by E. Franklin Frazier in 1957. These people came of age in an era when classism even among blacks was more overt and accepted. Integration was the watchword, such that middle-class blacks modelled themselves on white customs and had little interest in Africa or in retaining as much "street" in their essence as possible to avoid "becoming white." That set sits uneasily in our consciousness today. Even I never know quite what to make of them when I occasionally meet surviving examples, very old, usually light-complexioned people who seem to have no perceptible "black identity" according to what that has meant when I have lived. But whatever one thinks of that grand old "Our Kind of People" set, they contrast starkly with most middle- and upper-class blacks today.

Repeatedly, Anderson and Cashin depict post–Civil Rights middle-class blacks as if they hold their noses while fleeing poor ones—one imagines a portly high-yellow dowager in 1950 with a flowered hat sniffing, "Well!" as a black "ruffian" passes by. But this is a caricature of what modern middle-class blacks are like, and Cashin, in particular, is well poised to know this, having grown up middle class in the seventies just as I did. Successful suburban blacks tend to have nuanced views of why some blacks are left behind. Yes, they are known to say occasionally that the welfare Mom had no business having all those kids, or that their wayward young cousin needs to get himself a job. But they also have compassion—they bristle to hear a white person say that ghetto blacks are just lazy, vote Democratic almost to a man, and quite often are involved in activities assisting less fortunate blacks. Yet, while Cashin often refers to poorer blacks as "folks"—an affectionate term—she writes of middle-class blacks with an air of suspicion; blacks with nice houses are, apparently, no longer "folks."

To people like Cashin and Anderson, would the Black Bourgeoisie perhaps seem a little less blinkered if one of the "folk" made their case? Katherine Newman quotes a struggling inner-city resident talking about how "all those people moved."

> They probably moved out because of the block. If you lived on that block for a month, you would want to go too. You would definitely

want to leave. The streets are bad. . . . They had a body over there a few days ago, shot like eight or nine times. Our building is a hundred years old—it's disgusting, roach-infested. The neighbors are loud, very loud. Always cursing at their kids, playing their music loud, fighting.

Now—there's a sister doing what Anderson and Cashin desire, in showing America the awful conditions that too many people in this country live in. But she also has no problem with the fact that luckier people were, as she puts it, "doing very well and just left." At this point, sociologists often decree where wisdom fades into naïveté. The idea here would be that where the interviewee paints a picture of ghetto ills she is an enlightened reporter, but that she is sadly uninformed in not understanding that middle-class people could have been role models for her and her kids, and that she would be a more morally advanced person in resenting those middle-class escapees. But many of us, I suspect, will see basic human empathy and realism where social scientists claiming to speak for her perceive ignorance.

Scholarly work that calls attention to the plight of poor blacks and examines how systemic factors can keep them from making the best of themselves is enlightened. However, scholarly work that drifts from this into branding successful blacks as unfeeling for deciding not to live in the slums is barstool antiauthoritarianism masquerading as constructive cognition. This kind of unreflective smugness has helped to marginalize the social sciences from policymaking over the past thirty years, rendering fields like sociology and anthropology hothouse realms of radical ideology, compelling largely to academics and leftist activists but ignored by people in power. Sadly, we cannot look to these people for meaningful advice on how to get beyond our societal problems. Their counsel is rooted in affirming their own moral fiber as either opponents of The System or as noble victims of it, so insistently as to let pass lapses in logic and willful neglect of history.

SCHOLARLY WORK ON BLACKS PLACES DOOMSAYING OVER THE CONSTRUCTIVE

Academic work on black America also disqualifies itself as humanistic—or perhaps, humane—in offering us nothing but bad news, with an implication that our problems must necessarily sit static unless there is vast upending in the American political and sociological fabric, which they and we all know will never occur. So much of this work is therapeutic alienation set in ten-dollar words: The goal, while nominally constructive, is actually the doomsaying in itself.

Academic sociology is a particularly useful example. Reading books and articles by these people, a foreigner could genuinely come away supposing that race relations in the United States have barely inched beyond what they were in 1950. If in 1950, an African villager got a scholarship to spend a year in the United States and some missionaries decided to prime him for the kinds and degree of racism he would encounter, then they could give him no source more useful than all of the articles on black America that appeared in the *American Journal of Sociology* from 1990 to 1999!

I mean that, and to show you why, let's actually take a look at those articles. *American Journal of Sociology* is one of the most prestigious journals in the field, and thus we can assume that what made it onto its pages is representative of what was being done in the discipline during this recent ten-year period, when the state of black America was very much like what it is as you read this text. And yet, when I say that its portrait of black America sounds like the fifties, I do not mean that something like every second article takes this tone, or that it is just a matter of hints and concluding paragraphs and the like. I mean that the journal resonantly demonstrates an orthodoxy in article after article, issue after issue, that the state of race relations in the United States remains as brutal as it was fifty years ago. I can prove it only by taking us through every single black-oriented article that appeared from 1990 to 1999. Let's go. I'll be as brisk as I can.

Ten Years in the Life of a Flagship Journal

In 1990, there was an article by none other than Douglas Massey, principal author of *American Apartheid*, and Mitchell L. Eggers. It was a kind of tie-in to the book; the title says it all: "The Ecology of Inequality: Minorities and the Concentration of Poverty, 1970–1980."

In 1991, *The American Journal of Sociology* taught us three things about black America. Black women have a smaller choice of marriageable men to choose from than white women. We must be thankful to sociological methodology for revealing that—get this—social pathologies have a way of spreading in the worst neighborhoods. Not in the better neighborhoods, mind you, but the *bad* ones. Remember that. Also retain that these social pathologies—so unexpectedly of phenomena that are not individual but social—have a way of *spreading from one person to another*. Like, say, an "epidemic." And the author provided the truly unanticipated policy conclusion that "the epidemic theory suggests that we should target two types of neighborhood for policy interventions: neighborhoods that have already undergone epidemics and neighborhoods that are at high risk of doing so." Then, the more blacks look like whites in terms of skin tone, the better they tend to do in terms of education, occupation, and income.

In 1992, we learned that black infant mortality only goes down in cities according to how many black people there are in high places in the municipal government. But then there was some better news: Racist sentiment did not increase in the 1980s.

But no such exceptions in 1993. Even in 1910 single motherhood was hardly unknown among poor black women, which questions why we speak today of an "underclass." Thanks again to modern sociology, for letting us know that among the lowest caste in American society in the old days, all families were not like *Father Knows Best*. Zounds! Then, another article letting us know that blacks are more segregated from whites than from other groups—i.e., that there are more than a few large black ghettos in the United States. Finally, a little secret: Bad neighborhoods are bad for people growing up.

The year 1994 was more bad news. Opposition to busing black students into white communities increased the longer blacks had been present in the communities and was highest in all-white communities. Thus, "we interpret these results as indicating that whites will be more likely to mobilize where integration threatens the legacy of white privilege." After the Fair Housing Act of 1968, blacks lived apart from whites less because they wanted to live with one another than because of continued discrimination. In 1995, we got something that only the rigors of academic cogitation and statistical analysis could have teased out from the complexities of real life: that (drum roll, *please!*) whites tend to leave poor neighborhoods when there are a lot of robberies in them. Of course, "We are not trying to argue that violent-crime rates are the only cause of racial change. Far from it"—that is, racism remains a major player.

The year 1996 was a big year for black issues in *American Journal of Sociology*. We learned that the black *Los Angeles Sentinel* covered the Rodney King riots differently from the *Los Angeles Times*: "While it was construed in the *Los Angeles Times* as the beginning of a narrative of a crisis, in the *Los Angeles Sentinel* it was inserted into the middle of an ongoing narrative about civil rights and police brutality." Another article comes out with "Interracial contact is more common than it was during the late 1960s, especially for whites," but as one marvels that an article in this journal would posit such a positive conclusion, one is not surprised to find the authors quickly adding that the interaction "still consists primarily of brief, superficial encounters." Oh well—short of *intimate* contact with whites, blacks must, we all know, remain in the toilet. And meanwhile, there was even discrimination within the Civil Rights movement, in that women were shunted into middle levels of leadership. Then there was another staggering revelation that black women were often single mothers even before 1967. Oh, and in case you were wondering, lynchings tended to decrease in areas near ones where lynchings had previously taken place, either because whites were satisfied that they had made their statement or because blacks' behavior changed. (Am I alone in wondering exactly what present-day benefit would motivate scholars to investigate this oddly particular point, of all things? But then linguists are hardly immune from the same, perhaps even myself at times.) But another piece tells us that these days "prejudice" has decreased—but not opposition to "race-targeted policies" that is, opposition to affirmative action means that whites haven't woken up as much as we might think.

On to 1997. "Blacks are substantially less likely than whites to escape poor tracts and substantially more likely to move into them." Or—a William Julius Wilson protégé recounts how a gang he studied did some community work while they were selling drugs—in almost astonishing neglect of the fact that these were hoodlums addicting people to crack. Wise scholars warn us that large cuts in welfare will barely reduce the number of female-headed families—never mind that soon after they wrote, welfare reform would at least leave most women who used to live on welfare as working members of society, even if not married or middle class. Another article praises pioneers of affirmative action activism for wangling black-focused policies out of legislation worded in race-blind fashion. This is a major slap-down to anyone who would contest a claim that modern sociology is founded on political ideology rather than empirical assessment; otherwise, why would an article like this appear in one of the field's refereed flagship publications? And then we got a condemnation of the work requirements in AFDC programs of the late 1960s as punitive and racist, since no one had proposed such requirements when welfare was not yet associated with black people. Never mind that welfare of the late sixties was a vast expansion and relaxation of welfare before this, or that the work requirements were modest, fitfully enforced, and virulently opposed, as we saw in Chapter Four.

In 1998, we got that the police tend to kill more black people in neighborhoods where most people are black and poor. Next was a tricky mathematical argument that desegregation can often lessen actual contact between people of different races. After that, a paper showing that even in neighborhoods with a healthy racial mix in overall numbers, small streets can still have strong concentrations of one race. Since one's ambience is most immediately who is "down the street," this is possibly an "ominous" development in terms of how crucial it is for blacks to not live only among their own *even when it comes to single blocks*, on the pain of sinking into degradation as we all know nig—I mean, black Americans do under such conditions. Then, 1998's envoi was a kind of response to the "conservative" observation that blacks murder whites more than whites murder blacks: Namely, white neighborhoods tend to direct violence against minorities most when minorities are moving in.

The *American Journal of Sociology* saw out the nineties with three observations. First was a paean to the black panhandler who suffers from the dismissal of white female passersby less than enthusiastic about their attempts to cadge money from them and chat them up: "They are stuck talking to someone who does not want to talk, and the indignities, usually tacit, such people deliver to show it," they "endure a gauntlet of 'small insults',," and "the women appear to the men as beyond human empathy." Second, some startling news: Middle-class white flight has increased the number of poor neighborhoods in America. Finally, apparently whites and blacks kill one another more often when engaged in competition for the same jobs, and blacks kill less in cities with black mayors.

Ten years of this journal, then, teach us nothing but doom and gloom about the state of black America. Perhaps outright "prejudice" is down, and perhaps there is more contact between blacks and whites in a broad sense— but only that. Otherwise, we come away with no cause for hope and only perfunctory counsel for getting beyond the sinkhole we are mired in.

Ah, but that's just one journal. Is it that its editors happen to be especially pessimistic? Can we really judge a discipline based on just one of its journals? Even if that journal is one of its tippy-top representatives that sociologists fight to appear in? Well, suppose we looked at the same ten years of another top sociology journal, *American Sociological Review*? Maybe there we would find that there is a "diversity" in sociological work that is for some reason hidden in the pages of *American Journal of Sociology*. Or maybe not.

However, justifying that conclusion puts me in an awkward position as a writer. On the one hand, for me to cover all fifty-one of the race articles that *American Sociology Review* ran from 1990 to 1999 would qualify as literary Sominex. But on the other hand, to spare the reader is to leave a certain contingent under the impression that I have not done my homework.

In this case, I am forced to resort to the appendix strategy: In the Appendix I cover all of the relevant articles for those few readers who want to check up on my judgment here.

For the rest, suffice it to say that the articles are more of the same dogged doomsaying, depicting an America difficult to recognize as the one we actually live in. There were exactly four articles during the ten years of the run whose findings were explicitly presented as showing the sun peeking through the clouds, as opposed to the two during the same ten years of *American Journal of Sociology*. Thomas Daula, D. Alton Smith, and Roy Nord admitted that there was no racial discrimination in promotions in the military. As I mentioned in Chapter Three, Reynolds Farley and William H. Frey showed that in the eighties blacks were founding new middle-class developments in the West and South in which white flight was irrelevant because the houses and neighborhoods were new, and Paul A. Jargowsky noted that nationwide, middle-class blacks in that period were increasingly less likely to live among poor ones. Similarly, David R. Harris acknowledged that white resistance to black people moving into their neighborhoods was based on class more than race. And then, there was Mary Pattillo-McCoy's observationally neutral article noting that the church has played a central part in black communities and uplift efforts.

Wisdom from Our Thinkers

Based on these works, I conclude that modern academic sociology has the following to share with black America and American policymakers.

Racism relentlessly proscribed black lives in the past. Although overt racism has now vastly receded, other forms of racism persist today. These include subliminal personal biases against blacks. Whites tend to disavow these, but they are detectable in questionnaires and polls. Also, there is the more subtle operation of systemic racism. This is difficult for the layperson to perceive but is identifiable by academic quantitative study that reveals statistical discrepancies that can only be due to racism, as "cultural" explanations stem from blinkered ignorance. These forms of racism exert a powerful check upon black advancement and well-being, such that alerting white America to their existence is an urgent task that must center and guide all valid addresses of race in America. Signs of black advancement merit formal acknowledgment, but neither celebration nor even sustained interest because they invariably cloak concurrent signs of continuing oppression, reversal, and/or new problems emerging in their wake. Solving the race problem in America will require profound transformations in governmental policy. This will include suspensions of the capitalist impulse that the nation's economy is founded upon, and federally funded and societally bolstered mechanisms via which whites will be cleansed of their residual biases against blacks. Especially important in the latter mission will be to disabuse whites of the idea that individual effort (often termed *agency* in the literature and amply analyzed and debated) will play a significant role in black uplift, as the system is too deeply set against blacks for this to be a realistic or humane requirement.

I intend this characterization as sincere. I fully expect that just about any sociologist would concur with all of those propositions, with at most minor reservations. I expect this within a particular assumption: that all sociologists will understand that the existence of a few exceptions among sociological thinkers to this description does not refute my general characterization. Just as they do not see non-racist whites (such as, for example, white sociologists) as counteracting the idea that racism is dominant in America, they will not see the occasional sociologist who does not parse America the way I show them to as invalidating my portrait of the field's consensus as per the above. I am and they are referring to what we all see as very strong tendencies—them, the prevalence of racism among whites; me, sociologists' commitment to the characterization above, precisely as I have put it. So, for example, the existence of Orlando Patterson refutes me here no more than ostriches refute a statement that birds fly.

And on that subject, one wonders what influence the exceptions have on the trajectory of the field. For example, in Chapter Three, I discussed Reynolds Farley and William Frey's unusually positive article in *American Sociological Review* showing that middle-class suburbs are emerging in the South and West. But we must ask: Twenty years from now, will there be sociological papers and books analyzing the trend Farley and Frey identified? Based on what I have read from this field, it is very hard to even imagine beyond parenthetical asides and footnotes, so primed are sociologists to call attention to the worst. Rather, I would not be surprised to find a paper or two in 2015 examining the 2010 census data from these neighborhoods and fashioning some way to mine bad news from them. Potential topics will include, say, the fact that blacks in these communities might vote Republican in higher numbers than poor ones (which is necessarily *hideous* news, of course); that leaders in neighborhoods like these are statistically more likely to resist Section 8 housing than leaders in more "rooted" black neighborhoods adjacent to ghettos; or even perhaps that Latinos are not benefiting from the housing in these new neighborhoods as much as we might like and that this suggests a racism on the part of blacks. One imagines that if local newspapers start writing celebratory articles about these neighborhoods as beacons of black achievement in the face of obstacles, sociologists will "worry" that such coverage will detract Americans from "understanding" that racism continues to "shape" the American experience.

And as such, I cannot help but state that a discipline with this message to black America is not one that we can look to for counsel on how to uplift less fortunate blacks and get beyond race at last. Ideology, indeed, is key here. We all have it. And the ideology of modern sociology is hard left. These scholars operate upon a bedrock assumption that even residual racist bias decisively blocks black advancement, and upon a sense that it is logically plausible that an America could exist where the playing field is level for all comers. That is, they seek a profound transformation of society, in which hierarchy and power would play much lesser roles than they do now. Naturally this, a leftist ideology, guides their choice of projects, what data to examine, what conclusions to draw from it, and what advice to present on its basis.

But my ideology does not accept their bedrock assumptions. My ideology stipulates that residual racism is not a block upon the advancement of a group, and that a perfectly level playing field is therefore a fantastical distraction in a society in which hierarchy and power will always thrive. I believe this not out of a self-modelled, grousing sense that people must just "pull themselves up by their own bootstraps" and that those left behind just need to get real. I am endlessly thankful that overt discrimination was outlawed in the sixties, such that, for example, I have never had to pull myself up by said bootstraps and thus have no story to tell of that kind. And, as far as I am concerned, claims that blacks could, or should, have climbed their way upward without the Civil Rights revolution are academic at best. America evidenced a resonant moral sophistication in giving blacks at that time a boost.

However, I indeed believe that the Civil Rights and Voting Rights acts were enough to allow us to thrive, especially with affirmative action emerging in their wake. I believe this not out of influence from conservative "ideologues," but for a simple, empirical reason—that thousands of other human groups throughout history have managed to thrive despite the ruling class's contempt and subjugation, even without Civil Rights Acts— including, to a considerable extent, black Americans before the 1960s.

Thus, where sociologists think of South Central and shake their heads, I think of thriving Bronzeville at its height between the wars and shake my head, assuming that something extra turned Bronzeville into the Chicago inner city in the seventies, in which a proud term like "Bronzeville" could only seem irrelevant. It is precisely this something extra that I hold American society responsible for helping poor blacks to get past today. There is no "black bashing" here, since I consider concerned whites in the sixties major culprits in helping that something extra, the meme of alienation, to take root in black America. I am almost nauseated at the thought of white liberals teaching urban blacks in the late sixties to apply for welfare and to take offense at calls for them to work for their payments if possible. It was this "crack" that the government shunted into South Central, and for this reason I consider the late 1960s to be a chillingly repulsive period in American history.

Utopianism Is Cheap Advice

Yet in the end, this also means that I see no constructive value in the ideology that modern sociology presents as enlightened truth. Regretfully, I sense these people as telling us that solving black America's problems will only happen with a vast upending of procedure in a nation where no one could reasonably believe that this could ever happen. Cases that black Americans alone will need this upending of procedure will never achieve a consensus beyond the academy, liberal bureaucrats, and scattered leftist activists. If sociologists hope that somehow things may ever be otherwise, then it is unclear upon what logical grounds they suppose so; forty years of their books, editorials, and public speeches have failed to change a general consensus that while obstacles exist, responsibility is key—a consensus sociologists readily rue year after year.

A particular problem is that in our era, poor immigrants, many African-descended, are working their way upward year by year in full view of the populace. The Immigration Act of 1965 was brand-new during the War on Poverty, and so the success of such immigrants did not yet stand as an inconvenient contradiction to welfare activists' insistence that the new economy made it impossible to work one's way up from the bottom. Another result of the role that immigrants play in modern America is that a Latino segment now outnumbers blacks. The days when race issues in America were a simple matter of black versus white while Latinos and Asians and the others hovered in small numbers at the margins are gone forever. It will be increasingly difficult to motivate a newly diverse American populace to focus on black issues the way it did in the sixties and sev-

enties. This will be especially since Latinos often suffer from similar problems and yet are more diverse politically than blacks (splitting their vote
about down the middle for Kerry versus Bush in the 2004 election, for example).

The revolutionary prospect is even bleaker given a government that
has shown sincere and sustained interest (as opposed to the quickly scut-
tled gestures of Reconstruction) in turning racial policy upside down precisely once, forty years ago—and even then, in the view of most
sociologists, to an insufficient extent. And that government evidences not
a whit of interest in fostering another revolution, especially since such political revolutions occur in the wake of nationwide changes in consensus.
Brown v. Board of Education, for example, could not have happened ten
years earlier. After blacks served in World War II, their demands for desegregation in the workplace and the military in the 1940s had a unique resonance that bore fruit, and then, *Brown* and images of Civil Rights protests
on television became part of a context that allowed the Civil and Voting
Rights acts a decade later. But today, partly because of the very progress in
black advancement that sociologists are so distressed to see us paying attention to, there is not, and will never again be, a national consensus that
would condition the government to make such another ideological
U-turn.

Is this fair? That argument could go on forever. The sociologist wants
us to see the murderous thug with five kids by four mothers and recruiting
twelve-year-olds to sell crack as the product of factories moving away and
black doctors and lawyers moving to the suburbs in 1969. I disagree, but
just maybe the sociologist feels that he could defend his case if given the
opportunity, if only America would listen. He also feels that if he could
make his case, then whites and middle-class blacks would move back to
the ghetto where this thug lives, enticed by tax breaks encouraging successful people to pick up stakes and move to the slums, and help sway this
thug's children into more moral and productive lives. I consider that scenario hopelessly utopian. But he feels that utopianism is worth indulging
in, in our moment, since if Washington somehow adopted his vision and
fostered it via policy, then as well, corporations would be not just suggested but also required to move into depressed areas and hire the thug and
his friends, regardless of whether this relocation and a uniquely challenging, underprepared, and alienated workforce would allow the company to
reap profit, contrary to centuries of capitalist endeavor deeply entrenched in
the essence of the American polity. I can't help seeing the probability of

this kind of corporate policy ever becoming a norm in our society as distinctly minor.

Fine, though. Whether the sociologist is right or I am, we all agree, I would think, that at the end of the day, speaking up for a race with problems requires a realistic vision of what can be done. We will all shudder to think that sociologists might have drifted into supposing that masturbatory self-congratulation is truly a worthy goal of an academic discipline. And as such, we must ask, along with the sociologist, what the chances are that his vision is one that will bear fruit in America as we know it. After all, our interest here is in human beings and their children, not cogitating upon idealistically advanced brands of consummately informed moral awareness that give little or no indication of ever swaying the people at the levers of power in our nation.

It's not that I am against the idea of the "scholar-activist"—the question is simply what one's activism is aimed at. Is activism pointing the way toward feasible pathways to improvement in people's conditions, or is it pointing out eternal infelicities of human nature that will never change? The former brand of activism seeks change that might actually happen. The latter brand displays a personal higher awareness and seeks to inculcate it in others—but to what end?

Once when I gave a talk, one of the people in the audience was, as it happens, one of the authors of the paper in *American Sociological Review* showing that even small children perceive race. I had argued, among other things, that racism had been typical in all human civilizations past and present, and that we misdirect our energies in supposing that there will ever be a human polity in which there are no biases of any kind based on racial categories. I argued that the elimination of institutionalized discrimination was crucial, but that in the wake of this, we must rid ourselves of the idea that the revolution is not finished until even residual racist bias does not exist—because it always will, and in the meantime, humans regularly succeed despite it, including black Americans.

The author of the paper misheard me as saying that racism is extinct in America—a common mistake. Hearing this from what I said suggests being uniquely primed to refute such a claim, eagerly waiting to object to it as proposed by a "controversial" person—exemplifying my assertion that today's sociologists take the idea that all racism must be extinguished as a central commitment. But in any case, the author—quite genially, it should be said—gave me a copy of the book that the paper was a summary of, as evidence that racism is real. More precisely, the author engaged me with gentle joshings and nudges backed by a certain iron fist underneath the boxing gloves, that made it quite clear that the goal—or, I might say, mission—was to gently dissuade me of my understandably, but grievously, uninformed positions.

I asked: "I assume that in perhaps the final chapter of the book, you outline what we can do about children's early awareness of race. What are the suggestions?" The author replied that there were no such suggestions and that this might someday be a topic of future research.

I did not sense that the author was terribly concerned with change. Rather, the job was done once the "racism" was identified. Objection trumped process. Indicating how we uplift black people *despite* racial perceptions was not important.

But that's rather odd if you think about it. A whole book about how children perceive race early, and then, well—just that. If the authors were so disturbed by that phenomenon, then wouldn't we expect them to have an equal commitment to pointing the way beyond?

Imagine a convention of professional exterminators where someone gave a presentation showing that somewhere in Columbus, Ohio, there are some census tracts where there are a whole lot of roaches and termites. Period. Nothing about how to get rid of them. Now, maybe I am being unfair in depicting that presentation as being given at a convention of people trained to *exterminate* vermin. But here's the thing—can you even imagine a convention of people trained to do nothing but track where there is a lot of vermin and then just go home? "Well, ladies and gentlemen, this year we have found a new aphid infestation in two contiguous neighborhoods in Richmond, Virginia, and here are our statistical predictions as to where and to what extent the aphids will spread over the next five years. And now, please enjoy cheese cubes and Zinfandel out in the lobby."

I see no difference between this and sociologists identifying "racism" and going home. What is the purpose? If the purpose is to make it that racism somehow becomes utterly unknown in human interaction, then they give us little or no indication of how that would happen. Which means that all they are genuinely driven by is just telling us that there are a lot of roaches.

After all, since Americans will always perceive race to some degree— a proposition that even black lefties and their white comrades tend to concur with readily—the sociologist's argument would seem to signify that a disproportionate number of blacks will remain poor forever. I find this an unimaginative approach to an issue so tragic and urgent. It even seems lazy, until we see that the very goal itself is not to solve a problem at all, but to strike a sociopolitical orientation considered noble in certain circles.

I fail to see why academic sociology sees it as beside the point to apply mental power to shedding light on how black people can overcome, rather than applying that mental power to an almost macabre fascination with how black people can *be* overcome. Or better, I do see why—but only in that modern sociology is peopled by well-intentioned souls overcome themselves. They are overcome by the meme of therapeutic alienation— the same one that has overcome the people they analyze in their work.

Calling on America to turn upside down in 1956, when black Americans were casually and legally treated like lower beings, and recent history concretely showed that America was ready to listen if we just stuck to our guns, was realistic. Calling on America to turn upside down in 2006, when most black Americans are making the best of themselves, the remaining issues are so much more complex than they were in 1956, and there is no logical reason to suppose that any turning upside down will ever occur again, is performance art.

Modern Sociology: Mutual Admiration Society

I am fully aware that I could be accused of stepping out of bounds in making these summary claims about academic sociology without having devoted my career to participation in the field. I have not spent a decade or more reading the books, reading from several journals, attending conferences, conversing regularly with career sociologists, doing my own projects, knowing the up-to-the-minute work. Having spent a career in another academic discipline, linguistics, makes me especially aware of the fact that only doing these things over a long period of time can one truly claim to know a field. No one could convince me that he or she was anything approaching an expert on the science of language from having gone through ten-year runs of two linguistics journals, made his or her way through a textbook, read a fair number of other books, and made some assessments on the basis of this plus general knowledge and his or her own perception—no matter how carefully reasoned—of common sense.

Yet, even with this acknowledged, I would not be quite sure what to make of a claim that my verdict on the discipline's perspective on what black America needs is not representative of the consensus in the field. For example, if there were a significant strain in sociological work taking a less leftist perspective, then we would expect leading articles of the type I have examined to address this alternate school, aggressively attempting to rebut their conclusions. But the articles in ten years of both *American Journal of Sociology* and *American Sociological Review* evidence no such alternate school. Rather, the authors cordially cite and address fellow writers of their persuasion, engaging in moderate, in-house disagreements as to, for example, just how or to what degree racism affects a particular topic of address. I see the same tendency in articles in other sociology journals my research happens to lead me to, as I try to engage the sources that books and articles refer to in order to get as full a picture on a given topic as I can.

The only reference sociologists seem to make to thinkers seriously opposed to the basic "racism forever" paradigm is not of a "renegade" school of other sociologists, but of people who work outside of academic social science like Shelby Steele or Stephen Carter. And even they are generally acknowledged only in quick genuflective citations or brief potshots rather than engaged substantially, likely considered unworthy of serious engagement because they do not do statistical surveys. But even if we decide that this dismissal is valid (although I would disagree), the point remains that there would appear to be no alternate school of card-carrying sociologists that refutes my characterization of the field. These people work without serious criticism of their philosophical underpinnings, all rowing together in one boat, convinced that there is no sensible alternative to the way they think. Of course, some might suppose that this is because these people's convictions are unassailable truth. But black America past and present leads me to think not, as I have tried to get across in the previous chapters. Moreover, I will venture the assertion—albeit ready to see it contradicted with logical argument—that nothing I have seen by way of chi-squares and regressions in sociologists' arguments deep-sixes the conclusions I have come to. We might recall, for example, the statistical "predictions" in *American Apartheid* based on post-1960 conditions, as if the first slaves were brought to America around 1948 or blacks experienced a collapse in the economy for the first time in the 1970s, having somehow been immune to the effects of, say, the Great Depression or the Panic of 1893.

This is not to say that the articles in the journals I have examined do not address real phenomena. Certainly professional sociologists consider some articles more compelling arguments than others and can point out lapses in literature coverage, statistical analysis, use of data, and the like— but this would be beyond me. I assume that all of these articles, having passed peer review, are at the very least legitimate and deeply informed addresses of their topics. I will not deny that whites tend to leave neighborhoods when blacks reach a certain proportion of the population, that the number of black men in prison or on the ropes leaves black women with fewer marriage choices than is ideal, that growing up poor in a ghetto makes it harder to make the best of oneself as an adult, that before the seventies black women were hardly strangers to giving birth without being married, and so on.

The problem, however, is that the frames of reference on race now entrenched in academic sociology address only a part of the scene they claim to report from. That is, there is nothing in these works, individually or collectively, that belies a basic observation: They misrepresent the reality of the state of black America, in favor of stressing the bad and almost willfully neglecting the good, or even the possible.

CONCLUSION

When black legal theorist Regina Austin praises black lawbreaking in all seriousness with:

> A new politics of identification, fueled by critically confronting the question of the positive significance of black lawbreaking, might restore some vitality to what has become a mere figure of speech . . . drawing on lawbreaker culture would add a bit of toughness, resilience, bluntness, and defiance to contemporary mainstream black political discourse, which evidences a marked preoccupation with civility, respectability, sentimentality, and decorum.

. . . she is not engaging any reality she knows, such as one in which her comfortable life as a University of Pennsylvania law professor were perhaps interrupted by a "black lawbreaker"—perhaps one of Elijah Anderson's "boisterous" men from "Northton"—carjacking her at an intersection. She is placing sticking up her middle finger over all else. She is writing in therapeutic alienation.

When black New York University sociologist Troy Duster speaks against targeting drugs at specific races even when BiDil is found to prevent heart attacks in blacks much more than whites, he is placing playing the Cassandra to the White Man over black health. The only thing that justifies his being allowed to live outside of a mental institution is that he is led by a very coherent thought pattern: therapeutic alienation.

There is something grievously wrong with an academic orthodoxy whose favorite thing to tell black people is that we are right in keeping fury at whitey front and center. It's wasteful of good minds. It's condescending to people who deserve better. It will be regarded, a century from now, as a low moment in the history of American social scientific inquiry.

And it only makes any kind of logical or moral sense as the gestures of people caught up in alienation that serves to heal themselves rather than the people they claim to be concerned about. This includes both blacks healing a sense of racial inferiority and whites who gain a sense of moral legitimacy by shaking their fists at the Suits, having selected the black racket as their chosen brand of this kind of self-medication.

Reading through this literature I have a constant sense of, first, *J'accuse!*—couldn't such smart people claiming to have blacks' interests at heart do better than channeling their mental energy into such inert defeatism? Second, always resonating in my head is, well, *À quoi ça sert???*— what is this *for*? What *use* did these authors think this had?

Nevertheless, I do try my best to attend to what people who do not think like me have to say about race in America. I dare say that the bibliography of this book includes proportionally more books and articles by strange bedfellows, as my politics go, than the bibliography of just about any book by a black writer from the left would. I would feel starved to *only* read Steele, Sowell, Ellison, and the Thernstroms. I want to know as much as I can. After all, it's not uncommon to learn something valuable from writers who don't think like you.

However, I do not accept counsel rooted in a psychological tic that is, however understandably, disconnected from empirical experience. For that reason, I do not see the leftist orthodoxy in academia as presenting a case of any significant use to people who are seeking to solve black America's problems. And more germane to this book, I have encountered nothing in such work that speaks against the conclusions that I have presented.

ERASING IT

If it's not about The Man anymore, how do we process what is going on in Black America and think about moving ahead? The lens has changed.

The last time it changed was in the late sixties: Through the new lens in those days, what was once a token black became a "diverse" person.

So now we're changing the lens again. What will ideas like "hip-hop revolution" look like now? Or "black students fail because white teachers don't love them"? Or a Congressional Black Caucus that spearheads no significant legislation?

CHAPTER EIGHT

Therapeutic Alienation Meets Hitting the Books: "Acting White" and Affirmative Action Revisited

I f we understand that black American attitudes and behaviors can be determined by a meme that does not always correspond to modern reality, then we are in a better position to understand the notorious achievement gap between whites and blacks and to judge the wisdom of racial preference policies.

Namely, the reason for the notorious achievement gap between even middle-class black students and white and Asian ones is not economics or racism, but a cultural factor: a facet of black peer culture that senses school as something separate from black culture.

The best known instantiation, where black students openly assail diligent peers as "acting white," is a particularly clear manifestation of therapeutic alienation. The obvious harm of scholarly mediocrity becomes tolerable damage under a guiding embrace of setting oneself off against an oppressor, this celebrated by black teenage peers as a badge of racial identity.

But just as often, black students harbor a quieter sense that school is something that merits only a certain amount of commitment because it is something spiritually separate from being a black person. Here, the alienation is less overt: It is less a conscious rejection of achievement than a lack of spontaneous inclination to pursue achievement with the near obsession that separates the men from the boys in schoolwork. That self-imposed ceiling on how hard one pushes is, while not deliberate, an expression of a fundamental sense of separateness from the essence of the endeavor. The question is why such a disproportionate number of students belonging to one group have that sense, rather than it being a mere happenstance trait of a certain number of individuals within that group.

When we see that the disproportion holds constant even among privileged middle-class black students, we cannot help concluding that the barrier in question is not one of class or opportunity but of race.

A common response here is to note that the students' parents may well be of blue-collar origins even if they have achieved middle-class status in the financial sense, and thus unable to pass on the skills and orientations necessary to doing well in school. But that explanation neglects history. If it were true, then we would expect certain things to be true.

One, the "acting white" charge would have arisen shortly after the Civil War. In fact, *it only began in the late sixties*. I have yet to encounter a single documentation of it before then; old heads regularly describe it as a "new" problem, and the mountain of testimonials I have received about it since *Losing the Race* was published even allows placing its emergence at about 1966.

Two, we would expect that black students would have been underperforming compared with white students of similar backgrounds shortly after the Civil War. But again, this performance gap *only began in the late sixties*. Sure, poor black students in substandard segregated schools in the South did only so well. But there were a great many solid black public schools across the nation where black kids gave white students across town a run for their money, as Thomas Sowell has repeatedly called attention to.

Thus, the now familiar problem where black students from solid backgrounds mysteriously tend to hover at the bottom of the class and baffle educators is a late twentieth-century problem. Black students who reject school as "white" do so while ones who lived when lynching was ordinary pursued education obsessively. Black parents who do not instill in their children a sense that failing in school is unacceptable, and are more inclined to complain about "subtle racism" at the schools than to make sure their children do their best despite it, are a new phenomenon: The priorities were more often the reverse for these parents' own parents and grandparents. Clearly, a great many black people are approaching education differently from the way they did before the late sixties. Crucially, although their approach would have seemed natural before the sixties, it was in fact marginal—but then although their approach seems peculiarly disconnected from *modern* conditions, it thrives nevertheless.

It's that meme again, where an orientation lives on regardless of external stimulus. Like any successful meme, the sense of school as something separate from true blackness is passed from one peer generation to another even among black kids receiving solid educations from white teachers deeply devoted to helping them.

Then, some suppose that this sense of separation from school is based on fear or jealousy—upon which, see the previous two pages. Why not the same sentiment when whites could call blacks *nigger* with no fear of prosecution on the basis of hate speech codes or even social propriety?

To understand that we are dealing with therapeutic alienation rather than racism brings us to implications for grappling with the black-white achievement gap in the present and future. Namely, it sheds light on the wisdom of racial preferences. To set the bar lower for black students out of a sense that the achievement gap is due to socioeconomics is mistaken. Because the factor is not socioeconomic but cultural and self-perpetuating, the lowered bar only deprives black students and parents of any reason to learn how to hit the highest note. Much of the time, there is not even any way for black people to know what it would actually be to perform at that level—because they never have to.

Making sure black students get good educations in an economy that will be increasingly hard to take advantage of otherwise requires clear-eyed, honest approaches. There remains a contingent of people whose views on this issue are not based in reality and therefore can help no one. We will understand why these people have been led to think this way. But we must also, gently but firmly, exclude them from any discussions we intend as constructive.

DOUBLE-TALK IN THE ACADEMY

The current standard of discourse on blacks and education is, to put it lightly, problematic. This is especially the case regarding racial preferences. Discussions of this topic are as deeply coded as liturgical debates in the Middle Ages. In the future, painstaking analysis of social history and cultural context will be needed to comprehend the motivations behind positions that appear oddly incoherent until one understands what is behind various buzzwords and phrases. The reason for the cognitive dissonance is a failure to understand that the reason for the rarity of even middle-class black students able to submit top-flight applications to colleges is a cultural meme that thrives independently of racism or inequity.

Intelligent people earnestly discuss making black students feel "welcome." Administrators soberly genuflect to the notion that they have not yet done "enough" to foster a black "presence" on campus. Everyone "wants to know" why selective college campuses don't "look like America." But there is always an elephant sitting in the middle of the room that no one talks about—the reason why it is so "challenging" to get a representative number of black students on campus: namely, that so few of them have grades or test scores high enough to qualify under the regular evaluation procedure. In response to claims from the occasional whistleblower that standards are being lowered for black students, administrators are trained to insist that this is not true. Yet, simple and readily available data show that each year, there is but a sliver of black students with the grades and test scores considered sine qua non for serious consideration if students were white or Asian.

For example, admission to a top-ten law school requires a GPA of at least 3.5 and an LSAT score of at least 165. In 2002, 4,500 out of 91,000 law school applicants met that standard. Of them, exactly twenty-nine were black Americans—and that pool had to spread across all ten top schools plus other ones just below them in ranking. Pure logic requires that having a first-year class that is even 6 or 7 percent black requires each selective school to subject blacks to lower standards. Among undergraduate cohorts, it has been shown that black and Latino students were being admitted according to lower standards in university after university: UC Berkeley, The University of Texas, The University of Georgia, Rutgers University, and most notoriously, the University of Michigan, where in 1999, 93 percent of black and Latino students were admitted with combinations of grades and test scores that gained less than one in five white students admission.

To the extent that someone acknowledges that standards are lowered for black applicants, they switch into a different ritual: assuming that to discuss black students is to discuss people who are either poor or at least grew up on the wrong side of the tracks. Thus, one is to assume that the reason for the lower grades and scores is that the typical black student went to school under the tough conditions familiar from Jonathan Kozol's *Savage Inequalities*: broken homes, two students to one antiquated textbook, schools with peeling paint and metal detectors at the doors. But this again requires turning a blind eye to empirical experience.

It was one thing for affirmative action debates to proceed this way in, say, 1969, when to be middle class and black was still to be "fortunate," as it was then often put. But for students, faculty, and administrators to imply this in the 1990s has been, frankly, absurd. Black student bodies at selective colleges are overwhelmingly middle class. To the extent that we quibble about what middle class means, white and Asian students from homes that weren't exactly rolling in dough are quite common on such campuses as well. Once again, it is painfully clear that different standards have been applied not to struggling inner-city survivors, but to the children of the first generation of affirmative action babies. And one of the prime defenses of affirmative action is that it allowed this now graying generation to become—middle class.

Thus, we sing of racial preferences as giving disadvantaged blacks a break, appended with claims that black students we call middle class actually are not because, for example, blacks have yet to accumulate the stock portfolios that whites often have. But then the same people making these arguments sing paeans to affirmative action as having created a middle-class black generation who sent their kids to top schools, with mutual funds suddenly absent from discussion. This is, simply, double-talk.

The question is why children of this new middle-class black generation so often post GPAs and test scores that would bar any white or Asian student from consideration, while Asian children of shopkeepers come up with applications so sterling that admissions committees have to worry that their minority group is crowding out black and Latino applicants. Basic human intuition leads one to suppose that there is something about black culture—likely a legacy of slavery and segregation—that makes the difference between the Asian kids and black ones.

But under the Dadaistic regulations of discussing such issues in the brie-and-Zinfandel world, arguments attempting to uncover the cultural realities that cause these discrepancies are dismissed as conservative "rhetoric" and tarred as threatening "resegregation." Instead, university whites, who examine themselves for underlying racism more diligently than any people on the planet, let float the implication that universities, of all places, harbor some kind of mysterious anti-brown racism that infects admissions processes. The "How can we make black students feel 'welcome'?" incantation is especially deft here, with its hint that the issue is that some folks somewhere up in the Ivory Tower just don't much like black students. Lord protect the poor soul who observes that the issue is whether we want to "welcome" middle-class black students by admitting them under the bar (i.e., someone who addresses the issue according to simple logic rather than the dutiful elisions typical of religious faith). Given the almost rabid policing on college campuses of the slightest hint of "racist" sentiment, the studious soul-searching on such issues typical of the modern academic, the conversion of whole disciplines into crusades against discrimination, the diversity workshops freshmen are required to attend, the requirement that college presidents and provosts toe the party line on "diversity" in all public statements, and the vast resources devoted to wooing promising black students every spring, it would seem a distinct challenge to identify just how racism plays its hand in admissions, and few ever even venture explanations in this vein. Yet, I have witnessed black PhDs proclaiming at university forums that without affirmative action, campuses would quickly revert to being all white, with an implication that this would be because whites would drop their commitment to having a black presence on campus. Inevitably, comments like this get vigorous applause, with even white audience members joining in. This assent is purely visceral: It corresponds to no current reality that the people clapping know.

Then one more example of blatant contradiction masquerading as constructive thought is the common complaint by black students and new professors that their white colleagues automatically assume their qualifications are suspect because of affirmative action. But more often than not affirmative action does play a large role in admissions and hirings in universities. So wouldn't a natural solution, at least up for discussion, be to eliminate the cause for the suspicion?

But one who suggests this is tarred as "racist"—but only along the lines of twisted logic. Ellis Cose, for example, addresses this possible solution but then dismisses it for not taking into account society's "underlying attitudes," quoting a black professor sonorously saying, "I will still be perceived as a token until you bring in a significant number of blacks." The idea here is that blacks' abilities would be questioned even if there were no affirmative action. But there is no proof of this, and it is in fact by no means an obvious point.

Here and elsewhere, the rituals under which we discuss racial preferences in college admissions make no logical sense whatsoever—unless we realize that what is at work is the meme of therapeutic alienation. Blacks indulge in speaking up for the eternal victimhood of their brothers and sisters, and this is so seductive, as a leading meme of our era, that it is allowed to trump simple reasoning. This is only abetted by a private sense among these people that in the end, hitting the highest scholastic note is tangential to being "really black." For them this means that at a top university as everywhere else, one's "blackness" is the first consideration and one's humanity the second, rather than the other way around. Meanwhile, whites are equally under the sway of an era that elevates exaggeration of victimhood, and pretending to concur with it, as permissible suspensions of common sense. Thus, they get to congratulate themselves on being "aware" and "concerned"—and go home to take care of children whom they wouldn't dream of allowing to be used as tokens amid a smoke screen of Orwellian double-talk. This will not do.

THE "ACTING WHITE" CHARGE AS A MEME

What would put a block on much of the operations of the therapeutic alienation meme in these rituals would be a full awareness that the key issue is a different expression of that same meme. There are plausible reasons other than poverty or racism that could keep even affluent black students from doing their best. Over the past several years, there has grown a mountain of evidence that culture is the issue here.

For example, in *Losing the Race,* I referred to the middle-class Ohio suburb Shaker Heights, where even in fine, well-funded schools, where there is no ability tracking and students decide whether to take Advanced Placement classes, and where there are mentoring services set up to help minority students in danger of falling behind, black students from middle-class backgrounds regularly perform at the very bottom of their classes. But Shaker Heights is only one example amid a generality.

It was examined as part of a larger project conducted by the Minority Student Achievement Network, which since 1999 has identified similar problems in more than twenty middle-class districts across the country, including Amherst; Ann Arbor; Arlington; Mount Kisco, New York; Bellevue, Washington; Cambridge, Massachusetts; Champaign, Illinois; Chapel Hill; Cherry Hill, New Jersey; University Heights, Ohio; Eugene, Oregon; Evanston; Farmington, Minnesota; Green Bay; Hamden, Connecticut; Madison, Wisconsin; Montclair, New Jersey; Oak Park, Illinois; Brookline, Massachusetts; White Plains, New York; and Windsor, Connecticut. There have been similar reports from other districts, such as Prince George's County, Virginia; Maplewood, New Jersey; and Nyack, New York, and readers may well have read of an achievement gap problem where they live.

In one place after another, educators are baffled as even middle-class black students perform much more poorly than we would expect year after year. And reports are rife with such teens recounting having been teased for "acting white" when they embraced school and often even checking out of scholarly achievement to have friends. Why?

The History of the "Acting White" Charge

What helps us to peg this phenomenon as a symptom of the meme this book is about is that it only began in the mid-1960s.

Traditionally, anti-intellectualism was distributed in black American culture precisely the way it was in general American culture. In fact, in many ways there was less anti-intellectualism among blacks. During and after the Civil War, blacks were starved for education, and the idea that loving to learn was "white" was unknown. The chaplain of a black Civil War regiment recounted: "A majority of the men seem to regard their books as an indispensable portion of their equipments, and the cartridge box and spelling book are attached to the same belt." Freedmen's Bureau superintendent John W. Alvord reported in 1866 that "everywhere some elementary text-book, or the fragment of one, may be seen in the hands of Negroes" and that "Two colored young men, who but a little time before commenced to learn themselves, had gathered 150 pupils, all quite orderly and hard at study." One Alabama observer recounted a rally raising money for a schoolhouse: "One old man, who had seen slavery days, with all of his life's earnings in an old greasy sack, slowly drew it from his pocket, and emptied it on the table," saying, " 'I want to see the children of my grandchildren have a chance, and so I am giving my all.' "

After this, there was no achievement gap of note between blacks and whites. Unsurprisingly, blacks who went to underfunded backwater schools tended not to come out as learned citizens. But when conditions between blacks and whites were equal, there was no problem. The University of Massachusetts at Amherst admitted thirty-four blacks between 1892 and 1954, and seven (more than a quarter) were Phi Beta Kappas. Up through the fifties and beyond, black public schools were often excellent, as fondly recalled today by older blacks perplexed by the "acting white" charge. The most famous example was Washington, DC's, Dunbar High, where in 1899, students outscored all white schools in standardized tests. Other fine black schools included Atlanta's Booker T. Washington High, Baltimore's Frederick Douglass High, and New Orleans's McDonough 35 High.

Ironically, the demise of segregation in this era helped pave the way for the "acting white" charge. With the closing of black schools after desegregation orders, black students began going to school with white ones in larger numbers than ever before, which meant that whites were available for black students to model themselves against. That was not an inevitable response to their presence. Hypothetically we can imagine black students taking on whites competitively—recall the sadly obsolete adage blacks used to pass on among themselves that black people have to be twice as good as whites to be treated as normal.

But treating the act of doing well in school as disloyal became attractive under the new way of thinking that was settling into the black community. An open-ended wariness of whites became a bedrock of black identity, among a people deprived by history of a more positive, individual source of security and purpose. If this had not led black kids to start turning away from school as "white," it would have been surprising.

The meme, like so many cultural factors, expresses itself to varying extents in individuals. The spirited clique leaders who hurl the "acting white" charge most openly are deeply impacted by the meme. In most black kids, however, it operates more subtly, fashioning a basic sense that one's blackness and "the school thing" are different. One may plug away, but not go as far as the virtual obsession with the material that makes a top scholar; going that far would go beyond what it is to be "really black." This too is the operation of a meme, in that the same black students before the late sixties did not feel this way: We are dealing with a new kind of self-conception among blacks, a new kind of thought pattern that most of the students at Dunbar High did not have. This has decisive effects on how one performs scholastically. Certainly, plenty of white kids feel a sense of separation from school. But with black kids, the feeling is rooted in racial identity, which means that the sense of separation will be much more widespread among people of said race.

"The urge which drove Negroes away from education was whites'; it took Jim Crow to turn blacks against hope," Debra Dickerson has written, but this is only true if she means that black kids turned against hope in the *aftermath* of Jim Crow, as a protective strategy. *During* Jim Crow, black kids hitting the books were teased as "walking encyclopedias," like all American nerds, but not for the more trenchantly injurious sin of "acting white." That charge thrives today regardless of treatment from whites. As a meme, it replicates itself by passing from mind to mind and parasitizing itself upon preexisting mental configurations favorable to its entrenchment. In black teens' cases, these configurations are the insecurities of, first, youth and second, membership in a race whose sense of self remains, predictably, damaged just a few decades after the horrors of which we are all aware. To put "blackness" over school, actively or passively, offers one an escape from being an individual when doing so feels threatening. Stanley Crouch notes that the problem is not, as many misunderstand this issue, a fear of school. The problem is a sense that being a black individual is not good enough: "Children then seek to be good automatons, not individuals, and feel terrible when they don't do well at erasing their human qualities."

Many are viscerally revolted by claims that the "acting white" charge has anything significant to do with black student underachievement. Yet, the fact remains that the charge is extremely common; it is, quite simply, a familiar and deeply entrenched part of black American teen culture. Since the late 1960s, one simply could not grow up black in America and miss it, unless life happened to limit one's exposure to black children. One might even wonder just why it would *not* be a factor in underachievement. How could that charge be prevalent and yet somehow have no impact on performance worth mentioning? That would, in fact, be quite strange.

But for many, allowing that logical disjunction to pass is preferable to "blaming the victim." In fact, they needn't worry. It's not that black kids mysteriously started rejecting school for no reason in the sixties, or that there is anything inherently anti-intellectual about black America. What created the "acting white" charge was a normal psychological response to facing a new America while still riddled with generations of abuse. It is part of a protective mechanism. Our response must be one of compassion, not of dismissal. But our response cannot be one of what we might call compassionate denial. Otherwise, we waste our compassion upon false leads and efforts more symbolic than constructive.

Academics and "Acting White": Society Versus Culture

It is my impression that the fact that culture plays a large part in the achievement gap is seeming less heretical to many concerned people than it was ten years ago. A new "culture matters" meme is getting out there. The Minority Student Achievement Network's addressing the problem in middle-class districts is a clear indication, and an emblematic moment was when, at the 2004 Democratic Convention, Barack Obama called on us to "eradicate the slander that says a black youth with a book is acting white" and the audience went nuts. There are still people around who think that black students' problems in school are only or mostly because of lousy ghetto schools and biased teachers condemning black students to low ability tracks. But these days, these are usually either people who have come through education school indoctrination, or people who have not had occasion to examine the issue very closely, reciting a wisdom of the seventies and eighties and unaware that the debate has progressed since.

More and more people are realizing that admitting the obvious reality of the "acting white" problem does not mean disrespecting black students or black culture, and that one can understand that while race matters, culture matters as well.

However, a major exception is, predictably, many social scientists, who devote careers to decrying the "culture matters" perspective as a harmful illusion. Committed to the depths of their being to painting blacks as noble victims, their hair stands on end to see "conservative" writers getting what they see as inappropriate media attention, given that they consider themselves to have disproven the idea that "oppositional culture" affects black scholastic performance. They see books like my *Losing the Race*, the late Berkeley anthropologist John Ogbu's *Black American Students in an Affluent Suburb* (with Astrid Davis), and even statements like Obama's as underinformed dogma, misleading a populace whose resistance to academics' grim conclusions about blacks' conditions is already frustrating enough.

But the question is whether such people have actually proven that black teens' tendencies to hear that doing well in school is "acting white" has no effect on performance. And the truth is that despite the statistics that social scientists tend to consider so authoritative, these people have not even begun to disprove the thesis.

A useful example is James Ainsworth-Darnell's and Douglas Downey's *American Sociological Review* article purportedly showing that the "acting white" explanation is a myth. The study is based on a survey of 17,000 high school sophomores done by the National Center for Education Statistics in 1990, encompassing 2,197 black students. Ainsworth-Darnell and Downey find that on the average, black students report more positive attitudes toward school than whites and that black students who report being popular also tend to do well in school. They take this as refuting the idea that the "acting white" charge plays a part in depressing black students' performances.

But Ainsworth-Darnell and Downey present their conclusions as if certain problematic discrepancies in the larger world did not exist. Clearly, if all there was to be said was that black students say they like school and that they are popular when they do well at it, then across America, black students would be notorious as plucky high achievers, and this is not the case: Asians occupy that slot. Even the authors have to admit that the black students in the sample have the poorest grades however much they say they like school, and that even when socioeconomic background is taken into account, the grade gap between them and other students is lesser but still robust. Also, black students report doing the least homework—including the best ones.

There is, then, a lack of fit between what black students report and how they actually perform. Ainsworth-Darnell and Downey are empirical enough to at least address this at length—but in the end, they are too imprinted by the leftist imperative of sociology to avoid drifting into incoherence. They report that even good black students report doing an average of 3.9 hours of homework a day compared with white students' 5.4 and Asians' 7.5. Their response is that "there is no definite number of hours students who work 'as hard as they can almost every day' are *supposed* to spend on homework." That's nice, guys—but black students still do less, period. They come up with the athletic surmise that perhaps white and Asian students are overreporting how much homework they do, but without an explanation as to why black students would not do so as well. Might this not mean that there is something about black student culture that uniquely discourages such overreporting—that the scholarly does not have as much status among them as it does among other students? In this part of their discussion section, the authors' usual smooth, linear argumentation falters noticeably; one senses them as grasping at straws, faced with an inconvenient snag in their data that muddies their quest to paint black students as the new Asians.

When they close it with "Whether one 'tries hard in school' may mean different things to black students and white students because they are surrounded by different sets of peers with varying norms and expectations regarding school-related behaviors," they rather mysteriously shoot themselves in the foot, chiming in with precisely my observation in *Losing the Race*. Namely, I argued that the sense of cultural separation from school means that it can be hard for black students to spontaneously understand what doing their best would really entail because there is so little model for that kind of near-obsessive commitment in the culture, including the middle-class one. The issue is not only the overt one of being accused of "acting white," but also the larger effects of a meme, one of which inevitably casts school as "other." Ainsworth-Darnell and Downey would appear to agree with me here, and as such, support the idea that culture is key.

In a later response to a critique of the article, Ainsworth-Darnell and Downey also note that among the black students surveyed, the only ones who reported more teasing for doing well in school than whites were fourth graders and only a portion of them. But we are still faced with the simple reality of the grade and test score gap that concerns so many. Even if all students are teased for liking school to some extent, apparently white students' response to this teasing differs from black students' in significant ways. There is a cultural issue in play. This appears even more the case from something else tucked into Ainsworth-Darnell's and Downey's article, that teachers report that black students are more likely to be disruptive in class and to put forth less effort in homework—the latter, recall, confirmed by the black students themselves. The same problems apply to an oft-cited article analyzing the same data set as Ainsworth-Darnell and Downey, by Philip J. Cook and Jens Ludwig.

In any case, isn't it rather odd to see professional social scientists claiming that we illuminate psychological reality by simply asking people what they think? The same academics who wrote this article would dismiss out of hand a study that claimed to show that racism is extinct in America by asking a thousand whites whether they were racists. Surely, we would need subtler questioning and careful examination of actions as well as statements—and just as surely, these authors suppose that in doing this we would find that America Remains a Racist Country.

The sense of separation from school is, like racism, a subtle affair, that students are unaware of as often as not. If Ainsworth-Darnell, Downey, Jens, Ludwig, and company consider themselves to have proven that black teens are not united in an overt and proclaimed conviction that to apply oneself in school is "acting white," then they are correct. But this is a cartoon version of, for one, my argument, as well as Ogbu's and that of anyone who sees the "acting white" issue as a problem. Nothing this stark is necessary to create the achievement gap. I, for example, have argued not that every black student who tries to get good grades is shouted down as thinking he or she is white, but that a new sense of black identity in the sixties has led to a quiet cultural disconnect from "the school thing." Asking black students whether they subscribe to a bald assertion of this disconnect, given that most students of any color will be reluctant to openly say for public consumption that they do not value being good students, and that most of them are not consciously aware of the difference between them and students they tend not to socialize with anyway, has nothing to do with addressing a quiet habit of the heart.

It is hardly impossible to fashion tests that reveal that habit of the heart. One was Clifton Casteel's, surveying 928 white and 761 black students from twelve classes in nine schools: 81 percent of black females and 62 percent of black males said that they did their homework for their teachers, while just 28 percent of white females and 32 percent of white males did; white students tended to say that they did homework for their parents. This showed that black students tend to process schoolwork as something external to the realm of the heart—their parents and family; for them it is a task, a duty, to a greater extent than among white students, for whom school performance was something connected to home and hearth.

This was an ingenious study, and it is indicative that Claude Steele has been celebrated for applying a similarly careful technique to identifying "stereotype threat" among high-achieving black students, with a procedure in which the subjects did not know what was being investigated. Steele did not just sit the students down and ask them, "Do you feel insecure about your intellectual abilities in comparison with white students?" We all know almost all interviewees would say "no," and if Steele had presented such a study as showing that "stereotype threat" did not exist, it would have been roundly condemned as hopelessly crude. But when scholars like Ainsworth-Darnell and Downey use the same flimsy methodology and present it as evidence that black students are done in by The Man, they cop top journal slots. This is not scholars seeking truth; an ideological bias here is clear.

Then there has been a study by Karolyn Tyson, William Darity Jr., and Domini Castellino that the *New York Times* glibly featured as disproving the "acting white" thesis. But, in fact, the study soundly confirms that the phenomenon exists—it simply nuances the issue of what kinds of schools it is most likely to play a part in. The authors found that out of five high schools, the one where black students regularly reported being ostracized as "white" for doing well in school was 1) the largest, such that there was an especially robust and separate black student community, and 2) the one where there were the fewest black students in honors and Advanced Placement classes. At the other schools, which were either mostly black or were smaller and allowed more interracial contact, black students did not report this. In a different ideological climate, the paper could easily be publicized as proving the "acting white" thesis—especially as it reports things like a new assistant principal at one of the latter schools mentioning that the phenomenon was prevalent at the school she previously taught at.

Of course, the authors cannot allow the data to speak for itself. They want us to see the kids treating school as white as—drum roll, please—responding to racism rather than expressing a cultural meme. They have it that the absence of black students in the AP classes means that the classes are unjustly "the property of white students," and that if the black students' responses to this are cultural, then we must define culture as a tool kit rather than an ingrained folkway. Here, the tool kit allows the students to cope with the racist dismissal that their absence in the AP classes must be due to. But is racism really the reason for this absence when there are plenty of black students in AP courses in various schools across town? And why did black students in mostly white schools not resort to this "tool kit" before the late 1960s? These are yawning holes in their argumentation, which could only be let pass by academics and journalists out of a bedrock commitment to avoid confronting a phenomenon that stubbornly keeps making its presence known even to those who are dedicated to pretending it doesn't exist.

And joining Tyson, Darity, and Castellino as another nuanced but conclusive demonstration that there is no acting white "myth" is work by, of all people, a top social scientist, Harvard economist Roland Fryer. Fryer refers to data on ninety thousand students nationwide but assesses their popularity not according to self-reporting, but how wide their networks of friends are, first as reported by them, naturally—but then confirmed by checking whether the people in that network indeed report the subject as a friend. As I have heard Fryer put it, asking teenagers whether they are popular is like asking them whether they are having sex. (Certainly, that remark applies more gracefully to male teens than female ones, but still.) And Fryer's results ringingly show that among black teens, one is *less* likely to be popular the *better* one does in school—*to much more of an extent than among students of other races*. The findings also confirm two basic points I have often made about the issue: The problem is worst starting in junior high school (when racial identity starts kicking in seriously); and—as Tyson, Darity, and Castellino show—it evaporates in all-black schools (where there are no whites to set oneself off from).

Fryer is a black wunderkind whose phoenix-out-of-the-ashes working-class background disqualifies him from any charges of being a "bourgeois" sort out of touch with his roots or contemptuous of blacks who have not come as far as he has. Moreover, Fryer even takes issue with some previous analyses of the problem. He sees the "acting white" psychology as the result of a subconscious cost-benefit analysis rather than "oppositional identity" (although from my reading of his work, it seems to me that oppositional identity is the direct reason for the cost-benefit analysis in question, but so be it). He also treats my thesis as that black students "sabotage" one another in grand old "crabs in a barrel" style and politely dismisses it—upon which I feel moved to note: No hurt feelings, but while the word *sabotage* happens to be in *Losing the Race*'s subtitle, my thesis has nothing to do with crabs in a barrel. It is in fact one about oppositional identity—it's that which Fryer disagrees with me about.

In any case, we come back to the other scholars on this subject, presenting supposed analysis of a subtle problem like this based on what teenagers say about themselves, or running up against the problem they hoped not to find and laboriously fashioning swiss-cheese arguments tracing it to racism. This is flat-earther work. These scholars are not investigating the world without preset bias. They are seeking to confirm what they already regard as truth, and purport to have done so even in the face of glaring counterevidence such as the achievement gap itself, and do so via methodology they would laugh out of the room if applied to a thesis that did not support raging against The Machine. They are infected by the meme of alienation forever, caught in the same thought patterns that inform our twisted discussions of racial preferences.

The Blind Leading The Blind

At times, such scholars even harbor the very sense of separation from the scholarly that underlies the entire problem. An example is New York University scholar-activist Pedro Noguera, in whose work a particular strain in his reponse to my *Losing the Race* is especially revealing. Noguera has often claimed that in that book, I spend a lot of time singing of my own accomplishments and presenting them as a model for other blacks, wondering why they can't be like me.

Now, there are any number of criticisms of that book that, however we might judge them, address what is actually between its covers. But that is not true of Noguera's charge. The book does have personal anecdotes aplenty, but I think few who have read the book would claim that they are written as attempts to crow about my own accomplishments. Noguera has it that "McWhorter attributes his professional success to his talent and his intelligence." This truly sounds almost like Noguera read a book with my name on it that I didn't write. I am baffled as to where in the book I boasted about my abilities in this way. I might add that where in Chapter Seven of this book I contrast my reaction to racism to other blacks', even there, as I specified, the point is not, "Why can't you be like me?" but, "You are not like me and lots of black people I know and legions of blacks nationwide, and the reason is that you are hurting inside." My aim there is showing that hypersensitivity to racist "slights" is a personality type among blacks, not a universal, and analyzing why that personality type is so common. I do not devote my books to something as shallow and in-consequential as bragging.

However, since the anecdotes in *Losing the Race* do reflect my life, they inevitably mention things I have done, and as a university professor, those things inevitably have included learning, studying, making presentations, and writing books. That's what professors do. But here is the rub. Noguera spontaneously reads my even mentioning these things as boasting, and this could only be because he himself has a deep-seated sense that a black person only does such things as a kind of stunt. I write an anecdote about how when I was reading *Jane Eyre* a black friend said she would never read it: I intended the story to demonstrate the friend's sense of separation from "whiteness," but I think Noguera thought I was bragging about reading *Jane Eyre!* I mention that a black grad student wondered about my racial identity when I gave a report about a non-racial linguistic topic; I intended the recollection to demonstrate the sense of separation from the scholarly, but Noguera thought I was bragging about having done the report!

But he could only read me that way with a quiet sense that this kind of thing is not what normal black people do. Only then would he sponta-neously assume that in my scholarship or pleasure reading beyond the black realm, I have been consciously "striving" to make a mark—as if a black person could only read *Jane Eyre* to show off for whites or to show blacks how sophisticated they are, rather than because it was something he wanted to read as a human being that year (right after having enjoyed, for the record, Alice Walker's *The Temple of My Familiar*). I try to get at the heart of a social phenomenon by describing things I have seen, but Noguera thinks, "He was reading *Jane Eyre?* He was doing a report on something about language and it wasn't about Ebonics or hip-hop?"

I have received about four thousand letters and e-mails about *Losing the Race,* and I cannot think of a single one, even negative, that accused me of asking black people why they couldn't be like me. Naturally, I have seen plenty of criticism of *Losing the Race,* often stridently *ad hominem.* But Noguera is alone in the particular criticism that the book is about me telling black people to be like me. He first levied it in a debate we had at UC Berkeley in 2001, and because the charge is so unconnected to the book, I was almost surprised to find it repeated in his book on public schools a few years later.

At the end of the day, the truth is that Noguera's criticisms of *Losing the Race* fall so far from what I actually wrote that I find it almost impossible to imagine that he ever actually read it, rather than skimming it for the "anecdotes." But that would mean that he is an academic who considers it unexceptionable to pronounce upon someone's opinions without actually engaging them closely. If Noguera did not actually read the book before devoting so much ink to it, this reveals, again, a sense that the scholarly is separate from the self.

Overall, I am aware of no academic study claiming that the "acting white" problem is a myth that even begins to address the issue with methods that withstand scrutiny. Since *Losing the Race*, every claim I have seen or heard along these lines is levelled by people coming to the table with an indignant leftist commitment impatient with the full range of evidence germane to the problem, and sometimes as chary of race-neutral scholarly achievement as the students they write about. This is the blind offering to lead the blind. I cannot accept this as refuting my claim that black students harbor a historically conditioned sense of separation from the scholastic that lives on independently of a changing America.

The "Acting White" Problem Is Real

But am I not a bit too sure of my own conclusions here? Frankly, I think not.

For one, there is an almost overwhelming amount of testimony about the "acting white" charge, which academics denying its significance downplay with brief citations of Signithia Fordham and John Ogbu's single article from two decades ago, or of my *Losing the Race* without engagement with the data or argumentation I presented.

To be sure, the testimony classifies as anecdotal in the strict sense. But to dismiss it out of hand requires also dismissing, for example, Ellis Cose's *The Rage of a Privileged Class* as a mere storybook. If Cose's book is considered a legitimate analysis of the black experience in presenting a journalistic collection of blacks' feelings and experiences regarding racism, and if sociologist Joe Feagin can even get an article into *American Sociological Review* presenting a similar array of personal testimonies on same, then we must allow that the almost overwhelming volume of personal attestations of the "acting white" charge and its power corresponds to something real.

Even black *New York Times* columnist Bob Herbert, for example, who is otherwise no stranger to tossing off theatrical claims as to the prevalence of racism in American society, has acknowledged the "acting white" problem. In one column he spoke to a twenty-two-year-old black student who grew up in Washington, DC.

She noticed when she came home on visits from school, some of her friends treated her differently. "I don't know if it was out of jealousy or whatever," she said, "but they would actually say to me, "You're acting white now." They'd say that. They'd say, "You act white." Or, "You act proper." . . . "I knew that it would happen because other friends had told me it would happen," said Ms. Jhingory. "But I was surprised that it would happen with friends that I was so close to, people I had grown up with from the time I was maybe 6 or 7. I actually ended friendships because of comments like that. We just couldn't connect anymore because it was just a really negative situation."

According to social scientists who want to distract us from the role of "oppositional culture," the people Jhingory encountered were oddballs shouting from the margins; Jhingory apparently just had some peculiar friends. But Herbert's report joins countless others—newspaper stories about black students treating one another similarly are almost a cliché. The *Times*'s own Tamar Lewin described it in a story on teens in Maplewood, New Jersey, noting that students "develop a corrosive sense that behaving like honors students is 'acting white,' while 'acting black' demands that they emulate lower-level students." Black Harvard psychiatry professor Alvin Poussaint, a prominent media commentator on black issues and hardly a conservative, has said, "A lot of black youth now are anti-education and anti-intellectualism, who feel that getting an education is being white, is acting white. We never had that in previous generations; this is something new." Is Poussaint, of all people, zeroing in on something trivial? Is *Dr. Alvin Poussaint* merely stereotyping his own people? Hugh Price, when he was head of the National Urban League, wrote, "Pressure from peers not to achieve can undermine the best efforts of teachers and parents. Many have succumbed to the message that achievement is tantamount to 'acting white.' " Hugh Price has devoted a career to uplifting his people; he is a wise, temperate, and vastly experienced veteran of the race scene in America. Is what *Hugh Price* reports a mere myth? Al Sharpton has told the *New York Times* about a black woman who was the first in her family to go to college, and recounted, "When her brothers and sisters learned that she was making straight A's, they said to her 'Oh, you acting white now?' Like there is something black about flunking." Can we dismiss *Al Sharpton* as co-opted by "conservative" ideology?

Or—after *Losing the Race* was published, I received an avalanche of testimonials over years' time from people attesting to the reality of the "acting white" problem and also have spoken to countless people on radio shows or in real life who confirm the same. This has included blacks who were subjected to it as well as teachers black and white who attest to seeing its prevalence and effects. These testimonials were quite unsolicited by me—I did not contact these people myself, nor were any of their testimonials the result of my asking leading questions after they wrote me. I have kept a file of all of them, carefully restricting it to accounts of black students being tarred specifically as "acting white" for doing well in school—not just teased, not just accused of being "nerds." That file includes more than a hundred entries, from all over the United States, across four decades since the sixties—and if I were less stringent and included the less precise testimonials, then the file would include a good two hundred more. I could easily use this file to compose a book-length account along the lines of Cose's *The Rage of a Privileged Class*, replete with gripping stories of black students given grief for liking school.

A white Harlem resident recalls a smart black girl teased so hard as "thinking she's white" that her parents decided to move away. A black woman of Caribbean heritage is a child of good old immigrant pluck and loves school—and suffers endless abuse from black American kids for "thinking she is white" (a sadly common account I have received from black immigrants' children). A black woman of modest circumstances goes to college and starts fine but then slips because her friends are telling her that college is making her "white." A white adjunct professor at Southeast Michigan University hears black students say that the program called "'Study Skills' is where they teach us how to be white." A black teenager started as a top student but plummeted to D average in high school because of peer pressure and a desire to fit in with black kids, who had also taunted her for speaking standard English. A white undergrad served as a tutor for college students falling behind; only two of sixty regular visitors were black, and both reported being ostracized for "acting white." A Savannah teacher says that smart black boys have told her, "I'm tired of being told I'm trying to be white." A teacher in Troy, New York, recounts a black girl dropping out of her foreign language class to "be with my friends." A black girl in the projects of East Los Angeles is teased for being "white" when she likes school. School principals in Oakland tell their friend that the "acting white" problem is real when she is skeptical about it after reading about yours truly in the newspaper. In Los Angeles a white woman's daughter says that she watches black students pull down their friends' performances in school by telling them that doing well is "acting white." A teacher for a self-selected high ability track class in a Portland, Oregon, school reports that it is hard to keep black boys in her class because of how other black kids treat them for being in it. A white calculus teaching assistant doesn't know what to do when a black student tells him that math is a "white" thing. A black man of Caribbean parentage recalls that black American students told him to never admit having studied for exams, but that white ones never did. A black professor of history at a small college tells me that when he read my statements about the "acting white" charge in *Losing the Race* he at first thought it must be nonsense, but then found that one school principal after another in his area told him that the phenomenon was real.

Yet, apparently, the "acting white" issue is a mere "myth" because some studies have a stranger ask black kids, "Do you think it's 'white' to work hard in school?" and maybe check to see whether they tell the stranger that they think of themselves as popular. But the testimonials go on and on; it is hard to even decide which of them to include in one paragraph because they all tell the same story so clearly. And we cannot assume that for some reason I have been apprised of the sum total of such events. Obviously, for each event someone happens to have been moved to inform me of, there have been countless others: Most people, after all, do not write authors. Many assume that when we hear of an isolated episode of police brutality, we can assume that it is just one manifestation of a national generality. The same applies to my file of "acting white" cases.

One might reasonably ask why I accept these testimonials as valid while dismissing studies like Ainsworth-Darnell's and Downey's for being based on just what subjects say. But the analogy is off. The black sense of separation from the scholarly is a subtle, usually unconscious psychological trait, and as such, usually requires carefully designed questioning to reveal. But the testimonies I have received are of something different: simple, concrete memories of experiencing or seeing the "acting white" charge. It is also important that the testimonials I have received were unsolicited.

Then, in Chapter Seven I indeed argue that at least some "Ellis Cose" stories, even when unsolicited, appear to be filtered through a thought pattern that renders ordinary nuisances as "racism"—recall the black dean on the hotel room at the end of the hall, and other stories. But that analysis does not apply as gracefully to "acting white" stories. If someone recounts being subject to the taunt, what possible "filter" could be in operation? They were told they were "acting white," period—it has only one meaning; there is no alternate meaning of the charge, such as that they were actually being told that they might enjoy taking some bassoon lessons. We can only dismiss the claim by saying that the person is lying outright.

And as to suspicions that the teachers recalling seeing the charge levelled at black students or hearing black students recount it are filtering their memories through racism, this doesn't work either. As many of the teachers I have heard from are black *and* white, and most of the teachers, as modern Americans, pad their recollection with ample indication that they are loathe to stereotype. The white teachers, in particular, usually express regret at having to report such things, and often write that they resisted admitting it for a long time.

Thus it is, quite simply, a fact that the psychological operations of "oppositional culture" exert a decisive effect on black students' performances. Social scientists coyly pretending to think that this is refuted by interviewees saying that they value education and are popular cannot be responsibly treated as seriously addressing something sitting so clearly right under our noses. People who treat studies like this as showing that there is an "acting white myth" reveal themselves as placing alienation over reality. People who ignore reality, despite their benevolent intent, offer us no useful counsel for moving ahead in the the world as we know it.

MOVING AHEAD

There are many ways to address the achievement gap, and it remains to be seen which ones will be most effective. Commonly, culture changes as the result of the combination of assorted efforts and happenstance developments.

For example, the Civil Rights Act was spurred partly by how starkly segregation stood out as unjustifiable after blacks had served in World War II, when the Establishment was taking communism to task for suppressing human dignity, and the invention of television meant that the nation watched racist thugs abusing blacks on film instead of just reading about it on page 15 of the newspaper. We cannot know at this point what will tip the scales on black students and school.

Charter schools, embraced by the Bush Administration's No Child Left Behind program as an alternative to hopeless public school disasters, may bear enough fruit to change the general conversation. Over the next decade, we will watch minority student admissions rebound despite bans of racial preferences in one university after another: Already, at the University of Washington, there were 124 black freshmen in 1998 before racial preferences were banned there; two years later there were 119. At the University of Texas at Austin, before the ban in 1996 there were 266 black freshmen, and after the ban in 1999 there were 286, under a system admitting the top 10 percent of high school graduates. As "resegregation" fails to occur on campus after campus, consensus may drift away from quota programs and toward constructive efforts to teach minority kids how to get into good schools as individuals rather than as tokens. It remains to be seen what the counsel of the Minority Student Achievement Network will accomplish district by district, and I myself have helped initiate a program at the Manhattan Institute think tank bringing together influential people concerned about the achievement gap to fashion a nationwide program to close it. As Malcolm Gladwell taught us in his magnificent *The Tipping Point*, ultimately change happens when a consensus has emerged in the general culture that transforms what is thought of as normal.

As late as the sixties, it was normal for an ordinary American couple to put out cigarettes for guests at a dinner party because most people smoked at least to some extent. There was little room in the culture for people who found cigarette smoke intolerable; I remember sitting in backseats in this era when I was little having to endure adults up in the front seat puffing away. Today, smoking is no longer a norm in America to remotely this extent. Personally I know no one who puts out cigarettes for guests or who expects their kids to inhale their smoke in the car. We cheerfully arrange things so that the chain-smoking European visitor can puff out the kitchen window. Sure, there is a class difference here, but there was a time when cigarettes were a cross-class universal, as is clear in old movies when they were associated with, of all things, aristocratic elegance.

This kind of gradual but decisive shift is likely what will happen regarding the achievement gap. The day will come when black students do as well in school as white ones, with class being the only factor dragging performance down for both white and black students. Our articles and conferences musing on The Achievement Gap among even middle-class black students will seem antique curiosities.

That is, unless we continue viewing black students through a lens held in front of our eyes by people committed to alienation rather than progress. This will only hinder, and perhaps prevent, real change. Black students' sense of separation from school is a habit of the heart. In the same way, there are three habits of the mind on blacks and education that we are constantly presented with as hallmarks of being good people. We must teach ourselves out of them to be truly committed to helping black students connect to school without feeling culturally inauthentic.

HABIT OF MIND NUMBER ONE:
BLACK STUDENTS ARE POOR

There is an iconic image ingrained in the minds of many, of black children crammed into classrooms in crummy ghetto buildings being taught by underqualified, disengaged teachers and dodging knife fights in the hallway. "How can learning take place in such an environment?" we are asked. Of course, it barely can. But the idea that this scenario explains the achievement gap is illogical. The gap persists even with black kids who never knew an environment remotely like this.

There are certainly analysts who face this squarely. A report by the Roy Wilkins Center for Human Relations and Social Justice concluded that in Minnesota, "Poverty is not at the root of racial gaps in test scores." The report specifies that "measures of school poverty do not exhibit consistently negative impacts on test scores, once other factors such as racial composition and ranking of schools is accounted for. . . . Moreover, the marginal impacts of neighborhood poverty are negligible, and often statistically insignificant." We see a real-world reflection of this in accounts such as a black girl at Friendly High School in Fort Washington, Maryland, middle-class and mostly black, being praised for making a 950 on the SAT.

Beware the Filter

But clear-eyed conclusions like these are rare in the mainstream of academic work on the achievement gap. Leftist commentators on the subject seem almost neurologically incapable of processing that the problem is cross-class for longer than a few seconds because it is incompatible with the blame game. People well aware that the black middle class gets larger every year and that the income gap between blacks and whites continues to narrow, who are up in arms at the slightest hint from a white person that black equals ghetto, talk about the achievement gap indignant that anyone would propose a cultural explanation when "most" black students go to bad schools—regardless of the fact that almost none of the black students at the university where they are proclaiming this went to such schools.

This is because of a mental filter—a meme, specifying that one must conceive of black students as poor people. A nice example is a letter that happened to appear in the *New York Times* from a concerned person: "What good is it to debate who is admitted to Harvard and the like if such students, the descendants of slaves or not, are ill prepared because of years of neglect in our public schools?" This writer assumes that even black students at Harvard went to awful schools, out of a sense that this is the default experience for young blacks in America decades after the sixties.

I am not being rhetorical in designating the problem as a filter on reality. I once did a television interview on affirmative action and made my usual point that while I espouse preferences for students who grow up in lousy conditions, that I disagree with lowering standards for middle-class black students because I think that their performance problems are due to cultural identification. The cameraman was a middle-age black man, and as he packed up his equipment, he commented on the issue. His take on it was that when he looked at kids in the crumbling schools in his town sitting in classrooms sharing textbooks, he couldn't imagine how anyone could not approve of affirmative action. He was technically civil, but his tone made it clear that my views did not make me his favorite person. But the thing was, I had not simply mouthed something along the lines that people just needed to make the best of the worst regardless of the cards life had dealt them. I had said very clearly that I agreed that kids like the ones he described deserved preferences. My objection regarding middle-class black students had not registered, even though it was the heart of what I was talking about, he had stood a few feet away from me as I said it just minutes before, and the Asian American interviewer had immediately understood my point about middle-class black students and engaged me on it before the cameraman made his point—again, right in front of him. He genuinely could not hear me. There was a filter at work.

I have noticed a similar filter with many audiences. I have learned that when speaking on racial preferences, to make the audience understand my point it is necessary to remind them repeatedly throughout the address that I am referring to middle-class black students and not poor ones. Otherwise, almost always, a black questioner recounts having grown up poor, having to work while in school, and so on, and wants to know why I don't think he or she deserves affirmative action. This is a kind of *Savage Inequalities* meme—black students are poor students.

It must be eliminated from our public discourse. The disconnect is not an issue of socioeconomics, but of culture. The problem is that we have been seduced into a particular habit of thinking on the issue, argued so commonly, and with such indignant, intimidating passion, that we feel heretical to allow ourselves to perceive an obvious reality.

The Stereotype Fetish

Another example was a conversation I had with a national television producer, a white man, doing a special on Shaker Heights. The people making the special had extensive footage of black students saying quite explicitly that they had taken in a sense that doing well in school was for white people, and this had affected their grades. Getting this footage, the reporters had spent weeks in a tree-lined community in which the schools were almost caricatures of what the No Child Left Behind Act would have all public schools be.

And yet even so, in our conversation this very intelligent and well-meaning person could barely resist slipping into castigating himself for "stereotyping" in allowing that there was a cultural factor at work. "Sixteen percent of black families living at the poverty line—wow, we have to keep that in mind!" he kept saying. But here was that suspension of logic again. Yes, one in six of the black students are poor. But what about the other five? And did the students you interviewed over weeks give you the impression that, say, two or three out of those five were, even if not poor, children of bus drivers and factory workers?

Then, there are cases where if someone can admit that the problem is not one of class, then the therapeutic alienation imperative shunts them into another form of grievance, proposing that the problem is not a "black" one. One sociologist I spoke to long ago on the issue could only object that there are white slackers too. Okay, but we all knew that—*Animal House, Fast Times at Ridgemont High, The Simpsons*—but the issue is that black performance lags to an extent that suggests a nagging disproportion. That is, apparently there are vastly *more* black slackers proportionally. The sociologist was grounded in a commitment to warn us against stereotyping, as always. But the data clearly show that there is a statistical difference in performance here, such that objecting that calling attention to it is stereotyping technically makes no sense at all.

Imagine saying "a lot of people born in China are a little hard to understand when they speak English" and having someone say, "Well, I know some full-blooded Americans who don't enunciate too well." Yes, we all do—but obviously there is something about learning English at thirty-five that makes it somewhat more likely that one's English may be a little hard to parse than if one grows up in St. Louis, just as is the case with English-speaking adults learning Chinese compared with Chinese natives.

Besides, why the trip-wire alertness to the stereotyping issue at all in 1998? People like the CNN producer make it rather clear that an aversion to true stereotyping is now hardwired into the American consciousness to a considerable degree. No, all whites do not consider blacks the perfect equal of whites. But they never will, and black students do not require an America utterly devoid of stereotyping to excel—again, take Dunbar High while lynching, a rather obvious product of stereotyping, was ordinary. Why, then, would someone with a PhD so casually snap into illogic, responding to an observation of a sharp discrepancy in performance by adopting a battle pose against stereotyping, a foe long marginalized among the kinds of people making the argument that discomfits him, and with little relationship to the topic at hand anyway?

It was that filter again, typifying our times—victimhood is key, even in the face of reason. Next, the sociologist referred to the literature showing that even successful blacks don't have as much accumulated wealth as whites. I cannot resist mentioning that he was so committed to teaching me out of my misinformed heresy that he took me to the bookstore next door to the café we were at to show me two books on this subject (Berkeley residents will recognize the "Classical Music Café" abutting and sharing a restroom with the University Bookstore on Bancroft Avenue). But we were back to the illogic. What about the working-class immigrant kids—many Caribbean and African—who regularly submit such excellent dossiers to top schools, despite their parents rarely having generations-deep stock portfolios to pass on to them or use for frills like test-preparation classes or fancy private schools? Students like this are rife at Berkeley where this man and I taught; no professor could miss them.

Object that it is unfair to use immigrants as comparisons because they are uniquely driven to succeed—and it snaps us right back to culture. Obviously, too many black students and their parents are *not* driven enough to foster scholastic success—and *to an extent much more than white kids*. And if this traces to the demoralization and alienation created by slavery and segregation, then we are now right back at, essentially, my argument. We can quibble about the exact cause—I would say alienation is more important than demoralization—but the present reality is a cultural sense of separation from school, even in black kids who grew up in *Father Knows Best* homes. In modern America, savage inequalities are no longer the only issue facing us.

And none of this is difficult. Realizing it requires feats of imagination or reasoning no greater than figuring out the highway routes from New York to Montreal. There is a meme putting a block on engagement with these simple realities. Namely, we have been taught that to engage empirical reality and to be a moral citizen are different things. It has been drummed into us that convincing ourselves of counterintuitive positions on the state of our sociological fabric is the essence of higher awareness. Hence, we listen to black kids saying that their friends tell them that doing well in school is racially inauthentic, but insist to ourselves that the reason they get low grades is because their parents don't subscribe to *The Economist*.

Now, to be sure, it is the soul of education to learn to be wary of our gut impulses in processing ourselves and the world around us. The world is not flat. A German shepherd has more genes in common with a Chihuahua than with a wolf. Greasy food that tastes great clogs your arteries and kills you.

But when it comes to race issues, our public culture has taught us to distort intelligent caution into an embrace of religious dogma—religious in being considered beyond intelligent question regardless of empirical evidence, to the extent that anyone resisting the gospel must be dismissed as unfit for polite society.

Object Lesson

Pedro Noguera exemplifies this thought pattern, useful to my argument one more time because of how explicitly he lays out his views. He is infuriated by the very idea that anyone would attribute the achievement gap to culture rather than society, but his fury is based not on careful logical engagement with the world, but in a psychological identity rooted in opposing Power at all costs.

This is clear in that in his writings, Noguera is especially critical of my positions in *Losing the Race* but makes barely any gesture toward addressing the data or lines of argument in the book. Rather, he seems to consider general condemnations of "cultural" explanations as a coherent response in itself. But this, in the guise of intellection, is advocacy driven from the gut.

Typically of people under the influence of the therapeutic alienation meme, Noguera is even comfortable making no sense at all as long as the music is right. In the debate Noguera and I had at Berkeley, he announced that as to the "acting white" charge, "I've never seen it." But this would be odd of a veteran observer of public schools with heavily minority populations, as well as of a brown-skinned person who grew up in the sixties and seventies. In fact, he had openly acknowledged and discussed black kids' wariness of school—and its ill effects—in a lengthy newspaper profile just a few years before. Of course, he traced it to racism and inequity, but still, he had indeed seen it.

Claiming not to have seen it, in the role of an academic providing informed and considered counsel on the topic, would seem puzzlingly irresponsible in a professor who at the time was employed by Harvard. But if one's main commitment is to rebellion for rebellion's sake regardless of outcome, then inevitably some facts will have to be shunted aside because the real world is too complicated for Speaking Truth to Power to always be appropriate or even logical. Noguera's claim, then, made perfect sense in that way. It is no accident that Zachary Karabell, profiling various college professors in a book examining the purpose of a college education in modern America, judged Noguera's classroom lecture style as indoctrination into anti-Establishment ideology rather than instruction on how to think for oneself. Karabell is a good liberal; but he is also an honest one.

This sense that black America needs protection from white dismissal has only fitful connection with actually helping black America get to the point that no one would even venture such dismissal. All responses to the "acting white" thesis that are motivated primarily by an outdated and recreational opposition to "blaming the victim" should be treated with extreme caution. Noguera criticizes people such as John Ogbu and me because we "continue to propagate the idea that culture determines academic performance." But we have done this because culture does determine academic performance to a considerable degree. We would not be responsible thinking people to pretend otherwise, and the "insatiable appetite" for such statements that Noguera deplores is due to the fact that thinking people are interested in the truth.

When it comes to race and academic achievement, we have reached a point where, as Sam Harris aptly has it in reference to religious faith, "the rules of civil discourse currently demand that Reason wear a veil whenever she ventures out in public. But the rules of civil discourse must change."

On race and education, the rules of civil discourse must disinclude the outdated idea that all but a sliver of black students grow up in the 'hood. To embrace this shorthand notion is to disrespect the massive black middle class so obviously living among us all, and to minimize the tragedy that so many of its children have been hobbled by peculiarities of social history from being able to show what they are made of in school. Our job as concerned citizens is not to pretend that nine out of ten black students grew up in the ghetto, but to address the fact that so many black students who didn't can earn grades and test scores that make it look like they did.

HABIT OF MIND NUMBER TWO:
BLACK STUDENTS UNDERPERFORM BECAUSE
RACISM IS NOT DEAD

Another idea that distracts us from effective thinking about race and education is that what does black students in is white teachers' racial biases.

It is, in its way, comforting to harbor this idea. Black people are victims, we are on the side of the angels in realizing it, and it's easier to condemn the teachers than to address something trickier such as self-defeating cultural patterns, especially with all the people with alphabet soup after their names growling about how evil it is to see black culture as anything less than a noble and coherent survival strategy.

But *are* we on the side of the angels? The academic literature does not draw a link between the achievement gap and teacher bias in any remotely conclusive way. For example, Ronald Ferguson, professor at Harvard's Kennedy School of Government (and for the record, black, liberal, and overall more warmly inclined toward the black students lobbing the "acting white" charge than toward the Urkels who suffer it), concludes in one study: "If the benchmark for bias is unconditional race neutrality, most teachers are biased, but evidence shows that this is mainly because their perceptions of current performance are correct." That is, where teachers are biased it is because they have had ample experience with a real performance difference. Ferguson continues, "I have found no clear evidence on whether teachers' expectations or behaviors are racially biased for students whom they perceive to be equal on past or present measures of performance or proficiency." Then in another study, Ferguson surveyed the literature on whether black students do best when taught by black teachers and found only flutters of support. For example, the most that relatively recent and comprehensive surveys offer on the point is that *working-class* black teachers are just *slightly* more effective in raising *math* (but not verbal) scores for black students. In the end, we might reasonably read this almost arbitrarily particular result as showing that the race of the teacher is, really, irrelevant to the problem facing us.

Indeed, one wonders how much time people who blame white teachers for the achievement gap have spent in the classrooms in question. For example, Bob Herbert once wrote a *New York Times* column claiming that black students in New York are done in by white teachers who just don't "care" about them. But while surely such teachers exist, it is unclear to me upon what basis Herbert implies that such teachers are a norm, or even half, or a third, of the instructors black students are exposed to. And Herbert is ignoring the almost deadening procession of reports he surely hasn't missed, of teachers white and black struggling daily just to get minority students to sit down, be quiet, and pay attention. This standard portrait of inner-city schools corresponds in no logical fashion to a verdict that black students would achieve if only white teachers would "love" them—especially since the students behave this way even when the teachers are black.

I have spent some time in schools like this, such as one in West Harlem. Kids sassed and ignored teachers and gabbed casually while teachers were trying to impart information. I had to stare down a particularly rambunctious guy schoolyard-style just to get him to sit down in his seat and let the class begin—which likely only worked partly because I am male and partly because I was a novel presence. To the teachers of the school, white and black, he was an eternal nightmare, and surely depressed the GPAs and test scores of countless kids who had the misfortune to be in classes with him—and he was one of a type, not a unique scourge. Discipline was most of what the teachers did all day. Getting a few hundred kids down two flights of stairs to an assembly required traffic control that one teacher (Latino and ghetto-identified, not a "racist" white girl) called reminiscent of herding cats. The assembly was an end-of-year recital, kicked off by the director warning the performers that "we know everything will be in good taste." Obviously this suggested a precedent otherwise, and two acts into the show, a teenage girl launched into a hip-hop-inflected belly dance so lubriciously suggestive that as a grown man I was uncomfortable even watching her; of course, the kids were elated. Authority wasn't doing too well at this school, exactly the kind of urban public school that a contingent encourages us to "support."

Clearly, there was something besides *racism* going on, and no one who has spent any time in urban school settings would consider this school at all unusual. Bob Herbert is empirical enough to know that culture matters to at least some extent, as he showed in his column on "acting white." But he is too imprinted by therapeutic alienation to understand how very *much* culture matters—such as realizing that beating up on the white lady teacher for being prejudiced is no longer Doing the Right Thing.

Then, there is the notion that even in college, black students' performances suffer because of the pressures of racism. Claude Steele, for example, depicts a hypothetical black student at a university bedeviled by racism in the air, such as discussions as to whether affirmative action is a sound policy. His idea is that exposure to such unpleasantness depresses such students' performances planting in them an awareness that whites may think blacks are less intelligent than them. But if it were true that this kind of thing plays a significant role in why black students underperform compared with whites, then we would expect that at colleges where all the students are black, the achievement gap would disappear. This is not remotely true.

For example, in 2003, out of seventy-six Historically Black Colleges and Universities (HBCUs), at almost half of them, two-thirds or more students had not graduated after six years. The picture is much better at a few of the top HBCUs, but the aggregate situation remains. Over the years, I have heard from about twenty-five professors at such schools dismayed over the anti-scholarly attitudes among the student body as well as much of the faculty and administration. I have also received quite a few anecdotal but indicative snapshots, such as that one year at Hampton University, in an economics class, the top student was black—but the second- and third-highest ranked were white students visiting the school. Once again, then, we are faced with a cultural issue that exists independently of racism, although racism surely exists.

One of the most tragic fallacies that has hindered truly progressive Civil Rights work since the sixties has been the idea that black people's salvation will be the end of "racism." When we suppose that fixing the achievement gap will require cleansing white people's souls of all glimmers of bias, we effectively condemn black students to lag forever. No matter how many articles and books and seminars and forums and newspaper editorials continue to be churned out about teacher bias, there will come no great day when such biases are entirely absent.

And—there is no indication that black students are incapable of rising above them.

There is, in fact, a clear indication that they can: Two-thirds of the black undergraduates at Harvard are of Caribbean and African parentage rather than being what on the campus is called "Descendants" of black Americans. This is typical of the Ivies according to anecdotal evidence I have encountered from administrators and professors working at several of them. The PC response here is to say that the immigrant parents had a special "pluck" that they passed on to their kids, unfair to expect of blacks who have been here for centuries enduring the degradation of slavery and segregation. But then, we must admit that the success of these immigrants' children shows one simple thing: that *racism* is not a decisive factor in keeping black students from getting into Harvard. The immigrants' kids managed despite *racism*, which means that what hinders the black American kids is something else.

Still, though, one might insist that it is unfair to expect black American students to cope with *racism* when their parents were not immigrants giving them a strong sense of self that equipped them to let *racism* roll off of them. But then, think about this: Black kids with Caribbean and African parents are quite often given to claiming that university campuses are *racist*, taking their cue from the sentiments of native black American students as well as orientations in the air in university culture. But in such cases, they lob these charges while having done excellently in high school and doing just as well in college. Here, we see that their sociopolitical orientation is an after-the-fact sartorial kind of attitude, unconnected to the effect that reality has upon their ability to succeed in school—they claim that the white establishment at the university is opposed to them or unconcerned with them even when their scholastic performance shows no effects from the purported evil. *One can express feeling besieged by "racism" while not being hindered by it in any way.*

This is important because it shows once again that alienated attitudes can thrive independently of what current reality would condition by itself. That disconnect is, I believe, also what does in so many middle-class black American students. So many of them underperform not because current conditions force them to, but because young black peer culture has internalized an attitudinal tic treating not only "society" but also something as immediate and concrete as school as the province of an alien other. For children of black immigrants, the disconnect between orientation and reality occurs beyond the realm of concrete achievement: Their parents' influence tends to make doing their best a requirement, such that the disconnect is restricted to airing alienated sentiments while still getting A's. Black American students' parents do not have a recent history that would lead them to push their kids so hard, and so the disconnect can permeate to a deeper level, infecting not only sociopolitical sentiments, but also commitment to achievement.

So—we have a choice between teaching black Americans how to be like black immigrants or hoping that whites will rid themselves of even the subtlest of biases. Choosing the latter makes for great theatre, partly in its tragic futility. Choosing the former would seem to be a way of expressing the black strength we supposedly cherish—especially since we see that it is feasible: Those two-thirds of Harvard undergrads are concrete testimony that whatever the nature of white *racism*, it is surmountable by students with black skin.

Therapeutic alienation makes the notion of black students held down by racism compelling to many. But this does nothing for the students in question. Not a single black student in the country will ever gain anything from one more article pretending that a white teacher who watches black students failing for years is a racist. Our job is to teach black students to succeed despite bias. Anyone who thinks of that as backward or unenlightened is placing hating whitey over loving black people. You do not love someone whom you distract from coping with obstacles.

HABIT OF MIND NUMBER THREE:
FOR BLACK STUDENTS, NOT BEING WHITE IS MERIT

If we are truly committed to closing the achievement gap, then we must only be interested in "diversity" among people with equal qualifications.

In practice, we have been taught that creating "diverse" student bodies is important enough to justify lowering standards and that understanding this is a moral advance. But this is a condescending peculiarity of American discourse over just the past twenty-five years. Not only is it condescending, but it also helps to leave black America without the one thing that makes human beings or cultures change in any significant way: incentive. As long as black students have to do only so well, they will do only so well. Romantic notions of blacks as "diverse" exotics do not justify allowing this.

The History of "Diversity"

Before the eighties, the very meaning that "diversity" has acquired for us in education did not exist. Racial preferences were justified on a different basis: that once underqualified black students were brought to college campuses, they would excel given their new opportunities. Schools openly admitted that black applicants were ranked only among one another, according to lower standards than those applied to whites, such as the American Association of Legal Scholars' simple assertion that blacks must be evaluated separately since subjecting them to competition with whites "would exclude virtually all minorities from the legal profession." Thinking Americans were proudly rejecting a still-recent time when "cultural" explanations about gaps were typically couched in naked bigotry. Many sincerely thought that remedial programs and good intentions were all that were needed to remedy the injustices of the past. But they did not: In the seventies, countless black students crashed and burned trying to perform at levels that were beyond them.

The modern notion of "diversity" traces to Supreme Court Justice Lewis Powell's opinion in the *Regents of the University of California v. Bakke* case in 1978, as the failure of just bringing underqualified black students to competitive schools was becoming too clear to ignore. A white applicant to the medical school at the University of California at Davis charged that he was denied despite qualifications that would have gotten him in if he were a minority candidate. Powell supported UC Davis's admissions procedure, calling for assessing applicants based on an "array of qualifications and characteristics of which racial or ethnic origin is but a single though important element." But elsewhere in the opinion, Powell repeatedly warned against using this as a rationale for quota systems: "If a petitioner's purpose is to assure within its student body some specified percentage of a particular group merely because of its race or ethnic origin, such a preferential purpose must be rejected. . . . Preferring members of any one group for no reason other than race or ethnic origin is discrimination for its own sake. This the Constitution forbids."

But college administrators ignored these passages, and the result was the idea that racial preferences served not only to give black students opportunity to excel, but also to create "diverse" student bodies. Like Price Cobbs's interracial confrontation sessions, this idea was uniquely situated to take root in a culture in which therapeutic alienation had become acceptable. For whites, claiming that a student body was illegitimate when composed of too many people like their capitalist, white-bread, oppressive selves was an automatic way to feel enlightened and to assuage white guilt. Whether you would submit your own kids to such tokenism veiled in pretty words was less important than chalking one up for showing it to the Establishment that had lied about Vietnam and turned firehoses on blacks in Birmingham. This made you a decent person; acknowledging the tokenism was something to look off into the distance about, mumbling that "It makes you think . . ." (but not much).

For blacks, the idea that one's value as a black American was one's difference from whites, including a mission to teach them about racial injustice, fit right in with a new black identity based too often on being in opposition to The Man. To value oneself as "diverse" from whites is, actually, to avoid being an individual actor, in favor of joining a herd of people united in cherishing *not* being something, rather than *being* something—attractive when one is not sure whether one is good enough to *be* something.

Thus, the "diversity" cult is a direct manifestation of the therapeutic alienation meme: This is why it is argued for so desperately despite something that makes no sense on its face. Namely, being cherished for one's color and how it contributes to the local diorama used to be called being a token black. It is no accident that "token black" is now a virtually obsolete term: Since the eighties, therapeutic alienation has driven legions of people to *embrace* tokenism. Why in the world? Because the meme means that alienation trumps all else. Even in the face of an institutionalized dismissal of blacks' abilities to compete seriously on an academic level, the oppositional bedrock of the "diversity" rationale—celebrating being different from whitey—is so seductive that it becomes a mantra warmly cherished.

No one puts it that way. Whites do not proclaim that they feel a need to work out their guilt, especially since they are rarely aware of it on an everyday level. Blacks do not proclaim that they lack a sense of legitimacy without thinking of themselves as noble victims, especially because they are barely aware of it. The public advertisement is that diversity enhances the educational experience somehow.

Based on that, we might decide that to make an omelette you have to crack some eggs and that these educational benefits compensate for both the condescension and the repression of incentive. But in fact, the evidence is overwhelming that diversity confers no such benefits.

Diversity Bites

For one, the idea that black students are valuable in being able to give "the minority perspective" falls to pieces upon the slightest scrutiny.

It is unclear just what a "black" opinion is. Even the most doctrinaire radical shies away from supposing that in the real world, pigment and politics walk in anything approaching a lockstep. After all, if there really are "black views," then couldn't professors just learn them from a gathering of black students over a summer and then recite them from their own notes during the school year? Besides this, the entire notion applies logically only to a mere sliver of any curriculum. What is the "black view" on systolic pressure? *La Chanson de Roland*? Contract law? Musical counterpoint? And what, pray tell, are the distinct Latino views on these subjects?

And as we would expect given the fact that there is no such thing as The Black View, Terrance Sandalow, former dean of the University of Michigan's law school, has said, "My own experience and that of colleagues with whom I have discussed the question, experience that concededly is limited to the classroom setting, is that racial diversity is not responsible for generating ideas unfamiliar to some members of the class." Pointedly, Sandalow writes, "Even though the subjects I teach deal extensively with racial issues, I cannot recall an instance in which, for example, ideas were expressed by a black student that have not also been expressed by white students." My experience as a professor has been similar. Maybe things were different, say, thirty years ago, but on today's college campus, a white student can easily pick up the entire gospel of racial awareness and sensitivity from other white students, and this was already true by the early eighties when I was an undergraduate. (I first heard the term *politically correct* used by a white left-leaning roommate in 1984, at which time the term was still new enough that he used it without the loaded irony it has since accreted; he meant it as a term of sincere praise.)

Meanwhile, while we warm to black students for their "diverse" "contributions," they themselves do not cherish being museum exhibits as much as "diversity" fans assume. With almost numbing regularity, black college students decry the fact that they are asked for their special opinions in class (or out). "We are not here to provide diversity training for Kate or Timmy before they go out to take over the world," insists the *Black Guide to Life at Harvard* written by undergraduates. I have heard similar comments from countless young black questioners over the years. Ironically, the comments often come couched as support for the idea that black students remain besieged by "racism" on college campuses. A typical question goes something like, "Professor McWhorter, you say that black college students don't experience enough racism on campus to really matter, but what about when I am called on for my opinions as a black person in classes? Is it fair that I have to deal with that burden?" "Diversity" fans pride themselves on working against racism, only for the students thusly assigned to perform their "diverseness" to grumble about this as making their campus experience a racist one.

Nor do minority students see listening to the aggrievements of their fellow minorities as crucial to their own classroom educations. In a poll of minority graduates of the University of Michigan's law school from 1970 to 1996 asking which of seven aspects of their education they had most valued at the school, the top two were "faculty ability as teachers" and "intellectual abilities as classmates." Against those purporting that "diversity" is so vital to the worth of a diploma, the people polled rated "ethnic diversity of classmates" and "being called on in class" at the very bottom.

As to such surveys, there is in fact a damning weight of them that show the hollowness of the diversity rationale again and again. These surveys are by no means suppressed by the liberal wing of the media, but instead of attending to them, college administrators and "diversity" fans continue rattling off the same justifications as if this work did not exist. Indicatively, the authors of the surveys have often started out expecting to find support for the benefits of diversity only to come up short.

Mitchell J. Chang examined whether degree of racial diversity at a university affected students' GPAs, social self-concepts, intellectual self-concepts, likelihood of earning degrees, and satisfaction; whether one discussed racial issues; and whether one socialized with people of a different race. Big surprise—diversity only affected the latter two: When there is a decent number of black students, then (brace yourself) white students end up talking about race and meeting some black students. And with black students, even the seventh factor, socializing with students of different races, was not significantly affected by degree of diversity. This suggests that their discussions of racial issues were with one another, some of it likely in the vein of decrying the racism of other groups—hardly what most of us would consider a benefit.

Similarly, Stanley Rothman, Seymour Lipset, and Neil Nevitte surveyed 140 campuses and found that the more diversity there was on a campus, the *less* satisfied students are with their college experience. Stephen Cole and Elinor Barber's *Increasing Faculty Diversity* reveals that "diversity" can even be downright harmful to minority students' prospects: When minority students are placed in schools beyond what their qualifications would ordinarily have allowed, their lesser grades discourage them from pursuing PhDs and going into academia. Cole and Barber did not even expect this result, much to the discomfort of their funders, the Mellon Foundation. Another study by Eric A. Hanushek, John F. Kain, and Steven G. Rivkin indicated that generally, higher-achieving black students' performances are lesser the more black students there are on the campus. Wherever one decides to put that unfortunate result, it can hardly be treated as support for a "diversity" policy proposed as helping blacks or anyone else.

Sander Claus

Then UCLA law professor Richard Sander has argued in a rigorous and closely reasoned study that in the name of diversity, black law school applicants are regularly admitted to schools whose requirements are beyond their preparation. This mismatch makes them end up doing disproportionately poorly as a result: A survey of 163 law schools showed that 51.6 percent of black law students ended the first year in the lowest 10 percent of their classes as opposed to just 5.6 percent of the white students, and that this gap did not improve over the next two years. In addition, black students fail the bar exam at a much higher rate than whites. Sander concludes that racial preferences actually decrease the number of black lawyers, since students admitted to schools where discussion is paced in a fashion that their qualifications and preparation allows them to keep up with are better prepared to pass the bar exam and establish practices.

Sander, for the record, has worked as a community organizer on the South Side of Chicago, wrote his master's thesis arguing for desegregation in housing policy, later cofounded a Fair Housing organization, married a black woman and has a biracial child, and started out in favor of preference policies, until he saw their effects over years of teaching. He is no racist, nor is he a "conservative" bent on questioning the wisdom of the Civil Rights movement.

Nevertheless, unsurprisingly quite a few were after Sander's head after the article appeared, with the curious directed regularly to Emily Bazelon's gloating piece on *Slate* claiming that a collection of responses in an upcoming issue of the *Stanford Law Review* "debunked" Sander. As to Sander's rejoinder article at the end of the journal, Bazelon crowed, "What does Sander have to say for himself, once the bloodletting is done? Not much that helps him."—obviously not having actually read the piece, which in fact methodically made smoking little heaps out of all of the critique articles, so clearly that I seriously doubt most observers could resist any other conclusion after reading the whole issue.

Sander's article was the most substantial address of affirmative action since William Bowen's and Derek Bok's *The Shape of the River*. Because its findings are so central to understanding the hoax in the "diversity" notion, and because few have time to wade through long, dense law review articles, we should take a quick look here at how very soundly Sander refuted his critics.

One part of Sander's argument is that overall, black students do as well as white ones with similar grades and test scores, meaning that black students' sad rankings within the schools they go to are *only* because they have been placed higher than their qualifications designated—that is, among white students with better grades and test scores. David L. Chambers, Timothy Clydesdale, William Kidder, and Richard Lempert object that actually black law students do underperform slightly compared with similarly qualified whites—which they interpret as meaning that the performance gap Sander refers to is not due to the mismatch, but to more general things that the liberal consensus is more comfortable with, such as "stereotype threat." But the performance gap between equally qualified whites and blacks that they demonstrate is modest, whereas Sander shows that *half* of black students in *163 schools* end up in the *lowest 10 percent* of their classes. No one anywhere has ever claimed that "stereotype threat" and other subtle results of racism have this massive an effect upon black students. Chambers and his colleagues do not even venture to argue that they do, content with pretending that the same-old, same-old is "what we really need to be talking about" without addressing the painfully obvious issue of degree. Moreover, it is almost an insult to black intelligence and spiritual resilience to imagine that subtle obstacles must unequivocally kick to the curb all but the occasional young black genius. Obviously, the mismatch Sander documents has the much, much greater impact.

Michele Dauber pretends that Sander refuses to allow other researchers to use his data to check his conclusions—when Sander posted almost all of it long before the article was published. Also, Dauber would likely never grill William Bowen and Derek Bok as to the availability of their data, and if she found out that in fact, they do not share their data—a policy many of the book's critics have run up against—she would likely be distinctly less disapproving.

David Wilkins does an end-run around Sander's presentation and tells us that grades in law school don't matter anyway because a school's prestige is what determines a lawyer's career. But Sander shows that grades do play a significant part in hiring decisions, and besides, Wilkins seems mysteriously unconcerned about the bar exam part of the issue. In fact, the sense that making top grades is an eternal goal and special honor for a group of people is oddly absent from Wilkins's piece. Or maybe not so oddly; Wilkins is a black liberal, and as for many such people, a policy's "acknowledgment" of racism is so crucial that it doesn't matter if it lowers black people's grades! Meanwhile, Wilkins rues that blacks are such a small proportion of law firm partners—a problem exacerbated, presumably, by the mismatch Sander identifies. But never mind: Wilkins has done his job by exploring *racism*.

Sander also shows that the black students who are accepted to top schools because of preferences but decide to go to a lesser-ranked school that better matches their grades and test scores have much higher graduation rates than other black students and are 50 percent less likely to fail the bar exam. This refutes a claim otherwise made by Ian Ayres and Richard Brooks.

Then Daniel Ho, in a *Yale Law Review* piece, supposes that Sander errs in holding law school grades constant in his analyses because since the caliber of the law school affects grades, we can assume that school caliber therefore ultimately determines career as much as grades. That is, Ho accuses Sander of a mistake along the lines of holding lung damage constant in a study investigating the link between smoking and death, when smoking in fact causes lung damage. Ho's line of reasoning carries the implication that we must retain the idea that racial preferences are necessary because degrees from top schools are key to success. But Ho merely states his methodological objection, in an almost oddly brief article. In the formal sense, Ho is correct. But Sander, admitting this, shows that when he actually runs his numbers in various ways, in this particular case, law school grades have a conclusive impact far beyond that of school caliber.

"Those who argue against the mismatch theory have thus far been silent about alternative explanations or solutions," Sander observes. But

Sander's critics indeed have an "alternative explanation," which they consider too obvious to need spelling out: racism. They do have a "solution": to shield black students forever from serious competition because of racism, whatever the collateral damage. But the evidence we have seen from so many studies, including Sander's, makes this rationale for "diversity" an increasingly tough sell to anyone beyond these true believers.

Look, for example, at what can happen when legal writ forces us to place black students according to their dossiers. The University of California at San Diego has given us such a case after racial preferences were banned in the UC system—and the sky did not fall. The year before the ban, there was exactly one black freshman honor student (i.e., with a GPA of 3.5 or better) in a class of 3,268. *One*. After the ban, black students who once would have been let into Berkeley or UCLA through the back door were admitted instead to the second-tier but fine UC schools like UC San Diego and UC Santa Cruz. By 1999, one in five black freshmen were making honors—20 percent, compared with 22 percent for white freshmen. UCSD was now, for the record, more "diverse"—but the diversity coexisted with excellence, rather than founding a two-tier system as had been the case at Berkeley before racial preferences were banned in the system.

The Gurin Report

Nevertheless, one survey has commonly been assumed to show that diversity does somehow improve undergraduate education. During the Supreme Court's assessment of affirmative action in the cases against the University of Michigan in 2003, the mainstream media were abuzz with the idea that a study by the school's professor of psychology and women's studies Patricia Gurin somehow "proved" the scholastic benefits of diversity. But because what became known as The Gurin Report appeared only in obscure academic venues, few had occasion to actually read it. In actuality, it proves nothing.

Gurin did not, as one might suppose, show that degree of diversity leads to higher grades or test scores. She admitted in the report that diversity has no such effect and this had been conclusively demonstrated ten years before by Alexander Astin, director of the Higher Education Research Institute at UCLA, who compared degree of racial diversity at 184 schools with grades, graduation rates, test scores, and admission to grad schools, and found no correlation.

Instead, Gurin concocted her own metric of educational benefit. It was:

1. whether students prefer simple rather than complex explanations
2. whether they think about the influence of society on other people
3. how much they valued general knowledge, problem-solving, and foreign language skills
4. how personally important it was to them to write original works and create artistic works
5. whether they were intellectually satisfied with their work at the university
6. whether they expected to attend graduate school
7. whether they wanted to attend graduate school
8. whether they thought they had a greater drive to achieve and an intellectual self-confidence than the average person their age
9. whether they had greater academic, listening, and writing abilities than the average person their age
10. whether they thought they were more prepared for graduate school than when they entered college
11. whether they had more general knowledge and skills in problem-solving, thinking, learning, and foreign languages than when they entered college

For one, that all of these things are self-reported is almost flabbergastingly irresponsible of someone purporting to address as grave and crucial an issue as diversity on university campuses. We come back to how someone of Gurin's profession would feel about a survey of whites asking whether they were racists: Psychologists have been at the forefront for decades in showing that racist bias must be teased out carefully, given a gap between self-perception and reality. But suddenly this report, although neglecting such a basic tenet of investigating human minds, was celebrated nationwide as "proof" that diversity was crucial to an education.

In any case, the first four "benefits" are a mere matter of whether the students have become a very particular kind of left-leaning Blue-America sort that university culture values. Whether or not becoming exactly this kind of character out of a Woody Allen movie automatically means that education has been a success is hardly a simple question, no matter how much Gurin may find such people attractive. The middle three would be much more interesting if Gurin had investigated whether these students' satisfaction with their education was reflected in having performed at a high level in the relevant coursework, and whether they eventually did go to graduate school. And as to the last four, it is almost impossible to imag-

ine anyone answering "no" to these questions, which is also true of most
of the others.

The basic problem here is that Gurin presented no actual case, argument, or line of reasoning. What was presented as eleven "questions" was
actually eleven statements of Gurin's impressions of what diversity is
good for—rosy, PC propositions that only the most idiosyncratically contrarian undergraduate would venture to disavow. It is hard to imagine
Gurin's questions eliciting anything that would confuse or displease her.
It's as if she asked a hundred people, "Do you believe in being nice to others?", got 97 yeses, and considered her results as compelling evidence that
human beings are inherently kind. An amicus brief examining the Gurin
Report that was submitted to the Supreme Court by the National Association of Scholars observed rightly that

> Nowhere in society—not in graduate school admissions, college
> rankings, job recruitment—do we measure a student's academic suc-
> cess by asking him how much he personally values artistic works or
> whether he enjoys guessing the reason for people's behavior. Very few
> parents would be likely to accept a transcript that reported not
> grades' but their child's self-rating of his abilities and drive to achieve.

Thus, there has been no proof that "diversity" enhances anything except whites' sense of benevolence toward an aggrieved race and blacks'
tendency to seek legitimacy in opposition to whiteness rather than in embracing themselves.

From what I have seen, a great many people who consider themselves
fans of "affirmative action" are not aware that what the policy has often
meant on the ground is lowering standards for black people regardless of
their circumstances in the name of "diversity." This even includes august
figures like Harvard Law School Professor Charles Ogletree. His politics
are apparent from his participation in the movement for reparations, serving as Cornel West's spokesperson during the famous contretemps between West and Harvard President Lawrence Summers in 2002, and trying
to bar Clarence Thomas from speaking before the predominantly black
National Bar Association in 1998. Yet, in a debate I did with him, his response to my stating that standards were lowered for black students was
one of what seemed to be actual perplexity. He had apparently never realized the nature of the practice, likely thinking that "affirmative action"
only meant outreach efforts or letting race break a tie in qualifications.

His leftist embrace of "affirmative action" was *not* based on approval of lowering standards.

John Hope Franklin, an eminent, long-lived black historian considered a seasoned bard of the race, revealed the same thing when cross-examined as a witness for the defense in the University of Michigan trial. Franklin's politics are clear from when he, heading Bill Clinton's Dialogue on Race in 1997, rejected Ward Connerly's participation on the grounds that Connerly couldn't possibly have had anything to contribute to the discussion. Yet, presented with the University of Michigan's undergraduate admissions policy in which being black added 20 points while a perfect SAT score added just 12 and being a "legacy student" added 4, he was stunned, unable to even believe that such a system had arisen.

And ordinary black people often reveal the same state of mind. Black Americans demand equal opportunity, but do not equate this with lowered standards in the name of "diversity" to nearly the extent that one would think listening to academics and journalists. Typical was a poll by *The Washington Post* that showed 86 percent of blacks opposed. In *Black Pride and Black Prejudice*, Paul Sniderman and Thomas Piazza report that 90 percent of 715 blacks rejected admitting a black student over a white one when their difference in SAT scores is 25 points.

Smart People Who Cherish Diversity

In that light, we should cast a gimlet eye on all proposals on race and education with roots in the notion that blacks' "diverseness" should, in any way or at any time, be ranked above how they perform according to the metrics we consider unexceptionable for other students.

Take, for example, Susan Sturm and Lani Guinier's argument that admissions should be based on a lottery system that ensures that minorities are represented in numbers equal to their proportion of the population. The authors' commitment to justice is admirable. But their neglect of history and culture is a logical lapse. It could be that certain minority groups in this country labor under the effects of, first, centuries of disfranchisement, and then two—and this is just as important—self-perpetuating cultural patterns resulting from those abuses that no longer correspond to modern conditions.

That is, it could be that there are not only positive, but also negative traits in black culture. The fact that this is true of all human groups worldwide suggests that it is true equally of black Americans, and there is no logical reason that because black Americans have had a sad past, that their culture today is for some reason the first one in the history of our species whose facets are all constructive responses to the here and now. Despite that our past was imperfect, we remain human beings, and as such, remain imperfect, as we, like all human beings and all human cultures, always will. If we understand that, then we understand that when people tell us that racism must be the only reason that blacks and Latinos are not attending top universities in precisely the proportion that they represent in the national population, they are presenting a blatant and unreflective oversimplification as truth. Race matters, but so does culture. Culture matters, in fact, just as much, if not more.

I think most people spontaneously understand that, but have internalized a sense that to be good people, they must resist acknowledging it in favor of a higher wisdom that people like Lani Guinier are often presented as possessing. But to admit that Sturm and Guinier are neglecting history and cultural realities does not require leaving black students to stew in their own juices. Rather, our progressive efforts will be ones that face that one problem to be dealt with is an unwittingly ingrained sense of separation from the scholarly endeavor. That is, we are not moral troglodytes to admit that the people who concern us are often saddled with antipathy, of various forms and degrees, to what we would like to usher them into.

A lottery system would make sense if universities were still run by bigots. A lottery system makes no sense if the issue is cultural barriers. Our job is to make it so that no one would be moved to exempt black students from real competition by tossing them into a lottery system. We want to teach black students how to show what they *can* do, instead of others just talking about what they *could* do.

A different kind of example is the take on admissions of UC Berkeley law professor Linda Krieger. Krieger extends the diversity concept to the very standards used to evaluate students. She states the following:

> If those who control the definition of merit in a particular social context belong to the same social reference group, and if members of that group tend to excel on one of the relevant performance dimensions in relation to the others, social identity theory predicts that those who determine merit will tend to overvalue performance in the domain where they collectively excel.

I must admit that the linguist in me loves the language that law review articles are often couched in; that quotation is not Judith Butler "bad writing," but deliciously precise use of the highest register of the English language. But still, what does Krieger mean? Well, she refers to a study showing that when an "insider" outperforms an "outsider" in a task, they stick up for rewarding people based on good old-fashioned rankings, but that when the "outsider" outperforms the "insider," then the insider tends to suddenly embrace "fairness" and hope that reward will be split equally between winner and loser.

What Krieger is getting at is that perceptions of merit are subjective. No polemicist, she only hints at implications of that for issues such as affirmative action. She mentions that although law professors are responsible for teaching, research, and service, that in practice only research is determinative of appointments and promotions: that is, one might consider an alternate law school universe where people rose to the top for being good in the classroom even if they rarely published. Or more specifically, on the LSAT, she wonders whether it would be relied on so extensively if whites tended to do less well on it than students of other groups. However, in a debate I had with Professor Krieger in 2002, she was clearer in her view that these issues of subjectivity and fairness lead her to question the whole superstructure of evaluation that university admissions are based on.

Krieger is a top-ranking legal theorist and my debate with her was thoroughly cordial. However, I cannot concur with the idea that the way blacks should deal with the lag between their grades and scores and others' is to agitate for changing the rules. Krieger wants to get past the messy and uncomfortable debates over whether black students with lesser grades and scores are "qualified" via opening our minds to the possibility that the standards themselves are of questionable validity anyway. I see where she is coming from, but ultimately it strikes me as too formal and idealist to serve as useful policy in the real world we know.

This is because it would be, basically, impossible to rid American society of a basic sense that what grades one gets and how one does on tests measures something real, or at least that such measures are, despite their imperfections, the only way to decide who gets what in a society whose population is too vast for it to be practicable to assess all applicants on the basis of long-term contact and carefully reasoned holistic judgment. And because of that, simply decreeing that such measures are invalid would leave real people still under the influence of intuitive senses of what merit is. Whites' sense that their efforts were being underacknowledged would continue, as would blacks' tendencies to hide in oppositional identity, bereft of being able to found their sense of place on numerically demonstrable achievement of the sort that they were raised viewing as basic ways of separating the men from the boys. As often, my ancestors put this better than I can. Zora Neale Hurston once nailed exactly what I mean.

> It seems to me that if I say a whole system must be upset for me to win, I am saying that I cannot sit in the game, and that safer rules must be made to give me a chance. I repudiate that. If others are in there, deal me a hand and let me see what I can make of it, even though I know some in there are dealing from the bottom and cheating like hell in other ways.

Note that Hurston knew The System wasn't perfect: the "dealing from the bottom" today could be considered to be affluent kids' greater access to test coaching and advanced placement classes. But plenty of less-than-affluent whites, Asians, and even black immigrants put their best foot forward despite this. So can black American kids, if we provide them with a university establishment that lets them—which it only can by *requiring* them to.

The Supreme Court's upholding of the University of Michigan's racial preference policies in its law school was widely celebrated as ending the affirmative action debate for the time being. But, in fact, the court did not uphold the school's undergraduate admissions policy, which was more overtly based on quotas than the law school's. And in the wake of this, we will continue to see universities taken to court to defend racial preference programs that lower standards for black students. Whites listening to defenses based on "diversity" should ask themselves a simple question: Would you allow this of your own children?

Ralph Ellison would have asked the same question, criticizing whites who "publish interpretations of Negro experience which would not hold true for their own or for any other form of human life." There is no more eloquent testament to the remaining hint of racist dismissal of blacks in America than how rarely it occurs to white racial preference supporters that they are espousing a policy they would likely consider condescending if applied to their own "Kate or Timmy"—actually, I'll use Joshua or Caitlin.

CONCLUSION:
BLACK STUDENTS ARE HUMAN BEINGS

After writing in the *Atlantic* that middle-class black students underperform out of anxiety that whites think blacks are dumb, Claude Steele appends advice that teachers let such students know that they have faith in their abilities. However, this reminds me of Damali Ayo's counsel that whites learn about blacks from books instead of asking blacks about themselves. Wouldn't Steele's advice set the stage for a new complaint that white professors presume that black students will fail? Wouldn't black students feel uncomfortably singled out if treated this way? It is difficult to even conceive of exactly how white professors would heed Steele's advice without winding up assailed in campus newspaper editorials as racists of a new stripe.

Steele likely appends the "advice" as a perfunctory gesture because of a traditional journalistic requirement that writers at least pretend to offer solutions as well as analysis. But his primary interest is clear: revealing the operations of racism beneath the surface of an America that seems so open-minded on the surface. And Steele's thesis has been a hit on the school circuit for fifteen years now because his audiences share his frame of mind. They receive his findings as implying that the underperformance problem will only cease when there are no racial biases in America and cherish his work for that. Steele's work on the subject is processed not as progressive but as static, as one more useful indication to white America that racism remains real and that only when it is entirely absent will blacks be able to show what they are made of.

That is valuable if racism is really the cause of the problem. But Steele's thesis suffers from a fatal flaw. He showed that black students underperform when faced with a test labelled as assessing blacks' mental prowess—but he never addresses the question as to whether schoolwork on the everyday level comes with such a label. Obviously, it does not, and it is a logical jump to assume that it is general stereotypes in the air that cause black students to choke in this way. Steele considers it beyond question that black students could not perform despite the stereotype, but he is wrong. We must consider, for example, the black students at Dunbar High in Washington a century ago, batting a thousand in school in a time when whites quite openly considered blacks to be lesser beings. Steele, like Douglas Massey in his *American Apartheid* work, treats blacks ahistorically, as if the things he notes today were the same in the past. This is a grave lapse in argumentation: The thesis on race that neglects the histori-cal is, quite simply, invalid.

We seek a cause that explains why the problem only set in during the late twentieth century. That cause is, as so much evidence indicates, a sense of remove from the scholarly endeavor, in which the post–Civil Rights ver-sion of racial identity that young blacks often acquire entails taking on a sense of mainstream America as an alien threat. This wariness thrives re-gardless of personal experience, instead being parasitic upon adolescents' natural insecurities, and the desire this creates for a sense of belonging. White students channel this in various ways—becoming potheads, "goths," or even professional nerds. In this they will easily find plenty of comrades. For black students, a readily available way to channel this quest for a com-forting "us against them" identity is to retreat from whites. The meme is available, and it kicks in. The meme rarely manifests itself a conscious, overt antipathy toward whites. Rather, it can operate more quietly. But it is there.

So—if the problem is not whites' contempt but black students hold-ing white norms at arm's length because of a sense of group membership, then it would seem that white professors taking them aside and saying that they have faith in them is beside the point. It isn't that the students fear white teachers. They have just been passively imprinted by a sense of separation from the tasks at hand. That sense thrives independently of anything whites do today. It has been passed on from peer group to peer group since the late sixties because the comforts of belonging are seduc-tive enough to thrive even when the opponent group has long since laid down its arms. Memes can thrive independently of necessity—recall bot-tled water.

And so how do we lend new muscles to people whose identities leave them feeling spiritually unmoored in attempting the sport?

Well, how do we teach a reluctant person to dance? How do we teach someone to really speak a language? How do we teach someone to drive? We do not ask them to come to our office so we can tell them that we know that they will be good dancers, German speakers, or drivers. Or at best, we are fully aware that this alone would have precious little to do with realizing the goal of lending them the ability to perform in the activ-ity to the height of their abilities. What we do, without questioning it for a minute, is *challenge* them. We make them show what they are made of. We do not torture them or set the bar unrealistically high. But surely we do more than take them out into the hallway and tell them that we know they will do well.

One assumes that fans of Steele's idea do not consider that hallway chat the total of what challenging black students means. But what else do they mean? To assume that the student's performance is tied in any meaningful way to that Old Devil Racism cannot help but color one's conception of what degree of challenge is appropriate. Are we really prepared to challenge black students? I mean not to challenge them to battle racism but to simply do as well as other students. Because challenging them to battle racism means clapping when they do okay, and falling over when they manage better than okay. After which most of them will—big surprise—have trouble getting beyond better than okay because no one ever required it of them. Upon which we are back to even middle-class black American students hitting the top note so rarely that we need torturous preference algorithms to have more than two or three in an entering class at a selective university.

Are we genuinely interested in "challenging" middle-class black students to do not just better than okay but to hit the highest note? Oh, yes, we are—but wait: Are we committed to this to the extent that when a middle-class black student does not, for whatever reason, hit the highest note, we place him or her in the admissions hierarchy exactly where they would be placed if he or she were white? Are we really free of residual notions that where we place that *middle-class*, not poor, black student must be informed by issues of payback, of what we owe black people, or of making sure we, in making the decision, are morally legitimate persons? Do we fully understand that what is therapeutic for us may be mere tokenism for the black applicant? Do we fully understand that if so, in soothing our souls we insult black people, while in the bargain bar them from the kind of serious competition that is the sole thing that brings out the best in human beings regardless of their color or history?

This is what I mean by challenge. When I was a tot in school, there was a kind of science fair every year. In those days, for some reason I had a blazing interest in what children's books call "The Human Body"—something turned me on about learning about the pancreas, the hyoid bone, the ureters. So in third grade my science fair project was a primitive "book" about The Human Body—a little picture drawn in ballpoint pen of the spleen on one page, the intestines on another, and so on. I got a top prize. Then the next year I drew a picture on a big piece of cardboard of the whole Human Body—a skeleton with the bones labelled, hung with the various organs all labelled as well. I still have it—it was as gloopy as one would expect of a nine-year-old, but it did take some work. I got another top prize.

But then in fifth grade, I presented a plastic model called "The Visible Man" (they still make it), consisting of bones pinned together and plastic organs that the instructions direct one to paint with Testor's model paints and situate in their proper places, all of this encased in a transparent plastic shell of skin, with the whole model then mounted in slots on a base. (People who remember TV commercials from the seventies may recall the Anacin commercials that featured a similar model used to demonstrate how the aspirin goes from the head throughout the body.) That took work, too. Some work, at least. But I was hardly the only boy of that era who liked assembling and painting plastic model kits his mother bought at Sears.

Still, though, I was stunned when the teacher—quite white—did not give me a prize that year. I asked her why. She said that it was basically the same kind of thing I had done the other two years and that I wasn't stretching myself into learning anything new.

Even though putting that model together and painting it had taken a certain amount of time and effort, she was right, and I knew it even then. It was a crucial lesson in my life, which helped to teach me what pushing myself really meant. Putting that model together and painting it was not pushing myself, whatever my color, and whatever injustices had been levelled against people of that same color even recently at the time— Reverend King had been assassinated just eight years before, as recently as the Monica Lewinsky scandal will be by the time this book hits the stores.

The only way I could have truly learned the nature of serious effort was by not being given a prize that year, and I remain thankful to Ms. Karen Russo for the lesson. She did not indulge my delicate status as a Negro by rewarding me for just doing what was, black though I was, an ordinary job.

The next year I brought in some snails living on some plants in a "biosphere" (bought at Sears). I don't remember whether I got a prize that time, but at least I had rubbed my eyes and ventured beyond what I was most comfortable with. No more small intestines. The one thing I recall thirty years later about breeding those little snails is that I wasn't sure whether I would get a prize, but that I did my very best to fashion the project to the top of my ability. I would not have exerted that effort if I had not been denied the prize the year before. I was, in short, dealing with Real

Life, and the fact that I was not being given a pass because I was black only made me a stronger person.

If anyone suspects that this experience shows that my writing books like *Losing the Race* and this one stems at least partly from personal experience, they are absolutely correct. I wish more young blacks had experiences like the one I described—and I mean ones that they have no reason to process as, even "possibly," due to racism.

Pedro Noguera and his ilk may hear the story above as me bragging. But if I wanted to brag, I would not draw the reader's attention to tacky juvenile projects and my approval of the dismissal of one of them by a figure of authority. I do not consider it at all extraordinary that as a child, black though I was, I was interested in random things unconnected to my "identity" and put effort into them—although, for the record, I also had my black history flash cards and *Color Me Brown* coloring book. In this, I was simply a typical human being. My purpose in telling that story was to show what it really means to challenge a black student, period. To me, getting reminiscences like that "out there" is as urgent as sharing tales of run-ins with racism are to other black writers. Tell me that you have encountered racism, and I say, "That was awful." Tell me that you have been taught to be the best that you can be *despite* racism, and I say, "Keep talking." And if *that* means that I'm bragging, then it's high time more black people bragged along with me.

Here is why. There are two possible scenarios. One is that we commit ourselves 24-7 to fostering a sense of self among black students that sees doing well in school as something black people do just like everyone else. We commit ourselves in full acknowledgment that black students often feel otherwise even when attending excellent schools. We commit ourselves with full understanding that black students do not need the total eclipse of *racism* to get past this, given that they did so even in the segregated America of yore. And if we really understand what we are facing, then we commit ourselves to facing that for a while, black students may well be "underrepresented" in many competitive student bodies as the race becomes accustomed to dealing with the rigors of true competition. In this, whites will swallow their guilt in the name of helping black people rather than soothing their egos. Blacks will let go of payback fantasies and let their brothers and sisters ply away as individuals rather than as cannon fodder for identity theatrics.

The other scenario is that we thrill to the rhetoric of people medicating themselves by decrying that anyone would venture that black culture is less than perfect. Max Weber, pioneering social scientist who wrote before his comrades had been detoured into self-serving performances, had some choice words for such people: "Nowhere are the interests of science more poorly served in the long run than in these situations where one refuses to see uncomfortable facts and the realities of life in all their starkness." And while we wait for the magical revision that these people's counsel calls for of how America has operated for four hundred years, the achievement gap will sit forever exactly where it is as I write.

The accomplishments of black Americans over those very four hundred years show that we can do better. Let's stop just talking about how we could. Let's teach our young people how to show that we can.

CHAPTER NINE

The Hip-Hop "Revolution":
Therapeutic Alienation on a Rhythm Track

ew would accuse Henry Louis Gates Jr., chairman of Harvard's Afro-American Studies department, of not loving the black community. Yet, he has had some choice words about hip-hop music.

> The popularity of hip-hop trades off of voyeurism, right? So you're watching something illicit in a keyhole. The white kids watch illicit sexual activity in the keyhole, and they go back to their rooms and do their algebra and go to Harvard. The black kids, somehow, are trying to crawl through the keyhole. What I'm trying to figure out is why our kids, metaphorically, want to crawl through that keyhole and embrace those modes of behavior as authentically black. It is killing our people. And it makes me sick.

But under a cool idea that has gained steam since the early nineties, Gates's observations qualify as the out-of-touch rantings of an old man.

The new idea is that in all of its cuss-laden, woman-hating, violent splendor, hip-hop is a political statement from below. The music, we are told, is "revolutionary," putting the urgency of black poverty in white America's faces and pointing the way to a better future for poor blacks in America.

This is nonsense.

It's fine for people to listen to this music and to make money from it. But the idea that it is progressive or constructive is an incoherent, after-the-fact rationalization by people who are merely intoxicated by the rhythms and politically inclined to thrill to black voices from the street. They seek to cobble together concern about black progress with a mere sensual embrace of hip-hop's surface appeal, aware that the sociopathic nature of so much of the lyrics is not something a King, Powell, Rustin, Evers, or even a Malcolm would recognize as useful.

The result is torturous confection in the name of scholarship and hazy bloviations by rappers in interviews. None of this refutes that a music that celebrates gunplay, has no constructive political counsel to offer, and depicts women as animals has nothing to do with moving a people forward. Any proposal otherwise is senseless—unless what actually draws these people to the music is nothing but the fact that it is couched in alienation.

SLAMMING ON HIP-HOP?

I am sincere in saying that I have no problem with the idea of people just listening to and enjoying this music. I like and listen to some of it, although for me, the endless anger and put-downs and, especially, the pitiless comments about women are not something I could adopt as the sound track of my life. But that's just me.

Yet, the idea that this music is some kind of beacon for a new black America is something that I would be irresponsible in remaining silent about.

For the first few years after I started commenting publicly about race, I deliberately avoided broaching hip-hop. As far as I am concerned, claims that it *creates* violence or *fosters* black misery put the cart before the horse. The music is a symptom of larger factors, and it was those that I was more interested in addressing. Not to mention that there is little point in telling anyone that there is something wrong with their favorite music. We feel music so subjectively that hearing it attacked cannot help but feel like a personal affront. I regularly turned down requests to knock hip-hop in print, on radio or TV, or in speeches.

I at first made one exception, in a piece for *The New Republic* on Tupac Shakur. But I valued the opportunity to at least think about the music and write something about it once. I learned early on that it was television appearances and newspaper editorials that reached the most people immediately, such that a piece in *The New Republic* would only get around so much, not distracting from my statements on issues I thought more important. Also, in 2001 the blog culture was still in its infancy, such that although the magazine puts their articles online, the Tupac piece was not instantly linked throughout cyberspace, and I sense that few recall it today. And even then, I deliberately refrained from including it in my essay collection *Authentically Black* in 2003 because I knew that the nature of the

media and the trip-wire nature of the issue would mean that this one essay would end up being the main thing a lot of people were interested in
about that book. I didn't want the subjective temptations of that one easy,
"hot" topic to distract readers from engaging reparations, affirmative action, "the N-word," and the other things *Authentically Black* was about that
I thought of as *real*.

But at talk after talk that I gave in those years, a young black person
would stand up and ask how I felt about the "revolutionary" potential of
hip-hop. Once when I was addressing a smallish group of educated, urbane black writers and activists, I noticed that the second I uttered Tupac
Shakur's name there was an actual hush in the room. And finally there
was the night in 2003 that I was doing one more talk and a black woman
fresh out of college, well-spoken, poised, and intelligent, asked me once
again—in complete civility—about the possibility that black America
could forge a revolution through hip-hop.

For some reason, it was that night that I realized I needed to speak up.
I had harbored no animus against hip-hop; I thought it wasn't a big deal.
I thought that by and large, people knew that it was just a kind of theatre.
But it turned out that I wasn't hip enough. I was wrong.

Countless people black and white today think that this music is *politics*.

So that's when I started writing on the subject, including in a piece for
the Manhattan Institute's *City Journal*. Before spring 2003, I would have
waved away an offer to debate Russell Simmons on HBO (which ended up
being with Damon Dash; Simmons didn't show at the last minute), but
after that I leapt at the chance. I even allowed some interviews with writers
who I knew wanted to hang me in print because I have learned that the
readers I want to reach know how to distinguish what I am quoted as saying from the potshots the journalist gets in. (One of these pieces that
seems to have gotten around is one in the London *Guardian*, and I do feel
moved to note that, for the record, my hair is not graying in the least.)

I am still ambivalent about the fact that since 2003, my statements on
hip-hop have become what I am best known for among black reading
people and beyond. Since by 2003 the blog culture we know was a new reality, the *City Journal* article elicited more mail than anything that had ever
appeared in that magazine in its fifteen years. Much to my surprise, on the
basis of the Damon Dash interview, for more than a year afterward I was
recognized in public several times a week, including by bridge toll collec-
tors, security guards, supermarket cashiers, and people at bars. One of these
days I need to actually watch that debate; I might note that while HBO

trimmed it to something like twelve minutes, it actually lasted an hour, with the crew and staff gathering to watch a battle I thoroughly enjoyed.

But overall, I never thought I would be associated with hip-hop, of all topics. I started pitching in on it nevertheless because it worries me to see young black America distracted by the notion that helping people get ahead has anything to do with the lyrics of their favorite rappers. The notoriety I have attracted by speaking out on the music only reinforces my sense of urgency. I will never forget the day after HBO first broadcast the debate with Dash, when I could barely get down the street: Clearly, this issue is very much a live one among black Americans under fifty. And if people are so attuned to the issue of where hip-hop fits in with Civil Rights after the year 2000, then it is my responsibility to point out that fashioning hip-hop as progressive leaves black activism like an inner tube with a pinhole puncture. Pump it up and it's half flat again ten minutes later because of air seeping from a laceration that needs to be patched for good.

The lyrics of rap music are therapeutic alienation set to a catchy beat. This includes, for the record, the "conscious rap" often claimed to refute a statement such as that one, as I will discuss. Therapeutic alienation takes people nowhere; it holds people right where they are because it is all about alienation for its own sake rather than doing anything about it. For us to be under any impression that hip-hop is a new Civil Rights revolution will only siphon off energy from the real work that needs to be done.

FIGHT THE POWER:
EXCUSE ME, BUT HOW?

Smart people writing on rap are basically united in a claim that the music is a political statement, not only depicting poor black America but also pointing in the direction of changing it somehow.

Tricia Rose, American studies professor at UC Santa Cruz, designates hip-hop as a "liberatory, visionary, and politically progressive" music whose lyrics "continue to articulate the shifting terms of black marginality in contemporary American culture." Apparently, "rappers are constantly taking dominant discursive fragments and throwing them into relief, destabilizing hegemonic discourses and attempting to legitimate counter-hegemonic interpretations. Rap's contestations are part of a polyvocal black cultural discourse engaged in discursive 'wars of position' within and against dominant discourses" (whew!). Robin D. G. Kelley, anthropology and African American studies professor at Columbia, chimes in about "the young people who fill the deadened, congested spaces of the city with these sonic forces," forces that we must hear "to know the political climate among urban youth." William Van Deburg, Afro-American studies professor at the University of Wisconsin at Madison, thinks hip-hop has "the potential to invigorate a liberationist ethic that had fallen on hard times." Rutgers-Camden law professor Imani Perry swells to hip-hop offering a "counterhegemonic authority and subjectivity to the force of white supremacy." In his autobiography, hip-hop impresario Russell Simmons says that hip-hop "communicates aspiration and frustration, community and aggression, creativity and street reality, style and substance," and that embracing hip-hop is part of maintaining one's instinct toward "rebellion and change." Statements like this occur with numbing regularity, in a literature devoted to showing that what so many people think of as vulgar noise is actually worthy of attention and, in fact, "deep."

But it is hard to see anything utilitarian in what these people are saying. "Counterhegemonic"—I see. But what is the *counsel* that our counterhegemonic heroes offer, other than yelling? There is, in fact, none.

Pretenses otherwise are now piled so high and deep that we need to have a closer look at the "literature" in question.

HIP-HOP IS REVOLUTIONARY BECAUSE . . . (PART ONE) IT'S BLACK AMERICA'S CNN

Behind many celebrations of the "counterhegemonic" nature of hip-hop is an assumption that rap lyrics are precious in being so very "real." The idea would seem to be that it is an artistic and political advance to depict on a regular, and even fetishistic, basis that which is actual, even when repugnant.

In academese this is rendered as follows:

> The MC usually occupies a self-proclaimed location as representative
> of his or her community or group—the everyman and everywoman
> of his or her hood. As a representative, he or she encourages a kind of
> sociological interpretation of the music, best expressed by the con-
> cept of the "real."

That is, for the record, Imani Perry. More prosaically, we hear Chuck D calling rap black America's CNN. Presumably, the artists give us vibrant poetry showing the circumstances that poor blacks endure. Grandmaster

Flash's seminal "The Message" of 1982 was the most prominent kickoff of this strain in hip-hop, with its masterful strophe, "It's like a jungle sometimes, it makes me wonder how I keep from going under." The song gave us a cinematic scan of the hardship of ghetto blacks' lives, and in its wake, countless rappers since have echoed it in tracks covering poor black misery. Tracks of this kind are all but required of any rapper taken seriously. Tupac Shakur's iconic status is driven significantly by his "ghettoscape" interludes, for example, and today's "conscious" rappers contribute soaring equivalents such as Talib Kweli's miniature epic "Respiration" on his joint album with Mos Def *Black Star*.

But even this is not as unequivocally proactive as we are told. Thinking within our own moment, it might seem the soul of morality to obsessively promote how badly things are going for people on the bottom. But that is actually a simplistic notion. "Real" human beings living in decidedly "real" circumstances of poverty have been known to be somewhat uncomfortable seeing the negative aspects of their lives presented in public as their essence or as the most important thing to know about them.

Recall, for example, the letter that the Marian Anderson *See It Now* episode elicited from a black viewer in 1957, complaining that focusing on segregation unfairly left out the blacks making the best of themselves despite it. To show that this is a human and not "black" issue, in 1947, in Italy, Vittorio De Sica directed the film *Shoe Shine* (*Sciuscià*), about destitute Italians. Interestingly, the kinds of people he depicted did not approve of De Sica's Neo*real*ist approach. To them, this kind of "realism" put them on the big screen at their worst rather than their best, and they didn't like it, Neo- or not.

There is a book or two in the difference between Italians living hand-to-mouth in 1946 hating *Shoe Shine* and tenured black Americans in universities in 1996 celebrating sonic cartoons of young black men shooting up and shooting one another. But the point is that this fetish of the "real" is not a universal among poor human beings, nor is it the only possible brand of progressive politics. Something more specific is going on. Why is it so important just for the descendants of slaves in America to cherish the "real" in their popular music?

Well, taking the hip-hop intellectuals at their word, it seems that they think that the "reality" is valuable in *showing* whites who don't know the score what it's really like to be black, especially poor and black. In an interview, Tricia Rose gave some riffs on this idea, common among blacks on the left, that it is a problem that poor blacks are "invisible" to "white

America." Rose commented after moving to Santa Cruz from her former teaching position at New York University that the car culture in Santa Cruz leads to "unfettered whiteness" in contrast to whites having to rub shoulders with "rowdy" black people in the subway in New York.

There is a certain music to that comment, although one can only imagine a white professor casually disparaging "unfettered blackness" anywhere. But the question is: What does Tricia Rose want to happen in the case that whiteness was dutifully fettered and blacks got to show whites what they usually don't see?

Here is a white woman from Rockland County, New York, and here are five "unfettered" black kids from the 'hood. Let's sit them down in a room. The white lady is all ears. What is it that the kids have to tell her that will be a revelation to the white woman?

Or is it that there is something *about* them she needs to know that the kids would be unlikely to spontaneously articulate themselves? Well, then let's have her just observing them for four weeks, day in and day out. What is it that she will learn? She already knows some people have less money than others. She has heard of bad ghetto schools. She knows women get pregnant early in the ghetto. She certainly knows about ghetto violence. Anyone who claims that this woman is as naïve about black America and race as she would have been in 1950 is neglecting seismic changes in America since the Civil Rights era. So, what more is she supposed to be taking in?

Is it that she is supposed to inhale the gospel of *American Apartheid* and its ilk that if poor blacks do anything negative more than other people then it can only be because of the evils of industry and racist bias? For one, I hope not, since that gospel, that when inner-city blacks act up it is because factories and middle-class blacks moved to the suburbs in the seventies, is fiction. But then, here is the most important thing, whether or not you have been convinced by my previous chapters: Given how hard leftists like Rose have always found it to get Mr. and Mrs. America to really think that way, *how would just "seeing" poor blacks manage the trick?* Don't people like Rose think that even white New Yorkers seeing "unfettered blackness" every day on the subway are "blind" to urgent reality?

What, precisely, do we *mean* by the idea that thinking whites need to have "contact" with blacks, in terms of actual human beings and actual social policies? When a rap fan celebrates the lyrics as "showing" us black America, what does he or she think the purpose of the "showing" is?

When Imani Perry titles her exploration of hip-hop *Prophets of the Hood*, exactly what does she suppose the artists are prophesying?

What, again, is these people's *constructive counsel*?

Here, we move into things that show that there is no counsel at all.

HIP-HOP IS REVOLUTIONARY BECAUSE . . . (PART TWO) IT PREACHES DEFEATISM

On its face, the idea seems to be that America will see how poor blacks live and decide to fix it, moved by rappers' eloquence and charisma. Reviews sing of fat tracks and catchy riffs and the "flow" of the rapper's delivery, while academics and journalists sing of it as a wake-up call to the Establishment.

This all makes it sound like the hip-hop albums you see on display at Tower Records and announced on posters are basically a kind of hopped-up Tracy Chapman. One imagines vivid but perceptive aural paintings of what it's like growing up hard, with a certain tension between portraying the ghetto and glorifying it. We are to pardon this glorification as evidence of these men's self-confidence despite what they grew up in, which was, after all, the only thing they ever knew.

But the reality is quite different. Actually listen to the work, and the glorification of ghetto self-sabotage is usually front and center. There are the "deep" insights about life in da hood. But they are garnish, often tacked on almost as an apology for the savagery of the rest of the CD.

Down to Cases: Hip-hop as Album

Because this tends to get lost in a tendency in the hip-hop literature to discuss individual tracks more than whole albums, we might take a look at a typical Tupac Shakur recital, his second album *Strictly 4 My Niggaz* (1993).

Certainly hip-hop fans will have dozens of other albums I might take as "typical," but I can address only one without bloating the chapter. *Strictly 4 My Niggaz* is an entry by a lionized rapper, thoroughly typical of his work, and well entrenched in popular evaluation as a classic. No one could dismiss it as exceptional: It is bread-and-butter rap music, period.

So—it opens with "Holler If Ya'Hear Me," which superimposes a swaggering call to armed inner-city rebellion ("Keep your hands on your gat") upon a sinfully infectious rhythm track. Next is an interlude, "Pac's Theme," which crosscuts an excerpt from an anti-rap statement by Dan

Quayle with gradually coalescing segments of a spoken manifesto by Shakur: "I was raised in this society so there's no way you can expect me to be a perfect person. I'm 'a do what I'm 'a do. That's how I feel. I'll do whatever I like. I'm not a role model." Then, "Point the Finga" is a proto-Eminem moment in which Shakur decries his mistreatment by the media ("That's why these mothafuckas [ha ha ha] point the finga"). This song also includes rap's trademark misogyny: It crosscuts a female voice mercenarily wheedling, "Can we get some?"

The next triptych, "Something 2 Die 4," "Last Wordz," and "Souljah's Revenge," returns to the street riot theme of the title track. A leitmotif running through these three songs is "One nigga / teach two niggas / teach fo' niggas / teach mo' niggas." A bit of "conscious" rap here, in that liquor, jealousy, and recklessness are not "something to die for"—but rising up against police brutality ("*Fuck* the police!") is. Then "Peep Game," "Strugglin'," and "Guess Who's Back" mine the vein further, stirring references to "bitches" and general macho strutting into concentrated running down of police forces as occupying armies. A noted moment in "Peep Game" is the famous "Vice President Dan Quayle, eat a dick up," with Shakur cannily ending the track by repeating the last four words *sans* accompaniment.

"Representin' 93" is a kind of wave from the stage, paying tribute to assorted black pop stars of the period and including a "holler to my niggas in the pen."

Then comes a change in tone with the slower groove of "Keep Ya Head Up," a tribute to welfare mothers. This is the kind of ghetto anthem that Shakur admirers are often so taken by, typified by passages like saying of babies that, "Since a man can't make one, he has no right to tell a woman when and where to create one."

But this elegy does not stand unleavened. Just three tracks later comes "I Get Around," where Shakur joins some guest rappers in telling women to stand in line, given that "2Pacalypse Now don't stop for no ho's." And before this we get the title track (more invective against the police), and a corollary observation, "The Streetz R Deathrow," justifying thuggish behavior as an inevitable product of fatherlessness ("So call me crazy but this is what you gave me").

"Papa'z Song" is another time-out for family issues, indicting and rejecting an absent father who reappears. Tupac is afraid that since his mother is always away at work he is in danger of becoming like his father. His mother even does some whoring to pay the rent and grows to hate her child because he looks like the father. Shakur then allows the father to explain himself: He left because there was no way to make more than a pittance legally, and thus he took off to try to make a big score for his family outside of the law. Thus, everyone—Shakur, the mother, and the father—are caught up in currents beyond their control.

It's a marvelous aural drama in its way. But—the only solution is therefore a return to the race riots of the late 1960s: The CD goes out on the gutbucket loping swing of "5 Deadly Venomz," a final upturned finger at the police. Shakur brings the rhythm track back up briefly after the fade-out before fading back to black for good. As the CD player goes back to 1, the message has been that, in the vein of James Baldwin, we better not forget the fire next time: Just when you think we're gone, we'll be back—with our hands on our gats.

Now—what is the "message" of this CD, or the countless other ones of similar tone and with a similar mixture of content, such as NWA's *Straight Outta Compton*, Dr. Dre's *The Chronic*, and Snoop Dogg's *Doggystyle*, that writers like Nelson George consider apotheoses of recorded sound? The "message" analysis is especially hard for the albums where outright celebration of thuggishness is driven hard, such as 50 Cent's debut recording, *Get Rich or Die Tryin'*, one of the national best sellers of 2003, Lil Jon and the East Side Boyz's stunningly nasty *Crunk Juice* of 2004, or Cam'ron's debut album, *Come Home with Me*, with multiple tracks in which he raps of selling drugs with stony-faced pride.

Hip-hop as Utopianism

Hip-hop writers celebrate the music's *reality* because it *shows* whites an injustice and points the way to *change*. But what kind of change does this music *counsel*? A kind that the rappers and the rest of us know full well will never happen.

Rather, it would seem to be that poor blacks are mired in a situation that will *not* change—unless there is some kind of Marshall Plan of aid from the federal government, and that meanwhile, this exempts poor black people from any standards of morality. But since we all know that no Marshall Plan of this kind will ever happen, by implication these artists are actually saying that there will be no change, and that poor blacks will remain eternally stuck where they are.

I would be interested to see what other implication one could draw from these albums: This genuinely seems to be the Message, and I assume that chants along the lines of "Keep ya head up" are not considered "activism," however catchily they sit on a steady beat. No doubt, hip-hop lyrics are festooned with spiky addresses not only of the police, but also with criticisms of Clarence Thomas, George Bush I and II, and Bill Clinton, and paeans to the beauty of far-off Africa. But alienation and political activism are not the same thing. How effective are these observations in making change? To take one problem, AIDS is now as much a scourge in black communities as crack. But hip-hop, with its hypermasculinized and often homophobic substrate, would be about the last musical genre we would expect to address this epidemic in any sustained way.

It isn't that hip-hop does not include occasional hints in a different direction. On his debut album, Mos Def says, "It ain't where you're from; it's where you're at." But Shakur's message is that where you're at *is* where you're from and that message is typical in the genre. That basic idea, often expressed in hip-hop lyrics via the word *legacy*, is considered sage, compassionate wisdom. One way hip-hop scholars duck having to call this "progressive" is to claim that the issue is a matter of "debate" in the "hip-hop community." But if there is a "debate" in hip-hop over the extent to which early experience determines one's future, then the pessimists won it long ago. Tupac and Jay-Z and 50 Cent and their ilk sell much, much better than Mos Def. Yes, Shakur was known to come up with things like his idea that NIGGA stands for Never Ignorant, Getting Goals Accomplished. But the main goal in his lyrics was raging against the Establishment and leaving it there to go on with a new track about where "niggaz" are *from*, not where they had gotten *to*.

"One nigga / teach two niggas . . ."—but just what are said niggas supposed to be teaching one another? To Shakur chronicler Michael Eric Dyson and many others, this is *the* voice of black America. But what that voice counsels is hopelessness. Dyson attempts a religious spin, noting that today's despair can become tomorrow's redemption and bringing Jeremiah and the Psalms into the equation. But these sources, as well as Jesus—whom one suspects Dyson would consider an apt comparison with the rapper he calls a "ghetto saint"—counseled more constructively under equally difficult conditions. They have more to say to us than merely "Rage!"

Shakur had no love for the black "bourgeoisie," whom he considered to have lost touch with "their own people" down there purveying the 5 Deadly Venomz. Thus, his "message" becomes painfully clear: It is not even progressive for black people to become middle-class and, horror of horrors, become somewhat more culturally akin to whites than ghetto blacks are. Yet Dyson, in his ongoing crusade against black middle-class views, adores Shakur in that he "thrust the sharp edges of his lyrics into the inflated rhetoric of orthodox blackness, challenging narrow artistic visions of black identity." "Many critics," he writes, "are unable to acknowledge the ingenuity of artistically exploring the attractions and limits of black moral and social subcultures. They endorse a 'positive' perspective that is as artificial and uncomprehending of the full sweep of black culture as is the exclusive celebration of pimps, playas, hos, macks and thugs." Which means, I suppose, that when M. C. Eiht of Compton's Most Wanted claims, "I ain't punchin a clock," he is progressive—in dismissing behavior that puts food on the table for a family.

Therefore: Hip-hop's writerly fans celebrate the music as pointing us in some progressive direction. But in being founded on utopian visions of an America that shows no signs of ever coming into being, the music cannot support the progressive analysis. In essence, it points black America neither backward nor forward, but nowhere. (I believe this also to be true of conscious rap; I'll get to it later.) Tricia Rose has a neat passage that exemplifies this idea, breaking down the essence of the music into three components, "flow, layering, and rupture." Rose treats the latter "rupture" effect—sudden interpolations breaking the regular rhythm—as a reflection of the revolutionary potential of the music: "These effects at the level of style and aesthetics suggest affirmative ways in which profound social dislocation and rupture can be managed and perhaps contested in the cultural arena." We should therefore be "prepared for rupture, find pleasure in it, in fact, *plan on* social rupture. When these ruptures occur, use them in creative ways that will prepare you for a future in which survival will demand a sudden shift in ground tactics."

That is great writing. But what kind of rupture, and how plausible, how *humane*, is it to wait for it? Where writers like Rose acknowledge that so many of the lyrics are not constructive, they point out that the lyrics reflect the everyday nature of poor blacks' lives in which there is no identifiable "rupture," with the following passage by Nelson George typical:

> There is an elemental nihilism in the most controversial crack-era hip hop that wasn't concocted by the rappers but reflects the mentality and fears of young Americans of every color and class living an exhausting, edgy existence, in and out of big cities. Like crack dealing, this nihilism may die down, but it won't disappear, because the social conditions that inspired the trafficking and the underlying artistic impulse that ignited nihilistic rap have not disappeared.

I, for one, cannot help objecting that even the poorest blacks before the eighties produced no music like this. But whatever. George's point, and similar ones, still leave the simple fact that nihilism—however much it thrills leftist academics and journalists who think Dick Cheney and Rudolph Giuliani deserve it—is not activism.

Pop Star Politicians?

Finally there is the rather obvious fact that over the decades that hip-hop has been celebrated for its endless "potential" for political change, there has been so little indication that it will ever create any.

We must ask just how realistic it is that pop musicians are poised to forge realistic change in the political realm. Russell Simmons, attempting to spur legislation relaxing the Rockefeller laws, came a-cropper in the face of the byzantine and coded traditions of Albany politics, for example. We need not crow at him over this, as few people outside of the political arena would be equipped to just walk in and take on the painstaking, complex work of getting laws drafted and passed. But Simmons's experience cannot help but lead us to wonder just how well equipped the people turning it out on the covers of *Vibe* are to become effective agents of political change in between their recording sessions and tours (and, often, brawls, convictions, and spells in court and jail). No, Sister Souljah is not an exception—she was not a rapper who became an activist, but the other way around. She was an activist first, and her debut rap album was essentially an attempt at a souvenir tie-in to that. It never sold very well, and she has largely remained one of thousands of black people working in the trenches to make a difference. Her rapping stints have played no significant role in what she has done.

As I write, Simmons is proposing to channel his efforts into improving minority students' reading scores. If this bears fruit, then hats off to him. But it remains to be seen whether he tries to accomplish this through the channels available in America as we know it, such as piggybacking on the provisions of the Bush Administration's No Child Left Behind Act. Questions as to that program's generosity and execution are inevitable and will never disappear. But if Simmons's only approach to that is to decry it, or to embrace teachers' unions' resistance to changes out of a sense that this is the only possible way to be "progressive" or "black," then we will be right back to wondering whether a music that cherishes opposition over action can help people in the real America.

Meanwhile, I have had occasion to meet a few rappers in my time when I appeared with them on talk shows. E-40 was a quiet man, but I had conversations with Coolio and Lil Wayne. Good men both, but the impression I got was of ambitious people busy with making albums, touring, and doing TV appearances like the ones we were at, all aimed at mining money and attention from audiences thrilled by their menacing street postures. It was extremely hard to imagine them immersing themselves in spurring progressive legislation for black people, either on the ground or even in their lyrics.

This is often clear when interviewers probe rappers on their actual positions on politics. So often they come up with an unfocused kind of cynicism hard to fit into any kind of coherent philosophy or even concern. Nas doesn't even vote.

> I think I wasn't a part of Vote or Die [Sean Combs's voter registration drive in 2004] because I'm not a registered voter, and I don't agree with voting because of the examples out there, the thievery of an election, the so-called thievery, I can't tell people to stand on line to vote and they're still going to be found in jail tomorrow.
>
> Vote or Die is one way but we have to pull other resources. We need a representative in the United Nations that can make it a real issue to deal with. It's beyond a vote. The minority vote is not going to get anyone in office, it can't deal with middle America. Harlem can't do it alone.

The United Nations? Nas devotes his life to being a pop star, and all power to him for that. But his comments are those of someone who has chosen an avocation that makes sustained engagement with details of the issues of the day unlikely.

Mos Def, considered a leading "conscious" rapper, is disgusted rather than committed.

> When it comes to the presidential election, I'm not listening to those people. I heard those machines were broken. I think that they should fix them. I think they should fix all of those machines or throw them away and start over. Until then, I can't listen to those people talk. It's like listening to somebody lie all the time, and I have no use for that in my life.

It seems that he harbors the disgust as payback for white dismissal.

We built the global economy with our sweat, our blood, our bones. We've given this country many beautiful things: innovations in science, medicine, technology, art. And they don't give a fuck about us, for the most part.

You could almost set that as a good rap. Mos Def is a rapper. He is even an actor, and a damned good one based on what I saw in his performance in Suzi Lori-Parks's *Topdog/Underdog* in 2002. But where is the "progressive" counsel in his political insights? And why would we expect any in someone who has chosen a career as a performing artist?

It's not rocket science to see little hope for a new Civil Rights revolution in this kind of attitude. Plenty of even the most sympathetic chroniclers of the business know this. Black cultural critic Yvonne Bynoe, a committed activist, writes, "The leadership from the post–civil rights generation must be able to do more than rhyme about problems; they have got to be able to build organizations as well as harness the necessary monetary resources and political power to do something about them." Nelson George admits that hip-hop "doesn't present a systematic (or even original) critique of white world supremacy. Nor has it produced a manifesto for collective political agitation. It has generated no Malcolm X or Dr. King. It has spawned no grassroots activist organization on the order of the Southern Christian Leadership Conference, the Black Panther Party, NAACP, or even the Country Music Association."

Just after this point George notes, "Hip hop has actually had surprisingly little concrete long-term impact on African-American politics." But why the surprise? Imani Perry gives away the game nicely. She admits, "It is impossible to isolate, in any coherent fashion, a clear system of political critique with a traceable eschatology or teleology in hip hop." Indicatively, what the part about *eschatology* and *teleology* means in simpler English is that the music gives no indication of a game plan or coherent goal. Was Perry possibly wary of putting that too plainly? In any case, she follows up: "There is a kind of revelry present in the lyrical treatment of the prisons as a fundamental element to the identity construction of black male youth." But wouldn't you know, Perry approves of this: that is, of a music that teaches black kids that jail is a rite of passage, "real," I suppose. To her, you see, this is "a radical commitment to otherness." At which point wherever else we are being taken, we have departed from any conception of constructive politics.

One might object that I am putting too much of a burden on hip-hop—after all, in the end it's just supposed to be fun, to get the blood pumping, to remind us of "who we are" and to "keep it real." Okay—but then, one agrees with precisely my point. If it is unrealistic to expect hip-hop to address real-world concerns, then one thing it is not is political. Hip-hop is not a political statement. It is an attitude, and that's all.

HIP-HOP IS REVOLUTIONARY BECAUSE . . . (PART THREE)
RAPPERS LOVE TO HATE ON THE BITCHES

Something else that throws a wrench into the idea that rap lyrics are progressive is their notorious sexism. The words *ho'* and *bitch* are used so liberally that by now all of America is familiar with them as a kind of black male ghetto slang for women, and *ho'* has been a mainstream slang word among young Americans of all colors for about fifteen years. But it goes deeper than just name-calling.

Cam'ron opens *Come Home with Me* with a skit chuckling about *hitting* women. Hip-hop is about the problems facing black people, hmm? Well, later on in "On Fire Tonight" the civic problem we face that Cam'ron decides to address is the danger of getting VD from unclean women, the song preceded by a skit in which a man calls a woman to tell her she gave him VD only to have her blow him off unconcerned. Some cuts later in "Boy, Boy," I suppose in the name of the "keeping it real" that hip-hop fans consider so wonderful, Cam'ron describes things such as semen on a woman's face (which he then tells her to wipe off because, "I hate me a filthy ho' ") and plowing her so hard that she complains that the man is hurting her uterus, cervix, and ovaries. Yet, Cam'ron dedicates this album to his young son. I wonder if he really swells with pride at the thought of his son listening to this album when he gets old enough to understand it.

Hip-hop's fans cannot claim that Cam'ron is unusual or extreme; I have not chosen an especially raw or underground example. I once did a tutoring session with a fourteen-year-old black girl from a struggling neighborhood; she had been doing some creative writing, and noticing that its scansion seemed to owe something to rap, I asked her what her favorite music was—and her favorite album at the time was none other than Cam'ron's *Come Home with Me*. One runs up against the sort woman-hating on that album constantly in the supposedly enlightened lyrical art of hip-hop.

I know—it's just theatre. I may seem too humorless to "get" that all that happens is that fourteen-year-olds snicker about the stuff and then get on with their lives. But I do "get" that, and notice that I am not claiming that passages like this teach people to actually do such things.

But even so—tell me it's "political"!

We will also dismiss the more musically inclined writers' feint of noting that sexism was not unknown in earlier black popular music. We all know this, but the issue is one of degree. For example, Robin Kelley cites a 1965 "toast" on pimping, coldly instructing that the "bitch" must be stomped, tromped, driven, ridden, and shot through her "motherfucken head." But this was not *typical* of toasts. Old black bluesman Robert Johnson's work is not sold with an advisory label. His genre included plenty of "countercultural" attitude, but anyone who claims there is no difference between the salty strophes of these bluesmen and the in-your-face nihilism of their modern descendants hasn't heard much old blues music.

Beyond the rickety historical argument, the mental acrobatics that the hip-hop intellectuals and journalists go through to continue celebrating a music so chillingly misogynist are truly awesome. A common line is that we are stereotyping to locate sexism in these recordings because sexism is everywhere. As Rose puts it, "Few popular analyses of rap's sexism seem willing to confront the fact that sexual and institutional control over abuse of women is a crucial component of developing a heterosexual masculine identity." Kelley chimes in that "rappers merely represent an extreme version of sexism that pervades daily life." Rose also comes up with a neat side step: Black female rappers have been reluctant to speak out too loudly against hip-hop's sexism because they sense attacks on it from whites as attacks on black men rather than concern for black women.

But these sonorous, tribal incantations have to be seen against what we are really talking about. Joe Budden in the summer of 2004 did a remix of Usher's hit track "Confessions II" in which he raps of finding out that a girl-friend is pregnant and imagining kicking her in the stomach to make her abort. There was a similar image back in Ice Cube's "You Can't Fade Me" on *AmeriKKKa's Most Wanted*—"What I need to do is kick the bitch in the tummy," he muses: but decides not to *only* because he would be convicted for premeditated murder. In "One Less Bitch" on *Efil4zaggin*, Dr. Dre ties a hooker to a bed, has his "crew" gang-rape her, and then shoots her dead.

Sexism in America is one thing. Chanting about hurting a woman's cervix and dedicating it to your young son is another. Rap scholars' rationalizations suddenly pretend that all of life is based on simple binary alternations out of particle physics: It's either on or off, a proton or a neutron, sexism or not sexism. Suddenly there is no degree—although the same people are exquisitely sensitive to degree when preaching that overt bigotry is all but gone but the more subtle operations of "institutional racism" persist.

Hip-hop intellectuals tell us to consider that society itself is sexist— and we must respond by asking them where this kind of naked abuse of women is in the work of Billy Joel, Garth Brooks, or Bruce Springsteen. There is something going on in rap specifically, and it is not just a reflection of sexism as it plays out in everyday American life. It is a heightened, stylized iconography of callous brutality, disqualifying any CD it appears on as enlightenment of any kind.

Important—I am not condemning the sexual explicitness itself. Some of how women are depicted in rap lyrics is just a matter of, we might say, unbuttoning. In the top-twenty hip-hop songs of 2003, for example, sexual attraction was simply dealt with more honestly than in 1963. It's not that American pop in 1963 didn't know sexual attraction. Songs still familiar from that year's Hit Parade include "He's So Fine" and "My Boyfriend's Back," which limned a street-corner kind of hormonal heat that would have been unthinkable just ten years earlier—the rock revolution was already afoot, to be sure.

Fast-forward to 2003 and there was an obsession with the female posterior and remarks as to the wonder that the shapelier ones fit into pants, chanted vividly in songs like Sean Paul's call to "Get Busy," Lil Jon's advice to instead "Get Low," Chingy's "Right Thurr," and "Shake Ya Tailfeather" by Nelly, P. Diddy, and Murphy Lee, in which the feather in question is a metaphor for the bodily part that is shaking it. None of this would have gotten by in mainstream pop in 1963.

Yet, that stuff is *not* the problem. As to the burgeoning literature on how the celebration of big butts validates all the women "out there" who were given generous bottoms genetically, I say hooray. Men in 1963 were looking at women's behinds just like men today, and the fact that the topic was taboo in the era's pop culture now qualifies as curious puritanism. When Mary Tyler Moore on *The Dick Van Dyke Show* wore tight capri pants, there were angry letters—imagine—despite the fact that the show's male staff today recount delighting in her (modest) derriere. One era's "hot rhythm" is another era's "junk in the trunk"—it is unclear to me what effect a jolly public attendance to the back that baby got will have upon the progress of civilization. And even when things get even "realer" than that, such as tracks on *Crunk Juice* with lubriciously specific references to the vagina, it may not be what I personally would listen to while making dinner, but I see no fall of civilization in it.

But what about the *attitude* toward the women providing these pudendal and gluteal spectacles? "Now bring yo ass over here, ho', and let me see you get low if you want this thug," Lil John raps in "Get Busy." This kind of aggressively belittling stance toward women is ordinary in hip-hop. No, it isn't universal, but then it is never remotely a surprise—Tupac Shakur "don't stop for no ho's," Jay-Z says, "I don't love 'em; I fuck 'em," and so on.

As rap fans tie themselves up in knots trying to criticize and yet excuse rap's sexism in the same sentences, we must remember that rap is *the most overtly and consistently misogynistic music ever produced in human history*. Women are, after all, more than half of the humans on the planet. Which leads us back to the main question: How progressive can a music be that fits that description?

HIP-HOP: THERAPEUTIC ALIENATION FOR A NEW BLACK AMERICA

We are being told that a music is progressive that counsels stasis and deplores female people. Hip-hop scholars like to treat this as a "paradox." But the trendy words like "hegemonic" notwithstanding, attempts at societal and historical explanations leave the "paradox" standing. Tricia Rose notes the contradictions we run up against in calling hip-hop progressive. "Some rappers defend the work of gangster rappers and at the same time consider it a negative influence on black youths. Female rappers openly criticize male rappers' sexist work and simultaneously defend the 2 Live Crew's right to sell misogynist music. Rappers who criticize America for its perpetuation of racial and economic discrimination also share conservative ideas about personal responsibility." But Rose still feels that "Rap's contradictory articulations are not signs of absent intellectual clarity."

But that is exactly what they are.

And what's more, there is no "paradox" at all. Counseling angry stasis on the one hand, and putting a hex on "da bitches" that gave you birth, provide you love, and are your daughters on the other hand, have something in common, and it is not progressivism. Both are aimless kinds of alienation that do not correspond to reality, embraced as self-medication rather than constructive activity. Surely, it is not an accident that these two strains thrive and cross-fertilize in hip-hop year after year, regardless of calls from the sidelines for the artists to consider the impact of such things. Clearly these strains speak to the artists as well as to their listeners, even when the futility and nastiness are painfully clear. Hip-hop, then, is the musical rendition of the therapeutic alienation that has elsewhere had such an effect when channeled through political ideology. The point is acting up and only that. There is no other purpose, despite artful claims otherwise.

Russell Simmons comes right out and says, "Rick Rubin, who would later become my partner at Def Jam, used to say, 'Create the drama to make the theatrics. . . . What Rick saw was that rappers, just like wrestlers, took basic young male fantasies of power and inflated them into larger-than-life, over-the-top cartoons. For the kids who couldn't be superstrong or really hard-core, rappers and wrestlers acted out their fantasies for them." All the rhetoric about progressivism was, for Simmons, an add-on later: "There was no long-term vision then. We were all just making it up as we went along. But over time I developed a sense that this culture offered opportunities for economic, social and artistic growth like no other aspect of African-American culture." But here we return to whether that has borne fruit. It hasn't, and few of us would expect otherwise.

There are times when rappers reveal the prevalence of the attitude above all else right in their tracks. For all we hear about how "serious" and "deep" Shakur was, he repeatedly deflects the impact of the more ruminative moments on *Strictly 4 My Niggaz*. After telling his niggas how unwise it is to kill one another over trifles in "Something 2 Die 4," at the end of the track he injects a fatalistic, spoken "What do I know?" After "Papa'z Song," he giggles, "Heh, heh, we goin' platinum, nigga, we goin' platinum," and it is significant that this is the single time Shakur smiles on the entire recording. The message seems to be that the "deep" stuff is a kind of game—a gesture. The real deal is the sensationalistic evocations of violence, after which Shakur appends no such self-reflexive disavowals.

Thus, many considered Will Smith feeble as a rapper because he refrained from the gangsta routine. Ice Cube, after some of the most, in their way, articulate raps of the gangsta variety, has gone on to spearhead and star in movies about making the best of oneself in an unfair world. Clearly Ice Cube's *Friday* and *Barbershop* series are not rose-colored black bourgeois tableaus like *The Cosby Show* was. These are decidedly "real" people getting over as best they can, trying to keep morality front and center in neighborhoods that don't make that easy. But the themes in those movies have nothing to do with the world Ice Cube limned on the CDs. It was just playacting, attitude.

Coolio admitted this openly when I appeared on *Politically Incorrect* with him. A thoughtful person offstage, once the cameras were rolling he played the "thug" for his fans, cannily telling me during the commercial break that he was only pretending to disagree with my points to make good television. Work it, Coolio—but we're a long way from Michael Harrington.

As always, we must remember that the roots of therapeutic alienation in hip-hop are, as its roots are everywhere, spiritual insecurity. People embrace alienation as a way of hiding from facing the real world as self-realizing individuals. In an article in its series on race in America some years back, the *New York Times* portrayed an aspiring young rapper philosophizing about the problematic tendency for hip-hop to celebrate black pathology. He hit it right on the nose: The nasty lyrics are about the fact that "I'm valid when I'm disrespected." This guy *knew* this—only to later launch into a recording session of music so mindlessly abusive and profane that it chilled even the young white photographer for the article, despite her being comfortable enough with black culture to have had more than one relationship with black men.

I'll put it this way. Out of the many ways that people can air alienation, one is to craft angry cartoons about young black men "icing" one another, one is to revel in rapping of women as animals, and one is to toss off leftish observations that the white man is holding black America down. Hip-hop combines all three. The last strain is the "political" Tracy Chapman part that hip-hop chroniclers put front and center, claiming that this is the essence of the music.

But then they are faced with the other two strains, which submit to no analysis as "progressive," and are about just acting up for the sake of acting up.

One way of addressing this is to fashion charismatic double-talk claiming that we are faced with "complexity," optimally couched in elaborate terminology that gives an impression of authority and depth.

Another way of addressing it, especially given the aimlessness even of the political strain, is to admit that hip-hop is *all* about therapeutic alienation, and that pretending that the political strain is the essence is like saying that the "essential" color of a traffic light is red, and that the yellow and green lights are "paradoxes."

BUT ISN'T PERFORMANCE A KIND OF "POLITICS"?

Yet, to truly address what the hip-hop intellectuals are claiming, we get to the fact that much of their work implies that playacting is truly a kind of political activism. The work is couched within an assumption that readers already accept this, which I sense is much of why the literature is so thin on concrete prescriptives, not even beginning to show what the links between hip-hop and the Capitol Building could be.

We are to understand, then, that the rappers are playing characters rather than explicitly calling for us to pick up guns. Ice-T has said, "I'm singing in the first person as a character who is fed up with police brutality. I ain't never killed no cop. I felt like it a lot of times. But I never did it." Indeed, you don't "get" gangsta rap if you hear the lyrics as concrete advice. As Tricia Rose has it, rap is "contemporary stage for the theater of the powerless."

But—how is it "politics" to *pretend to tell us to do something*?

The Gramscian Legacy

This version of "politics" is ultimately due to a philosophical conceit cherished in academia, to an extent that in that world, one often picks up this way of thinking without even trying. The conceit traces back to Italian political theorist and activist Antonio Gramsci's revision of Marxism in *The Prison Notebooks*, published in 1946 and elevated anew by the academic left in the 1980s.

Gramsci argued that the ruling class creates ideological structures, such as educational systems, that support their interests while obscuring the evil underpinnings of society. Subordinate ("subaltern") groups accept these ideas and end up oppressing themselves. Thus, they must counteract the "hegemony" through attempts to revise cultural conceptions, with intellectuals at the vanguard in helping to foster "cultural resistance."

The source of a certain Ivory-Tower hothouse lexicon now familiar is clear here, and this provides a basis for the idea that rappers are presenting a new cultural paradigm, with their academic celebrants as conduits of that new "message" to the ruling class. Poor blacks are the subalterns; Washington, DC; William Bennett; and suburban whites who don't "see" blacks and preserve their "white privilege" are the "hegemony," and so on.

But Gramsci himself would be surprised to see how his ideas have been recruited for the subtle and complex race situation in America of the late twentieth century. He was a practicing Communist who wrote *The Prison Notebooks* from, well, prison, where he spent the last ten years of his life. He wrote in reference to working-class and peasant folk for whom the barriers to advancement were concrete and required no careful indoctrination to understand in the way that the black victim orthodoxy does today. And the problem is that in black America and beyond, as historian David Steigerwald puts it, "the more the intellectuals have analyzed cultural hegemony, the less real political effect their radicalism has had." He states, "Where the hard and gradual work of organizing revolution is dreamed away and the Left becomes willingly content with 'cultural resistance,' the best radicals can hope for is directionless, feeble, and scattered opposition to the state of things."

In other words, Gramsci, who never knew the mass entertainment "hegemony" so familiar to us today, did not mean that striking antiauthoritarian poses on pop recordings, videos, and posters was meaningful sociopolitical activity. This is how modern academics have distorted his argumentation and is the source of the idea that hip-hop's "subalterns" have accomplished something sublime because their lyrics disrespect authority. But the music simply does not fit into any serious program for change that Gramsci would have recognized. He gave us, as Steigerwald puts it, "a sophisticated program for revolutionary consciousness-raising" but what reappeared in the Ivory Tower in the eighties was the Cheshire Cat smile of "self-satisfied proclamations that the subversions of consumer culture amounted to substantive challenges to the status quo."

This is the mistake, then, in perspectives like that of (black) Syracuse English professor Greg Thomas, who has taught a whole course on none other than Lil' Kim, known for nakedly raunchy come-on lyrics. Thomas finds "her lyrical artistry nothing short of revolutionary. It's an art based on the most profound sexual politics we've ever seen." Then comes the Gramscian rhetoric:

> Contemporary society trains men and women to think that male domination is not only acceptable but 'natural,' logical and rational. Gender identity in Western societies is typically rigid, inflexible and fundamentally homophobic. As 'Big Momma/Queen B,' K.I.M. recasts gender and sexuality in a manner that radically challenges patriarchal and homophobic socialization—while embracing sexuality on her own terms, instead of rejecting it in terms of the status quo. Neither puritanical nor 'pornographic,' clearly grounded in Africa's Diaspora, her art works to radically redistribute power, pleasure and privilege in a world that would deny all of the above to most of us, the vast majority of the planet.

This is an upper division course, mind you—in spring 2005, the department was offering courses on Jane Austen, Geoffrey Chaucer, William Shakespeare, and Lil' Kim. The course's title is "Hip-Hop Eshu: Queen Bitch 101."

Note: "sexual politics"—but what kind of politics is this compared with Thurgood Marshall's "politics"? Whence this idea of "politics" as a matter of saucy posters and angry lyrics rather than directed action? Lil' Kim "recasts" gender and sexuality—but in image and attitude. What exactly is the impact of Lil' Kim "embracing" rather than "rejecting" the status quo in terms of her sexual practices, or more specifically, the imagery she projects of her sexual practices, on CDs and in videos?

Thomas lists "power, pleasure, and privilege" as elements that Lil' Kim's work purportedly "redistributes." But as to two of these things, power and privilege, how do CDs and concerts and videos "redistribute" them? Last I saw, in the wake of Lil' Kim's career, the power and privilege that people like Thomas have such a problem with remained "distributed" precisely as it was. Thomas seems to imply that Lil' Kim has shunted our way some of that power and privilege that the world would "deny" us. But where is the evidence for that? After all, for thinkers like Thomas, one of the focuses of their indignation is how eternal this denial of power and privilege is to us subalterns. If Lil' Kim has, in fact, made some kind of dent in this, then we expect Thomas to write papers delineating how since Lil' Kim's first CD, the oppressed have benefitted from a greater access to power and privilege, even if not to a revolutionary extent. But why, then, is Thomas's academic oeuvre devoted to decrying "coloniality's persistence," "white supremacy," and "Hellenomania"? Where is his work showing front and center how Lil' Kim's work has moved us toward a world where these scourges exert a lesser influence?

I suppose CDs, concerts, and videos can indeed "redistribute" one element in Thomas's list, the pleasure: I gather that we are to suppose that Lil' Kim has helped to teach women that they, too, deserve to be pleased in bed, and there have been similar claims about female rappers like Salt-N-Pepa. But where, exactly, is the evidence that Lil' Kim, Salt-N-Pepa, or any other female hip-hop artists have played a significant role in teaching women this? Many would say that the sexual revolution taught us this back in the sixties, before Lil' Kim was even born. To get down to it, reports these days do tell us that oral sex given both ways is now default and casual among teens in a way that it was not a generation ago. But I suspect that an attempt to trace this even in part to Lil' Kim—or even female hip-hop artists, or even pop music at all—would be fruitless. I venture that the notion of Lil' Kim as mentor here has something to do with, for example, a song of hers whose chorus (sung by Sisqo joining her on the track) goes, "How many licks does it take till you get to the center of the (oh oh oh oh oh!)" (the song is not about lollipops). But anyone who thinks that this doggerel created, rather than followed, a revolution in conventional sexual expectations did not experience the seventies and eighties past puberty.

Now, I could be accused of distorting Thomas's encomium. In fact, Thomas says that Lil' Kim *works to* "radically redistribute power," etc., etc. So—he means that it *suggests* that these things should be done. It doesn't *do* it; it just can be read as *suggesting* that it be done. That is—and here we are again—it represents an *attitude* that Thomas vibrates to. He likes seeing Lil' Kim project an *attitude* that he sees as valuable, in being the direction that he thinks America should go. Which brings us to wondering—when did we get to the point that attitude was *politics*?

The answer is that when thinkers like Gramsci—albeit distorted— became part of the canon that people like Thomas were nursed on in their scholarly training. A thoroughly brilliant and socially concerned person in 1937, high on the victories of the New Deal, would be bemused by someone claiming that theatrical poses and attitudes in the pop culture realm constituted progressive activity. If we could bring to life Franz Boas, founder of the legitimization of non-Western cultures now central in social science, or Michael Harrington, whose concept of "the other America" helped spark the Great Society program, I would be interested to see just what they would make of this idea that acting is politics. They did not mean that the self-indulgent "get over it!" jollies of acting out in dress styles and sexual adventurousness were a serious means of forging change in a complex society.

How could they have meant that? It is almost comical to imagine either of them arguing such points. Yet, we accept such "discourse" from people billed as advanced thinkers now. But is this because the frontiers of sociological expertise on how political change is fostered have advanced since the eras Boas and Harrington knew? Were Boas and Harrington, in spite of themselves, unenlightened? Does Greg Thomas have something on them? What, exactly, would Greg Thomas, faced with Boas and Harrington sitting before him, have to teach them? Really—what would he have the confidence to teach them, looking them in the eye and telling them that there was something they didn't know that he was going to impart to them, as a modern physicist would tell a resuscitated Newton? What counsel could he impart to these figures with a poster of Lil' Kim scantily clad with her legs spread? Crucially: What *results* could Professor Thomas refer to that showed where Boas and Harrington had fallen short?

Is it that Boas and Harrington would have been better off knowing that striking poses is a valid form of political engagement? Could Greg Thomas really look a living and breathing Franz Boas or Michael Harrington right in their vivid faces and tell them this? Or rather—come on, now—is it that Greg Thomas is a creature of his times, in which the cult of the individual, the cult of the unadorned, the cult of the "authentic" allows him to indulge in the notion that his visceral living-room enjoyment of Lil' Kim's catchy little attitude is a brand of intellectual endeavor?

Isn't it that a generation of "hip-hop intellectuals" have come of age in an era that teaches them that there is something deep in Madonna telling us to "strike a pose" in "Vogue"? And are the rest of us really so off-base, so unaware, to object that when Madonna told us to "strike a pose," it was fun on the dance floor but had not a thing to do with helping a poor black woman five months off welfare live a life beyond decent?

All About Me

Thus, writers are dressing up in Gramscian language a music that is about nothing but medicating the self: the self of the rapper's "character" as well as the self of his audiences. We are being taught that something is politically progressive that is actually just an expression of a tic of our times.

In 1963, the number one song in America was the Beach Boys' "Surfin' USA." As we all know, it was an Orangesicle-flavored bonbon about the beach and surfing and the notion that "everybody" was doing it, summoning the age-old custom in pop songs of imagining the whole country united in some hedonistic activity, usually dancing— "Everybody's Doing It," as Irving Berlin told us as far back as 1911.

Forty years later in 2003, the number one song in America was about doing something else and it wasn't surfing or even dancing. It wasn't even about all of us—it was about one person, top rapper 50 Cent, "In Da Club" with his "bottle full of bub," as well as Ecstasy if a woman happening by wants some, as long as she understands, if she sticks around, that what Mr. Cent is doing in the club is "havin' sex—I ain't into makin' love."

What was interesting about "In Da Club" versus "Surfin' USA" was not the profanity. As far as that goes, Everybody's Doing It now, and to decry it is as futile, and narrow, as the stuffed shirts who wrote editorials against songs like "Everybody's Doing It" because of what they saw as the "savage" syncopation of ragtime. Just as the young woman who thrilled to tunes like this was a sweet old lady fifty years later, some of nicest little "tweens" you'd ever want to meet were bopping their heads to "In Da Club" on their Discmans in summer 2003.

"In Da Club" does contrast importantly with "Surfin' USA," however, in being all about the person giving the message rather than summoning all of us. It's 50 Cent himself in the club with the bub, daring us to criticize him ("If it's a problem, pop off, nigga!" at the end). He, unlike most of *we*, has "mah crib, mah cars, mah pools, mah jewels." Unlike most of us, he has placed himself in a situation where he has been left with bullet wounds he refers to in the song (as well as displaying amply in his public persona). He isn't interested in embracing all of us in the joy of surfing or doing the twist (Chubby Checker's song on that subject had been number ten in 1960)—his interest in embracing is only of a transient and self-centered nature—no making love.

Now, we can harrumph all we want about how unsavory the "message" may be—and run up against a wall of people of all levels of education hotly objecting. Some will say that it shows a downtrodden black man who has conquered the system. Others will say that it is just a cartoon. Either way, a simple fact remains: No pop hit like this existed in 1963, neither as message nor comic panel. An America where "In Da Club" was common coin among people of all colors under age forty contrasts starkly with one where "Surfin' USA" was the song that parents didn't understand.

This is because "In Da Club" is about something Mr. and Mrs. America in 1963 did not yet thrill to: one person giving us all the finger. Crucially, in this, the song is normal of pop hits in our times, not an exception. By 2003, the song surprised no one, even if it shared space with vaguely androgynous *American Idol* winner Clay Aiken's sweet "This Is the Night" down at spot seven. "In Da Club" was, by 2003, apple pie.

The difference between the jangly ragtime of Irving Berlin and the jangly rock and roll of Little Richard forty years later was a mere change in fashion. But the difference between Little Richard and 50 Cent is evidence of a profound alteration in the national psychology. The vaudevilleans singing Berlin tunes and early rockers like Little Richard sang to America with a smile, a naughty one at times, but all in good fun, calling on everyone to have a good time. However, 50 Cent and his ilk rap to America with a cocky sneer, waving in our faces a personal good time unachievable by most of us since it would require breaking the law and/or embracing our worst moral impulses, and dare us to disapprove. This is alienation as sport.

Nelson George sings that "a powerful autobiographical impulse demands the exploration of the 'I' as 'me'" and links this to Richard Wright's *Black Boy*, Claude Brown's *Manchild in the Promised Land*, and Nathan McCall's *Makes Me Wanna Holler*. I'm sorry, Mr. George, but no. There is nothing of this kind of sustained and sincere gravity in hip-hop. The "I"-ness in this case is solely recreational and that is all it should be taken as. Wright and Brown, especially, worked too hard for it to be enlightened to pretend that gangsta rappers are their equals in any regard.

In 1937, white celebrity author Sinclair Lewis gave a speech to a serious radical political organization. Instead of giving sociopolitical insights, he pulled out some party imitations of prominent political rabble-rousers, and the young radicals roasted him for not seeming serious about forging change. Lewis had been flattered by their attention but was actually rather bored by politics beyond a certain point. What is the difference between Lewis in 1937 presenting as "politics" his "Hooey Long" imitation of Huey Long and a rapper sixty-five years later presenting as "politics" a track accusing George W. Bush of orchestrating 9/11? None, except that Lewis was received with stony faces, while today's rapper is feted as a prophet by not only audiences, but even also certain members of the intelligentsia.

THE DIVERSITY IN THE MUSIC: "PEOPLE WHO TRASH HIP-HOP NEED TO GET OUT AND LISTEN TO MORE OF IT"

The most common objection to any denial of hip-hop's majesty is to claim that gangsta rap is just one thread, while "conscious" rappers have a "positive message." The critic of hip-hop just doesn't know the music well enough to understand that there is this "diversity" in the genre.

The people levelling this objection seem to assume that anyone who has heard conscious rap would change their tune. But I have heard quite a bit of this kind of rap, and I remain, frankly, astounded at the weakness of the argument that it refutes criticism of the music as aimless acting up.

The General Versus the Specific

For one thing, in terms of what hip-hop "is," the gangsta work sells best. The critic of rap is addressing not the comprehensive CD collections of the aficionado, but the lowest common denominator of the music that impacts America most immediately, bought and played the most. And that is not the likes of Mos Def, Talib Kweli, Common, and The Roots. At the end of 2004, the top rappers on Billboard were Ludacris, Eminem, Lil Jon, Jay-Z, Snoop Dogg, T.I., Cam'ron, and Nas. For these artists "consciousness" is garnish at best. Kanye West's *The College Dropout* got around that year on the basis of its hit cut "Jesus Walks" and won a Grammy in early 2005. But that's just one record. The *generality* remains painfully clear.

Even conscious rappers complain about their sideline status. Mos Def has said, "I ain't mad at Snoop. I'm not mad at Master P. I ain't mad at the Hot Boyz. I'm mad when that's all I see." Talib Kweli tucks into the liner notes of his *The Beautiful Struggle*, "There are a lot of DJs that support my music, whether the industry does or not."

Which means that propping up conscious rappers against someone who calls the hip-hop scene a tantrum set to rhythm is a kind of debate team trick, where one studiously ignores an obvious generality in favor of dredging up exceptions. Let's imagine someone hearing the claim that America is a racist society and coming up with "Excuse me—there are some whites who aren't racist." Lips curl—we are to understand that racism is pervasive enough that the exceptions are not worth dwelling upon. The conscious rap school are also exceptions, shouting into the wind.

Back to the "Paradox"

And shouting indeed. Listen to "conscious" rap and what one hears is only slightly different in content and tone from the gangsta platinum albums.

Yes, Mos Def and Talib Kweli decorate their raps with calls to "stop smoking and stop drinking," starry-eyed time-outs where they sing the praises of their baby daughters, diligent paeans to the nobility of black women, and vague calls for black Americans to look sharp. But those things are hardly unknown even in much gangsta work, and overall, conscious rap is based on the same upturned middle finger that made Tupac an icon.

Okay, with the conscious crew, the pugnacious rhetoric is usually couched as challenges to mainstream rappers, as opposed to Tupac's call for black men to take over the streets. But this still means that Kweli on his first album, after a quietly wry introduction, busts out with angry, fists-high verses identical to the "It's on" tone of the likes of Jay-Z—"In the mike I'm unfuckwitable," "You get hit like a deer standin' still in the light," and so on. On Kweli's duo album with HiTek, he describes how in one competition he "smacked them in they face with a metaphor."

But why so violent? Why must "consciousness" sound like a street fight? Since the sixties, millions of black people have achieved in this country, and very few of them did so smacking anybody. In fact, they could not have gotten where they are with the warrior attitude that Mos Def, Talib Kweli, and their guest artists present so often on their recordings. In the name of being "deep," these rappers merely relocate 50 Cent's cops-and-robbers battle from the street to the slam contest.

So the "conscious" bonbons on these albums show a kind of schizophrenia, caught between "message" notions and a core commitment to sticking it to authority for the thrill of it. The result is contradictions that make it difficult to see just what the "message" is supposed to be, that hip-hop intellectuals so artfully rationalize.

On Mos Def's and Kweli's joint album *Black Star*, Kweli warns us against violence: "Keepin' it real will make you a casualty of abnormal normality," he says in "Respiration." The song is a rich lyric indeed, one of those "black CNN" reports. But then early on in his own *Quality* Kweli raps charismatically about how we need to make the streets "run red." Conscious rap fans are impressed as Kweli flags Du Bois, the Palestinians, the Ethiopians, and Norman Mailer—but he only mentions them in lists as inspirations to, well, make the streets run red. No, he doesn't mean it literally. But why that kind of violent metaphor at all? Exactly what kind of—let's look to Tricia Rose in all of her authenticity for an apt term—"rupture" is Kweli counseling us to foster on the basis of *The Souls of Black Folk*, the speeches of Yasir Arafat and Haile Selassie, or what Norman Mailer trots out for the *New York Times Magazine*? You've read all of these people—now, what? In real life, what? You like their attitude. But now—*what*?

Nor is the female problem completely absent from the "conscious" work. "For Women" on Kweli's joint album with HiTek is, in its way, a masterful lyric, praising black women for making the best of lives of abuse. But how sincere are we to think Kweli is when in "Put It in the Air" on *Quality* he has DJ Quik mimicking a woman saying, "All he do is disrespect me, keep callin me bitch" and then responding, "What the fuck you think I'm here for—not to love you I hope"? Jay-Z's "I don't love 'em; I fuck 'em" comes to mind. This is "for women"?

Of course, many claim that in-your-face belligerence is the heart of any genuine black progressive agenda—you know, after the slave ships (which Kweli is especially fond of mentioning) and so on. But we return to the danger of straying into charismatic utopianism. The idea that "real" black activism takes it to the streets, even metaphorically, hasn't helped anyone in forty years. Ever since the Panthers, black revolutionaries' dreams have been just that, dreams. Black people poor, rich, and everywhere in between get ahead by getting real and making the best of an unfair but workable capitalist—and yes, subtly racist—system.

Conscious of What?

I suppose we are to assume the conscious rappers have some advice to the contrary. But when Mos Def and Talib Kweli promise us on their joint album to "shine a light into the darkness," they illuminate nothing except the grand old idea that for black people—or, excuse me, niggas, an elevating term that conscious rappers embrace as wholeheartedly as any other hip-hoppers—politics is anger.

In "The Proud" Kweli teaches us that blacks are worn down by oppression, that the cops are corrupt, and that violent thugs either killed Tupac or know who did, and that what we do about this is—well, it's not quite clear; Kweli just reminds us that we are heroes and "we survive." This is just a step or two removed from Tupac telling us that "The Streetz R Deathrow," and how we get beyond that is, apparently, beside the point.

On *Black on Both Sides* Mos Def's "Mr. Nigga" first shows us the improper black thug we all could do without but then argues that whites see all blacks the same way many blacks see the thug. It's a great piece in the formal sense. But how many people's "consciousnesses" in our moment are unaware that racial bias still exists? How does saying it for the *n*th time teach anyone how to make the best of themselves despite the imperfections of reality?

On the joint album Kweli and Mos Def tell us of the "knowledge of self-determination." But again I dare anyone to come up with just what advice is meant to someone trying to help themselves. All we get is, "I feel the rage of a million niggaz locked inside a cage," "We're gonna take this hip-hop shit and keep it movin, shed a little light," "All my people, where y'all at, cause y'all ain't here." Kweli and HiTek tell us, "Don't prove somethin" but "Move somethin." But move what? What have Kweli and HiTek done but the same gestural "proving" that they pretend to consider inadequate?

The media celebrated Kanye West as "inspirational" because of the

"Jesus Walks" cut—but the rap is actually predicated upon the same old idea that black America is in a "war" against racism. And the album is not titled *College Dropout* for nothing: It includes a long skit ridiculing a man more interested in learning than money, a virgin by the end of college but proud that he can add up the change in your pocket, getting useless degrees throughout his life instead of working. Even if West means this as a joke, what kind of "joke" is it, given the problems with black students and the classroom? It is most certainly not a "conscious" statement of anything useful. Nor are other observations throughout the album, such as that crack makes white men rich or that blacks are only placed in high positions to serve as window dressing—typical of an America that West, born in 1977 and coming of age in the nineties, never even knew. *The College Dropout* is a catchy record and that's it. Its politics are a typical brand of self-perpetuating, unfocused leftism, telling us nothing we haven't already heard from the gangstas.

In conscious rap the key words seem to be *inspiration, destiny, eternal,* and *revolution,* with their mere utterance over catchy rhythms treated as marks of serious thought. A rapper could chant just those four words in random order for three minutes, and if the beats and cut-ins were catchy enough, one can almost imagine conscious rap fans eagerly trading the track via download, with academic fans treating it as hip-hop's version of Gertrude Stein. William Van Deburg treats the conscious rappers as "organic intellectuals—gifted grassroots individuals who possessed a profound, popularly accredited understanding of group history and who were well attuned to the requisites of oppositional politics." This is, really, an insult to black Americans' abilities to forge real political change.

No, we do not expect raps to provide detailed procedural prescriptives like government reports. But there are places raps could easily go, still blazing with poetic fireworks. Since welfare was limited to five years in 1996, there are now legions of black women dealing with life off of a dole that they grew up knowing little but. Tupac rapped that "Brenda's Got a Baby"—what about something about how these days Brenda's just off welfare? What about the black men coming out of jail and trying to find their way after long sentences in the wake of the crack culture fifteen years ago?

Or even, how about calling for the legalization of drugs? Much of Mos Def's latest album *The New Danger,* with its slurry chanting over endless riffs verging on rock style, is Music to Get High To. I get it—"Tune in and drop out." But that is not *exactly* new as "messages" go and is ultimately just one more call to show your strength by doing what The Man has made illegal. In these spots Mos Def, in all of his racial authenticity, becomes a kind of white rapper, joining countless white rockers who have been celebrating the weed for forty years. But millions of young black men are dying or going to jail smoking and selling what The Man has made illegal. Wouldn't it be more "conscious" to show our strength with lots of raps dedicated to the idiocy of drugs being illegal in the first place?

Why are conscious rappers so uninterested in the political issues that directly affect poor black lives? Could it be because those issues do not usually lend themselves to calls for popping a 'tude and smacking people and making the streets run red? If so, then chalk up one more for people who do not see hip-hop as politically constructive. Which is why when Mos Def decorates his albums with occasional insults to gay men, we will think about the AIDS crisis in black communities and unavoidably wonder whether he is committed most to serious compassion or to dissing whitey.

Mos Def is, in his way, especially articulate about where "conscious" rappers stand. In an interview for Michael Eric Dyson's exploration of Tupac Shakur, *Holler If You Hear Me*, Mos Def spelled out that his allegiance is not only to advice for blacks left behind, but also to anything blacks feel or say, gangsta or not: "They keep trying to slip the 'conscious rapper' thing on me," he says. "They try to get me because I'm supposed to be more articulate, I'm supposed to be not like the other Negroes, to get me to say something against my brothers. I'm not going out like that, man." So it would be "going out" even to question the theatrical savagery that hip-hop's critics fail to see the good in. He approves of Biggie Smalls and the like, which predicts that his lyrics often sound as cranky, menacing, and randomly dismissive as the gangsta ones do.

There's a reason why even conscious rappers pride themselves on, as it is put, "spitting" their rhymes. Ultimately, it's all about spitting in the eye of the powers that be—which is precisely what the millions of blacks making the best of themselves in modern America have not done.

And this means that while there is not a thing wrong with "conscious rap" fans enjoying the beats and the rhymes, and even valuing the sprinkles of an awareness of something beyond guns, Hennesey, and women's behinds, all arguments that hip-hop is not a constructive manifesto stand tall.

I suppose there are hip-hop fans out there who do not let anything but "conscious" rap by Mos Def, Talib Kweli, Common, and The Roots into their houses. But claims that this sideline genre means that treating the gangsta style as the heart of hip-hop is wrong are like telling someone that it's wrong to say that birds fly because ostriches don't. Try this: If there had never been anything but "conscious" rappers, then hip-hop would not have become a national sensation. It would be a minority taste, purveyed mostly in small urban clubs like Spoken Word poetry, with its rappers peddling their CDs as much via Web sites and downloads as in stores.

One car tape I wore out back in the day was Arrested Development's *3 Years, 5 Months and 2 Days in the Life of. . . .* Built on all of the typical features of hip-hop structure, including the cheeky vocal delivery central to the genre, there was nevertheless not a "bitch" or call to violence—cartoon or not—in it. Instead, it offered advice, affection, concern, and hope, while retaining the hip, spiky essence necessary to commercial success in our moment.

And they didn't last. Nastier rap artists like Public Enemy and NWA, the latter including its members' solo albums after their breakup, served up their "conscious" tracks between the usual violence and cussing and bitch-slapping. It was them who sold better than acts like Arrested Development and Digable Planets, and them who have gone down among the raposcenti as foundational beacons of the hip-hop genre.

THE BEAT GOES ON

My point is not that hip-hop should be stamped out. From things like a black Harvard Law School student getting through an eight-hour take-home exam by blasting Biggie Smalls (an anecdote from Imani Perry), we know that this music is now part of the warp and woof of America. Even if one wanted it to disappear, it would be the height of idle folly to call for it—rather like pretending that a certain "Revolution" will ever come.

What I "contest," as hip-hop intellectuals are fond of putting it, is the idea that it has anything to do with political philosophy. Hip-hop should be thought of as entertainment, pure and simple.

I do believe that the reason so many black people identify so deeply with music so nihilistic and so abusive toward females is the place of therapeutic alienation in the black American soul. In my opinion, to hear that music as a reflection of oneself in any way means that something deep inside of you feels inadequate, so assuaged by a notion of black identity based on *not being* white as opposed to *being* something else that it feels natural to let the guns and sexism pass.

But history makes this unsurprising, and if the music is left where it belongs—iPods, car radios, and nightclub sound systems—then there is no harm in it. Therapeutic alienation toward school is a problem because it depresses black achievement. Therapeutic alienation set to a catchy beat can be just an atmospheric remnant of the injury done to us. I presume that the music will change as our souls truly heal.

The superficial pleasures of the music are obvious. For example, as I have noted, many are deeply thrilled by "street" black voices having their say. As often, Imani Perry is especially explicit on this, writing that rap "primarily claims power through the voice of black males, and thus, given the dichotomized racial structure in the United States, takes power away from white America, even if only by operating through white American fear." If that's what you hear in it, great. Nothing wrong with a thrill. But it is problematic to assume that their mere speaking is necessarily constructive—that is, Perry going on that these voices are "champions of a particular kind of black empowerment." We have to think about *whether* they are, and I think that upon doing so, most of us will see that they are not.

Then, people are also moved by the devilishly infectious rhythms, which I doubt any more than one in fifty people under age sixty could resist. The ambrosial effect of these beats plays a large part in what grabs even its most reflective adherents. But again, we must assess what rhythm has to do with fostering change in the world as we know it once the rap is over.

When Sister Souljah recounts that as a young woman, she found that "Rap music could make me feel overtly sexual and controlled by the drum beat," she is describing a sensation harmless, but unconnected with anything Thurgood Marshall ever did. Why does Michael Eric Dyson readily condemn a new line of video games revelling in "gangsta" routines as "video crack" while anointing Tupac Shakur a "ghetto saint"? Because when the imagery is set to the beats, the visceral effect is so powerful that it starts writers like him to crafting rationalizations, rooted ultimately in just loving the way the music sounds and feels. I have debated Dyson and am moved to record that at one point in his rousing of the audience he even came right out and said, "Y'all know it's all about the beat!" Right—and leave it right there.

When Robin Kelley describes two years of research "rocking, bopping, and wincing to gangsta narratives," we cannot help but wonder how empirical and clear-eyed any political prescriptives growing from his rocking and bopping will be. Might the resultant notion be that black America's salvation will be, on some level, to rock and bop its way into revolutionary action based on the eternal truth connoted by the constancy and narcotic effect of those rhythms, African rhythms, the rhythms that have soothed black Americans dealing with the worst starting on the plantations and on through the churches and Dancing in the Streets in the Chocolate City of our dreams, that rhythm passed down generations of people of African descent and so real, so intimately tied to the primal act of sex that creates humankind, so much, well, so much, just *the shit* that it can't help but upend the mentality of the uptight, soulless white man with the weight of its ineffable Truth?

Heady stuff. But now, back to real life.

And in real life, we ask: When has anything this *easy* been how we helped ourselves in any real way?

Rock and bop in the car and leave it at that. Laborious attempts to elevate funky rhythm and upturned middle fingers into anything larger will lead us down garden paths we've all been down too many times before. "Deep in the American soul, it speaks to us and we like its voice," writes Nelson George of hip-hop. Good—but that's all it is. To pretend otherwise is a distraction from helping people who need it.

Even Kelley, in a strange volte-face after an extended piece on hip-hop as politics, presents a jolly dismissal of the whole idea. "Hip hop is first and foremost music, 'noize' produced and purchased to drive to, rock to, chill to, drink to, and occasionally dance to." (I wonder why he writes "occasionally" there; hip-hop's effect on the body is "off the hook," no questions asked.) He even dismisses the conscious rappers: "Save the 'PC' morality rap for those who act like they *don't* know. I'm still rollin' with Da Lench Mob, kickin' it with the Rhyme Syndicate, hanging out in the Basement with Pete Rock and the rest, and, like Das EFX, I'm coming straight from the Sewer."

Kelley puts that much better than I ever could.

In a way, the very fact that so many people pretend that the postures of hip-hop are a new form of The Struggle is a sign of how far we have come in fighting racism in American life. Only when oppression has become a whisper does space open up for dressing up trivial self-medication as societal concern.

We decry the criminalization of black men, the racialization of poverty, the subtle diminishment of black boys in schools, the high rate of teen pregnancy among young black women. Yet, millions of black Americans under age forty-five, regardless of class, income, or educational attainment, see a stirring reflection of their identities in a music that celebrates poor, violent, woman-hating young black men as heroes. This music, "conscious" or not, teaches that we must seek the wealth that the Civil Rights revolution gave us access to, but at the same time resist embracing an American identity in the spiritual sense, instead styling ourselves as embattled aliens in a strange land. In 1993, Ellis Cose criticized whites for stereotyping black men as criminals, with "As long as the dominant message sent to impressionable black boys is that they are expected to turn into savage criminals, nothing will stop substantial numbers of them from doing just that." Cose saw white America as the bearer of that "message," according to an opinion commonly expressed starting in the seventies that unremarkably lived on into the early nineties when Cose wrote the passage. But today, the main source of that message is none other than the music those black boys—just as impressionable as they were back in the day—live to, produced by black men who plug it as the heart of a progressive black identity.

Meanwhile, a coterie of black writers are building a small industry on celebrating how noble and "authentic" all of this is. Would we want black academics to utterly dismiss a music that is loved so deeply by most young people of their race, has its good points, and is, after all, not going away? No. But when "I Have a Dream" is considered less relevant than high-octane performances calling for armed riot and hurting women's cervixes, something isn't right.

Hip-hop, despite how its attitude stirs the guts of its fans inside and outside of the world of letters, will have nothing significant to do with the progressive efforts of those of us who are sincerely committed to social change. Black American thinkers do no one but themselves a favor in pretending an equivalence between "Eat a dick up" and *The Fire Next Time.* Unfocused antiauthoritarianism snarled over a delicious beat may be many things good and bad, but activism it is not, and never will be.

CHAPTER TEN

Therapeutic Alienation as a Plan of Action?
New Black Leadership for New Negroes

In the early twentieth century, progressively minded black Americans of the first generations not born in slavery were given to calling themselves "New Negroes." The New Negro was oriented toward making the best of the future, hungry for all information and training relevant to this journey. The New Negro had no interest in fashioning a wary, parochial "African" identity: Rather, the New Negro was proud to fuse the mainstream with his "colored" heritage—and had no sense that this would mean losing "himself."

Sure, we can see that idea as a little naïve in ways. The New Negro was on his way to finding that once blacks started leaving black towns in the South and becoming a healthy presence in Northern cities, whites made it extremely difficult for him to keep looking forward. Too often, the New Negro found himself barricaded by housing covenants into slum quarters. Too often, the New Negro earned a law degree only to find that no mainstream firm would hire him. Too often, the New Negro found herself quietly refused service at restaurants—even in the North.

Nevertheless, a great many modern black Americans today are a new kind of New Negro. If those proud black Americans marching in silent news footage were perhaps a little overly optimistic given that they lived in a deeply segregated country, we can hardly say that we black Americans today face the same obstacles. Our times have created a New New Negro, whose life experience and opportunities condition a different orientation than his forebears. In the old days, the difference was between those born into slavery and those born under freedom. Today, the difference is between those whom the aftermath of the Civil Rights revolution marked with therapeutic alienation and those born too late to suffer that fate.

The New New Negro is, once again, oriented toward a realistic, dynamically miscegenated future, not a mythical African past (or the Black Nationalist variation that dreams of multi-class all-black communities). The New New Negro knows that there is racism just as the Old New Negro knew so much more immediately. But the New New Negro processes this as something to wipe off of his shoe now and then, not as "most of what life is."

Naturally then, the New New Negro has a new conception of black leadership, both political and intellectual. For example, the leader that the New New Negro hearkens to will take a page from, of all people, a white law professor at the University of Pennsylvania.

THE WAY OUT VERSUS THE WAY IN: RACE LEADERSHIP THAT FACES THE MEME

In 2005, University of Pennsylvania law professor Amy Wax took some heat from the usual suspects when she published an editorial in the *Wall Street Journal* that made the simple point that while what white America did to blacks in the past was inexcusable and that compensatory programs are necessary and morally imperative, that in the end, these things will have no effect without blacks making inward efforts to help themselves.

Wax understands that while racism was the original cause of black America's ills, that "bad habits take on a life of their own, impeding the ability to grasp widening opportunities as society progresses, discrimination abates and old obstacles fall away. The victim himself has changed in ways that place him beyond the reach of outside help alone." Wax expresses what I have termed the setting in of new memes that thrive regardless of racism. She notes that while many think that "if racism is to blame, purging racism will do the trick," that actually, "this is the myth of reverse causation."

As such, she also keys into what I have described as the *path dependence* phenomenon familiar to social scientists, where conditions at a particular time set off a series of developments that eventually reach a point at which retracing steps is impossible. "In seeking solutions, we must look forward rather than dwell on the past because the way out of the present dilemma may not resemble the path in." That is an important sentence: She does not just say that we must stop dwelling on the past and just leave it there as a rhetorical incantation. What she wrote was that there is a specific reason why we must look forward: not because "look forward" just sounds good, not because "look forward" sounds positive and motivational, but because, as she explicitly stated, *the way out of the present dilemma may not resemble the path in.*

Attention must be paid to such a statement. Wax is saying that yes, the path in was racism's disenfranchisement of blacks, leaving too many at the bottom, and leaving too many vulnerable to temptations such as multigenerational welfare dependency when it was offered, and drug-based economies when pricing and technology made this possible. But Wax is saying that there is more, that there is something else equally urgent to be attended to even when we are aware of the first part. That is that at a certain point, an element of identity based on resisting mainstream standards as a badge of authenticity set in, and once that had happened, just withdrawing "racism" was no longer a feasible solution—there was something else to battle against.

She compares blacks' situations with someone who has been run over by a car and left crippled. The driver can provide financial restitution, but sadly and unfairly, only the victim can learn to walk again. In the same, she writes, "No one can force a person to obey the law, study hard, develop useful skills, be well-mannered, speak and write well, work steadily, marry and stay married, be a devoted husband and father, and refrain from bearing children he cannot or will not support. These decisions belong to individuals and families." She means this not as a finger-pointing moralistic slam, but as a coolheaded, logical observation—which millions of blacks readily agree with when it is put the right way: It is a virtual mantra in black communities that "we have to help ourselves."

And Wax makes clear what this means: that we must wean ourselves from the idea that until blacks' conditions are perfectly equal to whites', white America remains grievously culpable as "not caring" about blacks. "The persistence of racial disadvantage does not mean that society has failed to do enough. The greatest need at present may not be more government spending and new programs but a conversion experience. The victim must see that, although others have wronged him, his fate lies in his own hands. Justice may be forever elusive, but success is the best revenge." She did not say that government programs should be abolished, mind you—but that they alone will not do the trick. Again, few blacks would disagree with that point in itself.

Yet, predictably, Wax has been tarred as racist by a good number of black law students at Penn. Interviewed by Penn's newspaper, a black law student said that Wax does not understand that racism makes it impossible for blacks to heal themselves. For this student, the person in Wax's example is not run over once, but "the car is continuously running you over." The student states, "Before, you were being run over by an 18-wheeler. After a few hundred years of that, then it's something smaller than that, maybe just a full-sized pickup. . . . Nothing has really been done to address the 18-wheeler."

But the student's judgment of the effects of racism in today's America is mistaken. If the student thinks that the problem is "segregation" à la *American Apartheid*, then one wonders whether he elsewhere warms to notions of "black nationalism," under which blacks will live and network among their own—thoroughly "segregated." If so, the logical contradiction suggests alienation for its own sake rather than as an empirical response to life as it is.

If he thinks that black nationalism will only work when a certain proportion of the blacks are doctors and lawyers, then whatever his problems with the disloyal middle-class blacks who moved to the suburbs, the reason things are not now the way he would prefer is not white racism, but blacks who moved away from their brothers and sisters. That's a different issue that requires adopting a different story—in which the villains are people the same color as he is. So—"racism" is a dead letter.

And if he thinks middle-class blacks moved away because they had internalized racism and scorned lower-class blacks, then he is skating on thin ice indeed unless he happens to be one of the very few black law students at schools like Penn who grew up in the ghetto. Given that he is very likely the product of a middle-class black home, how readily would he tar his own parents as running over blacks with a "full-sized pickup"? If he cannot, then he must let go of treating the middle-class black exodus as "racism."

If the student thinks that limiting welfare to five years was racist, then we must ask him why black people are too weak to be expected to work for a living as a rule, even if needing to take a spell out of the workforce for five long years if necessary. If he, on the one hand, agrees that Black is Beautiful, but on the other hand thrills to the idea of multiple generations of black women on the dole, then there is that logical contradiction again, revealing being pissed off as the be-all and end-all. He can complain that Black is—in case you didn't know it, whitey—Beautiful, and at the same time complain that "society" condemns black women to dependency—while simultaneously complaining as well about programs designed to give black women the skills to get past dependency. This is therapy dressed up as politics.

If the student thinks that the increasing opposition to racial preferences in admissions is racist, then he is operating under the idea that most black students at Penn went to lousy schools and grew up in struggling households with few quiet places to study, where they had to help raise younger siblings while an uneducated single parent punched a clock over long hours every day. And since he is surrounded every day by a black student community where people of this profile are rare, he is arguing on the basis of a fiction. That fiction appeals because it allows eternal complaint.

If the student thinks that racial preferences are important in allowing him and his black friends to make Penn more "diverse," then he is embracing what blacks of his class two generations ago would have designated as tokenism. (Chapter Nine outlines my justification for that judgment of the "diversity" routine.)

If the student has taken in the Ellis Cose vision and thinks that occasional run-ins with bigots are equivalent to being run over on a regular basis by a pickup truck, then again, we wonder why he probably also thrills to the idea that black people are strong. We might venture that as a twenty-something black person in 2005, he may well get a kick out of hip-hoppers chanting charismatically about how in-your-face "niggas" are—that is, he thinks of Tupac Shakur as an arresting icon. Not to mention that if the student has sampled black history to any extent, we might think that he would pause before claiming that Emmett Till was run over by an 18-wheeler but that a black law student at the University of Pennsylvania is run over by a pickup truck.

At best, he finds a Matchbox car running up his ankle now and then, and processing that as a "full-sized pickup" is only possible through a psychological filter. That filter is what Wax attempts to cut through. White America needs to take a cue from her response to the usual criticisms she has received: "People have a credible fear of talking about these topics. They're afraid of being called a racist. That doesn't particularly strike fear in my heart. I don't think I am."

She isn't, and she is to be commended for saying so and leaving it there. Professor Amy Wax, in all of her "unfettered whiteness," is pointing the way ahead for black America.

So often, whites mouthing the usual post–Great Society pieties on race give away in facial and bodily cues that they are doing a performance rather than shooting from the hip. I notice it most often on racial preferences. A common symptom is the look into the distance, the same kind of look someone has as they perform a task like giving the numbers from one to ten in a language they have just started taking a class in. If they were expressing an opinion about their children's day care they would look you right in the eye. The person is switching into a different mental mode, where it is permitted that basic logic is suspended while buzzwords are treated as arguments in themselves. Amy Wax is honest enough, and sincerely concerned enough about black America, to step out of this mode. On race, leaders and thinkers must follow her model.

I cite her not to imply that black America will be best off sitting at the feet of white rather than black thinkers. There are black leaders who think like Wax, but she happens to have penned a piece that was usefully concise and explicit on the point. Wisdom knows no color.

THE NEW BLACK LEADER

Any black leader, political or writerly, who is to have any serious effect on black Americans' lives must openly and conclusively let the frameworks of the Great Society ideology, treating blacks as helpless victims of factory relocation, middle-class snobbery, buildings' heights, "segregation," and the rest, pass into history. To insist that this frame of mind is the only way to address our problems as humane, informed citizens is to, unwittingly, leave millions of people to languish in idleness, unfocused cynicism, and misery. Surely, the reasons they are in this condition now are beyond their making. But this is not because corporations moved to China or because all whites do not have precisely the same esteem for blacks as they do for their own. The reason was a cultural hijacking of a cultural consensus that once reigned, about the nature of honor, responsibility, and persistence. Yes, plenty of people fell short even in the old days—but they were not condoned by the larger culture as noble martyrs making a statement to the oppressor. This hijacking was larger than any individual and challenging to resist, and was even foisted upon us in large part by certain whites who were ardently devoted to black uplift.

If we really want to walk in the footsteps of the Civil Rights leaders of yore, we cannot shirk challenge for the easy score. Breaking down the walls of legalized segregation, and rendering casual and unquestioned racism socially unacceptable, was a challenge that seemed insurmountable in the fifties and sixties. But people died to make it happen.

Today, we face another daunting challenge, and it is not making sure all whites love all blacks, a mission that no black person saw as at all urgent even when black men were being lynched by the week. The work that remains to be done is dedicating ourselves to letting the "whitey has to pay" routine go, and filtering all of our race politics through a constant awareness of that, with a deeply felt moral urgency. We must open ourselves to this even though racism still lurks here and there and capitalism is a hard business.

After all, this time lives are not even at stake. Time was that black people could be killed for Living While Black without even knowing what Civil Rights was, such as Denise McNair, Carole Robertson, Addie Mae Collins, and Cynthia Wesley in the Sixteenth Street Baptist Church in Birmingham. And then Medgar Evers; Martin Luther King; Freedom Riders James Chaney, Andy Goodman, and Michael Schwerner in Mississippi; and countless others who gave their lives for our America to exist.

And we live in that America. In today's America there is a massive black middle class. Black people are in the highest reaches of government. In a great many places, the "interracial couple" is ordinary. The white intelligentsia fiercely defends affirmative action and is almost viscerally ambivalent about admitting that the results of welfare reform are preferable to Welfare As We Knew It. In this America, surely the black leader will not sit tight in spirited indictment of "white privilege" because it is easy, cathartic, and sits well on the infectiously confrontational rhythms of hip-hop and "slam" poetry.

The new black leader will refrain from this not because it is no longer "fashionable"—although blissfully it is indeed increasingly less so. The new black leader will refrain from this not because whites are increasingly deaf to it—although they are, and in the end this will only help us move on to true progressivism. The new black leader will refrain from this not because of clever arguments that because the Constitution bars discrimination according to race, we must reject policies that focus on black people—a point that is nimble, but too deaf to the realities of American history and human nature to ever speak to most.

The new black leader will refrain from this for one reason only: because "authentic" as it seems, it does not do a blessed thing for people who need help. They, and not self-medication, must be our concern. Think, for example: What important development in black America has the Congressional Black Caucus been responsible for since it was founded in 1969?

In short, we need no leaders whose goal, stated or tacit, is to call us to the barricades to fight for a Second Civil Rights revolution.

BLACK LEADER A AND BLACK LEADER B: A SCORECARD

1.

Black Leader A unabashedly celebrates our victories.

Black Leader B celebrates our victories only in parentheses, under the impression that trumpeting our failures is more important because it lets whites know they are "on the hook."

2.

Black Leader A is committed to eventually getting past race.

Black Leader B is committed to delineating us as a race apart, seemingly hoping that whites and other races will blend together but blacks will remain a separate group, since we were brought here against our will.

3.

Black Leader A is interested in cultural hybridity as evidence of progress.

Black Leader B is interested in cultural hybridity as evidence that whites "appropriate" blackness "and sell it back to us."

4.

Black Leader A identifies racism and discrimination after careful consideration.

Black Leader B identifies racism and discrimination as the cause of all statistical discrepancies between blacks and whites.

5.

Black Leader A is interested in blacks succeeding in the system as it is and considers us capable of doing so.

Black Leader B is interested in blacks succeeding in a system transformed by a revolution and considers us incapable of doing so otherwise.

6.

Black Leader A considers the equation between alienation and black identity a problem.

Black Leader B considers the equation between alienation and black identity a "wake-up call" to a benighted white Establishment by a people "denied love."

Black leaders and thinkers should be ranked on that scorecard. Some will prefer Black Leader B, but people of this kind will have no influence on the future of black America. No one ever got ahead by getting back. This does not mean that a number of such people will not be famous. Their theatrical charisma alone will assure them book sales and speaking engagements, especially since these both are driven considerably by the academic world—a cradle of the written word and public speaking events—where revolutionary politics are so popular. But the poses these people strike year after year have nothing to do with the legions of black people who are getting ahead despite the challenging but approachable realities of success in America, including with the slow climb upward that so many less fortunate blacks are making every year.

To be sure, forging true transformation in the nakedly racist America before the sixties had required rattling the pans and then some. Grand productions were urgent and indispensable. But they left behind an unintended by-product that confuses us to this day. When the show was over, drama queens—a human, not black, personality type—jumped up onto the set and dressed up in the costumes, acting up and savoring the pleasures of staged martyrdom. The drama queens are still up there going through their motions today. Because they are wearing the costumes and reciting the lines, these people can look quite a bit like the real deal, but all they are is mimics. The aftermath of the Civil Rights movement has become a kind of drag act. In this way, we got from Bayard Rustin's methodical, on-the-ground activism to Julian Bond censoring a white woman for using the N-word while *criticizing* it.

I try my very best to try to understand thinkers on race whose perspectives differ from my own. Nevertheless, more than a few black leaders and thinkers whose lives 90 percent of the world's citizens would envy, who got to where they are with human initiative and persistence, preach year after year that black America requires a second revolution in how the nation has operated for centuries and always will, despite painfully clear evidence that this second revolution will never occur.

This version of activism is not one I can sanction. With regret, I can only view it as an unwitting lapse into self-indulgent cruelty. This remains the case even when the rhetoric is presented in the seductive cadences of the black preacher, the black street, or a deft combination of the two. Articulate and affectionate though this can be in itself, when its message is to wait for something that will never happen, the contrast between the high-pitched volume of the event and the nonexistent impact it has on anyone's lives beyond delighting the audience that night is faintly gruesome. We could do so much better than this.

Forget the Idea of "Poverty Pimps"

However, the analysis I have presented in this book must not be read as the same old idea that black leaders taking the victim line are just cynically trying to line their pockets. My express intent has been to show that people of this sort are not callow charlatans—they are processing black America through a psychological lens that assuages an inner hurt. They may confuse and even annoy us, but they are not "poverty pimps."

This is, after all, a seriously trenchant charge to lob at a person, especially since we are talking about hundreds of thousands of black Americans in all walks of life who are raising families and doing what they see as the best they can in this world. Really, how sinister do we genuinely think so very many black Americans are?

Of course, sometimes life just isn't pretty. But the poverty pimp notion just doesn't hold up if we really think about it; it is, basically, unempirical. How many of us could say we have ever actually met a "poverty pimp"—that is, someone who was clearly crying wolf against reality to line his or her pockets or keep his or her job? No black person ever gives concrete indication that this is what he or she is about. No one ever admits it, even under questioning where one would expect them to let it slip. I, for one, have never seen a single black figure show that this was how they were thinking—not the slightest hint, inflection, or gesture. The only thing that stands out is a logical disjunction between what they say and what America is really like. But this does not require that they are hucksters: It could also be that something hinders them from processing reality. That is what this book has been about.

I also hope that the reader will not take from my argument that the problem is that "poverty pimp" leaders have pulled the wool over black America's eyes with speeches and statements.

First, this is logically implausible. Who among us really believe that a vast proportion of an entire race of people found their entire psychology upon a speech or two or three that they hear somewhere, or seeing someone spouting sound bites on television? We might think of the influence of anti-Western fundamentalist ideology on people like the Palestinians—but they are reinforced by real-life negative experiences with Israelis (which no one could deny regardless of one's position on which side started the conflict and/or bears the most responsibility for ending it). Since the sixties, in America, experiences of that kind with whites have been rare to nonexistent for most blacks. Yes, some young black men may have awful encounters with white police officers—but that is but a small segment of black America as a whole, and recall that privileged blacks of both genders in books like Ellis Cose's report the same antiwhite sentiments even without profiling anecdotes. Sure, the occasional person may be especially bedazzled by a firebrand African American studies professor or by reading Malcolm X's autobiography. But most people just take the class and forget it, read the book and forget it. To be permanently imprinted by such things is a matter of idiosyncrasies of personal psychology and experience—in other words, there is "diversity" among black Americans. To claim that speeches by people like Jesse Jackson or Louis Farrakhan infect black America as a whole makes it sound like there are about 600 black Americans all going to the same church.

Second, the idea is ahistorical. Marcus Garvey, preaching an antiwhite back-to-Africa rhetoric complete with theatrical showmanship and slogans over feasible plans, was a star in exactly the period when all-black districts like Bronzeville and black Indianapolis were thriving nevertheless. Black America can listen to, and even thrill to, rhetoric like this without going down the toilet. What messed black America up starting in the late sixties was not what people like Stokely Carmichael said here and there. It was that he and his comrades were saying it at a time when whites were open to hearing it and transforming it into new legislation (welfare's expansion) and social mores (the slightest hint of "prejudice" becoming as morally suspect as pedophilia). The culture had changed in a broader sense. I tried to be especially clear on this in Chapter Five, on how and why the therapeutic alienation meme took hold of black America.

In general, the poverty pimp analysis is recreational—which is not the same thing as accurate. If one is dismayed at what happened to black America after the late sixties, then it may feel good to pin it on some colorful characters. It's easy, it gives one something to feel above, and it is endlessly renewable as there are always a few such sorts to parse this way. But the question is whether the charge corresponds to reality.

Finally, the charge is simply unnecessary. I have tried to show that when black people present themselves as leaders but refuse to make sense, it is for a specific reason: *Their people were abruptly given the opportunity to be "selves" that they had never had a way of learning to love, and so they run from their "selves" and duck into the predictability of belonging to a cult.*

To wit: Black leaders who fetishize victimhood and pretend to be waiting for a "revolution" do not like themselves. Actual "poverty pimps" are rare. If we truly desire a higher awareness of what has gone wrong on the race scene, we must let go of that cartoon archetype.

Voting for the Leaders We Deserve

The New New Negro must also continue the current trend among younger blacks of questioning our allegiance to the Democratic Party. Quite often today, the programs that Civil Rights leaders of the past would have recognized as progressive are proposed by Republicans.

For example, in 2001, the Bush Administration proposed setting aside money for churches to apply for to help poor people, and dozens of prominent black ministers were chomping at the bit to get at the funds. Yet, most black Democratic leaders rejected the idea. They claimed to be worried about churches discriminating against people of other faiths or of no faith. But when affirmative action comes up, the same people argue that urgent realities sometimes require a bit of what we might call constructive discrimination, focusing assistance on one group more than others—as they did two years later when the Supreme Court was making its decision on racial preferences at the University of Michigan.

It was plain that their main commitment was to rejecting any idea Republicans came up with, out of a sense that being oppositional is the soul of being a black leader—regardless of whether the opposition helps anyone. Any black leader whose actions were truly based on concern for the poor would have jumped at the Faith-Based and Community Initiatives plan. Even if they were worried about allegations of race-based voting irregularities in Florida, or speculations at the time as to whether Attorney General John Ashcroft was a racist, they would have prioritized the availability of those funds, as the less fortunate of their race wandered in need of the help. But these leaders were less concerned with the poor than with chasing that ball of yarn. Therapeutic alienation is a drug. It's time we started calling people on this more clearly and more often.

Or: Is there perhaps a bit of therapeutic alienation in most blacks when we go to the voting booth? We are often taught that Republicans are racists, and hence we vote Democratic almost to a man. Now, opinions will differ, but do plans like the Faith-Based Initiatives and No Child Left Behind—that offers minority students in bad schools the opportunity of transferring to a good one and requires constant testing to make sure students are learning anything—really have no application whatsoever to black uplift? And whatever the imperfections of these programs, name one plan of similar scope that Democrats have presented over the past ten years. And now try twenty years, including telling us exactly what impact the "Enterprise Zones" idea has had upon poor blacks overall.

The problem here is that with Republicans having no reason to court people who won't vote for them, and Democrats having no reason to do anything for people who will vote for them no matter what, we are now the most politically powerless racial group in the nation.

Now, perhaps George W. Bush has been too polarizing a figure to expect blacks, as a group with a decades-deep tradition voting Democratic, to vote for him in significant numbers. And I feel it necessary to note here that I did not vote for Bush in 2000 or 2004—that is, this is not a partisan argument. But a hypothetical scenario of the future chills me to the bone.

A Republican candidate comes along who shows a sincere commitment to minority education and community development. The Democratic candidate does little besides speak before the NAACP, brunch with Al Sharpton, and say a little something to some black churches. But black writers and editorialists dutifully assail Republicans as racists, reminding us of Richard Nixon's "Southern Strategy" aiming to turn Dixie Republican by rousing it up about the blacks, Ronald Reagan's anecdotes about welfare queens, and something Trent Lott said about Strom Thurmond one night back in 2003. Assorted local activists tell NPR that blacks are "wary" of Republicans and are still "not sure" that the Republican candidate has "reached out." And even though increasing numbers of blacks bill themselves as Independents, and more than a few grouse about Democrats taking advantage of us, the morning after election night, the Republican's black vote barely cracks 10 percent. A consensus still reigns that real black people vote only for the Democrat, even if the Democrat has shown not the slightest genuine interest in our own black behinds.

That consensus is passive and outdated. Our vote must be based on the fate of our people, not a sense that the black way to vote is to show the finger to Republicans regardless of the potential impact of their proposals on people of our race. Lord forbid all of us vote Republican—then we'd be right back where we started. But if we are really so diverse a people, if it irritates us so much when whites imply that we are a monolith, then do we really show what we are in voting 90 percent for one party in election after election? We are today the only minority group with such a skewed vote: In 2004, Latinos went 53 percent for John Kerry and 44 percent for Bush; Asians were 56 percent for Kerry and 44 percent for Bush. They looked diverse. They looked like they think for themselves as individuals. We looked like sheep. I am afraid that we still will even if a Republican makes us an offer that we shouldn't refuse—if we continue in a quiet sense that to be really black is to be oppositional, regardless of reality. Therapeutic alienation retards genuine progress.

Something that might help: No doubt, as an employee of a free-market think tank and viewed as I am as a "black conservative," I have had occasion to meet quite a few black Republicans over the past five years. And I wonder if some out there may suppose that black Republicans are generally bow-tied, sociologically clueless people stuck in a simplistic old idea that they got theirs and poor blacks just need to "get real." Well, nothing could be further from the truth. Black Republicans are a highly "diverse" crowd, with all of the dreadlocks, Black English vocal inflections, hip-hop on their car radios, Zora Neale Hurston novels on their bookshelves, and even histories of welfare checks that we might think of as "authentic." They are different from black Democrats only in a spontaneous understanding that resonant catchphrases and buzzwords are not activism.

It's not enough to just tell a pollster that you are an Independent out of a desire not to be put into a box, but still harbor a basic revulsion at the notion of ever actually voting for a Republican. If the candidate is right, they should get the New New Negro's vote—even if the candidate is, well, on the right. Otherwise, we have no call upon the levers of power in our nation.

THE NEW BLACK THINKER

When it comes to black politicians, those who are interested in the future rather than the past are on the rise. It is getting ever more difficult to get elected or stay in office on the basis of the grand old theatrics, which make ever less sense to many blacks born in the sixties and afterward. Al Sharpton's dismal tallies in his run for the Democratic nomination in 2004 are Exhibit A: However good he is on the podium, he will likely never cop an elected post of any significance because almost everyone sees his lack of interest in changing anyone's life.

But the notion that blacks need a Second Civil Rights revolution remains more entrenched in the black thinking class. But what these people think of as a reasoned argument about rights has become what economists would call entitlements.

Economists Simon Gächter and Arno Riedl, although not addressing race issues, spell out this distinction: "Claims acquired in the past seem to generate strong entitlements, often in situations where the past is objectively irrelevant." Thinkers on black issues look to the Civil Rights revolution's accomplishments in fighting racism, deem them insufficient because black inner cities still exist that send far too many black men to jail, and suppose that continuing to oppose "racism" will make further progress. But as Gächter and Riedl put it in a more general sense, "the past is objectively irrelevant" today: Black America's main problem is no longer racism (which was, sadly, easier to address in a way). Another economist writing on the subject, Ekkehart Schlicht, spells out that entitlements are "the *subjectively* perceived rights that go along with a *motivational* disposition to defend them." In this vein, black warriors against "racism" are arguing less from sincere and sustained examination of how America is changing, but in a *subjective* animus, a *motivational* business based on their personal psychology.

Beware the "White Privilege" Rhetoric

An idea we must be especially vigilant against is one fashionable among black academics and white fellow travelers, that our problem is that America is based on "white privilege." This "white privilege" concept is bruited about as a hazy catchall concept that allows all manner of alienated claims along the lines that whites are culpable in having more of the chips than blacks, even when they are unaware of it, and that black America's salvation will only be the elimination of said "privilege."

We've seen some examples in this book. Damali Ayo, author of rent-a-negro.com, assailed white people asking her about her hair as abusing "white privilege." Greg Thomas, the professor doing the college course on Lil' Kim, cherishes her for redistributing "power, pleasure, and *privilege*"— he is using an established jargon.

In this, these writers are suddenly aware of how initial conditions can determine current ones, although blind to this when it comes to how cultural imperatives set in as gestures in the late sixties and detoured black America for decades afterward. The idea is that the overt racism of early Americans has left the foundations of modern America shot through with a legacy of bigotry that renders the entire American experiment a sham. Manning Marable tells us, in a passage typical of his writings, "Structural racism, the elaborate institutions informed by white prejudice, power, and privilege, predated the establishment of the U.S. democratic state. Consequently, most of America's political institutions and parties have been or are currently now compromised by white racism." As far as he is concerned, "We will never dismantle structural racism as a system unless we are also willing to address the transformation of the American social structure."

We might first ask Marable just how he is hoping we could accomplish something as massive as a "transformation of the American social structure." What are the steps he proposes? Really—in the real world we live in, what is he thinking we need to do? Even if he could get the ear of leftist victimologist Congressmen like John Conyers Jr., or could become the leading scholar-consultant for the Congressional Black Caucus, what would he propose? Or, more specifically—what would he propose that he would reasonably think the black congressmen could get the federal government to fashion into a bill, pass through both the House and the Senate, and have come out as something that would make a dent of difference in the lives of blacks left behind?

And why is it that in asking this I will seem to many to be pushing it a bit? Why am I pushing it? I thought we were interested in change. Change in the real world—like Powell, Rustin, King, and Farmer devoted their lives to working for. Say that it wouldn't work because the Feds are racists, and I ask again—is that where you want to leave it? Have you *established* that there is no conceivable change short of a "transformation of the American social structure"? Where are the position papers showing that the assiduous efforts of countless black community leaders nationwide are making no progress? Are some of us really interested most in just being angry?

And in the meantime, what about the basic proposition that the racist history has left a deeply racist present? Writers like Marable imply that this is unassailable truth. But are they attending to America as it actually develops?

Let's take a black American incensed by anthropologist John Ogbu's study of black students' performances in Shaker Heights, Ohio, who would probably read Marable as a sage. Here is this black American's letter to Berkeley, California's, *East Bay Express* in 2003.

> As a descendant of the "involuntary immigrants" called slaves, let me inform Mr. Ogbu of this fact. Every black child who is such a descendant is informed from the moment of his/her birth that he and his people have no culture; that the language of their ancestors was ooga-booga gibberish; that their religion was superstition and voodoo; that they never invented anything or accomplished anything; that the best thing that ever happened to us was to be dragged kicking and screaming into slavery; and that the most we could hope for is to become the best imitation white man we could be.

Few of us are unfamiliar with this kind of classic Malcolm X rhetoric, which has been a staple on the race scene for forty years. It is especially common on black talk radio and among African American studies scholars, especially ones working at nonselective colleges. However, it also has its place on "the street"—all black people, and all whites who have ample contact with the black community, know this type.

The incantations can sound like wisdom beyond logical engagement. It has become a kind of folklore, no more subject to cold reasoning than song, liturgy, mantra. But there is a short distance from this to "ooga-booga gibberish." How do this letter writer's observations stack up to reality?

In 2001, when the centennial of the Pan-American Exposition in Buffalo was celebrated, the organizers decided to include acknowledgment of racist aspects of the event. The white executive director of the Buffalo and Erie County Historical Society said that it had been decided that this was urgent: "You are better able to understand the present if you go back and look at some of the threads that brought us here."

President William McKinley was assassinated at the Buffalo event, and in 2003, a white historian brought back to light a lost aspect of that event—that a black man fought down assassin Leon Czolgosz after his first two shots and prevented him from hitting McKinley with a third one. As McKinley appeared to be rallying in the days afterward, Jim Parker was briefly a national hero. Eric Rauchway's book was published by a top house and well publicized, including on CNN's prominent *Booknotes* program.

The same year as the Buffalo anniversary celebration, artifacts discovered from the wreck of the slave ship *Henrietta Marie* travelled the country in an exhibition that attracted record numbers of viewers in twenty cities, and was extended to 2003.

In 2002, a Washington State representative agitated to have Jefferson Davis's name removed from a Seattle area highway and replaced by the name of William P. Stewart, a black Civil War veteran of the state. The representative, Hans Dunshee, was white. Meanwhile, among Underground Railroad buffs upset about distortions in a planned Cincinnati National Underground Railroad Freedom Center, the most vocal ones were white, while a white former radio host in Mississippi, of all places, publicized a huge collection of fifteen thousand slavery artifacts.

That same year, when white supremacists *travelled to* York, Pennsylvania, to hold a rally (they were not natives), the town sponsored a four hundred-strong interracial "unity rally" at the same time, with an Anti-Racist Action Group specifically opposing the supremacists. Meanwhile, interracial relationships are now common in the town.

The following year, on Strom Thurmond's one hundredth birthday, network and newspaper accounts regularly mentioned his having once been a segregationist; even the brief announcement that was looped all day on the half-hour on CNN's *Headline News* ran a film clip of him making a segregationist speech. The year after that, by the time the founder of Aryan Nations, Richard G. Butler, died, his organization was down to two hundred members scattered across the country. His yearly World Congress was by then drawing only one hundred attendants. His presence in the Coeur D'Alene area was considered a matter of shame and discomfort by local whites and spurred the emergence there of organizations against racism and anti-Semitism.

So now, let's hear again what our informed writer told us.

As a descendant of the "involuntary immigrants" called slaves, let me inform Mr. Ogbu of this fact. Every black child who is such a descendant is informed from the moment of his/her birth that he and his people have no culture; that the language of their ancestors was ooga-booga gibberish; that their religion was superstition and voodoo; that they never invented anything or accomplished anything; that the best thing that ever happened to us was to be dragged kicking and screaming into slavery; and that the most we could hope for is to become the best imitation white man we could be.

Obviously, the writer was unlikely to be aware of precisely the things I mentioned that I personally happened to come across over the years. But the writer also lives in the same America that I do, and writing to the *East Bay Express* suggests regular engagement with newspapers and the broadcast media. The writer cannot have been unaware of the *kinds of* things I mentioned, which are too common for any remotely literate, engaged person to be unaware of.

We all know that during these same years, racism still existed in America. But we also know two other things. One is that the manifestations of racism appeared, at least to most of us, as backward remnants of a receding past. The other is that when we heard of things like the ones I listed on the previous two pages, we did not marvel at them. They seemed typical phenomena of an America that is moving forward.

And this means that the letter writer's screed does not correspond to the reality that he or she knows. It corresponds to an America of roughly 1962, which the writer may well have never even experienced directly. The writer's mental program filters out evidence of good news as spam, devoted to maintaining a sense of aggrievement regardless of experience.

All rhetoric about "white privilege" suffers from this same problem. This writer has founded an identity upon feeling besieged by the White Man. But human beings do not embrace feeling oppressed in the face of overwhelming counterevidence—unless doing so conveys a psychic comfort that they find elusive when facing life as it actually is.

Beware a Social Science Uninterested in Black Leadership

And that brings us to taking a last look at what people considered the black people's thinking class must look to have to tell us. In Chapter Seven, I accused social scientists of being more interested in tearing down than building up. But surely we don't need academics to write just sunny reports about how great things are. So, what should they do instead?

The misrepresentativeness of the pessimism I refer to is clear from what gets covered versus what doesn't. For example, one would barely know from reading ten years of race articles in two leading sociology journals that there exist legions of organizations nationwide making a positive difference in black lives.

For example, in *Comeback Cities*, professional activists Paul Grogan and Tony Proscio show that in the 1990s, inner cities have been improving slowly but surely as the result of the efforts of Community Development Corporations and other bodies, shunting foundation funds into helping residents improve their neighborhoods one street at a time. There has been no magic—the 'hood is still with us, as a perusal of any newspaper makes painfully clear. But things are not as utterly hopeless as they seemed even fifteen years ago—there has been a crucial change.

In every large city with a major population of disadvantaged blacks, there are local organizations taking people by the hand and teaching them to help themselves in a way that federally funded bureaucracies never did. In New York, for example, there is the Harlem Children's Zone, covering a sixty-block area with a battery of uplift programs brought door to door.

Race Man extraordinaire Geoffrey Canada, a longtime dedicated community activist, founded the Harlem Children's Zone program. He identified the blocks most in need by seeking data such as which zip codes contributed the most people in prison upstate and which zip codes had the most high-school dropouts. The project includes a school designed to reach poor minority kids, as well as a range of programs giving poor black families counsel on economics and health issues. The HCZ's mission is to provide poor children in the neighborhood with nurturing environments as early as possible.

The programs are tailored differently according to age: Far from being a mere variation on Head Start, the HCZ is also committed to the difficult job of intervening with older children in whom patterns are already set. The Baby College teaches parents child care skills and is graded by the age of parents' children. The HCZ has placed supplementary teachers in seven Harlem schools to tutor students in reading and provide after-school activities. The Fifth Grade Institute gives support to kids just before the fragile phase of the "tween" years. Then, for older kids, the Employment and Technology Center offers computer classes and also connects young people to jobs. TRUCE (the Renaissance University for Community Education) helps teenagers graduate from high school: In 2004, its students were accepted to colleges such as Harvard, Yale, Bowdoin, Vassar, and Penn State. The students also produce a cable television program and a newspaper. TRUCE also has a fitness center. Community Pride mentors Harlem residents in improving rented properties as well as buying their own.

Meanwhile, the HCZ has recently opened its own charter school and is planning a Practitioner's Institute designed to disseminate the program's practices to other places.

So, this project is about not just making speeches, but knocking on doors—even housing project doors, no matter how tall the buildings are. When the people behind those doors resist, the project comes back. When the people behind the doors say, "Okay," but fade away, the project knocks again. The idea is to transform the lives of the many thousands of people living in the zone that Canada identified, tabulating what zip codes the unhealthiest people came from, what zip codes the worst students came from, what zip codes the most hardened criminals upstate came from. So many ask, "Where are the new black leaders?" with the same old musings about what's wrong with Maxine Waters and Kweisi Mfume and on and on—as the Harlem Children's Zone is currently serving almost ten thousand children.

The Harlem Children's Zone is not teaching white people not to be racist, and that very idea seems hopelessly irrelevant to the real-life people they are helping to help themselves. The people they help are imprinted by the cultural meme that reigned when they were children—it's okay to check out. The Harlem Children's Zone teaches them out of this. The Harlem Children's Zone is not waiting for a utopian America. It is helping people in a *real* America that will never know a Second Civil Rights revolution. This, and not picketing and psychological policing, is 2006's version of the Struggle.

It's happening nationwide. In Boston, Reverend Eugene Rivers's Ten Point Coalition is taking young black criminals off of the streets and into productive lives, mediating between them and the police. This has meant that since the nineties Boston—long known "on the vine" as a city where racism has a way of hanging on—has known no significant episodes where blacks rise up en masse in objection to the actions of white police officers. In Los Angeles, Operation Hope teaches disadvantaged blacks and Latinos how to buy their own houses. In Indianapolis, there is Christamore House, where the black leaders helping poor blacks would be surprised to hear that their charges have nowhere to turn to because of the blindness of whitey. The founders of these organizations and the people who work for them have devoted endless and heroic amounts of effort to changing what they saw as wrong, insufficient, and unjust, often having grown up knowing just what their current charges are suffering from.

Now: Where is all of this in the august academic literature on the black American condition?

Academic chroniclers of black America's modern reality seem, really, uninterested in these things. Now, make no mistake—the idea would not be for them to simply celebrate these developments and leave it there;

that's for the organizations to do themselves. There is only a slight overlap between cheerleading and thought. But still, the reason sociologists, anthropologists, and political scientists should look to these efforts is constructive. After all, I presume that intellectuals see themselves as constructive—that is, poised to apply intellection to forging social justice. But if so, then surely we would expect our top thinkers on race to be fascinated by which of these organizations have the best results and how (or perhaps even by which ones don't cut the mustard and why). Surely we would expect them to seek to spend months or years by the side of workers in these organizations, examining what methods work best in improving the lives of the unfortunate, submitting their findings to statistical analysis, and pointing us toward the best possible future efforts. Wouldn't we? Precisely why would this be, somehow, outside the bailiwick of a serious and concerned student of human social interaction, in a society where racial discrepancies stemming from a tragic history persist amid a permanently capitalist establishment?

Never mind that there might be an academic here and there who takes a sniff at such organizations. Really, after all, if academics were sincerely committed to helping the unfortunate, then these benevolent organizations would be nothing less than an obsession, one of the sexiest things that, say, a beginning sociologist could choose to study—that is, the organizations nationwide giving their all to help poor blacks would be *a front-and-center focus* among academics interested in race, by now a cliché topic at conferences. How America *might* be someday, somehow, would seem a kind of idle cogitation, a vision trivial and self-indulgent in view of the urgency of helping people whose lives are lousy today, right here and now, in an America as imperfect as we know it to be, and have all reason to suppose it always will be.

Yet, with the current state of academic inquiry on race, it is hard to imagine a scholar addressing these uplift organizations without a prime commitment to showing what they have trouble making a dent in, rather than what they succeed in. For example, the sociologist who stressed the good news would be condemned at his conference talks for neglecting his duty to warn Mr. and Mrs. America about the hidden perniciousness of racism and would have trouble getting articles published in prominent journals. One almost senses a genuine fear of this in sociology articles, as authors dutifully hedge and qualify good news to make sure they are seen to be, at heart, warriors against racism. But isn't that alone a rather narrow goal for people who are supposed to be committed to *thinking* in general? When identifying "racism" rather than showing how to get beyond it is a field's dominant watch-cry, isn't it a sign that the field has drifted into an ideology local to a certain few late decades in one century?

TAKE YOUR BUSINESS ELSEWHERE

The perspectives I have aired in this book stem ultimately from an amazement at how vastly different our ideas of black progressiveness were in 1970 from what they were in 1960. I openly avow that my sense of black history is based on a sense that the contrast between ten-year periods before the sixties was always moderate. There is no apparent "bump" between black America, 1910 and black America, 1920. Even between black America, 1950 and black America, 1960, the relevant "bump" is one perceived more by the historian than the ordinary citizen: *Brown v. Board of Education* and what Rosa Parks did were signature events, but *at the time*, they had a minor effect upon the daily experience of most black Americans. But between 1960 and 1970, black America went from the old days to the now days.

As it happens, I was born precisely in the middle of that period, which leaves me open to the charge that I am misled by an exoticization of "preme." But I don't think so—that I was born in 1965 and see things the way I do is, in my view, just an accident. Something truly seismic happened to black America exactly when I happened to come into this world. Certainly, much of it was good, and I am fully aware that my life would be impossible without them.

But so much of it was so very bad. Such as—the grand old professional indignation, the kind of rhetoric many blacks slip into that leaves most nonblacks quietly confused, which still lingers like a stray eyelash. It still holds considerable sway in the world of letters—your child is almost certain to get a dose of it in college, for example. It distorts basic analysis of modern black history, even among writers committed to progress and making sense. Schools of education are awash in it. In general, it exerts a quiet tug on general discourse. What begins as intelligent, useful exchanges gets muddled with eddies of incoherence and melodrama, as a certain kind of black participant drifts into an anger curiously detached from actual events or causes.

How we deal with individual citizens of this moment will vary according to circumstances and temperament. I personally prefer a kind of judo; once people reveal themselves to be of this sort, often the only useful response is to just quietly shut down and leave them to their business, sticking as much as possible to pleasantries and quickly agreeing with any further expressions of fantasy.

But the New New Negro, for his or her own sake and that of less fortunate fellow black Americans, cannot up and cast votes for this kind of person and cannot let the intelligentsia infected with this kind of thinking pass as bards of their race. Anyone purporting to have a valuable message to black America whose "message" is basically that nothing will change without a revolution that could never occur has nothing to offer us but the passing and idle pleasures of payback fantasies and stirring rhetorical formulas.

There is, most certainly, nothing New about that.

CHAPTER ELEVEN

Conclusion

My impression is that many readers came away from my *Losing the Race* wondering why black America took the turn it did in the sixties. People often took the message of that book as being "Black people need to look inward and help themselves." I have no major problem with that proposition, but my aim was to show *why* we had gotten to the point that this would be considered news at all. As far as I am concerned, we can leave it to the eight-hundred-word newspaper editorialists to just proclaim that something is wrong and leave us with a final sentence along the lines of "Maybe it's time for black America to wake up."

In this book I have tried to make clearer just what made the difference between black America in 1960 and black America today, and what this means in terms of where we go from here and why. Specifically, I hope to have shown that the nut of the issue is that black America turned upside down in a particular ten-year period, from 1960 to 1970, and that this era has left us a legacy much more damaging today than anything racism has left us.

My argument has been that it is not true that the reason for modern black America's ills is racism. The reason is a cultural shift now forty years old, that manifests itself in the form of a meme. This meme took hold of blacks and whites in the wake of the antiauthoritarian atmosphere of the countercultural revolution. After that revolution and the specific things that sparked it were over, the meme piggybacked on human psychology and stuck around. Namely, opposition as an identity gives a sense of purpose to people deprived of one for any number of reasons and is a handy way of refreshing even an identity less damaged. The result has been especially tragic in black America: a way of responding to the world and forming judgments that correspond fitfully to reality, if at all. To not understand this is to not understand black America's past, present, or future.

THE FUTURE IS HERE

The wonderful thing, however, is that therapeutic alienation is losing its mojo on the public scene. We are at a tipping point. For example, in Chapter Five, I mentioned some "High Victimology" statements by Beverly Daniel Tatum in an article in the *New York Times*. But just six years later, the whole article is a period piece.

It was a July 2000 editorial page dedicated to "A Conversation on Race," and beside Tatum's contribution, included black Columbia Law School professor Patricia Williams informing us of the "violently patrolled historical boundary between black and white in America" and Alvin Poussaint telling us that interracial dating is still something many "fear." The only black conservative contribution was from Ward Connerly making the rather academic point of his part-Irish ancestry. Otherwise, "black Martha Stewart" B. Smith admitted, parenthetically, that there is "a growing group of enlightened people who are beyond the stereotypical racial attitudes."

But today, if the *Times* ran an editorial page about race it would not look like this. Based on my sense of the paper over time, today the theatrics of Tatum and Williams in 2000 would be politely let pass as "overblown," while people like Clarence Page and Henry Louis Gates Jr. would be solicited for sensible calls for blacks to try to make the best of a less-than-perfect situation, as Gates did in columns for the paper in 2004 as well as in interview pieces in the *Washington Post* some months before.

The simple fact is that America is quietly getting past race despite the best efforts of the Soul Patrol to pretend otherwise. My sense is that the period when my *Losing the Race* was published, as the millennium turned, was a kind of last gasp of the Racism Forever routines. When the book was new in 2000 and 2001, my straying from the line expected of any black writer with a PhD predictably elicited assorted name-calling, especially from academics and journalists. But even then, I quickly saw a massive gulf between how these people tend to think and how most black Americans elsewhere think. I feel responsible for stressing that the black response to *Losing the Race* beyond academics and journalists has been very, very positive. I have heard from thousands of black people about the book over the past five years, and still hear from at least one a week as I write; the book is, much to my surprise, used in high school and college classrooms across the nation every semester. The haters I have heard from are a trickle. It is by no means a peculiar or brave view that sincere concern with one's people does not require focusing on lambasting whites.

On the contrary, these days, blacks taking the line of therapeutic alienation in overt argument are on the defensive rather than the offensive. They decorate their theatrical declamations about the perfidy of the White Man with dutiful acknowledgments of progress. The person often almost looks or reads almost as if they were saying it at gunpoint. But what is significant is that they do say it, aware that to be taken at all seriously beyond the fringe realm of local drive-time talk radio and assorted Web site chat groups, they must at least genuflect to reality.

The bans on racial preferences at the University of California and the University of Texas aroused aggrieved claims that "resegregation" was on the horizon, but this did not happen. For example, I taught at UC Berkeley for years after the ban and saw that the black student population dipped at first but climbed year by year afterward—in the late nineties and early 2000s, there was no perceptible eclipse of a numerous "black community" at Berkeley, while black students who would have been admitted to Berkeley before were doing quite well at UC schools like the one in San Diego, as I discussed in Chapter Nine. In 2003, the Supreme Court affirmed racial preferences in university admissions, but only half heartedly. The University of Michigan law school's preference procedure was let pass, but the brute quota system of the undergraduate school was deemed unconstitutional. This is the kind of system that reigns at most schools that still enshrine racial preferences, and across the nation they are refashioning their procedures to avoid litigation, and such litigation is awaiting any schools that refrain from doing so.

The reparations movement made its biggest noises yet starting in 2000, but when 9/11 and the wars in Afghanistan and Iraq detracted Washington's attention from all but the most pressing domestic issues, unsurprisingly, the reparations show soon lost its spotlight and will likely never regain it. If a few large companies end up coughing up some money for John Conyers and some black lawyers to put into some fund for scholarships or "community development," fine. But none of that business-as-usual will do anything significant in solving black America's problems, and the reparations agitation will become as much a historical curiosity as the Ebonics controversy of 1996 is now. I doubt we will again have to engage people insisting that black inner-city woes are a direct development from the plantation and that the Fed needs to pay black America retroactive wages from 150-plus years ago.

In 2000, there were still some people arguing that limiting welfare to five years was going to leave poor blacks huddling on sidewalk grates. But it didn't happen, and no one of influence is agitating for removing the time limit. Justice was done, and this becomes clearer by the year.

Both Jesse Jackson and Al Sharpton have been revealed as preaching morality in highly visible places while at that very time cheating on their wives and using solicited funds for cushy travel arrangements rather than helping poor blacks. As I write, Jackson is an irrelevance lately occupying himself with purported racist gestures in Mexico, while Sharpton is taking his proper place as a television entertainer.

Whereas twenty years ago mainstream media sources like *Rolling Stone* were celebrating rap as the vehicle of that ever-elusive Second Black Revolution, these days, that notion mostly thrills "hip-hop academics" and the undergraduates and scattered fans they get at. In real life, America understands that hip-hop is just a kind of agitprop theatre, especially as rappers, supposedly our new Malcolm X's, engage in senseless brawls at awards ceremonies and even on the streets. At the time of this writing, 50 Cent and his erstwhile protégé The Game were dueling in public not long ago to an extent that made Sharpton call for radio and television stations to stop playing rap for three months. Meanwhile, the rest of us saw that the whole battle was ultimately a publicity stunt by the two rappers, both of whom had new recordings out. Of the one by 50 Cent, *The Massacre*, Ethan Brown in *New York* magazine wrote "Hip-hop aspires (*or, at least, pretends*) to represent real life"—the italics are mine—a typical realization among the more clear-eyed scribblers on the music these days. Meanwhile, Lil' Kim, apparently in a time-out from radically redistributing power, pleasure, and privilege, is on her way to a year in jail for lying about not knowing that two associates of hers were involved in a shoot-out *right in front of her* outside of a hip-hop radio station in *Greenwich Village*, of all places—the very same station outside of which one of 50 Cent's "crew" shot one of The Game's in the behind during their duel. Rap insiders object that the media "stereotype" rappers as violent—well, okay. But the rest of us see clearly that, first, the members of Radiohead do not get shot in the butt, and that second, rappers, so familiar with either being shot or watching people in their posses take the bullets, are entertainers, not prophets.

Since 2000, one has talked about blacks being denied access to power only to have to explain away Colin Powell and Condoleezza Rice on television every night. In reality, some blacks don't think of Caribbean American, light-skinned Powell as really "black" at all, but that is a harder charge to lob at Alabama-born, dark-skinned Rice. And then, as I write, black Wilton Gregory has just finished a stint as president of the United States Conference of Catholic Bishops. The mayor of Atlanta—Atlanta!—is a black woman, Shirley Clarke Franklin. The CEOs of AOL-Time Warner, American Express, and Merrill Lynch are all black. Black Dennis Archer is the president of the American Bar Association. In 2004, black Audra Mc-Donald won her fourth Tony award at just thirty-three years of age. Two years before when she played the female lead at a benefit performance of Rodgers and Hammerstein's *Carousel* at Carnegie Hall, she and Hugh Jackman kissed passionately and no one batted an eye. Notably, she was doing the lead role of a New England mill girl written as lily-white by men who, racially enlightened as they considered themselves in writing "You've Got to Be Carefully Taught" for *South Pacific* in 1949, would surely have thought of a black Julie Jordan in *Carousel* as beyond plausibility. In 2002, Beyoncé Knowles was the Austin Powers girl in the "threequel" in that series and that same year Halle Berry was the Bond girl in *Die Another Day*.

Yes, during all of this, too many blacks have still been living stunted lives in inner-city hellholes. A study has shown that black ex-cons are less likely to be hired for work than white ones. Another one has shown that job applications with identifiably "black" names like Tamika are less likely to elicit responses even when the applicants' qualifications are identical to those of people whose applications got responses.

But to process these kinds of things as meaning that black American lives are bedeviled by "racism" is, really, to spit in the eye of your grandparents. Studies like this appear regularly, but what they show is that a given experience is more likely for blacks than whites, never that it is the only experience. That blacks may get slightly less cushy deals when buying cars is not great news, but there is no comparison between this and blacks being almost universally denied the vote in the South, as those who say "American society is still shot through with racism" imply. The inequities must be aired and stamped out, as happened when it was discovered—by whites, for the record—that black farmers had been denied loans disproportionately.

But this common sense does not mean pretending that such lingering discrepancies render trivial all of the triumphs I listed above, all of which would have sounded like science fiction as late as 1985. Things are changing, to a degree that has become too obvious to ignore or explain away.

Young people growing up in this world will be especially unlikely to grow up thinking America is a "racist nation." Not long ago I saw two small white children on a sidewalk here in New York joyously bouncing in a curiously butt-focused way in front of an elegant building with an awning and a doorman, apparently having a great time. They cracked me up so much that as I passed I asked them, "What are you *doing*?" They happily shouted, "Beyoncé!!!" I suppose certain informed sorts might object that these little kids were, as it is put, "appropriating" blackness. But I also suppose that the rest of us can see that these kids are the future.

ENGAGING THE FUTURE INSTEAD OF THE PAST

Make no mistake: When I hear someone say something along the lines of "Why do we have to always be talking about race? Why can't we just be people and let all that stuff alone?" I hear someone who hasn't had occasion to think very hard about how the past affects the present, or how real life does not always correspond to how we might wish things would be.

However, the Victimology Squad miss that the past can affect the present in ways other than leaving behind "systemic" socioeconomic disadvantage. The past can also leave behind culturally ingrained patterns of thought that no longer match current conditions. The Victimology Squad miss that real life departs from our wishes not in that real life is full of "racism" impeding our wish for black success, but in that real life presents "racism" as an occasional nuisance that need not impede the black success that we wish.

If we want to be people with a sincere civic concern about race issues, our responsibility is to do so without falling into the trap of supposing that racial authenticity (if we are black) or racial enlightenment (if we are white) requires initiating ourselves into a web of mantras and buzzwords designed to paint blacks as victims rather than victors. This includes realizing that claims that blacks will be victors when whites nationwide somehow "realize" something are, really, claims that blacks will be victims forever, since we all know that The Great Realization will never occur.

We must step around "dialogues" about race that are codedly founded on the question, "In what way can we continue to fashion ourselves as victims despite the fact that things keep getting better?" This includes, for example, radio and television host Tavis Smiley's annual State of Black America forums; I suggest the transcriptions of forums that Smiley convened at the Democratic National Convention in 2000 in his *How to Make Black America Better: Leading African Americans Speak Out* as a written record of this kind of thing. This way of thinking, quite simply, serves no purpose.

The Race Thang

We must get beyond the idea that the race problem in America is something vaguely occult, a higher wisdom possessed by black Americans as the result of a certain "experience" that only we can "understand." Only a meme of therapeutic alienation leads someone to claim that their lives are stained deeply by racism in 2006 via a mysterious liturgy that is considered a "deep" affair requiring long, tortured "conversations" where actually only blacks are allowed to talk, exploring "What I See" and "How I Felt."

As late as 1960, there was no such thing as "the race thang" that a white person "just wouldn't understand"—the "thang" of legalized segregation and denial of voting rights was too obvious for anyone to miss if it was presented. Many think that the problem is just as bad today but "subtle." In fact, the problem is not just "subtle" but lesser, and much, much lesser. Racism today is no longer "all life is," as Ellis Cose puts it, for any black person who is not psychologically primed to pretend that it is.

A useful litmus test is explaining "the race thang" to a foreigner. Often I have heard foreigners describe "the race issue" in America as a mysterious business that they have tried to understand but never quite have. They listen to a contingent telling them that racism remains a scourge on black lives in America but can't quite see what they mean in a country where they see so many successful blacks around them all the time and everybody they meet seems so repulsed by, well, racism.

Let's imagine a middle-class black man whose girlfriend is from Korea—where people are acutely conscious of "racism" against them by the Japanese, even today more naked than anything known in America since the 1960s. Or, let's imagine a middle-class black woman whose boyfriend is a Bosnian—who saw his town razed by Serbs who thought of his people as animals. The middle-class black person in the couple now explains to their foreign mate why racism colors their existence to the extent that they would even feel it necessary to initiate them into the "issues" in question.

If it would take the foreigner longer than five minutes to understand why their black mate is "oppressed" in America, then the black person is acting. Remember Bayard Rustin telling white leftists who wanted to hook poor blacks on open-ended welfare, "If you have an idea that takes two hours to explain, then you don't have an idea"? Sometimes, that's true, and this is one of those times.

We must view the very idea that race issues are "complex" with suspicion, as so often this is a fig leaf for the same old self-medicating indoctrinations. Take the following announcement:

> The University of Colorado at Boulder announced yesterday that it no longer would restrict an education course to minority and first-generation college students after receiving complaints that the restrictions violated equal-protection laws. Educators had limited fall enrollment for the Friday section of "School and Society" to "students of color" and first-generation college students, saying the restriction offered "a much safer and open environment" in which to discuss issues of race, class and the sexes.

Here is that notion that race issues are uniquely tricky, such that one must be "in on" a certain way of processing things to truly understand. It reminds me of the slow, mysterious initiation of Ralph Macchio into the mysteries of karate in *The Karate Kid*. Thus, these educators think a class where all of the students are "oppressed" will be "safer"—that is, with none of those uninitiated people whose middle-class existences mean that they can only "get it" after years of training.

But why "safe"? I thought the wisdom education schools like to impart was so clear. Or is it that they know that the kind of "discussion" they want to have, tracing everything wrong with minorities' education to whitey's hatred, is a fragile web of oversimplifications that is glaringly open to challenge by people engaging with the real world? Or more charitably, is it that they think that whitey just can't "understand"?

But it is these people who misunderstand, if they are going to teach that for poor blacks and Latinos, "agency" is useless—that is, that the problems in question must sit static until a Second Civil Rights Revolution. This is, after all, precisely what all claims that blacks have no "agency" mean, pure and simple. If this is not spelled out, it is only because the writer feels no need to because the assumption is processed as a long-established fact. Whatever private counsel such people want to give will—as we have seen for forty years—bear no fruit.

Demonstration Case

It's a sunny spring Saturday morning at a Starbucks in Oakland in spring 2000, in the Lake Merritt neighborhood, home to people of all races and all classes. The café is full of urbane, educated, successful middle-class black people. I will never forget a conversation I had that morning. A young black man, somewhere between about nineteen and twenty-two years old, was deeply committed to helping his people, preparing himself for a life dedicated to leading his people out of the mire. He was also grimly indignant about white people in America.

In the opinion of many, the latter position is a necessary accompaniment to the former. But what about when that meant that this guy was full of statements such as, "It seems like black men that the government doesn't necessarily approve of always seem to get sick or get cancer"? Or, "I see plenty of old white men but I never see any old black men"—the idea being that the government is killing black men surreptitiously or perhaps that the psychological ravages of racism pick off black men before age sixty.

After a few months from that day, black people in the Bay Area often recognized me from the local media based on *Losing the Race*. But that day, I was still anonymous, and so this young man was not taking a certain line to remind the "black conservative" that racism still exists. These were his spontaneous thoughts, and he clearly considered them a kind of wisdom in need of airing.

But what modern America was he referring to? There has been no mysterious string of illnesses among prominent black leftists, and old black men are all over Oakland. This guy often sounded rather as if he had been reading Eldridge Cleaver's *Soul on Ice*—but without looking at its date of publication. Cleaver was writing of an America thirty-five years before that morning, and this kid had missed that America by at least fifteen years. In terms of when his mature memories began, he missed that America by a quarter of a century.

He was, as they say, a "serious brother" in his way. He wanted to make a difference. But this was a serious brother who, although clearly having all of his marbles, was casually treating genocide against blacks as an issue worthy of discussion, when it in fact has no relationship whatsoever to real life. Even he must have known this on some level: No one who genuinely wants to help black Americans lobbies Congress to demand that the Feds stop poisoning old black men, and this young man would never indulge in such an action. But this means that the source of his anger was not things he was seeing that existed outside of him but something inside of him. He was engaging not with black America, politics, or justice, but with himself. He was satisfying himself. His alienation was therapeutic.

And it lent him such a vicious antipathy to "The White Man" that I couldn't help wonder how effectively he was poised to help anyone. Since whites are kind of thick on the ground and largely control the country, one must interact with them successfully to influence leading minds and channel resources. If you can break bread with whites only while holding your nose, it will show, and most whites will choose to break their bread elsewhere. Even if you do not truly believe whites are hatching evil plots out of a Batman movie, to the extent that you are convinced that they are on some level actively opposed to you and your people, you are that much less likely to be able to think outside of a certain Stokely Carmichael box and create effective ways for blacks to thrive in an America that will always be imperfect. Enjoy Maxine Waters for the authenticity of her indignation— and then notice that nothing she has done has made a bit of difference in the ills of black Los Angeles.

Here, then, was a black man with enough of a public commitment to want to make a difference for his people, but distracted by a tradition his times allow and often encourage: presenting self-assuaging fantasy as serious engagement. In similar ways, therapeutic alienation perverts our entire discourse on how to complete the Civil Rights revolution. Hovering ever in the background, it provides a standing excuse for mediocrity. Teaching many blacks a visceral wariness of whites divorced from personal experience, it discourages promotions, as blacks under its influence often cannot form the social bonds with white superiors and coworkers that partly determine who is moved upward. Lending a sense that school is the domain of The Man, it discourages black students from embracing knowledge for its own sake, and decreases even middle-class black students' test scores. It teaches other Americans that blacks consider themselves exempt from reason (i.e., are dumb and self-righteous). It keeps us from coming together—and does nothing to help black people move forward.

An Unstoppable Meme?

If this meme plays any part in our own psychology, can we get beyond it if the self itself is memes? Susan Blackmore considers this a tough proposition, largely possible only via feats of Buddhist-style meditation few could accomplish leading their daily lives, and ultimately suggests that our only spiritual freedom will be to accept that our consciousness is a conglomeration of memes that we cannot escape.

When it comes to the therapeutic alienation meme, I disagree. There are memes that are amenable to change. An old meme, for example, was for white Americans to openly and casually treat black people as lower beings. That meme is now all but gone, and while race-based biases still exist, I assume that only an unreachable fringe of blacks truly believe that the difference between 1926 and 2006 is only, or even close to only, a matter of what one is allowed to say and do in public. There has been a profound change, and it continues apace year after year. Middle-age people uncomfortable with that statement on the basis of interactions with their peers in their lifetimes might look at what is happening among Americans about twenty years and younger today, who in short order will, after all, be themselves middle-age—that is, functioning adults setting the tone in our national fabric.

In the same way, the meme conditioning blacks to fashion whites as eternal impediments to black advancement, a malevolent race smiling politely but quietly thinking of us all as niggers, is subject to change among a healthy proportion of blacks. A proportion indeed, of course. There are blacks for whom this way of thinking is so deeply ensconced that it has become a foundation of their entire mechanism for processing the complexities of American life. As such, it is unreachable by logic. If one could somehow subject them to a brain alteration that could reconfigure their synapses such that they no longer thought this way, they would be as at sea in coping with the world around them as if we had plunked them down in a remote village in Laos.

But then there are so very many other blacks for whom this meme is less a psychological foundation than a conditioned reflex. That is, for them it is a meme less like religious faith and more like loving disco in 1978. They embrace, or maybe only genuflect to, the meme because they have seen so many people around them doing it, it can feel good, and often it's easier to just go along with it than to challenge it, since at the end of the day they have bigger fish to fry. But it is not the essence of their being, and as fashion changes, they can change along with it. The "Black By Popular Demand" T-shirt can sit in the closet along with the 45 record of "Hot Stuff."

We can listen to the counsel of eminent Claremont psychologist Mihaly Csikszentmihalyi: "If you achieve control over your mind, your desires, and your actions, you are likely to increase order around you. If you let them be controlled by genes and memes, you are missing the opportunity to be yourself."

And watch out—resist the meme that says that for black Americans, being "yourself" must mean being perpetually pissed off about the white man and filtering your politics, intellectual inquiry, and cultural inclinations through this endless and futile bitterness. That, after all, is not a unique self—it is, today, the badge of a tribe of people thinking alike. If you fall into theatrical lines, routines, and attitudes laid out forty years ago that are now followed by legions of black people in a new America as a self-medicating habit, you have made no choice as an individual—you have joined a herd. More to the point, you have signalled no commitment to helping black people left behind by falling into lines, routines, and attitudes whose only result has been making black people who don't need help feel good.

Your "black identity" must be based not on not being white, but on being something positive. Ralph Ellison had some fine counsel on this score, suggesting that we embrace "that sense of self-discovery and exaltation which is implicit in the Negro church and in good jazz. Indeed, I had found it in baseball and football games, and it turns up in almost any group activity of Afro-Americans when we're not really thinking about white folks and are simply being our own American selves."

As Csikszentmihalyi counsels, only by stepping outside of prefabricated memes will you "increase order around you"—which in terms of our subject, means lending some "order" to the lives of disadvantaged blacks, as well as sometimes our own, in the world as it is. Neither articulate complaint for its own sake, nor articulate complaint intended as a call for a fantasy America, lend order to the world. Both types of complaint are merely hallmarks of an ideology divorced from reality or sincere compassion, embraceable only by people afraid to be themselves. Real selves, after all, face the complexities of the modern world—and, mind you, they do not recruit the notion of complexity as a proxy for wordier renditions of the same old blowing the whistle on whitey.

I opened this book describing the death of Robert Parsons, a father of four who was hardly a monster, but had been working only part-time and had a minor criminal record. As I noted, his murder was one in a string at the time of dismayingly cold-blooded and senseless exterminations of young black men by other men black or brown. The string continued a few weeks later when a black teen was stabbed to death by thugs his same age who were after his friend's iPod. That episode led Bob Herbert at the *Times* to write an editorial regretting that so many young black men grow up without fathers. "Black kids would be tremendously better off if the cultural winds changed and more fathers felt the need to come home," he wrote.

"Cultural winds"—with Herbert, you can read that many ways. Herbert, as we have seen, can write openly about the "acting white" charge as a cultural issue, but then later propose that black kids fail in school because white teachers don't love them enough. So did he mean that there is a cultural problem in black America that needs to be addressed as such, or that the problem traces to white neglect and that this is What We Really Need to Be Talking About?

My sense of Herbert is that his views fall somewhere in between. But the *Times* printed two letters in response to his piece, which neatly exemplified what I wrote this book to address.

First there was the noble lefty. He thought that black men leave their children because of "limited educational expectations, diminishing employment opportunities and the still-present specter of racism in finding work."

Wrong. The writer likely thinks that white teachers have "limited educational expectations" of black students, but pretends that the students themselves do not often associate school with being "white," or have "limited educational expectations" simply because so many around them do—recall the welfare mother Katherine Newman interviews who recalls thinking, "Whatever . . . ," when her mother told her to take school seriously. Meanwhile, on "employment opportunities," these deadbeat dads are physically surrounded by coal-black immigrants who work for a living. Okay, if you didn't go to college you aren't going to wind up as a stockbroker on Wall Street—but what is so unthinkable about the concept of the black American cabdriver in New York City, for example, when they are ordinary in Washington, DC? And as to the "specter of racism," I presume that even our enlightened advocate for the downtrodden agrees that black men in the old days knew the same "specter," and yet in the 1920s in Chicago, only 15 percent of black children were born without fathers at home. Our liberal letter writer is blind to the fact that culture can take root independently of societal factors. He is mired in a Root Causes paradigm that has helped no one for forty years.

The second letter was a more Fox News affair, ruing that Herbert would be accused of "washing dirty laundry in public" as Bill Cosby has been of late, and got in that "Embarrassment is no longer an excuse to stifle the truth." This is better than Mr. "Specter of Racism," but still not quite where we need to be. Leaving it as just that black men's irresponsibility is "the truth" has an air of "nyah-nyah" about it. It implies that there is something mysteriously "wrong" with these men, that they are moral degenerates to the bone, and, well, there it is. Some call this kind of opinion racist; I am more inclined to see it as just simplistic. In any case, this kind of rhetoric will get us no further than the leftist kind. Black people are not spineless victims of a System that almost everyone else makes the best of even when poor, not white, and barely speaking English. Nor, however, are black people amoral slobs who deserve smug tsk-tsking of the sort that Victorian burghers used to level at the "lower orders."

What Herbert described is a product of a transformation in the sixties of what was thought of as normal in black communities. The economy did not cause that transformation, any more than it had created anything similar in black America before then during its endless ups and downs from the mid-1800s onward. What changed senses of shame and responsibility in black America was the countercultural shift among whites. This relates to the black deadbeat dad epidemic in the creation of welfare as a lifestyle instead of as a stopgap. For the first time, a man could leave his children and know that the government would take care of them. Big surprise—as human beings, plenty of black men did.

Thus, there is indeed "dirty laundry," but the issue is a matter of how misguided benevolence can take a people down and leave new generations unable to imagine standing on their own two feet. Robert Parsons would likely have been perplexed and irritated if a social worker had insisted that he get a forty-hour-a-week job and stick at it until all four of his children were past eighteen, and Lord Forbid if someone had told him to work *two* jobs for sixty or seventy hours a week since there were, after all, four children. He never knew a context where standing on your own two feet like that was the norm.

And then standing on one's own two feet can also be elusive for more fortunate blacks. A black film industry executive says the following in 2005:

> I don't think much has changed for black films. They still think that we're monolithic, and mostly the films are limited to urban themes and comedy . . . when a black movie goes outside the box and does well, Hollywood doesn't follow up on it.

Well. Earlier that very year, *Hitch, Guess Who, Coach Carter, Diary of a Mad Black Woman*, and *Are We There Yet?* had been playing nationwide *at the same time*. The first three depicted not an "urban" "monolithic" black community but stable, middle-class folk. Plus—*Diary of a Mad Black Woman* split the difference between 'hood and buppie: Tyler Perry's Madea character lives in the ghetto, but in the film and in Perry's popular traveling plays with the character, successful blacks are also part of the mix and not dismissed as inauthentic. In any case, how is a film that brings back Cicely Tyson "urban" or "monolithic"? A few months before, Jamie Foxx and Morgan Freeman had won Oscars, and neither *Ray* nor *Million Dollar Baby* were "urban" (i.e., hip-hop-inflected à la post-1990) or "monolithic" in the slightest. Less than a year before our executive pronounced, Don Cheadle and Sophie Okonedo had starred in the decidedly non-"monolithic" *Hotel Rwanda* and both were nominated for Oscars. As for Hollywood not following up on black film hits as if racism trumps capitalism, when *Barbershop* went "outside the box" and did smashingly well in 2002, Hollywood made a sequel and then even a riskier gynocentric "threequel," *Beauty Shop*, with Queen Latifah, and a *Barbershop* television sitcom premiered in the fall of 2005. Meanwhile, just when the executive said this, the splashy mainstream blockbuster *The Fantastic Four* was opening, directed by the black man who had directed *Barbershop*, even though his film after *Barbershop* did not quite ring the bell. Hollywood doesn't follow up?

This man, too, is hindered by history from standing on his own two feet. He is willfully ignoring the heartening progress under his very nose because endlessly rehearsing the same old anti-whitey theatrics gives him a sense of comfort. He is part of a herd nurturing a predictable and eternally *self-affirming* ideology. He affirms himself via the presumed affirmation of that herd, not via affirmation of himself alone. He stays with that herd because he would not quite know how to affirm his sense of self-worth outside of a herd, as just an individual, himself, engaging with the complexities of the world as it actually is. This is not surprising given the history of his people. However, the fact remains that the worldview of people like this—with the injustices of history resoundingly acknowledged, regretted, and even reviled—does not correspond to current reality. I have ventured an argument as to why, and I do not mean it as a dismissive one. But I do believe that a truly progressive orientation toward black America must refrain from treating views like this as valuable counsel.

The view that what black America needs is for whites from the suburbs to the Capitol to face their inner racism and learn of remnant racial discrepancies is not complex. Nor is it even accurate, as our pre–Civil Rights ancestors knew so well. It is performance, by people who made the best of themselves with neither of those things even in the cards. But other black people need help now. As they sit mired in what American cultural history did to them, basic morality leaves no room for luckier blacks to nurture a self-indulgent tic passing as politics, thought, and compassion.

Forty years ago this same tic distracted white and black America into turning black communities across the nation into hells on earth. We're still living with the consequences. Under the influence of this tic, instead of overcoming, we condemn ourselves to merely undergoing. We must take a deep breath, rub our eyes, put our shoulders back, and let this tic go—free at last.

Appendix

I will first give a quick overview of the articles that make points of similar nature to those in *American Journal of Sociology*.

In 1990, Douglas Massey contributed another "American Apartheid Jr." article, teaching that middle-class blacks get only so far from the ghetto, leaving segregation unabated, and four years later was the main author for a paper in the journal on a similar theme. Over ten years, not one but two articles recapitulated Lincoln Quillian's point in his 1996 *American Journal of Sociology* article that whites continue to resist affirmative action claiming that individual effort is key. We learned more about lynching, including that blacks were more likely to leave counties where there had been more of it (would we expect different?). We learned again that black women do not have enough men to choose from as marriage partners and that single parenthood was something blacks knew long before the sixties. Black schools in the old South were usually substandard. No fewer than three studies explored that poverty and bad role models make it more likely that a black girl will get pregnant; another one showed that a chaotic home environment has a way of making it harder to maintain good grades even if one has made progress. There is a wage gap between blacks and whites. Race riots are more likely with interracial contact and spread "copycat" fashion from city to city. Children are aware of race early. People who feel racially alienated are more likely to feel threatened by outside groups A hard background makes it less likely for black women to work. Violent resistance can slow the progress of political movements. It's hardly cake for middle-class blacks to escape the ghetto. Again, robbery makes whites, of all things, move. The Rodney King rioters were motivated by pressure from immigrant groups. Whites get nervous when there are too many blacks in the neighborhood. And then, brace yourself—inequality persists.

But because *American Sociological Review* happened to run more articles on black issues during these ten years than *American Journal of Sociology*, naturally there were several articles that made points that stood out especially from the body of the ones in that latter journal. These were almost all variations on bad news.

On black history, Jill Quadagno covered the Family Assistance Plan I recounted in Chapter Four, but assailed its focus on working for a living as threatening to "reinstate male dominance over women in the household and retain white dominance over blacks in the labor market." In another article, Quadagno could not even see good news in Civil Rights activists cracking racist discrimination in unions, since it aroused blinkered political resistance: "Affirmative action has initiated its own dialectic, a political backlash that threatens to halt the progress made and eliminate the program underlying that progress." Aldon D. Morris observed that the Birmingham protests were successful because they attracted violent resistance from whites that moved viewers. Bernice A. Pescosolido, Elizabeth Grauerholz, and Melissa A. Milkie argued that the depiction of blacks in picture books since the mid-twentieth century has encouraged racism. Susan Olzak and Elizabeth West recounted that early black newspapers encountered racist hostility. Nancy S. Landale and Stewart A. Tolnay documented that when blacks knew little but sharecropper tenancy, they tended to marry earlier because of limited opportunities for job advancement.

Then there was the article by Gary LaFree and Kriss A. Drass that I mentioned in Chapter Three on the black middle-class exodus issue, which showed that black crimes go up with numbers of affluent blacks. Also already covered in this book, in Chapter Six, was Joe Feagin's article version of Ellis Cose's *The Rage of a Privileged Class*.

Stanley Lieberson and Kelly S. Mikelson came up with an analysis that saw doomsday even in the rise of African-sounding names among blacks (the Shiniqua and LaKweeshas), since even these are not precisely the names parents would give their children in Angola, but reflect in part the norms of English. Hence, a tragedy: "Their imagination, which has burst away from using 'standard' names, is still bounded by cultural practices," this being a "clash" between traditions.

On education, George Farkas, Robert P. Grobe, Daniel Sheehan, and Yuan Shuan assailed white teachers as "gatekeepers" for maintaining mainstream scholarly standards in "general skills, habits, and styles" that, apparently, give short shrift to poor black kids, although just how the alternate "skills, habits, and styles" would lend the same educational skills as white kids' orientations is unclear. James W. Ainsworth-Darnell and Douglas B. Downey proposed to show that black teens' propensities for treating scholarly diligence as "acting white" does not affect their scholarly performance. They based their analysis partly on asking black kids whether they think it is "white" to do well in school, suddenly leaving aside something sociologists are well aware of when it comes to asking whites whether they are racist: that there is a difference between the overt and the covert that direct questioning cannot reveal. Unsurprisingly they found black kids saying that they value education—while sweeping under the rug their finding that black students spend less time on homework. Doris R. Entwisle and Karl L. Alexander reinforced the idea that the difference between *ain't* and *isn't* or *I be goin' to school every Sunday* and *I go to school every Sunday* is why black students do not learn as quickly as white ones.

George S. Bridges and Sara Steen told us that the criminal justice system is biased against young black men once they come before the court having broken the law. Stephen Petterson told us that it is not true that black men are less willing to work, since when asked about it, they cite themselves as worth higher wages than what they settle for if they do work. Craig Zwerling and Hilary Silver claimed that blacks get fired from government jobs at higher rates than whites, and deemed racism as a likely cause, but with no engagement with the testimonials from white employers that a noble literature provides, such as in William Julius Wilson's work as treated in Chapter Four. David J. Eggebeen and Daniel T. Lichter noted that poverty correlates with single-head families—but dutifully observed, "Our results should not deflect attention away from the problems of persistent racial and gender inequality and employment hardship that may undermine family stability and exacerbate the child poverty problem in America."

Then Lawrence Bobo and James R. Kluegel were worried that whites prefer policies aimed at enhancing opportunity over ones aimed at equality of outcomes. For those of us who see this as just what we should want, Bobo and Kluegel feel that we are misled: "This research also points to the need to address the denial of contemporary racial discrimination and sense of group self-interest prevalent among whites if policies addressing persistent racial inequalities are to be pursued." Amy Binder decides that the reason the media have been easier on heavy metal than rap is racism.

And Donald Tomaskovic-Devey and Vincent J. Roscigno explore the strangely specific issue as to whether it is the elite or the working-class whites who benefit most from racial discrimination, sounding like Old Leftists smoking their way through long nights of argument about a revolution that never came—and never will.

Notes

Introduction

Black middle class: William Frey, "Revival." *American Demographics* (Web journal), October 1, 2003.

Interracial marriage: United States Census, 2002.

Crouch: Stanley Crouch, *The All-American Skin Game, or, the Decoy of Race* (New York: Vintage Books, 1995), 69.

"Robert Parsons": (I have changed the victim's name to protect the privacy of his family.) Information compiled from: Thomas J. Lueck and Ann Farmer, "Aspiring Hip-Hop Artist Killed at Brooklyn Barbecue." The *New York Times*, June 20, 2005; Jamie Schram and Tom Namako, "B'klyn Dad Shot Dead at Cookout." The *New York Post*, June 20, 2005; Robert F. Moore, "Dad Shot After Cookout." The *New York Daily News*, June 20, 2005; Daryl Khan, "Cops: B'klyn Father Knew Attacker." *Newsday*, June 20, 2005; New York Desk, the *New York Sun*, June 20, 2005.

poverty and race statistics in Crown Heights districts: United States Census, 2000.

substance abuse in Crown Heights: Eric Gershon, "Hooked: Drug Addiction and Crime in New York." Columbia University Graduate School of Journalism Web site.

Middle School 320: Clyde Haberman, "Role Models for the Future at School 320." The *New York Times*, April 15, 1997; www.emsc.nysed.gov/nyc/VPTAC/schools/ch85_sch.htm

Other murders: Abeer Allam, "Slain Boy's Family Grieves as Suspect, 13, is Charged." The *New York Times*, June 18, 2005; Thomas J. Lueck, "Manhattan: Man Shot at Restaurant." The *New York Times* (Metro Briefing section), June 20, 2005.

Robinson book: Randall Robinson, *The Debt: What America Owes to Blacks* (New York: Dutton, 2000).

University of Virginia episode: Kara Rowland, "Casteen Reacts to U. Va. Employee's Remarks." *The Cavalier Daily*, November 21, 2003; Jason Amirhadji, "Protestors Object to Employee's Comment." The *Cavalier Daily*, November 24, 2003.

Fifteen percent of births: St. Clair Drake and Horace R. Cayton, *Black Metropolis: A Study of Negro Life in a Northern City* (New York: Harcourt, Brace and Co., 1945), 589–90.

reading and math scores at Middle School 320: Clyde Haberman, "Role Models for the Future at School 320." The *New York Times*, April 15, 1997; Harold Levy, "A $13 Billion Disaster." The *New York Post*, March 16, 2001.

Dunbar: Thomas Sowell, "Patterns of Black Excellence." *The Public Interest* 43: 26–58 (1976), 51; or, more accessibly at this writing, Thomas Sowell, *Black Rednecks and White Liberals* (San Francisco: Encounter Books, 2005), 203–15.

dancers' comments: Guy Trebay, "The Clowning, Wilding-Out Battle Dancers of South Central L.A." The *New York Times Magazine*, June 19, 2005; Andrew Jacobs, "What Spins Around Comes Around: Break Dancing Makes Comeback, and Offers an Escape. The *New York Times*, August 5, 2004.

Byron Lee's murder: "In a City Numbed by Violence, the Death of a Young Boy Stirs Anguish," the *New York Times*, October 15, 2004.

Chapter One

Kain article: John Kain. "Housing Segregation, Negro Employment, and Metropolitan Decentralization." *Quarterly Journal of Economics* 82: 175–97 (1968).

Wilson on factory relocation: William Julius Wilson, *When Work Disappears: The World of the New Urban Poor* (New York: Vintage Books, 1996). Some signature articles representing the thesis include James Johnson and Melvin Oliver, "Structural Changes in the U.S. Economy and Black Male Joblessness: a Reassessment." *Urban Labor Markets*, ed. by G. Peterson and W. Vroman, 113–47 (Washington, DC: Urban Institute Press, 1992); John Bound and Harry Holzer, "Industrial Shifts, Skills Levels, and the Labor Market for White and Black Men." *Review of Economics and Statistics* 75: 387–96 (1993); and especially prominently, various works by John Kasarda including John Kasarda, "Industrial Restructuring and the Changing Location of Jobs." *State of the Union* (*Vol. I: Economic Trends*), ed. by Reynolds Farley, 215–67 (New York: Russell Sage Foundation, 1995). Wilson on black middle-class exodus: most summarily, *The Truly Disadvantaged*, 58–62.

Marable: Manning Marable, *The Great Wells of Democracy: The Meaning of Race in American Life* (New York: Basic Books, 2002), 46.

Anderson: Elijah Anderson, *Streetwise: Race, Class, and Change in an Urban Community* (Chicago: University of Chicago Press, 1990), p. 3.

Hollenback quote: Deborah Mathis, *Yet a Stranger: Why Black Americans Still Don't Feel at Home* (New York: Warner Books, 2002), 48.

Gates: Henry Louis Gates Jr., "Getting to Average." The *New York Times*, September 26, 2004.

Massey and Denton: Douglas S. Massey and Nancy A. Denton, *American Apartheid: Segregation and the Making of the Underclass* (Cambridge: Harvard University Press, 1993).

Massey and Denton: Douglas S. Massey and Nancy A. Denton, *American Apartheid: Segregation and the Making of the Underclass* (Cambridge, MA: Harvard University Press, 1993), 99–108.

black teen marriage: Christopher Jencks, *Rethinking Social Policy: Race, Poverty, and the Underclass* (Cambridge, MA: Harvard University Press, 1992), 131–2.

Shelby Steele: Shelby Steele, *A Dream Deferred: The Second Betrayal of Black Freedom in America* (New York: HarperCollins, 1998), 28.

canary metaphor: Lani Guinier and Gerald Torres, *The Miner's Canary: Enlisting Race, Resisting Power, Transforming Democracy* (Cambridge: Harvard University Press, 2003).

skeptics regarding "underclass": A typical example is Ishmael Reed, as in various comments in: Ishmael Reed, *Another Day at the Front: Dispatches from the Race War* (New York: Basic Books, 2003).

underclass definition: William Julius Wilson, *The Truly Disadvantaged: The Inner City, the Underclass, and Public Policy* (Chicago: University of Chicago Press, 1987), 7, 19.

old heads: Elijah Anderson, *Streetwise: Race, Class, and Change in an Urban Community* (Chicago: University of Chicago Press, 1990).

Goldwyn and *Dead End*: A. Scott Berg, *Goldwyn: A Biography* (New York: Alfred A. Knopf, 1989), 292–3.

bow to conventional culture: Massey & Denton, 175.

Cleveland comment: Kenneth L. Kusmer, *A Ghetto Takes Shape: Black Cleveland, 1870–1930* (Urbana: University of Illinois Press, 1976), 111.

Chiacago comment: St. Clair Drake and Horace R. Cayton, *Black Metropolis: A Study of Negro Life in a Northern City* (New York: Harcourt, Brace and Co., 1945), 48.

Detroit comment: Thomas J. Sugrue, *The Origins of the Urban Crisis: Race and Inequality in Postwar Detroit* (Princeton: Princeton University Press, 1996), 206.

Bronzeville achievements: Drake & Cayton; pp. 46–83 contain much indicative data, but there is valuable information throughout.

Bronzeville tenements: Alan Ehrenhalt, *The Lost City: Discovering the Forgotten Virtues of Community in the Chicago of the 1950s* (New York: Basic Books, 1995), 145.

black underworld in Bronzeville: Richard Wright, *12 Million Black Voices* (New York: Thunder's Mouth Press, 2003), 110–1, 135–6; Drake & Cayton, 570, 575, 584, 589, 595–99.

posterity comment: Ehrenhalt, 141.

"bunch of shacks": Ehrenhalt, 140.

flying squad: Ehrenhalt, 142.

employment rates in Bronzeville: William Julius Wilson, *When Work Disappears: The World of the New Urban Poor* (New York: Vintage Books, 1996), 19.

marriage rates in Bronzeville: Drake & Cayton, 584.

"quiet ghetto": Kusmer, 233.

corner men and employment: Elliott Liebow, *Tally's Corner: A Study of Negro Street-corner Men* (Boston: Little, Brown and Co., 1967), 34, 219.

Sea Cat: Liebow, 48.

corner men and marriage: Liebow, 103.

corner men and self-image: Liebow, 222.

corner men from South: Liebow, 74.

Hannerz portrait: Ulf Hannerz, *Soulside: Inquiries into Ghetto Culture and Community* (New York: Columbia University Press, 1969).

Jelly's scene: Elijah Anderson, *A Place on the Corner* (Chicago: University of Chicago Press, 1978), 2.

quote from "regular": Anderson 1978, 61.

"hoodlum" as derogatory: Anderson, 146.

"down" among Jelly's men: Anderson, 200–6.

killed for a gaze: Elijah Anderson, "The Code of the Streets." *The Atlantic Monthly*, May 1994.

refrigerator episode: Elijah Anderson, *Streetwise: Race, Class, and Change in an Urban Community* (Chicago: University of Chicago Press, 1990), 78.

knife click: Lee Rainwater, *Behind Ghetto Walls: Black Families in a Federal Slum* (Chicago: Aldine, 1970), 19.

residents' complaints: Rainwater, 10–12.

girls unconcerned with out-of-wedlock pregnancy: Rainwater, 310.

Bronzeville attitudes toward out-of-wedlock births: Drake & Cayton, 590.

girls with different view than above ones: Rainwater, 53–56.

Coolidge's critical comments: Rainwater, 19–20.

Coolidge caught between old and new ideology: Rainwater, 43–46.

Pruitt-Igoe and Newman: Oscar Newman, *Architectural Design for Crime Prevention* (U.S. Department of Justice: Law Enforcement Assistance Administration / National Institute of Law Enforcement and Criminal Justice, 1971), 1.

Joe's essay: Rainwater, 293.

Dyson: Michael Eric Dyson, "We Never Were What We Used to Be: Black Youth, Pop Culture, and the Politics of Nostalgia," *The Michael Eric Dyson Reader* (New York: Basic Civitas Books, 2004), 422–23.

Ellison: Ralph Ellison, "Remembering Jimmy," *The Collected Essays of Ralph Ellison*, ed. by John F. Callahan (New York: The Modern Library, 2003), 273–74.

Chapter Two

Black Expo, 1971: *The Indianapolis Star*, June 21, 1971 and June 26, 1971.

SoulFest shooting: *The Indianapolis Star*, June 11, 1993.

Lynn Ford: *The Indianapolis Star*, July 18, 1998.

SoulFest shooting in 1998: indystar.com/library/factfiles/organizations/black_expo/black_expo.html

general facts on black Indianapolis pre–World War II: from Emma Lou Thornbrough, *Since Emancipation: A Short History of Indiana Negroes, 1863–1963* (Indiana Division American Negro Emancipation Centennial Authority, 1964); Emma Lou Thornbrough, *Indiana Blacks in the Twentieth Century* (Bloomington: Indiana University Press, 2000); Richard B. Pierce II, *Beneath the Surface: African-American Community Life in Indianapolis, 1945–70*. University of Indiana PhD dissertation, 1996.

Recorder's list of black businesses: *The Indianapolis Recorder*, December 21, 1901.

Recorder's list of affluent blacks: *The Indianapolis Recorder*, June 21, 1902. (Thornbrough 2000 gives the date as June 27, but this was apparently a misprint.)

segregation of schools: Pierce, 25.

residential segregation: Pierce, 133–74.

The Klan in Indianapolis: Pierce 18, 27, 74–78; also indystar.com/library/factfiles/history/black_history/stories/1999_1223; indystar.com/library/factfiles/history/black_history/stories/1999_0404

1930 lynching: Thornbrough 2000, 67–69.

blacks in low-level jobs: Pierce 176–250, Thornbrough 2000.

black employment rates in 1940: Pierce, 188.

"Second Great Migration": Shane Davies and Gary Fowler, "The Disadvantaged Urban Migrant in Indianapolis." *Economic Geography* 48: 153–67 (1972).

factory location and transportation issues: Shane Davies and Melvin Albaum, "Mobility Problems of the Poor in Indianapolis." *Geographical Perspectives on American Poverty*, ed. by Richard Peet, 67–86 (1972). Worcester, MA: Antipode Monographs in Social Geography.

1969 riot: reconstructed from the following accounts: in *The Indianapolis Star*, "Sniper Hunted, 20 Arrested on Indiana Avenue," June 7, 1969; "City is Calm, Churchill Says," June 8, 1969; "Black Youth Leader Given Credit for Restoring Calm in Fracas," June 9, 1969; "Won't Tolerate Looting, Arson, Says Churchill," June 10, 1969; "Police Overtime in Disturbances Held to One Day," June 12, 1969; and the June 14, 1969 and July 5, 1969 issues of the weekly *Indianapolis Recorder*.

"Snooky" Hendricks: presence at the riot: *The Indianapolis Recorder*, June 14, 1969; other information from interviews with Indianapolis residents.

Mattie Coney: *The National Review*, October 22, 1968; interviews with Indianapolis residents. "Oh, you would have liked her," one interviewee told me. He was correct.

Margaret Moore: *Time*, June 23, 1967.

young peacemakers: "Black Youth Leader Given Credit for Restoring Calm in Fracas," *The Indianapolis Star*, June 9, 1969.

Fred Crawford: Thornbrough 2000, 166.

Ramsey: Andrew W. Ramsey, "A Voice from the Gallery," *The Indianapolis Recorder*, June 12, 1971.

Grover C. Hall: Grover C. Hall, "Some Truths Emerge On Rereading a Book," *The Indianapolis Star*, June 10, 1969.

housing projects 96 percent black: Thornbrough 2000, 204.

Indianapolis Commission on African-American Males data: *www.icaam.org/main-links/about/more_history*; Thornbrough 2000, 223–24.

violence in black neighborhoods: Edmund F. McGarrell, Steven Chermak, Alexander Weiss, *Reducing Gun Violence: Evaluation of the Indianapolis Police Department's Directed Patrol Project* (Hudson Institute: Crime Control Policy Center, 2002).

infant mortality: Thornbrough 2000, 205.

Better Indianapolis League letter: indystar.com/library/factfiles/history/black_history/attucks

Afrocentrism in schools: Thornbrough 2000, 228.

student test scores: Michael B. Katz, *The Price of Citizenship: Redefining the American Welfare State* (New York: Metropolitan Books, 2001), 119.

"lack of black male adult participation": the Web site of the Indiana Family and Social Services Administration, in.gov/fssa/icssbm/action

data on manufacturing facilities: U.S. Bureau of the Census, *County and City Data Book, 1967* (A Statistical Abstract Supplement) (US Government Printing Office, Washington DC, 1967), 102–13; U.S. Bureau of the Census, *County and City Data Book, 1972* (A Statistical Abstract Supplement) (US Government Printing Office, Washington DC, 1973), 150–60; U.S. Bureau of the Census, *County and City Data Book, 1977* (A Statistical Abstract Supplement) (US Government Printing Office, Washington DC, 1978), 150–61; U.S. Bureau of the Census, *County and City Data Book, 1983* (A Statistical Abstract Supplement) (US Government Printing Office, Washington DC, 1983), 158–71; U.S. Bureau of the Census, *County and City Data Book, 1988* (A Statistical Abstract Supplement) (US Government Printing Office, Washington DC, 1988), 154.

3.2 miles: Davies & Albaum.

Indianapolis factories in the fifties: Insurance maps of Indianapolis, Indiana. (New York: Sanborn Map Company, 1956.) (Vols. I, Ia, II, III, IIIa, IV, IVa, V, Va, VI.)

Indianapolis factories today: *Indianapolis, Indiana* (Skokie, IL: Rand McNally, 2004).

Blacks less likely to work at distant factories: Stephen Arnold Wandner, *Racial Pattern of Employment in Indianapolis: The Implications for Fair Employment Practices*. University of Indiana PhD dissertation, 1972, 64–73.

Blacks and cars: Davies & Albaum; Wandner, 73–75.

Crawford county: monitor.cbpa.louisville.edu/region/profiles/crawford.pdf

Brookins's commute: Pierce, 200.

"job information," "conception of distance"—Davies & Albaum.

Recorder want ads: those mentioned are from *The Indianapolis Recorder*, May 10, 1969,

May 17, 1969, April 24, 1971, May 1, 1971, June 13, 1971, September 4, 1971, and October 2, 1971.

Black employment in 1971: *The Indianapolis Recorder*, July 3, 1971.

Ruegamer: in her epilogue to Emma Lou Thornbrough, *Indiana Blacks in the Twentieth Century* (Bloomington: Indiana University Press, 2000), 232.

Rosier: Katherine Brown Rosier, *Mothering Inner-City Children: The Early School Years* (New Brunswick, NJ: Rutgers University Press, 2000).

extent of factory departures in late sixties: Davies & Albaum.

"office after office": Andrew Ramsey, "A Voice from the Gallery," *Indianapolis Recorder*, June 26, 1971.

busing: Thornbrough 2000, 154–60.

anti-discrimination business statutes: Thornbrough 2000: 181.

black business successes: Thornbrough 2000: 199.

most blacks left the ghetto: Thornbrough 2000, 220.

racial bias among realtors: Thornbrough 2000, 183.

Butler-Tarkington: Pierce, 164–69.

Detroit commutes: Kevin Boyle, *Arc of Justice* (New York: Henry Holt & Co., 2004), 111.

Chicago interviewee: William Julius Wilson, *When Work Disappears: The World of the New Urban Poor* (New York: Vintage Books, 1996), 39.

Lockefield housing project: Pierce, 145–6.

"Dignity Unlimited": from the *Indianapolis Star*'s fine black history Web site, at indystar.com/library/factfiles/history/black_history/index.html#king

Russell Lane: Pierce, 176–77.

Linthecome: Thornbrough 2000, 231.

Mmoja Ajabu: *The Indianapolis Star*, March 6, 1993; June 2, 1993.

tensions with police: Thornbrough 2000, 224–25.

Klan rally: *The Indianapolis Star*, January 10, 1999.

welfare concentrated in city center: Henry W. Bullamore, "Three Types of Poverty in Metropolitan Indianapolis." *Geographical Review* 64: 536–56 (1974).

data on AFDC recipiency, population by race, and poverty: U.S. Bureau of the Census, *County and City Data Book, 1967* (A Statistical Abstract Supplement) (US Government Printing Office, Washington DC, 1967), 102–13; U.S. Bureau of the Census, *County and City Data Book, 1972* (A Statistical Abstract Supplement) (US Government Printing Office, Washington DC, 1973), 150–60; U.S. Bureau of the Census, *County and City Data Book, 1977* (A Statistical Abstract Supplement) (US Government Printing Office, Washington DC, 1978), 150–61.

black employment after World War II: Pierce, 206, 214, 220–23; Thornbrough 1964, 76–81; Thornbrough 2000, 128–32.

blacks in city government jobs: Thornbrough 2000, 181.

Ninety-three percent of black men working: Pierce, 189.

late sixties economy and blacks: Thornbrough 1964: 76–81, Pierce 214.

welfare payments parsimonious: *The Indianapolis Recorder*, July 3, 1971.

welfare payments versus wages: Stephen Goldsmith, *The Twenty-first Century City: Resurrecting Urban America* (Lanham, MD: Rowman & Littlefield, 1999), 98.

blacks and charity in early black Indianapolis: Earline Rae Ferguson, *A Community Affair: African-American Women's Club Work in Indianapolis, 1879–1917.* (University of Indiana PhD dissertation, 1997).

work-chary person: Goldsmith, 99–100.

Bronzeville tenements: Alan Ehrenhalt, *The Lost City: Discovering the Forgotten Virtues of Community in the Chicago of the 1950s* (New York: Basic Books, 1995), 145.

bureacratic inertia: Goldsmith, 104; interview with Goldsmith.

"spatial mismatch": most summarily, John Kasarda, "Industrial Restructuring and the Changing Location of Jobs." *State of the Union* (*Vol. I: Economic Trends*), ed. by Reynolds Farley, 215–67. (New York: Russell Sage Foundation, 1995.)

"cold turkey": Deborah Mathis, *Yet a Stranger: Why Black Americans Still Don't Feel at Home* (New York: Warner Books, 2002), 169.

Chapter Three

Sugrue photo: Thomas J. Sugrue, *The Origins of the Urban Crisis: Race and Inequality in Postwar Detroit* (Princeton: Princeton University Press, 1996), 8.

Dyson: Michael Eric Dyson, *Holler If You Hear Me: Searching for Tupac Shakur* (New York: Basic Books, 2001), p. 192.

studies of deindustrialization: Harry Holzer and Wayne Vroman, "Mismatches in the Urban Labor Market." *Urban Labor Markets and Job Opportunity*, ed. by George E. Peterson and Wayne Vroman, 81–112 (Washington, DC: The Urban Institute, 1991); James H. Johnson and Melvin L. Oliver, "Structural Changes in the U.S. Economy and Black Male Joblessness: a Reassessment." *Urban Labor Markets and Job Opportunity*, ed. by George E. Peterson and Wayne Vroman, 113–14 (Washington, DC: The Urban Institute, 1991).

Loury quote: Glenn Loury, "Are Jobs the Solution?" (Review of *When Work Disappears: The World of the New Urban Poor*, by William Julius Wilson) *Wilson Quarterly*, Autumn 1996, 91–92.

Anderson quotes: Elijah Anderson, *Streetwise: Race, Class, and Change in an Urban Community* (Chicago: University of Chicago Press, 1990), 104, 110, 204.

Newman interviewee: Katherine S. Newman, *No Shame in My Game* (New York: Vintage Books, 1999), 99–100.

unemployment and crime in Detroit after factory closings: Sugrue, 144, 205.

Sugrue's conclusion: Sugrue, 271.

Gerald Reynolds: the *New York Times*, December 10, 2004.

housing discrimination surveys: Douglas S. Massey and Nancy A. Denton, *American Apartheid: Segregation and the Making of the Underclass* (Cambridge, MA: Harvard University Press, 1993), 99–108.

"cards stacked against them": Massey & Denton, 109.

increase in black suburbanites: Stephan Thernstrom and Abigail Thernstrom, *America in Black and White: One Nation, Indivisible* (New York: Simon & Schuster, 1997), 212.

decrease in number of blacks in all-black neighborhoods: Thernstrom & Thernstrom, 216.

studies on decline in residential segregation: Paul A. Jargowsky, "Take the Money and Run: Economic Segregation in U.S. Metropolitan Areas." *American Sociological Review* 61: 984–98 (1996); Reynolds Farley and William H. Frey. "Changes in the Segregation of Whites from Blacks During the 1980s: Small Steps Toward a More Integrated Society." *American Sociological Review* 59: 23–45 (1994).

Patterson: Orlando Patterson, *The Ordeal of Integration: Progress and Resentment in America's "Racial" Crisis* (Washington, DC: Civitas/Counterpoint, 1997), 47.

voluntary segregation: Reynolds Farley, Howard Schuman, Suzanne Bianchi, Diane

Colasanto, and Shirley Hatchett, "Chocolate City, Vanilla Suburbs: Will the Trends Toward Racially Separate Communities Continue?" *Social Science Research* 7: 319–44 (1978).

Gallup survey: Patterson, 44.

Farley study: Reynolds Farley, Charlotte Steeh, Maria Krysan, Tara Jackson, and Keith Reeves, "Stereotypes and Segregation: Neighborhoods in the Detroit Area." *American Journal of Sociology* 100: 750–80 (1994).

white tipping point in several cities: Massey & Denton, 93.

Massey and Denton passage: Massey & Denton, 118.

Massey article: Douglas S. Massey, "American Apartheid: Segregation and the Making of the Underclass." *American Journal of Sociology* 96: 329–57 (1990).

out-of-wedlock births among blacks: Thernstrom & Thernstrom, 240.

Steele: Shelby Steele, *A Dream Deferred: The Second Betrayal of Black Freedom in America* (New York: HarperCollins, 1998), 24.

Little Village vs. North Lawndale: Massey & Denton, 137.

racial composition of Compton and Watts: 2000 Census data of City of Los Angeles Population.

academics' "fear": Patterson, 48.

quote on exodus: Elijah Anderson, *Streetwise: Race, Class, and Change in an Urban Community* (Chicago: University of Chicago Press, 1990), 2–3.

perceptive youngster: *The Truly Disadvantaged: The Inner City, the Underclass, and Public Policy* (Chicago: University of Chicago Press, 1987), 56.

"out-migration" quote: Massey & Denton, 7.

Ishmael Reed, *Another Day at the Front: Dispatches from the Race War* (New York: Basic Books, 2003), 168.

community organizations among poor blacks: examples in book-length sources include descriptions of black social organizations in Alan Ehrenhalt, *The Lost City: Discovering the Forgotten Virtues of Community in the Chicago of the 1950s* (New York: Basic Books, 1995) and Kenneth L. Kusmer, *A Ghetto Takes Shape: Black Cleveland, 1870–1930* (Urbana: University of Illinois Press, 1976), 97–8; see also *The Indianapolis Recorder*, December 21, 1901, where a list of black-owned businesses is accompanied by an exhaustive list of the community's social organizations.

Newman quote: Katherine S. Newman, *No Shame in My Game* (New York: Vintage Books, 1999), 172.

LaFree and Drass study: Gary LaFree and Kriss A. Drass, "The Effect of Changes in Intraracial Income Inequality and Educational Attainment on Changes in Arrest Rates for African Americans and Whites, 1957–1990." *American Sociological Review* 61: 614–34 (1996).

access to job information: Massey & Denton, 166.

sho' nuff niggaz: Geneva Smitherman, *Talkin That Talk: Language, Culture and Education in African America* (New York: Routledge, 2000), 61.

housing project quote: Glenn Loury, "Race and Inequality: an Exchange." *First Things*, May 2002, 38.

number of urban renewal projects: Mindy Thompson Fullilove, *Root Shock: How Tearing Up City Neighborhoods Hurts America, and What We Can Do About It* (New York: Ballantine, 2004), 4.

number of public housing units: Fullilove, 68–69.

"root shock" analysis: Fullilove 14, 99, 124.

manufacturing jobs versus urban renewal: Fullilove, 46.

Cashin: Sheryll Cashin, *The Failures of Integration: How Race and Class are Undermining the American Dream* (New York: Public Affairs, 2004), 117.

Newman: Oscar Newman, *Defensible Space: Crime Prevention Through Urban Design* (New York: Macmillan, 1972).

"experience the space outside": Oscar Newman, *Architectural Design for Crime Prevention* (U.S. Department of Justice: Law Enforcement Assistance Administration / National Institute of Law Enforcement and Criminal Justice, 1971), 24.

Cabrini-Green: P. J. Huffstutter, "It's Bleak But It's Home." The *Los Angeles Times*, March 1, 2005.

1965 change in rules: Newman (1972), 188.

Rosen Apartments: Newman (1972), 193.

"howl of amputation": Fullilove, 224.

Hill District description: Fullilove, 61.

Lodge Freeway: Sugrue, 48.

Highways in Sunset Park and East Tremont: Robert A. Caro, *The Power Broker: Robert Moses and the Fall of New York* (New York: Vintage Books, 1974), 520–25, 850–94.

black gangstas in the old days: a useful source between two covers is: Rufus Schatzberg, *Black Organized Crime in Harlem, 1920–30* (New York: Garland, 1993).

studies of 1960s ghettos: Lee Rainwater, *Behind Ghetto Walls: Black Families in a Federal Slum* (Chicago: Aldine, 1970); Ulf Hannerz, *Soulside: Inquiries into Ghetto Culture and Community* (New York: Columbia University Press, 1969).

Good Times episodes: "JJ's Fiancée" (Part One), January 6, 1976;, "JJ's Fiancée" (Part Two), January 13, 1976.

Nelson George on heroin: Nelson George, *Hip Hop America* (New York: Penguin Books, 1998), 37–38.

mother's comment on her neighborhood: Jason DeParle, *American Dream: Three Women, Ten Kids, and Nation's Drive to End Welfare* (New York: Viking, 2004), 48.

Anderson quotes: Elijah Anderson, *Streetwise: Race, Class, and Change in an Urban Community* (Chicago: University of Chicago Press, 1990), 66.

Jencks on culture: Jencks, 18.

Jencks on blame: Jencks, 141.

women moving to Wisconsin: DeParle, 66–67.

Chapter Four

tighter restrictions on blacks: Robert C. Lieberman, *Shifting the Color Line: Race and the American Welfare State* (Cambridge: Harvard University Press, 1998), 120, 127–28.

Mother's Pensions: Jason DeParle, *American Dream: Three Women, Ten Kids, and Nation's Drive to End Welfare* (New York: Viking, 2004), 92–93.

black women's work in Bronzeville: Richard Wright, *12 Million Black Voices* (New York: Thunder's Mouth Press, 2003), 135.

welfare norms in Bronzeville: St. Clair Drake and Horace R. Cayton, *Black Metropolis: A Study of Negro Life in a Northern City* (New York: Harcourt, Brace and Co., 1945), 590.

Rainwater on welfare: Lee Rainwater, *Behind Ghetto Walls: Black Families in a Federal Slum* (Chicago: Aldine, 1970); an example of such a comment is on p. 408.

rise in welfare recipiency: Michael B. Katz, *The Price of Citizenship: Redefining the American Welfare State* (New York: Metropolitan Books, 2001), 5.

Forty-three percent were black: Lieberman, 129.

percentage of blacks and whites poor in 1960: Stephan Thernstrom and Abigail

Thernstrom, *America in Black and White: One Nation, Indivisible* (New York: Simon & Schuster, 1997), 233.

number of blacks on AFDC in New York: Vincent J. Cannato, *The Ungovernable City: John Lindsay and His Struggle to Save New York* (New York: Basic Books, 2001), 539.

number of blacks on AFDC in Milwaukee: Katz, 19.

Siegel quote: Siegel, 46.

black poverty and employment rates: Thernstrom & Thernstrom, 233, 246.

1956 forum: Gareth Davies, *From Opportunity to Entitlement: The Transformation and Decline of Great Society Liberalism* (Lawrence, KS: University Press of Kansas, 1996), 25.

Having the Power, We Have the Duty: Davies, 123.

Mobilization for Youth: Davies, 117.

NWRO women mostly black: Lieberman, 172.

Elman quote: Fred Siegel, *The Future Once Happened Here: New York, D.C., L.A., and the Fate of America's Big Cities* (New York: The Free Press, 1997), 60.

forty rallies: DeParle, 96.

two hundred protests a month: Siegel, 55.

Piven quote: Davies, 118.

Nation reprints: DeParle, 96.

Mitchell Ginsberg and New York: Cannato, 541–42.

welfare expansion: most schematically, Charles Murray, *Losing Ground: American Social Policy, 1950–1980* (New York: Basic Books, 1984), 164.

AFDC and politics: Lieberman, 175; Siegel, 60.

New York caseworkers: Siegel, 54.

Stephen Goldsmith, *The Twenty-First Century City: Resurrecting Urban America* (Lanham, MD: Rowman & Littlefield, 1999), 104.

jump in AFDC recipiency in late sixties: Davies, 7, 215.

rise in payment rates: Cannato, 541–42.

Wilbur Mills's suggestion: Davies, 161.

woman shouting at Lindsay: Siegel, 61.

Moynihan on Family Assistance Plan: Davies, 223–24.

Eugene McCarthy hearing: Davies, 229.

Civil War pensions: Theda Skocpol, *Protecting Soldiers and Mothers: The Political Origins of Social Policy in the United States* (Cambridge, MA: Belknap Press of Harvard University Press, 1992), 115, 143–48.

out-of-wedlock births doubled: DeParle, 41.

Ninety-three percent of AFDC families fatherless: Goldsmith, 100–1.

poverty rates according to family type: Thernstrom & Thernstrom, 236.

Star Parker: Star Parker, *Uncle Sam's Plantation: How Big Government Enslaves America's Poor and What We Can Do About It* (Nashville: Wind Books, 2003), 19.

Steele: Shelby Steele, *A Dream Deferred: The Second Betrayal of Black Freedom in America* (New York: HarperCollins, 1998), 29.

Goldsmith quote: Goldsmith, 97.

AFDC plus side work: especially useful is Christopher Jencks, *Rethinking Social Policy: Race, Poverty, and the Underclass* (Cambridge, MA: Harvard University Press, 1992), 204–35.

DeParle quote: DeParle, 79.

Angie's jobs: DeParle, 11, 72.

Angie on move to Milwaukee: DeParle, 81.

childbearing during the Depression: David E. Kyvig, *Daily Life in the United States, 1920–1940* (Chicago: Ivan R. Dee, 2004), 228.

Bronzeville out-of-wedlock births: Drake & Cayton, 589–90; years cited are 1923–28 and 1928–33.

marginal type: Drake & Cayton, 592–93.

woman crying: Elliott Liebow, *Tally's Corner: A Study of Negro Streetcorner Men* (Boston: Little, Brown and Co., 1967), 95.

Murray vs. Greenstein: cf. Robert Greenstein, "Losing Faith in Losing Ground," *The New Republic*, March 25, 1985; cf. also "The Great Society: an Exchange" (between Greenstein and Murray), *The New Republic*, April 8, 1985.

Jencks's objections: Jencks, 87, 130–31.

Wilson's objections: William Julius Wilson, *The Truly Disadvantaged: The Inner City, the Underclass, and Public Policy* (Chicago: University of Chicago Press, 1987), 109–24; William Julius Wilson, *When Work Disappears: The World of the New Urban Poor* (New York: Vintage Books, 1996), 164–78.

child poverty statistics: June E. O'Neill and Sanders Korenman, *Child Poverty and Welfare Reform: Stay the Course.* (New York: Center for Civic Innovation, Manhattan Institute, 2004.)

results of welfare reform: DeParle, 233–34.

Angie quote: DeParle, 210.

Ehrenreich book given to freshmen: Steven Malanga, "The Myth of the Working Poor." *City Journal*, Autumn 2004, 34.

Latoya quote: Newman, 161.

two-parent families in 1960: Thernstrom & Thernstrom, 238.

abortion story: Jason DeParle, *American Dream: Three Women, Ten Kids, and Nation's Drive to End Welfare* (New York: Viking, 2004), 70.

comment on the pill: "When Outcomes Collide With Desires," *The Washington Post*, January 29, 1986.

ex-slaves and education: James D. Anderson, *The Education of Blacks in the South, 1860–1935* (Chapel Hill, NC: University of North Carolina Press, 1988), 6–7, 162.

literacy rates: Anderson, 31.

Latoya on education: Newman, 125.

Burger Barn worker: Newman, 97.

Burger Barn managers hiring from other areas: Newman, 236–40.

Girl proud to work: Newman, 98.

Newman admitting that attitude matters: Newman, 167, 210.

Newark: Myron Magnet, *The Dream and the Nightmare: The Sixties Legacy to the Underclass* (New York: William Morrow & Co., 1993), 48.

study of employers' chariness of inner-city blacks: Joleen Kirschenman and Kathryn M. Neckerman, "'We'd Love to Hire Them, But . . .': the Meaning of Race for Employers." *The Urban Underclass*, ed. by Christopher Jencks and Paul E. Peterson, 203–32 (Washington, DC: The Brookings Institution, 1991).

Wilson's documentation of above: William Julius Wilson, *When Work Disappears: The World of the New Urban Poor* (New York: Vintage Books, 1996), 111–46.

Braddock & McPartland: Jomills Henry Braddock II and James M. McPartland, "How Minorities Continue to Be Excluded From Equal Employment Opportunities: Research on Labor Market and Institutional Barriers." *Journal of Social Sciences* 43: 4–39 (1987).

"I think one of the reasons": Kirschenman & Neckerman, 212.

testy demeanor: Newman, 183–84.
Wilson quote: Wilson, 144.
blacks vs. immigrants in labor pool: Wilson, 139–41.
drug trade as alternative: Wilson, 142–43.

Chapter Five

jugs in Cyprus: Philip Steadman, *The Evolution of Designs: Biological Analogy in Architecture and the Applied Arts* (Cambridge: Cambridge University Press, 1979), 103–23.

Allan Keiler, *Marian Anderson: A Singer's Journey* (New York: Scribner, 2000), 283, 287.

All in the Family episode: "Edith Writes a Song," October 9, 1971.

playlet: Thomas J. Sugrue, *The Origins of the Urban Crisis: Race and Inequality in Postwar Detroit* (Princeton: Princeton University Press, 1996), 169.

Rustin on new black politics: John D'Emilio, *Lost Prophet: The Life and Times of Bayard Rustin* (New York: Free Press, 2003), 363.

Randolph: Paula F. Pfeffer, *A. Philip Randolph: Pioneer of the Civil Rights Movement* (Baton Rouge: Louisiana State University Press, 1990), 276.

H. Rap Brown episode: Christopher Jencks, *Rethinking Social Policy: Race, Poverty, and the Underclass* (Cambridge, MA: Harvard University Press, 1992), 192.

Clive James: Clive James, *As of This Writing: the Essential Essays, 1968–2002* (New York: W.W. Norton & Co., 2003), 63, 365.

Lee Harris's friend: Lee Harris, *Civilization and Its Enemies: The Next Stage of History* (New York: Free Press, 2004), 4–5.

Elijah Wald: Elijah Wald, *Robert Johnson and the Invention of the Blues* (New York: Amistad, 2004).

Dickerson quotes: Debra J. Dickerson, *The End of Blackness: Returning the Souls of Black Folk to Their Rightful Owners* (New York: Pantheon, 2004), 169, 11, 26, 174.

Hoffer quotes: Eric Hoffer, *The True Believer: Thought on the Nature of Mass Movements* (New York: HarperCollins, 1951), 79, 81, 106.

Erikson: Erik H. Erikson, "Identity and Uprootedness in Our Time." *Insight and Responsibility: Lectures on the Ethical Implications of Psychoanalytic Insight* (New York: W.W. Norton, 1964), 93.

Black Rage and its aftermath: Elisabeth Lasch-Quinn, *Race Experts: How Racial Etiquette, Sensitivity Training, and New Age Therapy Hijacked the Civil Rights Movement* (New York: W.W. Norton & Co., 2001); quotation, 81.

path dependence: Ronald Aminzade, "Historical Sociology and Time." *Sociological Methods and Research* 20: 456–80 (1992); Paul David, "Clio and the Economics of QWERTY." *American Economic Review* 75: 332–37 (1985).

"collective memories and rituals": Aminzade, 463.

hints of path dependence in Wilson: William Julius Wilson, *When Work Disappears: The World of the New Urban Poor* (New York: Vintage Books, 1996), 71.

Wright on memes: Robert Wright, *Nonzero: the Logic of Human Destiny* (New York: Vintage Books, 2000), 81.

minimization: Faye J. Crosby, *Affirmative Action Is Dead; Long Live Affirmative Action* (New Haven: Yale University Press, 2004), 20.

Dennett quotes: Daniel Dennett, "Appraising Grace." *The Sciences*, Jan/Feb: 39–44 (1997); Daniel Dennett, *Consciousness Explained* (Boston: Little, Brown, 1991), 203.

meme as "self": Susan Blackmore, *The Meme Machine* (Oxford: Oxford University Press, 1999), 219–34.

welfare quotations: Gareth Davies, *From Opportunity to Entitlement: The Transformation and Decline of Great Society Liberalism* (Lawrence, KS: University Press of Kansas, 1996), 115–16.

alien abduction and sleep paralysis: Blackmore, 176.

Yale Law School episode: Jonathan Kay, "The Scandal of 'Diversity'." *Commentary*, June 2003.

Damali Ayo radio appearance: New York City National Public Radio affiliate WNYC, The Brian Lehrer Show, May 15, 2003.

Tatum quotation: "America, Seen Through the Filter of Race," the *New York Times*, July 2, 2000.

Harris quotes: Sam Harris, *The End of Faith: Religion, Terror, and the Future of Reason* (New York: W.W. Norton & Co., 2004), 72, 65.

latah: P. M. Yap, "The Latah Reaction: Its Pathodynamics and Nosological Position." *Journal of Mental Science* 98: 515–64; quote, 537.

Stanford takeover: my account is based on my memories as an observer, reinforced by specifics confirmed at seas.stanford.edu/diso/articles/takeover89-2.html.

Aaron Lynch, *Thought Contagion: How Belief Spreads Through Society* (New York: Basic Books, 1996), 25, 158.

Cooper: Marc Cooper, "Thinking of Jackasses." *The Atlantic Monthly*, April 2005.

Ellison: Ralph Ellison, "The Little Man at Chehaw Station," *The Collected Essays of Ralph Ellison*, ed. by John F. Callahan (New York: The Modern Library, 2003), 507–8.

Chapter Six

Cose quotes: Ellis Cose, *The Rage of a Privileged Class* (New York: HarperPerennial, 1993).

"in the real world": Cose, 40.

black opinion after the riots: Cose, 182.

"as awful as Rodney King's treatment": Cose, 185.

"a different set of rules": Cose, 183.

"cutting racial remark": Cose, 139.

psychologist's quote: Joe R. Feagin and Melvin P. Sikes, *Living With Racism: The Black Middle Class Experience* (Boston, MA: Beacon Press, 1994), 114.

college dean quote: Feagin & Sikes, 109.

"ignorance and arrogance": Cose, 60.

Oakland study: Geoffrey Grogger and Greg Ridgeway, "Testing for Racial Profiling in Traffic Stops from Behind a Veil of Darkness." RAND Corporation Working Paper (2004).

black police officers: Heather Mac Donald, "The Black Cops You Never Hear About." *Are Cops Racist?* (Chicago: Ivan R. Dee, 2003).

black university student: Joe R. Feagin, "The Continuing Significance of Race: Antiblack Discrimination in Public Places." *American Sociological Review* 56: 101–16 (1991).

Bryonn Bain: Bryonn Bain, "Walking While Black: A Bill of Rights for Black Men." *The Village Voice*, May 2, 2000.

Gerald Reynolds: the *New York Times*, December 10, 2004.

Moynihan quote: Cose, 33.

Tourist Motor Club: Alan Ehrenhalt. *The Lost City: Discovering the Forgotten Virtues of Community in the Chicago of the 1950s* (New York: Basic Books, 1995), 142.

housing development protest: Laurence Maslon, *Broadway: The American Musical* (Boston: Bulfinch Press, 2004), 312.

Golden Boy audience: Gary Fishgall, *Gonna Do Great Things: The Life of Sammy Davis, Jr.* (New York: Scribner, 2003), 241.

Chapter Seven

Newman quotes: Katherine S. Newman, *No Shame in My Game* (New York: Vintage Books, 1999), 167, 210.

Newman on reasons for early childbearing: Newman, 211.

Study Newman cites: Arlene T. Geronimus and Sanders Korenman, "The Socioeconomic Consequences of Teen Childbearing Reconsidered." *Quarterly Journal of Economics* 107: 1187–1214 (1992). (relevant passage on p. 1210)

Hannerz on culture of poverty: Ulf Hannerz, *Soulside: Inquiries into Ghetto Culture and Community* (New York: Columbia University Press, 1969), 180–81.

Myrdal and Ellison: Ralph Ellison, "An American Dilemma: A Review." *The Collected Essays of Ralph Ellison*, ed. by John F. Callahan (New York: The Modern Library, 2003), 328–340; relevant quotes, p. 339.

Orwell: George Orwell, "In Front of Your Nose." *The Complete Works of George Orwell, Volume 18: Smothered Under Journalism*, ed. by Peter Davison, 161–64 (London: Secker & Warburg, 1946), 163.

Anderson on the black middle class: Elijah Anderson, *Streetwise: Race, Class, and Change in an Urban Community* (Chicago: University of Chicago Press, 1990), 65.

Cashin quote: Sheryll Cashin, *The Failures of Integration: How Race and Class are Undermining the American Dream* (New York: Public Affairs, 2004), 128–9.

Anderson on "raucous behavior": Anderson, 175.

Anderson on men with loud radios: Anderson, 174.

"There are worse things": Cashin, 60.

Cashin advises middle-class blacks to move to slums: Cashin, 324–28.

Newman interviewee on middle-class black exodus: Newman, 170.

American Journal of Sociology articles in order of their citation in the text:

Douglas Massey and Mitchell L. Eggers, "The Ecology of Inequality: Minorities and the Concentration of Poverty, 1970–1980." *American Journal of Sociology* 95: 1153–88 (1990).

Daniel T. Lichter, Felicia B. LeClere, and Diane K. McLaughlin, "Local Marriage Markets and the Marital Behavior of Black and White Women." *American Journal of Sociology* 96: 843–67 (1991).

Jonathan Crane, "The Epidemic Theory of Ghettos and Neighborhood Effects on Dropping Out and Teenage Childbearing." *American Journal of Sociology* 96: 1226–59 (1991).

Verna M. Keith and Cedric Herring, "Skin Tone and Stratification in the Black Community." *American Journal of Sociology* 97: 760–68 (1991).

Thomas A. LaVeist, "The Political Empowerment and Health Status of African-Americans: Mapping a New Territory." *American Journal of Sociology* 97: 1080–95 (1992).

Charlotte Steeh and Howard Schuman, "Young White Adults: Did Racial Attitudes Change in the 1980s?" *American Journal of Sociology* 98: 340–67 (1992).

S. Philip Morgan, Antonio McDaniel, Andrew T. Miller, and Samuel H. Preston, "Racial Differences in Household and Family Structure at the Turn of the Century." *American Journal of Sociology* 98: 798–828 (1993).

Richard D. Alba and John R. Logan, "Minority Proximity to Whites in Suburbs: An Individual-level Analysis of Segregation." *American Journal of Sociology* 98: 1388–1427 (1993).

Joanne Brooks-Gunn, Greg J. Duncan, Pamela Kato Klebanov, and Naomi Sealand, "Do Neighborhoods Influence Child and Adolescent Development?" *American Journal of Sociology* 99: 353–95 (1993).

Susan Olzak, Suzanne Shanahan, and Elizabeth West, "School Desegregation, Interracial Exposure, and Antibusing Activity in Contemporary Urban America." *American Journal of Sociology* 100: 196–241 (1994).

Reynolds Farley, Charlotte Steeh, Maria Krysan, Tara Jackson, and Keith Reeves, "Stereotypes and Segregation: Neighborhoods in the Detroit Area." *American Journal of Sociology* 100: 750–80 (1994).

Allen E. Liska and Paul E. Bellair, "Violent-crime Rates and Racial Composition: Convergence Over Time." *American Journal of Sociology* 101: 578–610 (1995).

Ronald N. Jacobs, "Civil Society and Crisis: Culture, Discourse, and the Rodney King Beating." *American Journal of Sociology* 101: 1238–72 (1996).

Lee Sigelman, Timothy Bledsoe, Susan Welch, and Michael W. Combs, "Making Contact? Black-White Social Interaction in an Urban Setting." *American Journal of Sociology* 101: 1306–32 (1996).

Belinda Robnett, "African-American Women in the Civil Rights Movement, 1954–1965: Gender, Leadership, and Micromobilization." *American Journal of Sociology* 101: 1661–93 (1996).

Deanna Pagnini and S. Philip Morgan, "Racial Differences in Marriage and Childbearing: Oral History Evidence from the South in the Early Twentieth Century." *American Journal of Sociology* 101: 1694–1718 (1996).

Stewart E. Tolnay, Glenn Deane, and E. M. Beck, "Vicarious Violence: Spatial Effects on Southern Lynchings, 1890–1919." *American Journal of Sociology* 102: 788–815 (1996).

Lincoln Quillian, "Group Threat and Regional Change in Attitudes Towards African-Americans." *American Journal of Sociology* 102: 816–60 (1996).

Scott J. South and Kyle D. Crowder, "Escaping Distressed Neighborhoods: Individual, Community, and Metropolitan Influences." *American Journal of Sociology* 102: 1040–84 (1997).

Sudhir Alladi Venkatesh, "The Social Organization of Street Gang Activity in an Urban Ghetto." *American Journal of Sociology* 103: 82–111 (1997).

Daniel T. Lichter, Diane K. McLaughlin, and David C. Ribar, "Welfare and the Rise in Female-headed Families." *American Journal of Sociology* 103: 112–43 (1997).

Nicholas Pedriana and Robin Stryker, "Political Culture Wars 1960s Style: Equal Employment Opportunity-Affirmative Action Law and the Philadelphia Plan." *American Journal of Sociology* 103: 633–91 (1997).

Sarah A. Soule and Yvonne Zylan, "Runaway Train? The Diffusion of State-level Reform in ADC/AFDC Eligibility Requirements, 1950–67." *American Journal of Sociology* 103: 733–62 (1997).

David Jacobs and Robert M. O'Brien, "The Determinants of Deadly Force: A Structural Analysis of Police Violence." *American Journal of Sociology* 103: 837–62 (1998).

Scott L. Feld and William C. Carter, "When Desegregation *Reduces* Interracial Contact: A Class Size Paradox for Weak Ties." *American Journal of Sociology* 103: 1165–86 (1998).

Rick Grannis, "The Importance of Trivial Streets: Residential Streets and Residential Segregation." *American Journal of Sociology* 103: 1530-64 (1998).

Donald P. Green, Dara Z. Strolovitch, and Janelle S. Wong, "Defended Neighborhoods, Integration, and Racially Motivated Crime." *American Journal of Sociology* 104: 372–403 (1998).

Mitchell Duneier and Harvey Molotch, "Talking City Trouble: Interactional Vandalism, Social Inequality, and the 'Urban Interaction Problem'." *American Journal of Sociology* 104: 1263–95 (1999).

Lincoln Quillian, "Migration Patterns and the Growth of High-Poverty Neighborhoods, 1970–1990." *American Journal of Sociology* 105: 1–37 (1999).

David Jacobs and Katherine Wood, "Interracial Conflict and Interracial Homicide: Do Political and Economic Rivalries Explain White Killings of Blacks or Black Killings of Whites?" *American Journal of Sociology* 105: 157–90 (1999).

Thomas Daula, D. Alton Smith, and Roy Nord, "Inequality in the Military: Fact or Fiction?" *American Sociological Review* 55: 714–18 (1990).

Reynolds Farley and William H. Frey, "Changes in the Segregation of Whites from Blacks During the 1980s: Small Steps Toward a More Integrated Society." *American Sociological Review* 1994: 23–45 (1994).

Paul A. Jargowsky, "Take the Money and Run: Economic Segregation in U.S. Metropolitan Areas." *American Sociological Review* 61: 984–98 (1996).

David R. Harris, "'Property Values Drop When Blacks Move In, Because . . .' Racial and Socioeconomic Determinants of Neighborhood Desirability." *American Sociological Review* 64: 461–79 (1999).

Mary Pattillo-McCoy, "Church Culture as a Strategy of Action in the Black Community." *American Sociological Review* 63: 767–84 (1998).

Austin quote: Regina Austin, "'The Black Community,' Its Lawbreakers, and a Politics of Identity." 65 *Southern California Law Review* 1769 (1992).

Troy Duster: Nicholas Wade, "Race-based Medicine Continued . . ." *The New York Times*, November 4, 2004.

Chapter Nine

Sowell: Thomas Sowell, "Patterns of Black Excellence." *The Public Interest* 43: 26–58 (1976), 51; Thomas Sowell, *Black Rednecks and White Liberals* (San Francisco: Encounter Books, 2005), 203–15.

law school standards: Jonathan Kay, "The Scandal of 'Diversity'." *Commentary*, June 2003.

University of Michigan figures: Richard H. Sander, "A Systemic Analysis of Affirmative Action in American Law Schools." 57 *Stanford Law Review* 367 (2004), 402.

Cose: Ellis Cose, *The Rage of a Privileged Class* (New York: HarperPerennial, 1993), 122.

achievement gap study from national perspective: Ronald F. Ferguson, *What Doesn't Meet the Eye: Understanding and Addressing Racial Disparities in High-achieving Suburban Schools*. Harvard University, John F. Kennedy School of Government Working Paper (2002).

Post–Civil War observations: James D. Anderson, *The Education of Blacks in the South, 1860–1935* (Chapel Hill, NC: University of North Carolina Press, 1988), 282, 6, 165.

blacks at Amherst: Thomas Sowell, *Affirmative Action Around the World: An Empirical Study* (New York: Basic Books, 2004), 143.

Dunbar scores: Thomas Sowell, "Patterns of Black Excellence." *The Public Interest* 43:

26–58 (1976), 51; Thomas Sowell, *Black Rednecks and White Liberals* (San Francisco: Encounter Books, 2005), 203–15.

Dickerson: Debra J. Dickerson, *The End of Blackness: Returning the Souls of Black Folk to Their Rightful Owners* (New York: Pantheon, 2004), 209.

Crouch: Stanley Crouch, *The Artificial White Man: Essays on Authenticity* (New York: Perseus, 2004), 44.

Ainsworth-Darnell and Downey: James W. Ainsworth-Darnell and Douglas B. Downey, "Assessing the Oppositional Culture Explanation for Racial/Ethnic Differences in School Performance." *American Sociological Review* 63: 536–63.

Reply article: Douglas B. Downey and James W. Ainsworth-Darnell, "The Search for Oppositional Culture Among Black Students." *American Sociological Review* 67: 156–64 (2002).

Cook and Ludwig: Philip J. Cook and Jens Ludwig, "The Burden of 'Acting White': Do Black Adolescents Disparage Academic Achievement?" *The Black-White Test Score Gap*, ed. by Christopher Jencks and Meredith Philips, 375–400 (Washington, DC: The Brookings Institution Press, 1998).

Casteel study: Clifton Casteel, "Attitudes of African American and Caucasian Eighth Grade Students About Praises, Rewards, and Punishments." *Elementary School Guidance and Counseling* 31: 262–72.

Tyson, Darity, and Castellino: Karolyn Tyson, William A. Darity Jr., and Domini Castellino, "Breeding Animosity: The 'Burden of Acting White' and Other Problems of Status Group Hierarchies on Schools." Duke University Sanford Institute Working Paper (2005).

Fryer articles: Roland G. Fryer and Paul Torelli, "An Empirical Analysis of 'Acting White'"; David Austen-Smith and Roland G. Fryer, "An Economic Analysis of 'Acting White'." *Quarterly Journal of Economics*.

Claude Steele: Claude M. Steele and Joshua Aronson, "Stereotype Threat and the Test Performance of Academically Successful African Americans." *The Black-White Test Score Gap*, ed. by Christopher Jencks and Meredith Philips, 401–27 (Washington, DC: The Brookings Institution Press, 1998).

Dyson: Michael Eric Dyson, *Is Bill Cosby Right? Or Has the Black Middle Class Lost Its Mind?* (New York: Basic Civitas, 2005), 85–88.

Noguera: Pedro Noguera, *City Schools and the American Dream* (New York: Teachers College Press, 2003), 46, 57.

Herbert column: Bob Herbert, "Breaking Away." The *New York Times*, July 10, 2003; Herbert also wrote about the problem in his *Times* column of March 1, 1995.

Maplewood story: Tamar Lewin, "Growing Up, Growing Apart." *How Race is Lived in America* (New York: Times Books, 2001), 151–69.

Poussaint quote: *The Newshour with Jim Lehrer*, July 15, 2004.

Price quote: William G. Bowen and Derek Bok, *The Shape of the River: Long-Term Consequences of Considering Race in College and University Admissions* (Princeton: Princeton University Press, 1998), 85.

Sharpton quote: Joyce Purnick, "Kids Today? Sharpton Grimaces." The *New York Times*, November 7, 2002.

Wilkins report: "Summary of Results: An Analysis of the 1996 Minnesota Basic Skills Test Scores." University of Minnesota Humphrey Institute of Public Affairs: The Wilkins Center for Human Relations and Social Justice (1997).

Cashin: Sheryll Cashin, *The Failures of Integration: How Race and Class are Undermining the American Dream* (New York: Public Affairs, 2004), 143.

Letter to *Times*: June 28, 2004.

Karabell on Noguera: Zachary Karabell, *What's College For? The Struggle to Define Higher American Education* (New York: Basic Books, 1999).

Noguera against cultural explanations: Noguera, 46.

Harris quote: Sam Harris, *The End of Faith: Religion, Terror, and the Future of Reason* (New York: W.W. Norton & Co., 2004), 168.

Ferguson: Ronald F. Ferguson, "Teachers' Perceptions and Expectations and the Black-White Test Score Gap." *The Black-White Test Score Gap*, ed. by Christopher Jencks and Meredith Philips, 273–317 (Washington, DC: The Brookings Institution Press, 1998), 311; Ronald F. Ferguson, "Can Schools Narrow the Black-White Test Score Gap?" *The Black-White Test Score Gap*, ed. by Christopher Jencks and Meredith Philips, 318–74 (Washington, DC: The Brookings Institution Press, 1998), 347–50

Herbert on teachers: Bob Herbert, "Failing Teachers." The *New York Times*, October 24, 2003.

Claude Steele's depiction of student: Claude Steele, "Thin Ice: Stereotype Threat and Black College Students." *The Atlantic Monthly*, August, 1999.

HBCUs: "New Data on Graduation Rates at Black Colleges: A Dismal Performance Overall, But Two HBCUs Beat Harvard." *The Journal of Blacks in Higher Education* 45.

number of immigrant black students at Harvard: Sara Rimer and Karen W. Arenson, "Top Colleges Take More Blacks, But Which Ones?" *The New York Times*, June 24, 2004.

AALS on separate standards: Sander, 381.

Sandalow: Terrance Sandalow, "Minority Preferences Reconsidered." 97 *Michigan Law Review* 1874, 1906–7 (1999).

Black Guide to Life at Harvard: Sara Rimer, "Blacks' Guide to Harvard Covers History and Tips." The *New York Times*, February 1, 2003.

poll of Michigan minority graduates: Richard O. Lempert, David L. Chambers, and Terry K. Adams, "Michigan's Minority Graduates in Practice: The River Runs Through Law School." 2000 *American Bar Foundation* 395.

Chang study: J. Mitchell Chang, *Racial Diversity in Higher Education: Does a Racially Mixed Student Population Affect Educational Outcomes?* University of Michigan at Ann Arbor PhD dissertation.

Rothman, Lipset, and Nevitte: Stanley Rothman, Seymour Lipset, and Neil Nevitte, "Does Enrollment Diversity Improve University Education?" *International Journal of Public Opinion* 15: 8–26 (2003).

Cole and Barber: Stephen Cole and Elinor Barber, *Increasing Faculty Diversity* (Cambridge, MA: Harvard University Press, 2003).

Hanushek et al. study: Eric A. Hanushek, John F. Kain, and Steven G. Rivkin, *New Evidence about Brown v. Board of Education: The Complex Effects of School Racial Composition on Achievement*. National Bureau of Economic Research Working Paper 8741.

Sander's observations: Sander, 426–27, 434–36, 442–43, 468–75.

Slate piece: Emily Bazelon, "Sanding Down Sander." *Slate*, April 29, 2005.

Sander's responses: Richard H. Sander, "A Reply to Critics." 57 *Stanford Law Review* 1963 (2005); Richard H. Sander, "Mismeasuring the Mismatch: A Response to Ho." 114 *Yale Law Journal* 2005 (2005).

Sander on his critics: Richard H. Sander, "A Reply to Critics." 57 *Stanford Law Review* 1963 (2005), 2015.

Sander's critics: David L. Chambers, Timothy Clydesdale, William Kidder, and

Richard Lempert, "The Real Impact of Eliminating Affirmative Action in American Law Schools: An Empirical Critique of Richard Sander's Study." 57 *Stanford Law Review* 1855 (2005); Michele Landis Dauber, "The Big Muddy." 57 *Stanford Law Review* 1899 (2005); David B. Wilkins, "A Systematic Response to Systemic Disadvantage." 57 *Stanford Law Review* 1915 (2005); Ian Ayres and Richard Brooks, "Does Affirmative Action Reduce the Number of Black Lawyers?" 57 *Stanford Law Review* 1807 (2005); Daniel E. Ho, "Why Affirmative Action Does Not Cause Black Students to Fail the Bar." 114 *Yale Law Journal* 1997 (2005).

Heriot article: Gail Heriot, "Equal Opportunity Works." *The Weekly Standard*, April 17, 2000.

Gurin report: Patricia Y. Gurin, "Reports Submitted on Behalf of the University of Michigan: The Compelling Need for Diversity in Higher Education." 5 *Michigan Journal of Race and Law* 363 (1999).

Astin conclusion: Alexander W. Astin, "What Matters in College." *Liberal Education* 79: 4–15 (1993).

amicus brief: William H. Allen, Oscar M. Garibaldi, Keith A. Noreika, Dimple Gupta, Amicus Curiae brief submitted to *Gratz v. Bollinger* (2003), 16.

John Hope Franklin: Larry Purdy (lawyer for the prosecution in *Gratz v. Bollinger* and *Grutter v. Bollinger*, personal communication).

Sniderman and Piazza: Paul M. Sniderman and Thomas Piazza, *Black Pride and Black Prejudice* (Princeton: Princeton University Press, 2002), 146–50.

Sturm and Guinier: Susan Sturm and Lani Guinier, "The Future of Affirmative Action: Reclaiming the Innovative Ideal." 84 *California Law Review* 953 (1996).

Krieger article: Linda Hamilton Krieger, "Civil Rights Perestroika: Intergroup Relations After Affirmative Action." *California Law Review* 86: 1251–1333 (1998).

Hurston quote: Zora Neale Hurston, *Folklore, Memoirs, and Other Writings* (New York: The Library of America, 1995), p. 794 (from "Seeing the World As It Is" [appendix to *Dust Tracks on a Road*]).

Ellison: Ralph Ellison, "The World and the Jug." *The Collected Essays of Ralph Ellison*, ed. by John F. Callahan (New York: The Modern Library, 2003), 170.

Chapter Ten

Gates quote: Courtland Milloy, "A Challenging Analysis of Black America." *The Washington Post*, March 21, 2004.

Perry: Imani Perry, *Prophets of the Hood: Politics and Poetics in Hip Hop* (Durham: Duke University Press, 2004), p. 44.

Rose: Tricia Rose, *Black Noise: Rap Music and Black Culture in Contemporary America* (Middletown, CT: Wesleyan University Press, 1994), 24, 3, 101.

Kelley: Robin D. G. Kelley, *Race Rebels: Culture, Politics, and the Black Working Class* (New York: The Free Press, 1994), 225.

Van Deburg: William L. Van Deburg, *Hoodlums: Black Villains and Social Bandits in American Life* (Chicago: The University of Chicago Press, 2004), 199.

Simmons: Russell Simmons with Nelson George, *Life and Def: Sex, Drugs, Money, and God* (New York: Three Rivers Press, 2001), 5, 9.

academic version of "real" argument: Perry, 39.

"unfettered whiteness": *www.metroactive.com/papers/metro/07.10.03/rose-0328.html*

Dyson: Michael Eric Dyson, *Holler If You Hear Me: Searching for Tupac Shakur* (New York: Basic Books, 2001), 149.

Dyson on Shakur and middle-class blacks: Dyson, 96–120; quote: 104.

M.C. Eiht: quoted in Kelley, 195.

Rose on rupture: Rose, 39.

George passage: Nelson George, *Hip Hop America* (New York: Penguin, 1998), 49.

Nas interview: "Rap, Politics and God." cnn.com, January 12, 2005.

Mos Def on politics: Mos Def, "These United States." *The Fader* 25 (Nov. 2004), 143–44.

Bynoe quote: L. Yvonne Bynoe, "Hip Hop Politics: Deconstructing the Myth." politicallyblack.com, December 8, 1999.

Nelson George on hip-hop and politics: George, 155.

Perry: Perry, 47.

Kelley on toasts: Kelley, 214–15.

Rose on hip-hop sexism: Rose, 16.

Kelley on hip-hop sexism: Kelley, 222.

Rose on female rappers and feminism: Rose, 176–82.

Mary Tyler Moore's backside: "The Making of Season One" documentary on DVD set *The Mary Tyler Moore Show: The Complete First Season* (2002).

Rose on contradictions: Rose, 2.

Simmons on theatrics: Simmons, 70, xiii.

Times rapper: N. R. Kleinfeld, "Guarding the Borders of the Hip-Hop Nation." *How Race is Lived in America* (New York: Times Books, 2001), 218; "Knowing Your Subject, Knowing Yourself: Journals from the Writers and Photographers." Ibid., 356.

Ice-T quote: "Rapper Ice-T Defends Song Against Spreading Boycott." *The New York Times*, June 19, 1992.

Steigerwald: David Steigerwald, *Culture's Vanities: The Paradox of Cultural Diversity in a Globalized World* (Lanham, MA: Rowman & Littlefield, 2004), 203, 206, 208.

Greg Thomas on Lil' Kim: Joyce Wadler, "Boldface Names" column, *The New York Times*, November 3, 2004.

George comparisons: George, 51.

Sinclair Lewis: Richard Lingeman, *Sinclair Lewis: Rebel from Main Street* (New York: Random House, 2002), 423.

Mos Def on conscious rap vs. gangsta: Dyson, 91.

Van Deburg on conscious rappers: Van Deburg, 204.

Mos Def resisting "conscious" label: Dyson, 91–92.

Perry anecdote: Perry, 1.

Perry on rappers' voices: Perry, 47–48.

Souljah on rhythm: George, 172.

Dyson on videos: Michel Marriot, "The Color of Mayhem." The *New York Times*, August 12, 2004.

Kelley quote: Kelley, 183.

George quote: George, 49.

Kelley addendum: Kelley, 227.

Cose on stereotyping: Ellis Cose, *The Rage of a Privileged Class* (New York: Harper-Perennial, 1993), 110.

Chapter Eleven

Wax editorial: Amy Wax, "Some Truths About Black Disadvantage." The *Wall Street Journal*, January 3, 2005.

student objector: Mara Gordon, "Professor's Column Sparks Race Dialogue." The *Daily Pennsylvanian*, January 28, 2005.

Gächter and Riedl: Simon Gächter and Arno Riedl, "Moral property rights in bargaining." Institute of Mathematical Economics Working Paper No. 300, Fascicle 2 (2002).

Schlicht: Ekkehard Schlicht, *On Custom in the Economy* (Oxford: Clarendon Press, 1998), 24.

Marable quotes: Manning Marable, *The Great Wells of Democracy: The Meaning of Race in American Life* (New York: Basic Books, 2002), 323, 12.

Letter: *The East Bay Express*, June 11, 2003.

Buffalo exposition: Randal C. Archibold, "Buffalo Gazes Back to a Time When Fortune Shone: Much-Maligned City Celebrates the Glory of a Century Ago." The *New York Times*, September 7, 2001.

Rauchway: Eric Rauchway, *Murdering McKinley: The Making of Theodore Roosevelt's America* (New York: Farrar, Straus & Giroux, 2003), 61–66.

Henrietta Marie: Winnie Hu, "Relics of Slavery, Up From the Ocean's Depths." The *New York Times*, December 24, 2001.

highway naming: Sam Howe Verhovek, "Road Named for a Confederate Stirs Uncivil Debate." The *New York Times*, February 14, 2002.

Underground Railroad issue: Francis X. Clines, "Slave 'Railroad' Buffs Question Museum Site." The *New York Times*, June 24, 2002.

Artifact collector: Jeffrey Gettleman, "15,000 Objects Testify to a Peculiar Institution." The *New York Times*, November 30, 2002.

York rally: "White Supremacists Rally in York, PA." The *New York Times*, January 13, 2002.

Butler: Daniel J. Wakin, "Richard G. Butler, 86, Dies; Founder of the Aryan Nations." The *New York Times*, September 9, 2004.

Harlem Children's Zone: my description is based partly on speeches by Canada and a conversation with him; the organization's Web site is useful.

Chapter Twelve

Times "Conversation on Race": "A Conversation on Race: America, Seen Through the Filter of Race." The *New York Times*, July 2, 2000.

New York on 50 Cent: Ethan Brown, "The Half-Buck Stops Here." *New York*, March 14–21 (2005).

Beyoncé kids: 102nd St. and West End Avenue, New York City, spring 2004.

University of Colorado announcement: Valerie Richardson, "University 'Clarifies' Its Policy on Course." The *Washington Times*, August 3, 2004.

meme as "self": Susan Blackmore, *The Meme Machine* (Oxford: Oxford University Press, 1999), 246.

Csikszentmihalyi: Mihaly Csikszentmihalyi, *The Evolving Self: A Psychology for the Third Millennium* (New York: HarperCollins, 1993), 290.

Herbert: Bob Herbert, "Dad's Empty Chair." The *New York Times*, July 7, 2005.

Letters: "When Fathers Can't Be Found at Home." The *New York Times*, July 10, 2005.

black film executive: Let's just give him his privacy.

Ellison: Ralph Ellison, "Remembering Richard Wright," *The Collected Essays of Ralph Ellison*, ed. by John F. Callahan (New York: The Modern Library, 2003), 676–67.

Appendix

American Sociological Review articles:

Douglas S. Massey, "American Apartheid: Segregation and the Making of the Underclass." *American Journal of Sociology* 96: 329–57 (1990).

Douglas S. Massey, Andrew B. Gross, and Kumiko Shibuya, "Migration, Segregation, and the Geographic Concentration of Poverty." *American Sociological Review* 59: 425–45 (1994).

James R. Kluegel, "Trends in Whites' Explanations of the Black-White Gap in Socioeconomic Status, 1977–1989." *American Sociological Review* 55: 512–25 (1990).

Howard Schuman and Maria Krysan, "A Historical Note on Whites' Beliefs About Racial Inequality." *American Sociological Review* 64: 847–55.

Stewart Tolnay and E. M. Beck, "Racial Violence and Black Migration in the American South, 1910 to 1930." *American Sociological Review* 57: 103–16 (1999).

E. M. Beck and Stewart Tolnay, "The Killing Fields of the Deep South: The Market for Cotton and the Lynching of Blacks, 1882-1930." *American Sociological Review* 55: 526–39 (1990).

R. Kelly Raley, "A Shortage of Marriageable Men? A Note on the Role of Cohabitation in Black-White Differences in Marriage Rates." *American Sociological Review* 61: 973–83 (1996).

Daniel T. Lichter, Diane K. McLaughlin, George Kephart, and David J. Landry, "Race and the Retreat from Marriage: A Shortage of Marriageable Men?" *American Sociological Review* 57: 781–99 (1992).

Pamela Barnhouse Walters and Carl M. Briggs, "The Family Economy, Child Labor, and Schooling: Evidence from the Early Twentieth-Century South." *American Sociological Review* 58: 163–81 (1993).

Pamela Barnhouse Walters, David R. James, and Holly J. McCammon, "Citizenship and Public Schools: Accounting for Racial Inequality in Education in the Pre- and Post-Disfranchisement South." *American Sociological Review* 62: 34–52 (1997).

Karin L. Brewster, "Race Differences in Sexual Activity Among Adolescent Women: The Role of Neighborhood Characteristics." *American Sociological Review* 59: 408–24 (1994).

Clea A. Sucoff and Dawn M. Upchurch, "Neighborhood Context and the Risk of Childbearing Among Metropolitan-Area Black Adolescents." *American Sociological Review* 63: 571–85 (1998).

Scott J. South and Kyle D. Crowder, "Neighborhood Effects on Family Formation: Concentrated Poverty and Beyond." *American Sociological Review* 64: 113–32 (1999).

Doris R. Entwisle and Karl L. Alexander, "Summer Setback: Race, Poverty, School Composition, and Mathematics Achievement in the First Two Years of School." *American Sociological Review* 57: 72–84 (1992).

A. Silvia Cancio, T. David Evans, and David J. Maume Jr., "Reconsidering the Declining Significance of Race: Racial Differences in Early Career Wages." *American Sociological Review* 61: 541–56 (1996).

John J. Beggs, "The Institutional Environment: Implications for Race and Gender Inequality in the U.S. Labor Market." *American Sociological Review* 60: 612–33 (1995).

Steven Ruggles, "The Origins of African-American Family Structure." *American Sociological Review* 59: 136–51 (1994).

Daniel J. Myers, "Racial Rioting in the 1960s: an Event History Analysis of Local Conditions." *American Sociological Review* 62: 94–112 (1997).

Debra Van Ausdale and Joe R. Feagin, "Using Racial and Ethnic Concepts: The Critical Case of Very Young Children." *American Sociological Review* 61: 779–93 (1996).

Lawrence Bobo and Vincent L. Hutchings, "Perceptions of Racial Group Competition: Extending Blumer's Theory of Group Position to a Multiracial Social Context." *American Sociological Review* 61: 951–72 (1996).

Irene Browne, "Explaining the Black-White Gap in Labor Force Participation Among Women Heading Households." *American Sociological Review* 62: 236–52 (1997).

Kenneth T. Andrews, "The Impacts of Social Movements on the Political Process: The Civil Rights Movement and Black Electoral Politics in Mississippi." *American Sociological Review* 62: 800–19 (1997).

Scott J. South and Kyle D. Crowder, "Leaving the 'Hood: Residential Mobility Between Black, White, and Integrated Neighborhoods." *American Sociological Review* 63: 17–26 (1998).

Allen E. Liska, John R. Logan, and Paul E. Bellair, "Race and Violent Crime in the Suburbs." *American Sociological Review* 63: 27–38 (1998).

Albert Bergesen and Max Herman, "Immigration, Race, and Riot: The 1992 Los Angeles Uprising." *American Sociological Review* 63: 39–54 (1998).

Marylee C. Taylor, "How White Attitudes Vary with the Racial Composition of Local Populations: Numbers Count." *American Sociological Review* 63: 512–35 (1998).

Michael Hughes and Melvin E. Thomas, "The Continuing Significance of Race Revisited: A Study of Race, Class, and Quality of Life in America, 1972 to 1996." *American Sociological Review* 63: 785–95 (1998).

Jill Quadagno, "Race, Class and Gender in the U.S. Welfare State: Nixon's Failed Family Assistance Plan." *American Sociological Review* 55: 11–28 (1990).

Jill Quadagno, "Social Movements and State Transformation: Labor Unions and Racial Conflict in the War on Poverty." *American Sociological Review* 57: 616–34 (1992).

Aldon D. Morris, "Birmingham Confrontation Reconsidered: An Analysis of the Dynamics and Tactics of Mobilization." *American Sociological Review* 58: 621–36 (1993).

Bernice A. Pescosolido, Elizabeth Grauerholz, and Melissa A. Milkie, "Culture and Conflict: The Portrayal of Blacks in U.S. Children's Picture Books Through the Mid- and Late-twentieth Century." *American Sociological Review* 62: 443–64 (1997).

Susan Olzak and Elizabeth West, "Ethnic Conflict and the Rise and Fall of Ethnic Newspapers." *American Sociological Review* 56: 458–74 (1991).

Nancy S. Landale and Stewart A. Tolnay, "Group Differences in Economic Opportunity and the Timing of Marriage: Blacks and Whites in the Rural South, 1910." *American Sociological Review* 56: 33–45 (1991).

Gary LaFree and Kriss A. Drass, "The Effect of Changes in Intraracial Income Inequality and Educational Attainment on Changes in Arrest Rates for African Americans and Whites, 1957–1990." *American Sociological Review* 61: 614–34 (1996).

Joe R. Feagin, "The Continuing Significance of Race: Antiblack Discrimination in Public Places." *American Sociological Review* 56: 101–16 (1991).

Stanley Lieberson and Kelly S. Mikelson, "Distinctive African American Names: An Experimental, Historical, and Linguistic Analysis of Innovation." *American Sociological Review* 60: 928–46 (1995).

George Farkas, Robert P. Grobe, Daniel Sheehan, and Yuan Shuan, "Cultural Resources and School Success." *American Sociological Review* 55: 127–42 (1990).

James W. Ainsworth-Darnell and Douglas B. Downey, "Assessing the Oppositional Culture Explanation for Racial/Ethnic Differences in School Performance." *American Sociological Review* 63: 536–63.

Doris R. Entwisle and Karl L. Alexander, "Winter Setback: The Racial Composition of Schools and Learning to Read." *American Sociological Review* 59: 446–60 (1994).

George S. Bridges and Sara Steen, "Racial Disparities in Official Assessments of Juvenile Offenders: Attributional Stereotypes as Mediating Mechanisms." *American Sociological Review* 63: 554–70 (1998).

Stephen M. Petterson, "Are Young Black Men Really Less Willing to Work?" *American Sociological Review* 62: 605–13 (1997).

Craig Zwerling and Hilary Silver, "Race and Job Dismissals in a Federal Bureaucracy." *American Sociological Review* 57: 651–60 (1992).

David J. Eggebeen and Daniel T. Lichter, "Race, Family Structure, and Changing Poverty Among American Children." *American Sociological Review* 56: 801–17 (1991).

Lawrence Bobo and James R. Kluegel, "Opposition to Race-targeting: Self-interest, Stratification Ideology, or Racial Attitudes?" *American Sociological Review* 58: 443–64 (1993).

Amy Binder, "Constructing Racial Rhetoric: Media Depictions of Harm in Heavy Metal and Rap Music." *American Sociological Review* 58: 753–67 (1993).

Donald Tomaskovic-Devey and Vincent J. Roscigno, "Racial Economic Subordination and White Gain in the U.S. South." *American Sociological Review* 61: 565–89 (1996).

Acknowledgments

In Indianapolis, I thank John Hall, John Lands, Harry McFarland, and Olgen Williams for sharing their reminiscences and life experiences with me, as well as former Indianapolis mayor Stephen Goldsmith, who took time out of his busy schedule to endure my queries on issues surely rather oddly specific as viewed within his wide-ranging career as a public servant dedicated to making America better.

Nancy Kandoian of the New York Public Library taught me how to get a view of mid-twentieth century industrial locations in American cities via the miracle of Sanborn fire insurance maps, a source a career linguist had no way of being aware of. She was bracingly diligent in consulting connections of hers, among what appears to be a network of crack librarians, to inform me of even what is *not* available, information often as valuable to a researcher as positive data. Hats off to her for enduring the bizarrely particular efforts of someone who walks in and wants to know, of all things, exactly where factories were located in Indianapolis, of all places, specifically in the 1950s.

I am deficient in the ability to come up with names for things that live vibrantly as concepts in my head. As such, I owe the term "therapeutic alienation" to Micah Freedman (otherwise known to Equity as Michael Friedman). I had the "alienation" part but was hopelessly stuck as to the proper adjective. Also, a nod to Zander Teller for nudging Micah in that direction amid a conversation where I posed to both of them the question of what I should call what I was referring to in this book.

Endless thanks to Larry Purdy for sharing his research on affirmative action and the diversity concept, and to Marianne Coffey for some very important insights on what life was like in old-time black ghettoes, which helped me to present the most responsible picture of them that I could, as someone who did not live through the era.

I am grateful to Theodore and Vada Stanley, Elizabeth B. Lurie and the W. H. Brady Foundation, James Pierson and the John M. Olin Foundation, Joe Dolan and the Achelis and Bodman Foundations, and to Larry Mone and the Manhattan Institute for supporting the research for this book.

My little black cat, Lara, sitting on my lap as I wrote this book as she has while I wrote the others, deserves acknowledgment as well. Although she has frequently been designated "John as a cat," she is nevertheless illiterate and unable to understand more than a few words of English, which will prevent her from knowing of my salute. But it will be a sad day when I have to write a book without her reassuring warm ten pounds on my lap, and moreover I have been heartened while writing this book that Lara is black and yet is utterly disinclined to process her life as an oppressed one. Also, best and hopeful wishes to sweet little guy Onslow, so fascinated by the movements of the cursor on the computer screen while I typed this book—and sorry about him, pretty girl.

Finally, Martha Sparks, ever on the watch for anything in print or online that might be useful for this book, has contributed more than anyone to the final result. For one, she read the whole first draft. Then, she also let me hole myself up for countless evenings to write it. Now I know what authors mean on their acknowledgments pages when they thank their nearest and dearest for putting up with their frequent unavailability, and I am eternally grateful to Martha for her gracious forbearance of borderline workaholic behavior.

My mother made me read C. Wright Mills when I was a kid because she wanted me to have the "Sociological Imagination" he referred to. She was pleased when as a teenager I seemed to be developing one. I cannot be sure how she would feel about how mine has developed since then. But regardless, thank you to Schelysture Ann Gordon McWhorter, whose way of seeing the post-industrial American city around us was, ultimately, the foundation of this book.

Index